Heidegger and His Jewish Reception

In this book, Daniel M. Herskowitz examines the rich, intense, and persistent Jewish engagement with one of the most important and controversial modern philosophers, Martin Heidegger. Contextualizing this encounter within wider intellectual, cultural, and political contexts, he outlines the main patterns and the diverse Jewish responses to Heidegger. Herskowitz shows that through a dialectic of attraction and repulsion, Jewish thinkers developed a version of Jewishness that sought to offer the way out of the overall crisis plaguing their world, a crisis which was embodied, as they saw it, in Heidegger's life and thought. Neither turning a blind eye to Heidegger's antisemitism nor using it as an excuse for ignoring his philosophy, they wrestled with his existential analytic and what they took to be its religious, ethical, and political failings. Ironically, Heidegger's thought proved itself to be fertile ground for reconceptualizing what it means to be Jewish in the modern world.

Daniel M. Herskowitz is the Career Research Fellow in Jewish Studies, Wolfson College, University of Oxford.

Heidegger and His Jewish Reception

DANIEL M. HERSKOWITZ

University of Oxford

CAMBRIDGE
UNIVERSITY PRESS

Shaftesbury Road, Cambridge CB2 8EA, United Kingdom

One Liberty Plaza, 20th Floor, New York, NY 10006, USA

477 Williamstown Road, Port Melbourne, VIC 3207, Australia

314–321, 3rd Floor, Plot 3, Splendor Forum, Jasola District Centre, New Delhi – 110025, India

103 Penang Road, #05–06/07, Visioncrest Commercial, Singapore 238467

Cambridge University Press is part of Cambridge University Press & Assessment, a department of the University of Cambridge.

We share the University's mission to contribute to society through the pursuit of education, learning and research at the highest international levels of excellence.

www.cambridge.org
Information on this title: www.cambridge.org/9781108749954

DOI: 10.1017/9781108886109

First published 2021
First paperback edition 2023

A catalogue record for this publication is available from the British Library

ISBN   978-1-108-84046-0   Hardback
ISBN   978-1-108-74995-4   Paperback

Cambridge University Press & Assessment has no responsibility for the persistence or accuracy of URLs for external or third-party internet websites referred to in this publication and does not guarantee that any content on such websites is, or will remain, accurate or appropriate.

To Smadar and David

Contents

Preface

The philosopher wants to be everything at once: prophet, healer, savior, scholar, politician.[1]

Heidegger is a static thinker, I am a more dynamic one. He feels closer to the Greeks, I feel closer to the Jewish prophets.[2]

Martin Heidegger is one of the most important modern philosophers and certainly the most controversial. Indeed, the polarized reception of his work can be matched by none. Karl Popper, for example, proclaimed: "I appeal to the philosophers of all countries to unite and never again mention Heidegger or talk to another philosopher who defends Heidegger. This man was a devil."[3] Emmanuel Levinas, on the other hand, noted: "for me, Heidegger is the greatest philosopher of the century, perhaps one of the very great philosophers of the millennium."[4] Heidegger has garnered a long list of enthusiasts and skeptics, admirers and detractors. But the mixture of admiration and disdain is particularly blatant in one of the most intriguing, fraught, and complex strands of his reception: his Jewish reception.

Of course, "Heidegger and the Jews" is hardly an overlooked theme. To date, an overwhelming number of studies has been dedicated to this broad topic. The majority of these studies, however, take on a similar perspective: they examine Heidegger's view of Jews and deal with the question of his antisemitism and relation to the Nazi party. The recent

---

[1] Lehmann, *Die Deutsche Philosophie der Gegenwart*, 11. Unless otherwise indicated, all translations from German and Hebrew are my own.

[2] "Ihm liegen die Griechen näher, mir die jüdischen Propheten." A quote by Max Scheler, as recorded in Berl, "Begegnung mit Jüdischer Zeitgenosse," 333.

[3] Eugene Yue-Ching Ho, "At 90, and Still Dynamic."

[4] Levinas, "Philosophy, Justice, and Love," 116.

publication of his so-called *Black Notebooks* brought about another wave of critical scholarship that reinforced the urgency of this perspective. Yet the dominance of this narrow scholarly angle should not come at a price of losing sight of the intense conceptual engagement of Jewish thinkers with Heidegger, an engagement that began immediately after the publication of his masterpiece *Being and Time* in 1927, continued throughout the entirety of the twentieth century, and was wider and richer than is often acknowledged. Describing the early excitement around Heidegger among his fellow students, Hans Jonas writes: "Many of these young Heidegger worshippers were ... young Jews ... what emerged in that time in Marburg was, in any case, not a healthy atmosphere, but rather something like the relationship of the believers to the Lubavitsher [Rebbe], such as if Heidegger was a tsadik, a miracle-working rabbi, or a guru."[5] Heidegger's appeal was not limited to his students alone. Though far from being the bewitchment Jonas describes, the persistent and momentous engagement of many twentieth-century Jewish thinkers with Heidegger's ideas is an undeniable fact. This study thus aims to center the critical glance on the topic of Heidegger and the Jews from the opposite perspective, reconstructing and critically appraising responses to Heidegger from a self-consciously Jewish standpoint.[6]

To avoid false expectations on the part of the reader, I wish to be clear from the very beginning as to what is meant by "Jewish" in the title. In order to preserve a focused research theme and definite argumentative line, this book concentrates primarily on thinkers who used

---

[5] Wiese, *The Life and Thought of Hans Jonas*, 88.
[6] Methodologically, this work differs from other studies that explore various comparisons, intersections, and other exchanges between Jewish traditions and Heidegger. For example, Elad Lapidot explores connections between Heidegger and the rabbinic tradition in "Heidegger's *Teshuva*?"; and see also his "Das Fremde im Denken" and his "People of Knowers: On Heideggerian and Jewish Epistemico-Politics." See also Sergey Dolgopolski's "How Else Can One Think Earth? The Talmuds and Pre-Socratics." Zohar Atkins engages with Jewish and biblical sources to reveal a resonance between Heidegger's thought and Jewish existence in his *An Ethical and Theological Appropriation of Heidegger's Critique of Modernity: Unframing Existence*. Allen Scult develops a Jewish theology exploring the "strange affinity" between Heidegger's philosophy and the traditional hermeneutics of Torah in *Martin Heidegger and the Hermeneutics of Torah: A Strange Affinity* and *Being Jewish/Reading Heidegger: An Ontological Encounter*. See also Zarader, *The Unthought Debt*. Elliot Wolfson has found in Heidegger a hermeneutical key through which the philosophical dimensions of Kabbalah can be disclosed and discussed. See, among many, his *Alef, Mem, Tau: Kabbalistic Musing on Time, Truth, and Death*; his *Language, Eros, Being: Kabbalistic Hermeneutics and Poetic Imagination*; and his *Heidegger and Kabbalah: Hidden Gnosis and the Path of Poēsis*.

their engagements with what they took to be the religious charge of Heidegger's thought as a foundation for offering a philosophical or theological reconstruction of Judaism or Jewishness. It is important to remember that the German word *Judentum*, which is often employed in this context, does not directly and seamlessly translate to the English "Judaism," and that the term "religion" is ambiguous, particularly as it applies to Judaism. It would thus be most accurate to say that I am dealing with receptions of Heidegger that perceive themselves as drawing on or speaking in the name of Jewish heritage. As is fairly well known, Heidegger had a remarkable cohort of gifted students who were Jews by descent and later became distinguished figures in their respective fields. These former students will only be explored here insofar as they fulfill the above criteria, that is, only insofar as they present an encounter between a construction of Judaism or Jewishness and Heidegger's philosophy. To make clear the scope of figures that will be included in this study, Hannah Arendt can serve as an example. Surely one of Heidegger's most brilliant students, Arendt's political thought is rightfully read, at least in part, as a response to her former teacher. Her reflections are clearly grounded in her experiences as a Jew, and at times she directs our attention to theologically inflected moments in Heidegger's thought. While Arendt will by no means be absent from the present study, to the extent that she does not bring to bear a construction of Judaism through her engagement with the religious charge of his philosophy, she does not fall under the category of "Jewish receptions" in the sense that I intend and thus will not be subjected to a thorough analysis.

This book aims to go beyond the common perspective on the theme of "Heidegger and religion," which usually focuses on Heidegger's roots in, or impact on, Christianity, and bring to the fore the Jewish perspective. It is true, no doubt, that to someone with theological commitments, everything seems redolent of such commitments. But this is not just a case in which for a person with a hammer, everything looks like a nail.[7] For, as we shall see, Heidegger invites these kinds of readings – Heidegger's language, as Theodor Adorno proclaimed, "created a theological aura" – and the long list of people who read him so testifies to this. Indeed, the Jewish reception that will be examined in this book is part of a broader story of Heidegger's reception among various groups – Catholics, Protestants, atheists, Marxists, and others – and parallels

---

[7] I thank Babette Babich for this formulation.

and similarities between these readings certainly exist.[8] At the same time, no other philosopher has had more impact on twentieth-century Jewish European thought than Martin Heidegger. To be sure, such a claim may seem odd, even offensive, given the notoriety of his biography, particularly as it intersected with Jews. His maltreatment of his (formerly Jewish) mentor Edmund Husserl, his political and philosophical support of Hitler, and his silence after the Holocaust, among other things, generated a deeply dubious personal and philosophical reputation and turned him, quite justifiably, into the ultimate "bad guy" of the philosophical world, the philosopher everyone loves to hate. Given the ominous historical and political setting within which the encounter with his thought took place, it is understandable that Heidegger's Jewish reception is fraught from the very outset. Nevertheless, one of the aims of this book is to substantiate the above claim: more than any other thinker, Heidegger's philosophical innovations and challenges marked and fomented twentieth-century European Jewish thought in a profound, indelible way.[9] This means, notably, that many of those who found Heidegger's philosophy meriting serious consideration did not suffer, as it has been suggested, from "false consciousness," nor were they "unJewish Jews" attempting to "deny their own Jewishness," and none deserve the somewhat dismissive title "Heidegger's Children."[10] Indeed, we shall see that Heidegger's thought – with its non-rationalistic bent, its secularized Christian categories, its obscure references to "gods," and its possible links to nationalistic fascism – served as a key reference point in the various attempts to negotiate the boundaries between Judaism, Christianity, and secularism in twentieth-century Jewish thought. For this reason, particular attention will be given throughout this study to the thematic of secularization and to the employment of the paradigm of Athens and Jerusalem, the convenient structure often put to use in the context of Jewish thought to delineate its

---

[8] It seems that the "theological turn" in French phenomenological circles that Dominique Janicaud decried was not confined to France and not necessarily a "turn." See Janicaud, *Phenomenology and the "Theological Turn."*

[9] This point has already been made, albeit formulated differently, by Fleischacker, who rightly likens Heidegger's mark on twentieth-century Jewish thought to Plato's mark on Philo, Aristotle's on Maimonides and his followers, and Kant's on Cohen, Leibowitz, and Breuer (and one can add to this list also Nietzsche's on early Zionist thinkers). Fleischacker, "Heidegger's Affinities with Judaism," 1. Fleischacker's piece offers insights into moments of correspondence between Judaism and Heidegger.

[10] Wolin, *Heidegger's Children: Hannah Arendt, Karl Löwith, Hans Jonas and Herbert Marcuse.* See also Fleischacker, "Heidegger's Affinities with Judaism," 3.

boundaries vis-à-vis Christian thought and culture.[11] From the perspective of intellectual history, therefore, this book seeks to contribute to our understanding of Heidegger's general reception, and from the perspective of Jewish studies, it seeks to expand, and perhaps even retell, the narrative of developments in twentieth-century Jewish philosophy.

It should be emphasized that my aim is not merely to outline Heidegger's "influences" on some of his Jewish readers (although these certainly exist and will be duly noted). Rather, I seek to account for a wider range of intellectual exchanges, including identification, incorporation, negotiation, critique, and rejection. One of the features that will crystallize throughout the chapters of this book is that, in a comparable manner to Spinoza in the infamous *Pantheismusstreit* in Germany at the end of the eighteenth century, Heidegger's philosophy is often misrepresented, and the views he is claimed to hold do not necessarily accord with his actual position. His philosophy came to mean different things to different people, and the variety of distinct and often contradictory portraits of Heidegger indicate not only the richness, intensity, and even density of his philosophy, but also, and perhaps more interestingly, the concerns and ideological tendencies of his Jewish readers, specifically as they relate to their perception of the modern, and modern Jewish, predicament.[12] Another, related feature that will emerge in our forthcoming discussion is the way in which twentieth-century Jewish thinkers read Heidegger's philosophy as an implicit or explicit religiously charged framework – and as a response, they posited Judaism as the ultimate alternative to it. Indeed, because Heidegger's life and thought were often seen as symbolizing and encapsulating the philosophical, theological, ethical, and political pathologies of modernity, the accounts of Jewishness sketched in response served not only as alternative theoretical schemes but as alternative modernities, with appropriate philosophical, religious, and political implications that are said to be immune, or at least more resistant, to the pathologies he was seen as manifesting.

---

[11] The theoretical context is, of course, the famous debate between Karl Löwith and Hans Blumenberg over the efficacy of the term "secularization" for modern times. Löwith, *Meaning in History*; Blumenberg, *The Legitimacy of the Modern Age*. The secondary literature on this debate is abundant.

[12] Not to mention the relatively limited number of his works available at the time – certainly in comparison to what is available to us now, including the recent publication of Heidegger's controversial *Überlegungen* notebooks, as well as the ever-increasing philosophical works, academic lecture courses, and correspondences that have been published over the years.

A central challenge facing a project of this kind is navigating between "too little" and "too much." Heidegger's presence in twentieth-century European Jewish thought is prevalent and multifaceted; there is no denying that more can be said of the thinkers who are discussed, and others, who are either only alluded to or not discussed at all, could have been considered as well.[13] It should therefore go without saying that I have no pretension to exhaust the subject matter. However, in bringing together those who are without doubt among the leading Jewish philosophers of the twentieth century alongside many less known figures, from a number of different geographical locations and over an extended period of time, this study seeks to outline the main patterns and provide a rich and diverse tapestry of Jewish responses to Heidegger. While not comprehensive, this book aims to offer a breadth that is unmatched by any other study to date, and by introducing new materials and addressing new questions, it hopes to provide a historical and conceptual foundation for further scholarly explorations of the topic.[14]

I must admit that when I embarked on this project, I was hoping to deal with the issue of Heidegger's Nazism as little as possible. The importance of this issue is undisputable, yet given the astounding amount of scholarship already written on it, I thought that little more could be said that would be of interest. But not only were Heidegger's private philosophical notebooks from the time of the war, the *Black Notebooks*, published soon after, unleashing a tidal wave of renewed interest in, and research on, this theme, but I also quickly came to see that it would simply be impossible to write a study of the Jewish reception of Heidegger without addressing his political involvement. His Nazism and the question of its ties to his thought are stitched into the intellectual moment that occupies this book, and rightly so, for Heidegger's support of the party and his anti-semitism, "being-historical" (as Peter Trawny termed it), "metaphysical" (as Derrida or Di Cesare termed it), or otherwise, are well documented and can no longer be seriously questioned.[15] Nor is there any point in trying to absolve Heidegger of any of his political or philosophical offenses – though there is no sense in exaggerating them, as is sometimes

---

[13] Among these are Michael Wyschogrod, Emil Fackenheim, Jacob Taubes, Susan Taubes, and Margarete Susman, to name only a few. I hope to address at least some of these omissions in future studies.

[14] Throughout this book we shall see that the examination of Jewish approaches to Heidegger intersects frequently with the receptions of existentialism more generally, *Lebensphilosophie*, Nietzsche, Karl Barth, Kierkegaard, Carl Schmitt, and even Hegel. Fleshing these out constitutes strands for further scholarly exploration.

[15] Di Cesare, *Heidegger, die Juden, die Shoah*.

the case, either. But while his shameful politics constantly looms in the background – and in the foreground – of our theme, depicting the Jewish encounters with Heidegger as simply a confrontation with a Nazi thinker amounts to a grave misconstrual of the seriousness with which his philosophy was approached, and obscures the fact that these thinkers did not only share many of his theoretical assumptions and agendas, but also actively drew on his thought as a fertile source for their own purposes.

It is at this point that a methodological obstacle to which a study like this is susceptible ought to be flagged: given Heidegger's notorious ties to the National Socialist Party, there is an almost inevitable impetus toward examining the Jewish encounter with Heidegger through the structured symbolic paradigms of "German" versus "Jew," "Nazi" versus "Jew," or even "perpetrator" versus "victim." Understandably, these structures are an operative optic through which this episode can be, and has been, grasped. Throughout this book it will become clear, I hope, that these typologies are overly schematic and ultimately oversimplify the complexity and gravity of the intellectual encounter at hand. Indeed, these very contrastive paradigms constitute a crucial facet of the subject matter itself, and thus they themselves – how they are perceived, the content inserted into them, the analytical means by which they are sustained, and their implicit normative charge – are part of what is under examination here.

MISE EN SCÈNE

It is best to perceive the twentieth-century Jewish reception of Heidegger's philosophy dealt with in this book as bearing a centrifugal dynamic. While it ultimately occurs in a variety of different places and contexts, mirroring the diffusion and displacement of much of European Jewry, it is rooted in a common historical and conceptual frame of reference. All the thinkers addressed here, including Heidegger himself, bear the marks of the turbulent era of interwar Germany, and it is the conceptuality and historical experiences of this period which laid the foundations for the diverse developments that constitute these receptions. A brief sketch of this context would do well to set the stage for the discussion that follows.

Heidegger's philosophy took shape in a Germany gripped by a sense of decadence and crisis.[16] The political and economic disaster ensuing the humiliating debacle in the Great War went hand in hand with a deep-

---

[16] See the collection edited by Gordon and McCormick, *Weimar Thought: A Contested Legacy*; Gay, *Weimar Culture: The Outsider as Insider*.

seated cultural pessimism. The newly born and unstable Weimar Republic staged a conflict that was both generational and ideational. Dissatisfied with the dominant schools of thought taught in the academic lecture halls, such as historicism and neo-Kantianism, the younger generation voiced a desire for new and radical forms of thought. Reflecting an anxiety attached to the processes of rationalization and what Max Weber called the "disenchantment" of modernity, many protested the comprehensive and systematic philosophical structures that ignored the individual's subjectivity and concreteness of its temporal existence.[17] The liberal bourgeois values of progress, reason, and universalism of the older generation were increasingly viewed as superficial, mechanistic, and soulless. A diminishing faith in the West corresponded with an increasing fascination with "oriental" non-Western cultures and an enhanced appeal to the irrational and archaic. The *Bildungsidealismus* that commanded the old order was gradually stripped of its prominence, and in its stead, matters of ontology, theology, and self-actuality came to the fore. A growing sense of breach between an inadequate world and divine transcendence gave rise to what was termed Gnostic or Marcionite attitudes. The thematics of *Deus absconditus* and *Deus revelatus* figured largely, and Pauline theology, with the dualisms associated with it, was intensely and creatively explored. This dualistic picture was complemented by the rise of a secular depiction of a radically immanent world. New questions concerning the meanings and relations between secularism and religion presented themselves as urgent. Are these two positions incongruent, or are they in fact two sides of the same coin? Is secularism solely a rejection of faith, or can it be construed theologically? What is the moral status of the world absent of God? Is salvation possible in an utterly fallen world? Can the individual achieve self-actuality when its existence is governed by the experience of alienation and not-at-homeness? Can transcendence be found in immanence? With a palpable eschatological tension, it was a time that experienced itself as "Zwischen den Zeiten." The "world of yesterday" was crumbling, but a new order was not yet in sight.

Perhaps nothing manifested the temperament of the time better than the surge in popularity of Søren Kierkegaard.[18] In underscoring the

---

[17] Gadamer, "Existentialism and the Philosophy of Existence," 11.
[18] Much has been written on Kierkegaard's reception in the German-speaking world. See Malik, *Receiving Søren Kierkegaard*, especially 339–392; Schulz, "A Modest Head Start," 307–419; Moyn, "Anxiety and Secularization," 279–304. On Kierkegaard in the Jewish intellectual world, see Nowotny, *"Kierkegaard ist ein Jude!"*

"infinite qualitative difference" between God and humanity, in appropriating and redefining the scholastic concept of "Existenz" from its
traditional meaning of substantiation of "essence" to the basic human
situation of experience, decision, and life, and in leveling a decisive critique against the all-encompassing Hegelian idealism, the Danish thinker
struck a resonant chord. And within this fraught atmosphere, it was the
perspective of *Existenzphilosophie* and particularly Heidegger's existential phenomenology in *Sein und Zeit* (1927) that sparked a fire in the
young generation's already kindled soul.[19] Leo Strauss, who will occupy
us in Chapter 5, seems to capture Heidegger's defining role in the development of many of his peers' thought:

> Nothing affected us as profoundly in the years in which our minds took their
> lasting directions as the thought of Heidegger … everyone else in the younger
> generation who had ears to hear was either completely overwhelmed by
> Heidegger, or else, having been almost completely overwhelmed by him, engaged
> in well-intentioned but ineffective rearguard actions against him.[20]

For the Jews, the unsteady times of Weimar bore both great promise and
great peril. The liberal constitution granted the Jews unprecedented equality and freedom. As "outsiders" who became "insiders," Jews were
allowed participation in many cultural and professional spheres that had
been previously closed off to them. An explosion of Jewish creativity and
involvement in science, art, literature, religion, philosophy, and political
activism ensued. Yet alongside an indisputable Jewish flourishing, the
tumultuous Weimar period witnessed an aggravation of reactionary,
neoconservative, and antisemitic forces. The perceived delusion of
Jewish assimilation led many to Zionism and Socialism, and also spurred
a process of dissimilation and revival of Jewish self-assertion.[21] Culturally
and intellectually immersed as they were, the young generation of Jewish
intellectuals heralded an equivalent revolt against the previous generation's worldview, with its synthesis of Kantianism and Judaism and the
more general conflation of Judaism with the values of the Enlightenment,

---

[19] As Dan Zahavi writes, "almost all subsequent theory formulations in continental philosophy can be understood as either extensions of or reactions to phenomenology." Zahavi,
"Phenomenology," 102. As various scholars have shown, this is true with respect to
twentieth-century Marxism, critical theory of the Frankfurt School, and Christian
thought, Protestant and Catholic alike, among others. I argue that the same is the case
with the European-rooted tradition of Jewish thought as well.
[20] Strauss, "An Unspoken Prologue," 450.
[21] Brenner, *The Renaissance of Jewish Culture in Weimar Germany*.

which was so carefully fashioned by nineteenth-century Jewish liberal thinkers, and above all, by Hermann Cohen.

The protest against the philosophical worldview typified by Cohen and its complementary liberal political-theological position is central to understanding the conceptual drive fueling the various Jewish engagements with Heidegger, and thus deserves some elaboration. Cohen, the founder of the Marburg school of neo-Kantianism, was one of the leading philosophical voices of his generation. As a Jew, he was also occupied by the effort of depicting Judaism as compatible with and epitomizing German liberal values and sensitivities.[22] In his understanding, the German spirit was indebted to two sources: ancient Greece and Judaism. "Plato and the prophets," he asserts, "constitute the two most important well-springs of modern [German] culture."[23] For this reason, Judaism is not only compatible with the peak of European spirit, it is also indispensable to it. Using a Protestant conceptual framework and applying an optimizing idealistic hermeneutic to his sources, Cohen knitted the biblical prophets, Plato, Maimonides, and Kant into a narrative of a shared German-Jewish ethico-religious vocation. This theoretical construct supported Cohen's political-theological worldview concerning the so-called – and widely disputed – "German-Jewish symbiosis." According to this position, Jews are an essential part of German nationality, and hence for Germany to fulfill its historical destiny, the equal share of Jews in German culture must be admitted.

Cohen's apologetic efforts came as a response to a common accusation of Judaism's antiquarianism, irrelevance, and overall alien character, voiced by nineteenth-century *Religionswissenschaftlers*, with the effective theologico-political vision of de-Judaizing Christianity and Germany. In the nineteenth-century debates, for most Germans and particularly for liberal Protestant intellectuals, granting the Jews emancipation was a contract with provisions. Equality was the reward, and complete assimilation was the condition. Supersessionist theological positions merged with a desire for a unified national identity in which Germanism and Protestantism were conflated. Academic scholarship was harnessed to this end, and findings in the fields of biblical studies, archaeology, philology, and history validated present-day anti-Jewish positions and sentiments. At times, the recurring theme of Christianity's emergence through the negation of Judaism was blended with racial theory which drew

---

[22] Myers, "Hermann Cohen and the Quest for Protestant Judaism."
[23] Cohen, "Das soziale Ideal bei Platon und den Propheten," 618.

a strict line between the Aryan-German and Semitic-Jewish race. The implicit political-theological statement of this general intellectual endeavor was clear: Judaism is at odds with the Christian-Protestant character of Germany, and the Jews have no place in the German *Volk*. By presenting Judaism as the root of the prevailing values of contemporary Germanism, Cohen strategically countered these adversary voices.

Cohen's account of the Jewish-German fellowship was founded upon faith in progress, reason, and universal morality, principles that were the cornerstone of the predominantly *Bildungsbürgertum* German Jews' identity. However, this was precisely the order that was under attack by the younger Jewish generation, for whom Cohen embodied the inauthentic liberal and bourgeois Judaism that willingly surrendered itself for the sake of acceptance and clothed its Judaism with a Christian-Protestant garment. Moreover, the unstable social and political reality of Weimar made his treasured political-theological dream passé. In a dynamic that began before the Great War but accelerated throughout the interwar period, the desire for an authentically Jewish framework generated a rethinking of Judaism in light of present sensitivities. As part of this effort, Martin Heidegger's philosophy was frequently engaged with.[24]

The famous renaissance of Judaism was underway, driven by a new generation of intellectuals seeking to reimagine and reformulate Jewishness along more existential, experiential, and post-liberal lines. Indeed, among the cadre of thinkers who rebelled against nineteenth-century philosophy and theology, it was the profundity and pathos of Heidegger's existential phenomenology, with its penetrating analysis of actual, concrete human existence and with what Adorno famously called the "jargon of authenticity" which was so appealing to many Weimar Jewish theorists in search for their authentic heritage. Of course, it is important to remember that Heidegger's thought appealed to many, Jews and non-Jews alike, holding diverse and often conflicting ideological and confessional commitments. But the fact that Heidegger was a main spokesperson for the denunciation of metaphysics, liberalism, and idealism and for the superiority of the perspective focusing on historical existence, made him an attractive and readily available source for Jewish thinkers who envisioned their Jewishness according to similar lines.

---

[24] For an initial sketch of this, see the chapter entitled "Bemerkungen zur Ungeschriebenen Geschichte der Jüdischen Heidegger-Rezeption," in Meyer, *Zwischen Philosophie und Gesetz*, 273–308.

The new spiritual climate and fresh theoretical frameworks presented their own set of challenges, however. In its Christian manifestation, the rejection of nineteenth-century liberalism took the form of unstitching the synthesis of Christianity and culture. From the Jewish perspective, however, the rejection of liberalism was often framed as a denunciation of the foreign Protestant conceptuality that had been internalized by Jewish thinkers. Foreign, unauthentic, and ill-suited, the Protestant framework was to be discarded and replaced by an authentic form of Jewish expression. But were the philosophical and theological perspectives available to replace the deficient frameworks of the past themselves neutral? Do not the Christian undertones in *Existenzphilosophie* make it unsuitable for authentic Jewish thought? Moreover, the rise of Gnostic and Marcionite attitudes carried a reverberating anti-Jewish import of supersessionism and antisemitism. These complemented the rise of radical German nationalism and reactionary forces that perceived the Jews as the German "misfortune." In this respect, despite the revolt against earlier patterns of reflections, key strands of German interwar philosophy and theology continued the nineteenth-century objective of severing the historical ties between Judaism and Christianity and between present-day Jews and Christians.[25]

The collapse of faith in reason and in the liberal world of the nineteenth century, and the possibilities, challenges, and impasses that emerged as a result of this collapse, is the backdrop of this study. While Hermann Cohen died almost a decade before the publication of *Sein und Zeit*, his philosophical worldview and vision of Judaism continued to reverberate throughout twentieth-century Jewish thought, and covertly looms over a century of the Jewish reception of Heidegger. This is because the disillusionment with, and rebellion against, the Cohenian picture was shared both by Heidegger and the majority of the Jewish thinkers that we will examine, but the inspection of the possibilities and pitfalls of Heidegger's philosophy was part of the Jewish attempt to work out how it is best to proceed after the downfall of reason and liberalism. Thus, as we shall see, it is the political climate, the conceptual terms, and the pressing experiences of the interwar period that determine the ensuing twentieth-century receptions of the philosopher from Messkirch. That its determining terms were shaped in a period when an all-encompassing atmosphere of crisis took hold explains the sense of urgency, far exceeding the tensions of

[25] Tal, *Christians and Jews in Germany*; Schwarzschild, "The Theological-Political Basis of Liberal Christian-Jewish Relations in Modernity," 70–95.

common theoretical debates, that marked this intellectual encounter. For in the minds of many at the time, the stakes of philosophical disputes were almost apocalyptic, and what was debated was no less than the very nature and future of Western civilization. The coveted dream of one was the daunting nightmare of the other; where one saw hope, the other found nihilism. The urgency of this encounter is validated by Heidegger's public endorsement of the Nazi party only shortly after the publication of his magnum opus, and the general sense that in this case, philosophy and politics – and, as we shall see, also theology – were intimately intertwined. Engaging with his thought thus demanded coming to terms not only with the challenges it posed in the sphere of speculative reflection, but with its ethical and political ramifications as well – and with the shortcomings of the traditions of thought that made Heidegger's philosophy possible.

The layout of the study is as follows: Chapter 1 sets the stage for the following chapters by attending to the question of the relation between Heidegger's philosophy and Christianity. By focusing on his claim for neutrality toward theology and the theme of secularization, the chapter outlines the transitions of Heidegger's thought from his early theological endeavors to *Sein und Zeit* and to his later work. It also discusses the early Christian reception of *Sein und Zeit* by Protestant and Catholic theologians, framing the descriptive and evaluative examination of the analyses of the Jewish engagements with Heidegger that comes next.

Chapter 2 portrays how the intellectual and generational split in interwar German culture between "old," rational, and idealistic thinking, and "new," experiential, and existential thinking, is manifested in the early Jewish receptions of Heidegger. It does this by focusing on the battle over the legacy of Kant typified in the famous Davos encounter and by fleshing out the political and theological resonances of this encounter in terms of its bearings on the debate over the ties between *Judentum* and *Deutschtum*. As I show, Ernst Cassirer and Franz Rosenzweig can be seen as representing something like "typical" reactions to Heidegger from the perspective of "old thinking" and "new thinking," respectively. As part of this examination, I situate the common association of Rosenzweig and Heidegger within the larger context of Heidegger's Jewish reception.

Chapter 3 shows that the secularized Christian terminology and the presumption of *Dasein*'s godless existence in *Sein und Zeit* led a variety of Jewish thinkers in interwar Germany and Palestine to conclude that Heidegger's existential analysis of *Dasein* is caught up in Christian assumptions, outlines a Christian conception of human existence, and is thus ill-suited for Jewish expression. This reading of Heidegger is contextualized within the wider debate at the time regarding the theological inflection of the perspective of *Existenzphilosophie*, the juxtaposition of Heidegger, Kierkegaard, and Karl Barth, and the anti-Jewish political-theological reverberations of the "Gnostic" and "Marcionite" perspectives with which Heidegger was associated.

Chapter 4 is a critical examination of Martin Buber's decades-long fascination and confrontation with Heidegger's philosophy. This chapter expands previous scholarship's prime focus on Buber's conception of I–Thou in relation to Heidegger's notion of being–with (*mit-Sein*) and exposes Buber's far more extensive engagement with – and assault on – Heidegger's earlier and later works, including a latent quarrel over the appropriation of the German poet Friedrich Hölderlin. I show that Buber shadowboxed Heidegger for his entire mature life and sought to construct a Jewish-dialogical alternative, which I term "dwelling prophetically," to what he called Heidegger's monological thought and its ideal of "dwelling poetically."

In Chapter 5 I argue that one cannot fully grasp Leo Strauss's critique of Heidegger's philosophy, which he perceived as the greatest challenge to both philosophy and authentic Judaism, without understanding Strauss's critical attitude toward the Christian horizon and connotations he identified in Heidegger. Examining Strauss's early and later writings, I concentrate on Strauss's depiction of Heidegger as a historicist and a nihilist and analyze how Strauss both utilizes Heidegger to extend his critique of what he took to be the modern Jewish crisis and at the same time draws on his work to signal toward the overcoming of this crisis. The chapter also traces the hesitant shift in Strauss's critical approach toward Heidegger's later writings.

Chapter 6 aims to organize Abraham Joshua Heschel's otherwise unsystematic critique of and rejoinder to Heidegger, and present it as a coherent, unified theological argument. By reviewing Heschel's writings from his early years as a philosophy student in Weimar-era Berlin to his mature works in the 1960s, I demonstrate that for him, Heidegger puts forth a paganist framework of radical immanence that dehumanizes *Dasein* and deifies being. In contrast to this, Heschel advances his account of the biblical God of pathos, who is transcendent to the world but is also the concerned Lord of being.

Chapter 7 traces Emmanuel Levinas's lifelong struggle with Heidegger's philosophy, from the 1930s to the 1980s. It approaches the matter through the prism of the confrontation Levinas posits between what he considers to be Heidegger's paganism and his own account of Judaism and ethics. I argue that Levinas mimics Heidegger and develops an existential hermeneutic of being-Jewish in his early writings, as an alternative to Heidegger's "pagan" analytic, which then serves as the basis for the contrast between "ethics" and "ontology" in his mature writings. As I show, in both method and content, Levinas's philosophy is more dependent on Heidegger's scheme than he is willing to admit, as is his account of Judaism.

The Jewish engagement with Heidegger in the twentieth century is rich and varied. Through a dialectic of attraction and repulsion, Jewish thinkers developed a version of Jewishness that sought to offer the way out of the overall crisis plaguing their world, which was embodied, as they saw it, in Heidegger's life and thought. Neither turning a blind eye to Heidegger's antisemitism nor using it as an excuse for ignoring his philosophy, they came to grapple with Heidegger's existential analytic and diagnose where it had gone wrong in order to correct its philosophical and political errors, and while doing so, also to think through the place of Judaism and Jewish existence in the modern world. Perhaps ironically, then, Heidegger's thought proved itself to be fertile ground for reconceptualizing what it means to be Jewish.

Acknowledgments

Throughout this project I have benefited from the assistance and support of many teachers, colleagues, and friends, and it is a particular pleasure to be able to thank them. This book began as a doctorate dissertation written under the guidance of Graham Ward at the department for theology and religion at the University of Oxford. Special thanks go to Graham for his astonishing erudition, astute remarks, and constant support and advice. I was lucky to have Mark Wrathall and Paul Franks as my examiners, and their comments were crucial to the reworking of the dissertation into a book, which took place during my time as the Stanley A. and Barbara B. Rabin Postdoctoral Research Fellow at the department of Religion and Institute for Israel and Jewish Studies at Columbia University. The final touches on the manuscript took place in my current position as the Career Research Fellow in Jewish Studies at Wolfson College, University of Oxford, which has served as my home and community for the best part of the last six years. During my stay at Columbia, Elisheva Carlebach suggested organizing a workshop on an earlier version of the book manuscript, an idea that was then supported and set into motion by Gil Anidjar. I am deeply grateful to all the participants of the workshop – Gil Anidjar, Elisheva Carlebach, Michah Gottlieb, Eugene Sheppard, Babette Babich, and Edward Baring – for reading the entire manuscript in depth and for doing so out of a wonderful mixture of intellectual curiosity and good will. I am fortunate to have profited from their critical thinking, insightfulness, and creativity. I've incorporated many of their comments and suggestions for improvement and simply cannot thank them enough for their generosity. Miri Freund-Kandel, Johannes Zachhuber, Yiftach Ofek, Dror Bundy, Zohar Atkins, Judith Wolfe, Ehud Luz, Asaf

Ziderman, Megan Loumagne, Elizabeth Li, Sam Shonkoff, Bill Plevan, Jeff Bernstein, Ori Werdiger, Netta Cohen, and Michael Fagenblat have read either all or some chapters of the book, in various stages of the project, and have offered thoughtful and constructive comments. Beyond the rich intellectual input, Megan and Libby have been an endless source of sanity, encouragement, and support. I've also benefited from illuminating conversations on the topic of Heidegger and Jewish thought with Daphne Hampson, Ehud Luz, Michael Fagenblat, Zohar Atkins, and Elad Lapidot. Special thanks to Evan Parks for insightful reflections on this theme and for the experience of a genuine intellectual dialogue. Ido Ben-Harush has been a close friend and intellectual companion for years and is inscribed into this project in more ways than one. Hindy Najman has offered deft guidance and advice at various crossroads. Martin Goodman and Elliot Wolfson have been extremely generous and supportive of me and my work, and I am deeply grateful to them. I must also thank my family and especially my parents for their constant encouragement and interest in my scholarship, despite not entirely understanding what it is I actually do. Michal, Nir, Adam, Stéphane, Maria, Biel, Lina, Nomi, Netta, Benjamin, Marta, and Pierre were an essential part of the journey as well.

A word of appreciation is due to the staff of the various archives I've visited and consulted while conducting research for this book. These include Hila Tzur from Gnazim Archive in Tel Aviv, Gudrun Bernhardt from the Deutsches Literaturarchiv in Marbach am Neckar, Rachel Ariel from Abraham Joshua Heschel's Archive at Duke University, as well as the staff at Israel National Library in Jerusalem, the Hebrew University Archive, University Library Frankfurt am Main, the Institute for the History of the German Jews in Hamburg, and the Center for Jewish History in New York.

I wish to acknowledge the generous sources of financial support that have made this study possible: British Friends of the Hebrew University, Memorial Foundation for Jewish Culture, AJA/Karten Trust, Leo Baeck Fellowship Programme, Duke University Jewish Studies/Rubenstein Library Research Fellowship, Hensley Henson Studentship, Crewdson Award, Sir John Plumb Charitable Trust, the Polonsky Foundation, Wolfson College Bursary, Spalding Trust, the Rothschild Foundation Hanadiv Europe Doctoral Fellowship, and the Association for Jewish Studies Dissertation Completion Fellowship, generously supported through a grant from the Legacy Heritage Fund.

Herkunft and *Zukunft*: Heidegger, Christianity, and Secularization

Heid[egger] is right in one thing, the remnants of Christianity must be exorcized from Philosophy. Only he does not do it (does he?)[1]

In a particularly honest moment, Heidegger describes his struggle with Christianity as

affecting the whole path of my questioning so like subterranean, seismic shocks . . . and who should fail to recognize that my entire path so far has been accompanied by a salient engagement with Christianity: an engagement that has never taken the form of an explicitly raised "problem," but was rather at once the preservation of, and *at the same time* a painful separation from, my ownmost provenance – the childhood house, home and youth.[2]

Laying the groundwork to the ensuing discussion as a whole, the present chapter aims to explore the ambiguity characterizing Heidegger's relation to Christianity. While an exhaustive account of the evolution of Heidegger's thought and the knotty contours of "Heidegger and religion" are beyond its scope, we will touch on some key moments of this theme. Throughout this chapter we aim to establish the integral role of Heidegger's engagement with Christianity for the development of the ideas laid out in *Sein und Zeit*, examining in particular the transition from his early theological endeavors to the analytic of Dasein in his 1927 magnum opus. In the center of our discussion stand the themes of secularization and the self-professed theological neutrality of his philosophy. Second, we shall discuss the efforts in his later thinking to overcome the technological tradition of metaphysics, which he perceived to be interlinked with Christianity, and to prepare for a future advent of the

---

[1] Taubes, *Die Korrespondenz*, vol. II, 72.
[2] GA 66, 44–28, 415/Heidegger, *Mindfulness*, 368.

gods and the divine. Third, we shall survey some of the initial debates in Christian theological circles surrounding his early work. We begin with Heidegger's relation to Christianity – its role in the development of his thought and its role as a foil for the innovative theoretical path he sought to blaze – not only because it is fundamental to understanding the architecture, motivations, sources, and goals of his philosophy, but also because it is vital for coming to grips with his Jewish reception.

Since the publication of the "earliest" Heidegger's lectures and notes, it has become undeniable that the trajectory of his philosophy as a whole is thoroughly indebted to his Christian origins.[3] Biographically, the young Heidegger was raised in a devout Catholic home in the rural town of Messkirch in Baden. As he came of age, he aspired to become a priest and began formation in a Jesuit seminary. While his quest for priesthood was cut short, Heidegger remained a passionate disciple of the Catholic faith, publishing polemical and apologetic pieces in various conservative Catholic journals and enrolling as a student of Catholic theology at the University of Freiburg. His initial philosophical training was in neo-Scholasticism and neo-Kantianism, and he wrote his dissertation on psychologism (1913) and his *Habilitationsschift* on "Duns Scotus' Doctrine of Categories and Signification" (1915). Increasing dissatisfaction with the assumptions and efficiency of his philosophical commitments and his eventual marriage to the Protestant Elfride Petri in 1917 contributed to his estrangement from Catholicism and adoption of the Protestant confession. Correlatedly, he immersed himself in what was at the time regarded as the anti-metaphysical Protestant theological tradition, including the writings of Paul, Augustine, Luther, Schleiermacher, Overbeck, Kierkegaard, Dilthey, and others, which had an immense impact on the development of his original thought.[4]

---

[3] Much has been written on this topic, but the most authoritative works remain Van Buren, *The Young Heidegger*; Kisiel, *The Genesis of Heidegger's Being and Time*; *Reading Heidegger from the Start*, edited by Kisiel and Van Buren; *Becoming Heidegger*, edited by Kisiel and Sheehan.

[4] While there is no denying that Heidegger's Catholic upbringing and scholastic training left their mark on his work (cf. Ott, "Martin Heidegger's Catholic Origins"), I focus on the Protestant layers in his thought because it is mainly these that are picked up by his Jewish readers. Of course, the twentieth century is replete with Catholic thinkers who were attracted to Heidegger's thinking. Karl Rahner, Bernhard Welte, Hans Urs von Balthazar, Johannes Baptist Lotz, Richard Williamson, Max Müller, John D. Caputo, to

Heidegger's writings and lectures from this early period hold nascent formulations of much of his later work.[5] A central theme in his early intellectual endeavors is the rejection of the "Scholastic" attitude of *philosophia perennis*, with its ideal of static, a-temporal, and metaphysical abstraction, in favor of an attitude faithful to the factical lived experience. Metaphysical language, he believed, objectifies, de-worlds, and de-historicizes the immersive and unsurveyable flow of being. One correctly finds echoes of Wilhelm Dilthey's historical focus (drawn from Hegel) in Heidegger's rejection of the detached and a-temporal Greek metaphysics and his shift toward the historical, temporal, and factical existence. Heidegger also follows Dilthey in attributing the origin of this shift to the advent of early Christianity.[6] For Dilthey, the turn to history is rooted in the incarnation, wherein "God's essence, instead of being grasped in the self-enclosed concept of substance of antiquity, was now caught up in historical vitality. And so historical consciousness, taking the expression in its highest sense, first came into being."[7] Christianity validates history as the site of significance, Dilthey holds, for it is the realm in which the drama of Christ's life, suffering, and death unfolded. Mirroring this view, Heidegger states in the 1919/1920 lecture course "Basic Problems of Phenomenology" that "the deepest historical paradigm for the peculiar process whereby the main focus of factical life and the life-world shifted into the self-world and the world of inner experience gives itself to us in the emergence of Christianity."[8] One of Heidegger's first independent phenomenological undertakings is an attempt to explicate this originary inward religious experience from within. By approaching religion as a phenomenological lived experience, Heidegger intentionally rebels against the *Religionswissenschaft* school's approach to religion as an object of science. By this time, he had already departed from the phenomenological method of his mentor Edmund Husserl, with its transcendental phenomenological reduction and non empirical, pure

---

name only a few, drew to differing extents on Heidegger for their respective theologies. On the consequential pre- and postwar Catholic reception of phenomenology (in particular, Husserl, Heidegger, and Scheler), see Baring's rich *Converts to the Real*.

[5] This is fleshed out in Wolfe, *Heidegger and Theology*; Caputo, "People of God, People of Being"; Caputo, "Heidegger and Theology"; Crowe, *Heidegger's Religious Origins* and *Heidegger's Phenomenology of Religion*; Vedder, *Heidegger's Philosophy of Religion*; Kovacs, *The Question of God*; the collection *Heidegger und die christliche Tradition*, edited by Fischer and von Hermann; Hemming, *Heidegger's Atheism*.

[6] Heidegger, "Wilhelm Dilthey's Research."

[7] Dilthey, *Introduction to the Human Sciences*, 230.

[8] GA 58, 61–62/Heidegger, *Basic Problems of Phenomenology*, 47.

consciousness of transcendental subjectivity, and in its stead he developed an alternative phenomenology centering on the hermeneutics of facticity of Dasein's being-in-the-world. Heidegger found this model of phenomenology to be particularly potent for the task of uncovering the pristine existential disposition of authentic religiosity, found, he believed, in *Urchristentum*, which was unadulterated by "Greekanizing."[9] This is because, for him, phenomenology's liberation from the agglomeration of unnecessary preconceived conceptuality and its focus on the pretheoretical immediacy of facticity is comparable to the liberation of the immediacy of factical being-Christian from the restrictions of alien Aristotelian metaphysical categories.[10] As such, Heidegger perceived himself as reenacting the rare yet "powerful eruptions" of authentic Christian assertion, found likewise "in Augustine, in Luther, in Kierkegaard."[11]

Participating in the contemporary resurgence of Pauline theology, Heidegger turns to Paul's letters to the Galatians and to the Thessalonians – the earliest texts of the New Testament – in the winter semester lecture course given in 1920/1921, as part of his aim to unearth the experience of primordial Christian life. These texts are not systematic philosophical treatises, and deliberately so – they are external to the metaphysical-Scholastic tradition and, as epistles, convey the situation of a concrete, temporal existence. Consonant with the then-prevalent view, Heidegger presents an eschatologically centered account of early Christianity. In his reading of Paul, the coming of Christ as a moment of actualization is not to be understood as an event that will come to pass in a certain particular moment. "Paul does not say 'When,'" he observes, "because this expression is inadequate to what is to be expressed."[12] The indeterminacy of the Second Coming grounds a life of insecure anticipation, emphasizing the lack, the still-to-come of salvation. Authentic Christian life, Heidegger determines, subsists in the experience of not-yet, in the pending openness in the face of divine absence, in the eschatological suffering and fragility in light of the undetermined *parousia*.[13]

---

[9] GA 61, 6/Heidegger, *Phenomenological Interpretations of Aristotle*, 6.

[10] As Wolfe notes: "Heidegger discovered the phenomenological method, together with Protestantism, in large part as a means to adequately describing religious experience." Wolfe, *Heidegger's Eschatology*, 44.

[11] GA 58, 205/Heidegger, *Basic Problems of Phenomenology*, 155.

[12] GA 60, 102/Heidegger, *Phenomenology of Religious Life*, 72. An excellent collection of essays on these lectures is McGrath and Wierciński, *A Companion to Heidegger's Phenomenology of Religious Life*.

[13] On Heidegger's early eschatological horizon and its prefiguration of later developments see Wolfe, *Heidegger's Eschatology*.

Being Christian, according to this construal, consists of inhabiting a certain mode of temporality. More specifically, it is the unstable historical process of *becoming* Christian, whereby the anticipated eschatological future throws the believers back unto their "already-having-become" Christians, creating the uncertainty of the present "now being" which can reach its abrupt end at any given moment. In *Sein und Zeit*, one finds a replication of this tripartite originary Christian existence in the phenomenological construal of Dasein's ec-static temporality. The very conceiving of Dasein's existence in terms of temporality is modeled in accordance with the earlier eschatological hermeneutic of primordial Christian religiosity. We shall see that the configuration of temporality that is spelled out in his early lectures on Paul is de-Christianized in the Dasein analytic, where Dasein's being-toward-death replaces anticipating the *parousia*.

It this context, Heidegger contrasts the eschatological tendencies of early Christianity with "late-Judaism" (*Spätjudentum*), for whom the messianic anticipation is directed at the coming to pass of a particular futural moment.[14] This is an aside comment, stated almost inadvertently, but it is characteristic of Heidegger's overall treatment of Judaism: judgments are made, almost always in passing, with virtually no textual or historical substantiation, nor with any actual engagement with Judaism as a real textual, practical, and lived tradition. As will be discussed below, in the rare cases he refers to it, Judaism functions as a cipher and foil against which his proposal is positioned. In any event, with this judgment, Heidegger implicitly couples Judaism with Greek metaphysics, both of which betray what Kierkegaard calls the "vulgar" conception of temporality as the succession of present moments; time as chronology (*chronos*), *Historie*. As Heidegger explains soon after, on this account time undergoes a "homogenization" – "an assimilation of time to place, to Presence pure and simple."[15] As such it correlates with a defunct ontology of presence, as it presupposes that "to be" means "to have presence in the moment that now is."[16] In contrast to this rendition of time stands the authentic Christian *Augenblick*, time as eschatology (*kairos*), *Geschichte*. In *Sein und Zeit*, this temporal distinction is reproduced in the distinction between the inauthentic relation to death characterizing *das Man*, that of

[14] GA 60, 114; Heidegger, *Phenomenology of Religious Life*, 81. Wolfson critiques this understanding of Jewish messianism in *The Duplicity of Philosophy's Shadow*, 98–99.
[15] Heidegger, *The Concept of Time*, 18e.
[16] Heidegger, *Sein und Zeit*, 373, and *Being and Time*, 425–426. Hereafter cited as *SZ/BT*.

awaiting (*Erwartung*) a futural point in time in which death "comes to pass," and the authentic anticipation (*Vorlaufen*) toward death, in which Dasein's possibilities in the present are illuminated by its being-ahead-of-itself (*sich-vorweg-sein*).

The textual analysis of Paul is colored by perhaps the most crucial theological influence on Heidegger at the time, Martin Luther. Heidegger began reading Luther, to whom he refers as "a companion" in his quest, around 1918 in Freiburg and even taught seminars on his theology with Rudolf Bultmann in Marburg after moving there in 1923.[17] Heidegger was inspired by Luther's attempt to purge Christianity of the infiltration of Greek metaphysics. Luther's admonishment of the Scholastic belief in a natural and speculative access to the divine, as well as his emphasis on God's extreme externality, particularly impressed the young Heidegger. His portrayal of Christian existence in a world in which God is experienced only as absence and concealment reflects Luther's pessimistic anthropology of the postlapsarian human state of existence as *status corruptionis*. According to the dominant reading at the time to which Heidegger concedes, Luther held that the corruption of the Fall is so deep and constitutive that it completely eliminates humanity's prelapsarian character, generating an unbridgeable gap between a radically distant God and the utterly sinful human being. This view is contrasted to Scholastic theology's belief that while deeply marred by the Fall, something of the original prelapsarian state of human existence remains, and thus some form of continuum and connection between God and the human being is maintained. That Heidegger adheres to Luther's view is evident from a 1923 lecture course, where he defends Luther's radical anthropological view over against Max Scheler's idea of the human's natural orientation toward God. The human being is not a "God seeker," as per Scheler, but is by definition in a *status corruptionis*, a state of *ignorantia Dei* which is "a determinatively negative relation to God, in which man stands against God" – and Heidegger adds: "*this* is as such constitutive!"[18] By aligning himself with the implications of the doctrine of the radical otherness of God and the abyss between the world and God, Heidegger accords with the present-day "Gnostic" theological trend permeating Germany at the time. It should be noted, however, that unlike the

---

[17] GA 63, 5/Heidegger, *Ontology*, 4. See Van Buren, "Martin Heidegger, Martin Luther"; McGrath, "The Facticity of Being God-Forsaken," reprinted in McGrath, *The Early Heidegger & Medieval Philosophy*; Lehmann, "Sagen, was Sache ist."

[18] GA 63, 27/Heidegger, *Ontology*, 22–23.

typical "Gnostic" attitude, he maintains that through the focus on factical life, the absence of God does not lead to a devaluation of the world, but rather to the opposite: the anxiety embedded in the salvation-seeking historical temporality reveals, paradoxically, this world as the arena of meaning.

Luther's mark is also discernible in the lecture course, "Augustine and Neoplatonism," delivered in the following 1921 summer semester, dedicated to book X of Augustine's *Confessions*.[19] Carrying out the exegetical attempt to extract Neoplatonism from Augustine, Heidegger differentiates between "metaphysical" ("Greek") and "factical" ("Christian") layers in Augustine and parallels them to Luther's distinction between *theologia gloriae* and *theologia crucis*. The former, he maintains, is manifested in Augustine's hope to reach eternal and all-fulfilling peace in God, the *summum bonum*. This Scholastic-metaphysical God, Heidegger contends, following Luther, is an object of conceptual vision and thus a readily available, calculatable, and masterable God; a God of presence, an idol. The message of the Cross, on the other hand, is that the Christian God, the *Deus absconditus*, is not a God of harmony and serenity but of concealment, fear, and trembling. The historical facticity of the Christian in-faith is thus constituted by the struggle, guilt, and humility of finite existence in the face of divine absence. Here, as in his exegesis of Paul, it is the mood, the affordance (*Befindlichkeit*) – a notion Heidegger seems to have developed on the basis of Augustine's *affectio* – that is central, and it remains so in *Sein und Zeit*'s phenomenological hermeneutic of Dasein. Likewise, the feature of Dasein's guilt or debt (*Schuld*) is foreshadowed in the irreducibility of existential guilt to any religiously charged action, be it sin or partaking in Christ's suffering. And as Heidegger readily admits, the very characterization of Dasein as care (*Sorge*) was first uncovered in his reading of Augustine.[20] Indeed, it has been suggested that in *Sein und Zeit*, Heidegger turns Luther's *theologia crucis* into an *ontologia crucis*.[21]

[19] On Heidegger and Augustine, see for example, Coyne, *Heidegger's Confessions*. Coyne offers close readings of processes of de-theologization of Christian concepts in Heidegger's thought as they emerge from the philosopher's encounter with Augustine. See also van Fleteren, *Martin Heidegger's Interpretations of Saint Augustine*.

[20] *SZ* 199/*BT* 492; *GA* 20, 418/Heidegger, *History of the Concept of Time: Prolegomena*, 302.

[21] Van Buren, *The Young Heidegger*, 167. Van Buren also quotes Edmund Schlink, the noted Luther scholar: "Heidegger's existential analytic of human Dasein is a radical secularization of Luther's anthropology" (ibid., 159).

Shortly after the lectures on Paul and Augustine, Aristotle and Kant assume a more central stage in Heidegger's developing thought. There is, however, no question that his engagements with the canonical Christian texts markedly affect his approach toward these philosophers. Indeed, given that many fundamental categories of Dasein's ontological explication are prefigured in the configuration of "Christian existence" in these early commentaries on Paul and Augustine, they are to be rightly considered as core building blocks in the development of his thought toward *Sein und Zeit*.[22]

A-THEISTIC PHENOMENOLOGY AND THE QUESTION OF NEUTRALITY

Before we turn to discuss *Sein und Zeit*, a point about Heidegger's phenomenological method needs to be made. In the early 1920s, Heidegger adopts an a-theistic methodology, one which does not take a definitive stand on the question of God, but rather brackets it out of the philosophical purview. In his 1921–1922 lecture course "Phenomenological Interpretations of Aristotle," he exclaims that "Philosophy, in its radical, self-posing questionability, must be *a-theistic* as a matter of principle. Precisely on account of its basic intention, philosophy must not presume to possess or determine God."[23] With this Heidegger is following Husserl's "principle of presuppositionlessness" ("des Prinzip der Voraussetzungslosigkeit"), whereby metaphysical speculations and the positive teachings of all scientific fields are to be bracketed from the inquiry of phenomenology.[24] "The object of philosophical research," Heidegger maintains, "is the human Dasein as it is interrogated with

---

[22] Though Fergus Kerr's claim that "it may be said, without much exaggeration, that almost every philosophical innovation in *Sein und Zeit* may easily be traced to a theological source," is indeed an exaggeration. Kerr, *Immortal Longings*, 47. It is important to keep in mind, as Van Buren notes, that "Heidegger's ontology in the twenties was decisively influenced not only by religious sources by also by Aristotle, Husserl, Scheler, Jaspers, Lask, Natorp, and Bergson, as well as by such sources as Plato's dialogues, the ancient skeptics, Seneca, Tolstoy, Dostoevsky, Van Gogh's letters, and perhaps also Ortega y Gasset and Georg Lukàcs." Van Buren, "Heidegger's Early Freiburg Courses, 1915–1923," 141–142.

[23] GA 61, 197–198/Heidegger, *Phenomenological Interpretations of Aristotle*, 148). On Heidegger and Aristotle, see Volpi, *Being and Time*; McNeill, *The Glance of the Eye*; Brogan, *Heidegger and Aristotle*; Taminiaux, "The Interpretation of Aristotle's Notion of Aretê in Heidegger's First Courses."

[24] Husserl, *Ideas*, 188.

respect to the character of its being."[25] God is never given as a *Gegenstand* of phenomenological investigation, and as beyond the phenomenological horizon, any recourse to God must be excluded from philosophical reflection. Phenomenology is and only can be concerned with the immanent world of human existence, and is thus limited, from within, by human finitude. Not God or eternity, but death is the horizon of human existence. This position has its philosophical justifications, but we would do well to point out that Heidegger's methodological bracketing of God and his implicit premises that God serves only an ontic rather than ontological role in the constitution of human existence parallels the commitment to radical divine externality and acknowledgment of human forsakenness to which Heidegger subscribed at the time. For, from within the utterly sinful world, no recourse to God can be made; human existential structures are to be articulated on their own terms.

Following Luther, Heidegger's approach draws a clear line of demarcation between theology and philosophy. The result of this demarcation is the methodological emancipation of theology from the constraints of philosophy and of philosophy from dealing with claims of faith. "Could it be," he suggests, "that the very idea of a philosophy of religion ... is pure nonsense?"[26] Nevertheless, not unlike Husserl, who perceived his "atheological" phenomenological approach to be a way of arriving "at God without God," Heidegger intends this methodology to operate as a *preparatio evangeliae*.[27] "The more radical philosophy is," he remarks, "the more determinately is it on a path away from God; yet, precisely in the radical actualization of the 'away', it has its own difficult proximity to God."[28]

Heidegger held fast to this a-theistic methodology also after he parted company with Christianity in the mid-1920s. This is evident from his lecture "Phenomenology and Theology," delivered shortly after the publication of *Sein und Zeit*, to the Protestant theological faculty in Tübingen (and then in Marburg). In this lecture, he articulates his views on the relationship between philosophy (phenomenology) and theology in a more organized way. He proceeds by dismissing the common way of approaching the matter through the distinction of reason/faith, in favor of the distinction – so central to the entire project of *Sein und Zeit* – between

---

[25] *GA* 62, 348–349.   [26] *GA* 62, 363n54.
[27] Jaegerschmidt, "Conversations with Edmund Husserl"; Moran, *Edmund Husserl*, 16–18.
[28] *GA* 61, 197–198/Heidegger, *Phenomenological Interpretations of Aristotle*, 148.

the ontological ("existential") dealing with being and the ontic ("existentiell") dealing with beings. Ontic sciences, Heidegger determines, deal with their respective ontic subjects and take for granted the being of their researched entities. The subject of inquiry of philosophy, on the other hand, is being as such, and thus it serves as the ultimate foundation for all ontic sciences. Theology is a positive ontic science, dedicated to "the specific mode of being of the Christian occurrence," and as with all ontic sciences, any attempt at scientific systemization or reflection on its pre-Christian foundation must call upon philosophy. Theology needs philosophy only as the "science of faith"; in terms of its particular content and concepts, it functions autonomously. Theology is a "calling to faith in faith"; the disclosure of "theological knowledge" is grounded in faith itself and is not given outside of faith. Its self-attestation, as Heidegger asserts in *Sein und Zeit*, "remains closed off in principle from any philosophical experience."[29] In this regard, it is restricted to a specific realm of operation and is "absolutely different from philosophy"; or as he puts it, "faith is so absolutely the mortal enemy" of philosophy.

Two points are noteworthy in this context: first, Heidegger designates theology, as a positive science, to the ontic sphere. Theology, he maintains, is "closer to chemistry and mathematics than to philosophy."[30] Second, he claims that "God is in no way the object of investigation in theology," but rather the "believing comportment itself."[31] This positioning allows Heidegger to neutralize theology's common claim to probe into the nature of being, and thus to intercept in advance the potential competition with philosophy over its subject matter. In so doing, he can affirm that ontological structures are always ontically concretized and never free-floating universals, and that the concrete, "tainted" and "committed" ontic moments instantiate uncommitted ontological structures. When it is posited as a-theistic and undergirdingly prior to ontic theology – Christian and non-Christian alike – fundamental ontology emerges as neutral with regards to theology, *in principle*. As Heidegger writes in 1929, "the ontological interpretation of Dasein as Being-in-the-world does not determine against or in favour of a possible being-toward-God."[32]

Heidegger's claim for neutrality, thus, is predicated on the distinction and separation between theology and philosophy. This, as noted, has its

[29] *SZ* 306/*BT* 496.   [30] *GA* 9, 6.   [31] *GA* 9, 25/Heidegger, *The Piety of Thinking*, 15.
[32] *GA* 9, 159n56/Heidegger, *The Essence of Reason*, 91n56.

own internal logic and justification. However, here, too, it is worth asking whether this principle separation is itself neutral. As indicated above, the radical demarcation between theology's and philosophy's domains of operation, as well as the refusal to mix faith and thinking, matches the predispositions of a particular Protestant framework wherein the relation between philosophy and theology is problematized from the outset. Heidegger's claim that Christian philosophy is a "square circle" and that faith is the "mortal enemy" of philosophy bear a Lutheran ring as well. In contrast, other traditions, Christian and non-Christian alike, hold that philosophy supports and serves natural theology, and therefore partakes in the shared task of elucidating the natural relation between God and the world. Heidegger's early rejection of natural theology continues to reverberate throughout his philosophy well after he left his Christian faith behind.

The neutrality with regards to theological determinations is central to Heidegger's philosophical project as a whole. It is the underlying assumption of the existential analytic of Dasein in *Sein und Zeit* and remains largely unchanged throughout his later thinking. Continuing to insist on the uncommitted character of his thought, Heidegger confirms in 1946 that in ontology, "nothing is decided about the 'existence of God' or his 'non-being', no more than about the possibility or impossibility of gods."[33] In 1951, he reaffirms the decision to barricade God outside philosophical reflection, and the strict separation between faith and thinking, with an explicit evocation of Luther. Pressing once again that there is no intersection between God and being – God is no being, being is not God – Heidegger affirms:

God and being are not identical and I would never attempt to think the essence of God by means of being . . . If I were yet to write a theology, something that appeals to me at times, then the word *Being* would not appear in it. Faith does not need the thought of Being. When faith has recourse to this thought, it is no longer faith. This is what Luther understood . . . One could not be more reserved than I before every attempt to employ Being to think theologically in what God is God. Of Being, there is nothing to expect here. I believe that Being can never be thought as the ground and essence of God, but that nevertheless the experience of God and of his manifestedness, to the extent that the latter can indeed meet man, flashes in the dimension of Being, which in no way signifies that Being might be regarded as a possible predicate for God.[34]

In a similar manner, in a 1964 statement read *in absentia* to a convention of American theologians discussing the productivity of his thought to

[33] *GA* 9, 350/ Heidegger, *Pathmarks*, 266.
[34] *GA* 15, 436–437. Quoted in Marion, *God Without Being*, 61–62.

theology, Heidegger reinforces "the positive task of theology, viz., to discuss, within its own bounds, the bounds of the Christian faith, and out of faith's very essence, what it has to think and what it has to speak."[35]

Heidegger's insistence on the theological neutrality of his philosophy sits somewhat uncomfortably with the blatant critique that he levels at Christianity and the so-called Judeo-Christian tradition throughout his entire mature life, and which will occupy us below, though the brunt of this critique centers on the negative effect this tradition has on philosophy. And yet, his insistence on this point is worthy of emphasis because the question regarding the possibility of theological residues in his thought will be repeatedly raised in his Christian and Jewish receptions.

Sein und Zeit

In his 1927 masterpiece *Sein und Zeit*, Heidegger takes his task to be attaining to the forgotten question of being, or the meaning of being, the *Seinfrage*, and raising it anew in the right way. Being, he claims, comes into view only indirectly, through beings, and so it itself is not a being, it is no-thing. It cannot be approached through a disengaged conceptual examination, only from within historical life and the all-encompassing experience of being which constitutes our existence. In order to capture the pre-theoretical sense we all have of what it means to be, Heidegger embarks on a transcendental project outlining the ontological structures and preconditions of the entity whose being is its concern and is at stake, namely, Dasein, the being we are. Thus, "fundamental ontology, from which alone all other ontologies can take their rise, must be sought in the existential analytic of Dasein."[36]

Heidegger claims that Dasein's essential characteristic is disclosedness, that is, that Dasein is the site through which entities show up *as* meaningful, and for this reason he insists that Dasein is the access into the question of being. Crucially, the concretization of the ontological inquiry through the Dasein analytic has led to a fateful result in the general reception of Heidegger's philosophy. For, while Heidegger states plainly that "the analytic of Dasein is not aimed at laying an ontological basis for

---

[35] Heidegger, *The Piety of Thinking*, 30. This conference at Drew University became famous due to Hans Jonas's keynote lecture, at which he stood in for Heidegger and attacked his former mentor, to the surprise of his audience. Jonas, "Heidegger and Theology"; Montgomery, "Scholar Breaks with Heidegger." On Jonas and Heidegger, see Chapter 3.
[36] *SZ 13/BT 34.*

anthropology; its purpose is one of fundamental ontology"[37] many have read the rich portrayal of human existence in this work and concluded that Heidegger is an existentialist. Heidegger, to be sure, denounces this attribution frequently. For example, in his 1931 lecture course *Hegel's Phenomenology of Spirit*, he writes: "It was never my idea to preach an 'existentialist philosophy'. Rather, I have been concerned with renewing the question of *ontology* – the most central question of western philosophy – the question of being."[38] It is not difficult to see why Heidegger rejects the tag: the existentialist perspective restricts itself to the ontic concern of human existence and generally disregards his ontological purpose and interest in the meaning of being. Nevertheless, for a large part of the twentieth century, the existentialist perspective was dominant in the way Heidegger was understood and, indeed, was a central reason for the widespread success of his early philosophy.

What unfolds in the pages of *Sein und Zeit* is an overt attempt to provide an ontology bereft of crippling metaphysical assumptions and "residues of Christian theology."[39] And indeed, the myriad ontological features introduced in the Dasein analytic remain true to Heidegger's a-theistic methodology: withheld as a horizon of interpretation, God is not an "always already" in Dasein's being-in-the-world. At the same time, it is difficult to overlook the fact that *Sein und Zeit* is fraught with theologically impregnated notions. A number of examples will prove sufficient. Heidegger coins the term *Verfall*, a German rendering of Luther's *Corruptio*, denoting the irrevocability of the Fall, to indicate the default and inevitable immersion of inauthentic Dasein in *das Man*, its impossibility of its evading the uncanniness of its existence. The very idea of Dasein as always already outside itself, fallen and absorbed in a homogenizing social force, is a transposition of the Augustinian notion of the self as not- and outside-itself. The authenticating comportment toward Dasein's future, its being-toward-death (*Vorlaufen zum Tode*), uncoincidentally resembles Kierkegaard's "sickness-toward-death" (translated into German as *Krankheit zum Tode*) – a despair opposite to faith – which itself is almost a direct translation of Luther's Augustinian *cursus ad mortem*.[40] Heidegger also speaks of a "call of conscience" (*Gewissensruf*), a silent call that unveils Dasein's fallenness by summoning it to its authentic and ownmost potentiality of being. This calling, with its resemblance to an

---

[37] *SZ* 200/*BT* 244.   [38] *GA* 32, 18–19/Heidegger, *Hegel's Phenomenology of Spirit*, 13.
[39] *SZ* 230/*BT* 272.
[40] Wolfe, *Heidegger and Theology*, 87–88; Coyne, *Heidegger's Confessions*, 87–123.

epiphany or revelation, awakens Dasein from its existential forsakenness in *das Man* and individuates Dasein by alerting it to the constitutive negativity of its existence, its being-toward-death. It gives rise to guilt or debt (*Schuld*), a theologically charged term in itself, bespeaking Dasein's sense of existential indebtedness to its being-thrown-in-the-world.

While employing these notions, Heidegger is careful to distance himself from their theological undertones by stressing the a-theistically ontological and hence neutral nature of his framework. As ontic, he reminds, theological determinations "must come back to the existential structures which we have set forth."[41] His (curiously minimal) treatment of Kierkegaard exhibits this dynamic well. The Danish thinker, a major influence on Heidegger's thought in its formative years, is commended for his penetrative examination of existential phenomena and categories, and his definitive vocabulary, such as Angst, retrieval, curiosity, "crowd," the Moment, and others, is consistently utilized. Yet Heidegger affirms, in a controversial interpretation, that as a Christian theologian, Kierkegaard is restricted to the derivative sphere of the *existentiell* and alien to "the existential problematic," and hence falls short of significant philosophical contribution.[42] This strategy repeats itself throughout the treaties: structures and categories of discernible Christian origin are formulized and made neutral by stressing the ontic character of theology in contrast to the noncommitted character of fundamental ontology. In this way, Heidegger legitimizes his categories from a philosophical standpoint and frees them from what is otherwise taken to be a limited tradition of thought. Thus, he clarifies that "the call" of which he is speaking is "the call of Care," Dasein's most fundamental ontological structure, "a kind of discourse – in terms of the disclosedness that is constitutive for Dasein."[43] It should not be confused with any form of ontic "vocal utterance" because it "is prior to any description and classification of experiences of conscience."[44] He particularly warns against a theologically flavored interpretation of "the call": "[I]t is no less distant from a theological exegesis of conscience or any employment of this phenomenon for proofs of God or for

---

[41] *SZ* 180/*BT* 224.

[42] Cf. *SZ* 190n6, 235n6, 338n3/ *BT* 492, 494, 497; Heidegger, *History of the Concept of Time*, 292. Kierkegaard's role in the development of Heidegger's thought is widely debated, as is Heidegger's claim that the Dane touches only on the ontic. See for example Caputo, *Radical Hermeneutics*, 60–92. McCarthy, "Martin Heidegger," 95–125; Huntington, "Heidegger's Reading of Kierkegaard Revisited," 43–65; Disse, "Philosophie der Angst," 64–88; Wolfe, *Heidegger and Theology*, 71–75.

[43] *SZ* 271/*BT* 316.   [44] *SZ* 269/*BT* 313.

establishing an 'immediate' consciousness of God" (ibid.). In a similar manner, he cautions against understanding "the voice of conscience as an alien power by which Dasein is dominate," a power which could be understood "as a person who makes himself known – namely God."[45] Similarly, unlike Luther's dogmatic *status corruptionis*, the notion of *verfallen* "makes no ontical assertion about the 'corruption of human Nature,'" Heidegger explains,

because the problematic of this interpretation is *prior* to any assertion about corruption or incorruption. Falling is conceived ontologically as a kind of motion. Ontically, we have not decided whether man is "drunk with sin" and in the *status corruptionis*, whether he walks in the *status integritatis*, or whether he finds himself in an intermediate stage, the *status gratiae*.[46]

Likewise, the ontological condition of being-guilty "must be distinguished from the *status corruptionis* as understood in theology. Theology can find in Being-guilty, as existentially defined, an ontological condition for the factical possibility of such *status*."[47] Underscoring the noncommitted nature of this condition, he writes:

The existential analysis of Being-guilty, proves nothing either *for* or *against* the possibility of sin. Taken strictly, it cannot even be said that the ontology of Dasein *of itself* leaves this possibility open; for this ontology, as a philosophical inquiry, "knows" in principle nothing about sin.

In this passage, as in others, Heidegger seeks to ratify ontology's non-interference with regards to theology. It should be noticed, however, that this view is only possible on the assumption that theology is an ontic science and that its teachings are either irrelevant or derivative from a philosophical standpoint. After all, the claim for impartiality implied in the assurance that being-guilty "proves nothing for or against the possibility of sin" is only possible by the initial exclusion of sin from the realm of ontology, as conveyed in the statement that ontology "knows in principle nothing about sin."

SECULARIZATION IN SEIN UND ZEIT?

Both in terms of biography and in terms of textual genealogy, the stamp of Heidegger's engagement with Christianity is clearly present in *Sein und Zeit*. Notions of theistic origin are displaced from their traditional

---

[45] *SZ 275/ BT* 320.   [46] *SZ 179/ BT* 224.   [47] *SZ 306/BT* 354n1.

context, stripped of their religious content, and employed after having undergone a process of ontological formalization. Some of these are identifiable due to the Christian etymological lineage, while others can be traced to Heidegger's early reflections on sacred texts and themes through conceptual genealogy. How should this process be understood? Does the fact that Heidegger draws from the conceptual, structural, and terminological reservoirs of certain confessional traditions challenge his claim for theological neutrality?

Seeking to come to terms with the relation between the discernible Christian terminology in *Sein und Zeit* and its author's adamant insistence on the suspension of religious tradition from its analysis touches on a theme that will prove central to our discussion: the question of secularization. In this context, "secularization" can be understood in at least two different ways. According to the first, secularization means the clearing of any and all theistic determinations. The religious past is completely discontinued, even negated, and the result is a nontheological, utterly secular order. The second understanding of secularization is the notion that some prima facie secular traits of modern concepts have their genealogical roots in a religious framework and thus continue to possess the stamp of their past even after their de-theologization. Secularization strips away and disposes of the religious charge of its original meaning, but the outcome of the process, while seemingly discontinuous with, and even openly critical of, its theistic origin, is nonetheless determined by the repressed religious background and thus continues in some way to bear its mark – despite but also by means of its repression. Heidegger, to be sure, would reject the possibility that either understanding of secularization is an appropriate lens through which his philosophy could be illuminated. He stands firm that the categories employed in *Sein und Zeit* reflect formal and utterly noncommitted ontological structures. To say that his existential analytic reflects the biases of specific traditions amounts to misunderstanding the imperative and methodology of his philosophy. Evincing the ontological structure of human temporality disclosed, for instance, in Paul's letters, can be seen as liberating theologically, for it exposes its formal and thus universal, rather than local and theologically committed, character. In this sense, for Heidegger, the very fact that these ontological modalities are discernible in the ontic anthropological outlook developed in certain Christian traditions *confirms* rather than refutes their formal nature.

It is, as we have seen, difficult to deny that Heidegger's early theological interests set the tone for his "secular" phenomenological efforts, and that the fundamental theoretical framing and content of the Dasein analytic is pervasively impacted by the profundity of his encounter with Christianity. But this does not at all mean that the relation between some of the themes in *Sein und Zeit* and their Christian origins is simply one of continuity. In the complex, volatile, and tension-filled character of his work with regards to Christian tradition, this relation is marked by both formation and deformation. Continuities, discontinuities, and transvaluations are present simultaneously. For example, Heidegger's rendition of the Christian doctrine of the postlapsarian *status corruptionis* in the description of Dasein's *Verfall* and *Geworfenheit* retains the structure of permanence and the constitutive modality of lostness, of one's existence being beyond one's control. Omitted is the notion of a fall from a primordial and pristine state as well as its attachment to sin and its unquestionable negative undertone. Similarly, Dasein's being-guilty is removed from the theological connotation of transgression, although it draws on a predetermined understanding that being-guilty labels a distinct manner of being and that it is a primal basis of Dasein's being, reflecting a fundamental and inexpiable privation or debt unrelated and prior to any action or behavior.[48] Additionally, in the de-theologized configuration of the disposition of Dasein's being-toward-death, the "end" toward which Dasein's future-oriented life unfolds is not the second coming of Christ, but rather the nothingness of Dasein's death. Upended, moreover, is the link between death and sin so fundamental to Christian tradition. And yet the eschatological disposition, the structural futural anticipation toward "last things," is preserved.

The immanentism that features in Heidegger's philosophy also plays a role in this context, as it strips categories of their implicit appeal to what is beyond phenomenological givenness. For example, "transcendence," traditionally the attribution of the highest height of God, is ascribed to Dasein. In its specifically phenomenological register, Heidegger's notion of transcendence aims to counteract Husserl's "transcendence in immanence" as the intentionality of the subjective ego's consciousness, and he also clearly targets the traditional Christian-metaphysical notion of transcendence pertaining to a supersensory, otherworldly ultimate being.[49] He replaces the traditional conception of vertical transcendence associated with God and the cognitive horizontal transcendence of Husserlian phenomenology with his own version of the ecstatically temporal horizontal

[48] Coyne, *Heidegger's Confessions*, 144–156.
[49] Cf. Heidegger, *The Basic Problems of Phenomenology*, 299.

transcendence of Dasein.⁵⁰ In the introduction to *Sein und Zeit*, Dasein is said to be "simply the transcendent" (*das transcendens schlechthin*). Transcendence is "what is unique to *human Dasein*," a fundamental determination of its ontological constitution as being-in-the-world and as that which serves as "the open" in which beings are disclosed as intelligible. "To *be* a subject," he maintains, "means to be a being in and as transcendence."⁵¹ In the lecture "What is Metaphysics" (1930), he ties transcendence with Nothing: "if [Dasein] were not in advance holding itself out into the nothing, then it could never adopt a stance toward beings nor even toward itself."⁵² Because by "transcendence" Heidegger denotes Dasein's disclosive and ec-static openness toward beings, and immanence is commonly associated with an enclosed sealedness, he states in *The Basic Problems of Phenomenology* that "what is truly transcendent is the Dasein … The Dasein itself oversteps in its being and thus is exactly *not the immanent*."⁵³ Nevertheless, it is clear that transcendence for him is not a-temporal or otherworldly, but rather in the world and thoroughly temporal, a beyondedness within the confinement of *finis*. Indeed, in his *Kantbuch* (which will be discussed in the following chapter) Heidegger formulates this with radical simplicity: "transcendence is finitude itself."⁵⁴

His immanentism is likewise apparent in the notion of the "call of conscience." Heidegger is aware that this notion invites an analogy with the divine revelation and therefore accentuates its immanent feature. He highlights that "In conscience Dasein calls itself";⁵⁵ the self-calling that reveals the primordial openness of Dasein's ownmost interiority that has been concealed by the chatter of *das Man* does not erupt from without, but rather summons from within. At the same time, it is not something that can be intentionally or voluntarily performed. Instead, it happens *to* Dasein. In a manner that resembles a secularized version of Augustine's idea of God being "more intimate to me than I am to myself," Heidegger states: "'It' [*Es*] calls, against our expectations and even against our will. On the other hand, the call undoubtfully does not come from someone else who is with me in the world [*nicht von einem Anderen, der mit mir in der Welt ist*]. The call comes *from* me and yet *from beyond and over me*."⁵⁶ While Heidegger cautions against reading this notion theologically, the

---

⁵⁰ Cf. Moran, "What Does Heidegger Mean by the Transcendence of Dasein?"
⁵¹ GA 9, 138.   ⁵² GA 9, 115/Heidegger, *Pathmarks*, 91.
⁵³ Heidegger, *The Basic Problems of Phenomenology*, 299.
⁵⁴ Heidegger, *Kant and the Problem of Metaphysics*, 50.   ⁵⁵ SZ 275/ BT 320.   ⁵⁶ Ibid.

structure of being lost and then summoned by an abrupt call that induces
a redemptive existential transformation is a familiar theological trope.
The terms used to describe this also bear clear religious overtones:
Dasein's   foresakenness   (*Verlassenheit*)   and   abandonment
(*Überlassenheit*) in *das Man* are provoked by "an abrupt arousal," coming "from afar unto afar" as "something like an *alien* voice."[57] This call,
moreover, is not heard by just anyone, but "reaches him who wants to be
brought back."[58]

The place of Christian thought in *Sein und Zeit* is therefore a complex
and ambiguous one. On the one hand, Heidegger's project attempts to
reconceive Dasein in terms of its facticity and temporality in a manner
divested of, and at times even as an alternative to, Christian anthropology.
On the other hand, some of its central elements appear to be rooted in
close readings of Christian texts or determined by formally indicated
Christian experiences and categories, which are reintroduced as neither
religious nor nonreligious but rather ontological and hence universally
applicable structures.[59] The complexity is underscored when we take into
account that Heidegger himself was of the view that secularization of
theological notions into philosophy involves not only alteration but also
preservation and is therefore faulty. Indeed, he interprets the history of
philosophy precisely through this prism. Already in 1923 he charges
Descartes's formulation of the modern subject with de-theologization.
"What was previously established in believing consciousness' understanding is here secularized [*säkularisiert*]," he writes.[60] Earlier in this lecture
course, in the context of Descartes's concept of human freedom, he
similarly states that "Descartes transposes what is theologically desig-
nated as the working of God's grace to the relation of the intellect working
on the will."[61] He also points out that "Fichte, Schelling, and Hegel were
theologians, and Kant can be understood only in terms of theology."
These philosophers, he adds, "come out of *theology* and take from it the
basic impulses of their speculation. This theology is rooted in Reformation
theology, which succeeded only to a very small extent in achieving
a genuine explication of Luther's new basic religious position and of its
immanent possibilities."[62] This view is also voiced in *Sein und Zeit*, where
he writes that "in modern times, the Christian definition [of the human's

---

[57] *SZ* 277/*BT* 321.   [58] *SZ* 271/*BT* 316.
[59] On formal indication see Dahlstrom, "Heidegger's Method."
[60] *GA* 17, 311/Heidegger, *Introduction to Phenomenological Research*, 236.
[61] Ibid., 156–157/116.   [62] *GA* 61, 7/Heidegger, *Phenomenological Interpretations*, 7.

being] has been de-theologized [*enttheologisiert*]."[63] For Heidegger, the fault in de-theologizing Christian conceptions is that it breaches the fundamental incommensurability of theology and philosophy, leading to a flawed portrayal of human existence stemming from "inadequate ontological foundations." Moreover, from early on he develops an understanding of philosophy as always leading to questions, and of theology as always leading to answers. In his mind, theology cannot bring itself to pose the urgent questions with the appropriate radicalism and without already assuming to possess the answers. It has too many previous commitments – to tradition, to revelation – that predetermine its inquiry from the outset and preclude genuine questioning.

At this juncture, it is crucial to note that Heidegger recognizes that "all philosophical discussion, even the most radical attempt to begin all over again, is pervaded by traditional concepts and thus by traditional horizons and traditional angles of approach."[64] Even the most radically revolu-tionary philosophers are bound to the horizons and concepts bequeathed to them by tradition. In Heidegger's case, this would mean, inter alia, the Christian tradition, which for him is one with the philosophical tradition that has systematically concealed or forgotten the temporal character of being.[65] The task of beginning anew "from scratch" is impractical. What he proposes instead is a *destruction*, a very specific form of inquiry into the Western ontological tradition, an effort both negative and positive, a constructive dismantling. Stepping out of the conditioning of one's hermeneutic tradition is impossible; the path away from the inadequate inherited traditional ontology is necessarily through and by means of this tradition. "If the question of being is to have its own history made transparent," Heidegger writes,

then this hardened tradition must be loosened up, and the concealments which it has brought about must be dissolved. We understand this task as one in which by taking *the question of being as our clue*, we are to *destroy* the traditional content of ancient ontology until we arrive at those primordial experiences in which we achieve our first ways of determining the nature of being.[66]

Once these concrete experiences are laid bare, a new kind of ontology, one that is attuned to the temporality of being, can be constructed. Heidegger thus sets out to go through and dismantle the layers of impoverishing misconceptions handed down by Western ontology in order to allow for

[63] *SZ* 49/*BT* 74. Translation amended.
[64] GA 24, 23/ Heidegger, *Basic Problems of Phenomenonology*, 31.
[65] Cf. Mulhall, *Philosophical Myths of the Fall*, 46–47.   [66] *SZ* 20–23/*BT* 41–44.

repressed past possibilities to shine forth onto the present. In recasting theologically charged notions into purportedly noncommitted ontological structures, Heidegger intends to radically rethink their traditional application and disclose the primordial experience of factical life that gave rise to them in the first place.

The difficulty, of course, lies in the tension between recognizing that one is historically situated and that one's orientation is dictated by one's tradition, and the ambition for a radical *reorientation* from within that tradition. A manifestation of this tension can be seen in the very notion of *Destruktion*, which is directed against traditional ontology but bears the resonance of Luther's effort (inspired by his interpretation of Paul) in his "Heidelberg Disputation" to destroy (*destruere, destructio*) the "folly" of Scholastic theology of glory. Heidegger makes the distinction between an inauthentic comportment toward one's tradition, wherein tradition limits one's possibilities and weighs down on Dasein, and an authentic comportment wherein one's tradition is taken over as heritage, liberating Dasein to its possibilities.[67] When considering this distinction, one must remember Heidegger's insistence that the authentic/inauthentic division is not a binary of two distinct modes of being, because authenticity is a *modification* of inauthenticity. Dasein never exits the fallenness of its immersion in *das Man*. In the context of one's relation to one's past, this means that while an authentic comportment toward one's past as one's "heritage" gives access to possibilities that seemed obscured at first, it still does not release Dasein from its determining trajectory. There is no escaping one's thrownness, but there is, from within one's thrownness, the possibility of cultivating authenticity. As we shall see, there are indications that Heidegger continues to wrestle with the recognition that his philosophical and Christian upbringing continue to mark his efforts to transcend their conceptual path.

HEIDEGGER'S LATER WORK

Relatively soon after its publication, and despite its massive popularity, Heidegger came to identify shortcomings in *Sein und Zeit*, chiefly due to his realization that it is still too indebted to traditional ways of thinking. As he writes in *Contributions to Philosophy (of the Event)* (written between 1936 and 1938 but published much later), in which remarks on the strengths and weaknesses of *Sein und Zeit* are scattered, the way in

[67] *SZ* 383/*BT* 435.

which it conducted the search for being as a form of beingness and its transcendentalism as well as its prioritization of Dasein, make it overly subjectivist and metaphysical. Nevertheless, he notes, his overarching question remains the same and so *Sein und Zeit* should be considered an indispensable work of transition rather than simply false. In "Letter on Humanism," from the mid-1940s, he comments on the so-called "turn" (*Kehre*) in his thought and ascribes the failure of his early endeavors to, inter alia, the "help of the language of metaphysics."[68] Here he notes that "the ultimate error" of the philosophical tradition was approaching the human being "as if it were the secularized transference to human beings of a thought that Christian theology expresses about God."[69] In its oblivion of the difference between being and beings, metaphysics amounts to nihilism. "But where is the real nihilism at work?" he announces in *Introduction to Metaphysics*, "Where one clings to current beings and believes it is enough to take beings, as before, just as the beings that they are ... Merely to chase after beings in the midst of the oblivion of Being – that is nihilism."[70] From the beginning of the 1930s, thus, Heidegger reframes his path of thinking, and instead of producing an outline of a systematic account of the meaning of being in general, what increasingly comes to the fore is the place of language, the difference (*Differenz*) between beings and being, and what he calls the technological configuration of truth. Focusing on the giving of being as bearing import and importance, he no longer tries to think of being by way of Dasein, but Dasein by way of being, or better still, their co-respondence.[71] The notion of Dasein's historicity is expanded to a *Seinsgeschichte*, an eschatological sketch of the historical unfolding of different manners of what he calls "essencing" (*Wesen*) or world-disclosures throughout the course of Western thought.[72] The trajectory of his thinking, he announces in *Contributions*, is a move from the understanding of being to the happening of being, which appropriates Dasein in this happening.

This reframing, however, should not be exaggerated. There is much indication that the much mythologized "turn" in Heidegger's

---

[68] Heidegger, *Pathmarks*, 239–276.   [69] *GA* 9, 327/*Pathmarks*, 249.

[70] Heidegger, *Introduction to Metaphysics*, 203.

[71] Polt, *The Emergency of Being*, 28–29. This is the best work on Heidegger's *Contributions* I know of. An alternative view, stressing being as always prior to human meaning, is capably presented by Richard Capobianco in a series of works. See for example his *Heidegger's Way of Being*.

[72] A good overview of this development is McNeill, "From Destruction to the History of Being."

thinking – an alleged break between Heidegger I and Heidegger II, as William J. Richardson put it – is overstated, if, indeed, it even denotes a movement in his thought in the first place.[73] While the attempt to rearticulate the thought about being involves at times a critical engagement with the project of *Sein und Zeit*, Heidegger's early work constitutes the philosophical backbone for his later thinking; the latter grows out of the former – a development rather than a break.[74]

Heidegger's attempt to think beyond the nihilism of metaphysics and traditional faith does not mean he seeks to promote a godless outlook. Indeed, from the mid-1930s and onward, more explicitly than before, the *Gottesfrage* and the *Seinsfrage* are intimately interlaced. This is readily apparent when one comes across the many deeply religious terms in his later writings. Through an intense wrestling with Nietzsche and even more so with Friedrich Hölderlin's poetry, Heidegger begins to speak of "the Holy" which makes possible the appearance of cryptical "gods." These terms do not denote what traditional Christianity indicates by holiness or God, for these latter categories, Heidegger repeatedly affirms, are accessible only through faith. Despite his terminology, the distinction between philosophy and theology still stands. Rather, with this charged language, he wishes to contemplate and cultivate what he considers to be a genuine comportment to the holiness of being, an openness to the coming of other gods – silenced, effaced, forgotten gods. Later Heidegger intends to tread beyond the deformed notions of "religion," "secular," and "holiness" and prepare for an inceptive moment in which access to a more genuine and primordial sending of the holy can be gained. The present is "a time of need," he judges, "because it stands in a double lack and a double not: in the no-longer of the gods who have fled and in the not-yet of the god who is coming."[75]

Beginning in the early 1930s, Heidegger develops the notion that in this time "between the times," an objectifying technological disclosure of being, the *Ge-stell*, presently holds sway. As he explains, most programmatically in the later "The Question Concerning Technology" but beginning already before, he is concerned not with technological artifacts but with the "essence of technology," which "is not technological." In this

---

[73] Richardson, *Heidegger: Through Phenomenology to Thought*.

[74] The question regarding the relationship between his early and later work is among the most discussed and debated in Heidegger scholarship. For a deeply informed argument for continuity, see Sheehan, *Making Sense of Heidegger*. Another elaborate argument against the idea of Heidegger's *Kehre* is found in Hemming, *Heidegger's Atheism*.

[75] Heidegger, *Elucidations of Hölderlin's Poetry*, 64.

lecture he approaches the topic by reflecting on the difference between the Greek understanding of causation as "bringing forth [*Her-vor-bringen*]" out of concealment into unconcealment, and the modern-technological conception of causation as "manufacturing."[76] The former "responds" to being, while the latter is a violent imposition (*Bestellen*) on being, which shows up in beings as replaceable and standardized resources (*Bestand*), "standing reserve" or "stock," aimed at production and consumption and lacking inherent significance. Technology enframes our concern with the world through a coercive form of ordering which Heidegger terms "machination" (*Machenschaft*). The danger of technology as a modification of truth is that it forces a monistic and absolutized disclosure of beings that limits and impoverishes the abundance of being's possible manifestations. It is a denial of the possibility of the essencing of being. Reflecting on a poem by Hölderlin, Heidegger writes:

> The men of this earth are provoked by the absolute domination of the essence of modern technology, together with technology itself, into developing a final world-formula which would once and for all secure the totality of the world as a uniform sameness, and thus make it available to us as a calculable resource.[77]

In its reduction of the truth of being to a disclosure as a calculable resource and in its visage of finality and absolutization, technology forces a leveling onto beings that closes off the sensitivity to the richness of being's meaning and holiness.

As part of his critique of technology and metaphysics, Heidegger also brings to light what he terms ontotheology. Categorically, this is philosophical critique, pertaining to the constitution of metaphysics. In the ontotheological tradition, there is a tendency to conflate, and hence to confuse between, the science of being (ontology) and the science of the highest being (theology). The question of being is inadequately posed in the doubled manner: "What is being in general as a being?" and "Which being is the highest being and in what sense is it the highest being?"[78] This tendency begins with Aristotle and continues throughout, up to Leibniz, Kant, Hegel – the paradigmatic example of ontotheology – and even Nietzsche, who signaled toward its overcoming but finally succumbed to it. In this tradition, the entire metaphysical structure of reality gains its meaning from a single ultimate ground, a *causa sui* upon which the

---

[76] An excellent analysis is Rojcewicz, *The Gods and Technology*.
[77] Heidegger, *Elucidations of Hölderlin's Poetry*, 202.
[78] GA 9, 449/Heidegger, "Kant's Thesis about Being," 10–11.

structure is based.[79] In the essay "The Onto-theological Constitution of Metaphysics" Heidegger offers a list of notions that operated as such *Urwesen* in different metaphysics throughout the history of the West: "*Phusis, Logos, Hen, Idea, Energia*, Substantiality, Objectivity, Subjectivity, Will, Will to Power, Will to Will."[80] The ontotheological manner of thought perpetuates the original sin of Western thought: the forgetfulness of being (*Seinsvergessenheit*). In it the difference between being and beings disappears, which results in considering the most question-worthy question, the *Seinsfrage*, un-question-worthy.

In Heidegger's understanding, the theological-metaphysical God of the Judeo-Christian tradition is an ontotheological god. This god, he claims, lacks the exalted mystery of the divine; it is present-at-hand being, conceptualized, objectifiable, and available. The ontotheological god, as a technological god, is thought of through a specific understanding of causation, that of efficient causality.

Thus where everything that presences exhibits itself in the light of a cause-effect coherence, even God, for representational thinking, can lose all that is exalted and holy, the mysteriousness of his distance. In the light of causality, God can sink to the level of a cause, of *causa efficiens*. He then becomes even in theology the God of the philosophers, namely, of those who define the unconcealed and the concealed in terms of the causality of making, without ever considering the essential provenance of this causality.[81]

One example Heidegger repeatedly invokes to demonstrate the technological character of the Judeo-Christian tradition is the biblical-theological idea of "creation" and God as "creator." This idea perceives the world as produced and God as its manufacturer and cause. In *Introduction to Metaphysics*, he writes:

Christianity reinterprets the Being of beings as Being-created. Thinking and knowing come to be distinguished from faith (*fides*). This does not hinder the rise of rationalism and irrationalism but rather first prepares it and strengthens it. Because beings have been created by God – that is, have been thought out rationally in advance – then as soon as the relation of creature to creator is dissolved, while at the same time human reason attains predominance, and even posits itself as absolute, the Being of beings must become thinkable in the pure thinking of mathematics. Being as calculable in this way, Being as set into calculation, makes beings into something that can be ruled in modern, mathematically

---

[79] Thomson, *Heidegger on Ontotheology*; Thomson, "Ontotheology? Understanding Heidegger's *Destruktion* of Metaphysics."
[80] Heidegger, *Identity and Difference*, 66.
[81] GA 7, 30/Heidegger, *The Question Concerning Technology*, 331.

structured technology, which is *essentially* something different from every previously known use of tools.[82]

The monotheistic notion of the creator God and master of being is the
grounding principle of a uniform and stable understanding of being as
produced, which receives its meaning from a single capstone ultimate
entity. It is rooted in the technological notion of control over being and
the will to power. In this way, the biblical tradition unites with the Greek
tradition of metaphysics and generates a powerful hold on Western
thought. "With the assistance of Christianity," Heidegger writes in the
Black Notebooks, "metaphysics becomes explicitly biblical-theological,
and *ens* appears as *ens creatum*."[83] "The whole situation of modern
metaphysics" he states in 1935, arises from "the Christian representations
of beings as *ens creatum* and the fundamental mathematical character (of
thinking about beings)."[84]

Alongside its technological features, Heidegger subjects "the Jewish-
Christian idea of creation and the corresponding representation of god" to
special invective because it implies that the question of being has been
answered before it is even raised. Discussing in *Introduction to
Metaphysics* the difficulty of genuinely and radically accomplishing the
"originary power" of the question "why are there beings at all instead of
nothing?," he takes the faithful person as an example for someone who is
"just mouthing the words":

Anyone for whom the Bible is divine revelation and truth already has the answer to
the question "Why are there beings at all instead of nothing?" before it is even
asked: beings, with the exception of God Himself, are created by Him. God
Himself "is" as the uncreated Creator. One who holds on to such faith as a basis
can, perhaps, emulate and participate in the asking of our question in a certain
way, but he cannot authentically question without giving himself up as a believer,
with all the consequences of this step. He can act only "as if" – .[85]

The belief in the Bible as divine revelation denies the possibility of
a genuine *philosophical* inquiry into the fundamental ontological question. Alluding to 1 Corinthians 1:20, Heidegger states that it would be
foolish to re-raise the question from within a religious framework, for
doing so genuinely would necessitate "giving oneself up as a believer."
The postulation of creation as extended in the Bible solves, he believes, the
ontological question without actually attending to its horizons of

---

[82] Heidegger, *Introduction to Metaphysics*, 207.   [83] GA 97, 358.   [84] GA 41, 85.
[85] Heidegger, *Introduction to Metaphysics*, 7–8.

obscurity, and as such perpetuates the negligence of being. About this Heidegger is unequivocal: however which way it is interpreted, and mysterious and undetermined as it may be, the notion of "creation" constitutes an *answer* to the question of being and therefore is inimical to the kind of radical questioning and wondering he wishes to promote.

It is rather clear that Heidegger's attacks on the monotheistic biblical tradition target primarily Christianity. In the rare cases in which Judaism is mentioned, Heidegger commonly glosses it over as basically identical to Christianity. For example, in *Introduction to Metaphysics* he analyzes the meaning of *logos* in Judaism and Christianity in contrast to its meaning in Heraclitus. He explains that in the New Testament *logos* means "*one particular thing, namely the Son of God*" understood as "in the role of mediator between God and humanity."[86] This understanding of *logos* as mediator, he contends, is also "that of the Jewish philosophy of religion which was developed by Philo." Indeed, his occasional invocation of the problematic marker of "Judeo-Christian tradition" is a case in point as well. At the same time, it cannot go without mentioning that Heidegger does, at times, specifically single out Judaism, the Jews, and world-Judaism (*Weltjudentum*) as the embodiment of the cardinal sin of modernity, namely, the uprooting technological machination (*Machenschaft*) and the oblivion of being. In a lecture course from 1933–1934, Heidegger ontologizes the relation between a *Volk* and its *Heimat*, writing that "Every people has a space that belongs to it," and this "relatedness to space … belong[s] together with the essence and the kind of Being of a people."[87] A people's rootedness in a land bears ontological significance and thus "uprootedness" is ontologically inferior. Heidegger's ready example for those to whom nature "will perhaps never be revealed at all" is "the Semitic nomads."[88] The Jews, in other words, subsist in a profoundly impoverished, worldless, and uprooted ontological modality vis-à-vis being.[89] Likewise, in a number of disturbing passages found in his private philosophical notebooks, he associates the technological dominance of the era with the characteristically Jewish "empty rationality and calculative efficiency."[90] With their unique skill for calculativity and the calculative-biological relation to their ancestry, the Jews are technology incarnate and agents of machination: "*With their emphatically calculative*

[86] Ibid., 143.   [87] Heidegger, *Nature, History, State*, 54–55.   [88] Ibid., 56.
[89] A penetrating discussion of this point is found in Wolfson, *The Duplicity of Philosophy's Shadow*, 1–32.
[90] GA 96, 46.

giftedness, the Jews have for the longest time been 'living' in accord with the principle of race, which is why they also offer the most vehement resistance to its unrestricted application."[91]

In his notebooks Heidegger tries to justify himself by explaining that the "question of the role of the *world-Judaism* is not a racial question, but a metaphysical one"[92] and he repudiates biological racism precisely for betraying the perverse calculative rationality that should be rejected. Yet not only is "metaphysical" antisemitism equally inexcusable, it is clear that at times it draws on ethnicist and even racist logic. This can be seen in a 1939 entry from his *Black Notebooks*, where a connection is made between the Jewish ancestry of Husserl – who had converted to Evangelical Lutheranism on April 26, 1886 and lived and died as a faithful, unaffiliated Christian – and what Heidegger takes to be his former mentor's philosophical limitations. After ranting about the fact that "the temporary increase in the power of Jewry has its ground in the fact that the metaphysics of the West, especially in its modern development, served as the hub for the spread of an otherwise empty rationality and calculative skill," he turns to Husserl to claim that while the master has yielded contributions "of enduring importance," these fall short of "the domains of essential decisions." He then adds: "My 'attack' on Husserl is not directed against him alone, and in general is inessential – the attack is against the neglect of the question of being, that is, against the essence of metaphysics as such, on the basis of which the machination of beings was able to determine history."[93]

---

[91] *GA* 96, 56–57/*Ponderings, XII–XV*, 44. The revelations of Heidegger's *Black Notebooks* generated a flood of new publications on his antisemitism and notion of race, which could be added to an already large existing body of scholarship on these themes. For some recent contributions, representing a diverse of positions on the matter, see Homolka and Heidegger, *Heidegger und der Antisemitismus*; Nancy, *The Banality of Heidegger*; Farin and Malpas, eds., *Reading Heidegger's Black Notebooks: 1931–1941*; Di Cesare, *Heidegger, die Juden, die Shoah*; Trawny, *Heidegger and the Myth of Jewish World Conspiracy*; Heinz and Kellerer, eds. *Martin Heideggers "Schwarze Hefte."*

[92] *GA* 96, 243/*Ponderings XII–XV*, 191.

[93] *GA* 96, 46–47/*Ponderings XII–XV*, 37. On the Jewish origin of his mentor Husserl and the personal, philosophical, religious, and political aspects of their troubled relationship, see Herskowitz, "The Husserl-Heidegger Relationship in the Jewish Imagination." In *Contributions* Heidegger pushes back against the identification of calculative science with Jews, noting that "We would then have to resolve to number Newton and Leibniz among the 'Jews'" (*Contributions to Philosophy (of the Event)*, 127). See Trawny, "Heidegger, 'World Judaism', and Modernity"; Trawny, *Heidegger and the Myth of Jewish World Conspiracy*.

Heidegger's anti-Jewish sentiments are a conglomerate of familiar religious and social prejudices, reconfigured to operate within his philosophical scheme. It is certainly correct to argue, as many have, especially since the publication of his *Black Notebooks*, that with his anti-Jewish views Heidegger lapses into lazy and essentializing thinking that is not only ethically degraded but also philosophically vacuous. But it must also be admitted that at least with respect to the anti-Judaic aspects in Heidegger's thinking, he is in fact in *continuity* with many of his philosophical predecessors. The sad truth is that the debasing of Judaism and the depiction of Jews as inferior from a philosophical point of view is the rule rather than the exception in modern German philosophy. This tradition of philosophical degradation of Jews and Judaism includes, to differing degrees and in different moments, Kant, Hegel, Feuerbach, Schopenhauer, Nietzsche, and others.[94] This of course does not minimize the shameful scandal of Heidegger's explicit alignment of his philosophy and anti-Jewishness in support of Nazism. But it does allow us to notice that despite – or rather together with – his deeply disturbing utterances against the Jews and Judaism and his deplorable anti-Jewish political activities, what serves as the general rule with regards to Heidegger's attitude toward Judaism is an overarching *inattention*. This oversight is hinted at already by Derrida (before the publication of the *Black Notebooks*), when he referred in passing to Heidegger's avoidance of the Hebrew *ruah* and "a whole tradition of Jewish thought," in order to highlight the deep affiliations his philosophy holds with Christian theology.[95] While many of his teachers and students were of Jewish descent, it appears that Heidegger was barely familiar with Jewish traditions, texts, or customs (on his own admittance, he learned Hebrew in *Gymnasium* and later during his theological studies, but "unlearned" it soon after).[96] What is clear, however, is that in his

[94] See, for example, Mack, *German Idealism and the Jew*. Schelling, it appears, stands out for not participating in this tradition of debasement. See Brumlik, *Deutscher Geist und Judenhass*.

[95] Derrida, *Of Spirit*, 99–113. In an interview with Dominique Janicaud, Derrida says: "Heidegger silenced every reference to Jewish thinkers, from Spinoza to Bergson, to more originary Hebraic matters, and to what one calls the 'Old Testament'. One can perceive a factual violence, deliberate or not, with respect to the Jewish tradition." Interestingly, Derrida also admits that "paradoxically, I am still less knowledgeable about Judaism than Heidegger was. He encountered it by way of theological texts, but I did not." See Janicaud, *Heidegger in France*, 358–359.

[96] As Heidegger writes to Shlomo Zemach, the translator of *The Origin of the Work of Art* to Hebrew, on January 5, 1969. See Herskowitz, "Heidegger in Hebrew." Though there is reason to believe Caputo overstates the case when he writes that Heidegger "knew next

philosophical works, *Judentum* is an abstraction, bereft of actuality and content, and most often hyphenated to and swallowed by some other order of thought. Thus Heidegger speaks of the "Christian-Jewish doctrine,"[97] the "Hellenistic-Jewish,"[98] or the "Christian Hellenistic-Jewish and Socratic-Platonic."[99] Indeed, as noted, despite occasional evocations of "the Jewish," Heidegger's reflections involve virtually no engagement with Judaism as a form of life, culture, or textual tradition. One might say that Jews and *Judentum* are a phenomenological blind spot for Heidegger – they simply do not show up to him as themselves. It must of course be added that much of what Heidegger finds objectionable in Christianity may apply to central strands of Judaism as well, and it should not go unnoticed that by finding fault above all with the thematic of "creation," Heidegger aligns himself, intentionally or not, with a millennia-old tradition condemning the creator God of the Old Testament as the root of all evil.[100] This, however, does not change the fact that in many respects, his attack on Judaism is an indirect assault on Christianity, the real nemesis of the Heideggerian project. A dual act of concealment thus takes place: Judaism becomes a placeholder for the metaphysics of *Machenschaft* and is absorbed into Christianity. This leads to a paradoxical dynamic, whereby Judaism is reduced to a single principle only to then be applied expansively and identified everywhere. Through the intrinsic tie between technology, metaphysics, and Judaism, Heidegger's narrative of the history of the West as *Seinvergessenheit* unfolds as the *Judaization* of the history of the West, but this occurs while at the same time Jewish tradition is conspicuously omitted. This is the contradictory role of Judaism in Heidegger's thought: it is conflated with Western thought and at the same time sternly avoided; omnipresent while radically concealed. One might say, in Heideggerian parlance, that Heidegger's invocations of Judaism are a positive revealing that conceal the fact of Judaism's absence.

Ironically, the dynamic of the revelation of presence as concealment of absence which can be identified in Heidegger's treatment of Judaism is precisely the trait Heidegger attributes to the ontotheological Judeo-Christian god. The revelation of this technological and metaphysical god, Heidegger informs, is a positive form of concealment, because it

---

to nothing in a direct way about the Hebrew scriptures." Caputo, "People of God, People of Being," 95.

[97] *GA* 94, 475–476.   [98] *GA* 95, 339.   [99] *GA* 95, 322.

[100] We shall discuss different associations of Heidegger with Gnosticism below. See also Wolfson, *Duplicity of Philosophy's Shadow*, 109–130; and more extensively, idem, "*Gottwesen* and the De-Divinization of the Last God."

conceals the absence of the true divinity. In its absolutization it blocks off the realization of the possibility of other modes of disclosure, leading to the double negative state in which we presently find ourselves: we are oblivious to the absence of the divine gods. Beginning to sense the presence of the absence of the gods is the needed preparatory step for the possibility of our coming into the presence of an indeterminate forthcoming divinity. In "Letter on Humanism," Heidegger writes:

> Only from the truth of being can the essence of the holy be thought. Only from the essence of the holy is the essence of divinity to be thought. Only in the light of the essence of divinity can it be thought or said what the word "God" is to signify. Or should we not first be able to hear and understand all these words carefully if we are to be permitted as human beings, that is, as *eksistent* creatures, to experience a relation of God to human beings? How can the human being at the present stage of world history ask at all seriously and rigorously whether the god nears or withdraws, when he has above all neglected to think into the dimension in which alone that question can be asked?[101]

This, according to Heidegger, is the role of the poet, who must "remain near to the god's absence, and wait long enough in this prepared nearness to the absence till out of the nearness to the absent god there is granted an originative word to name the high one."[102] *The* poet, for Heidegger, is Friedrich Hölderlin. As he writes to Erhart Kästner: "What does Hölderlin's poetry say? Its word is: the Holy. It speaks of the flight of the gods. It says that the fled gods spare us. Until we are capable and of a mind to dwell in their vicinity."[103] The challenge Heidegger draws from Hölderlin is to achieve a certain vicinity to being, to cultivate a gratuitous responsiveness to being, attuned and attentive to the process of orderings through which beings come into presence as what they are. He terms this possibility of non-metaphysical thinking "being-historical" or "being-destinal" (*seyns-geschichtlich*) thinking, and it is in this sense that he states in his 1966 *Der Spiegel* interview "only a god could save us."

Rather explicitly, then, Heidegger perceived the later thought he was developing to be not only *by definition* non-Christian, but in an important sense antithetical to Christianity. Indeed, his rejection of Christianity is ubiquitous and sweeping. Overcoming ontotheology is tantamount to overcoming traditional philosophy and Christianity as such, because, in Heidegger's conceptualization, these are basically one and the same. Heidegger's insistence on the need for a radical separation between

---

[101] Heidegger, *Pathmarks*, 267.   [102] Heidegger, *Elucidations of Hölderlin's Poetry*, 46–47.
[103] Heidegger and Kästner, *Briefwechsel*, 59.

theology and philosophy as well as the rejection of metaphysical conceptions of God constitutes a continuation of his early Luther-inspired, anti-
theologia gloria impulse of his early years. Interestingly, he still perceives
his thought as a preparatory. "The godless thinking . . . is thus closer to the
divine God. Here this means only: godless thinking is more open to Him
than onto-theo-logic would like to admit."[104] Now, however, he is preparing not for a Lutheran version of Christianity, for his critique has been
radicalized to target Luther's nonphilosophical Christianity as well. This
is indicated in his claim that "All theology of faith is possible only on the
basis of philosophy, even when it rejects philosophy as the work of the
devil." This is a suggestive remark, because it speaks to the question of
the compatibility of Heidegger's thought with non-metaphysical
Christianity. While, as noted, the ontotheological critique is by definition
philosophical, it has been embraced by those wishing to retrieve the
"living God of Abraham" from the abstractions of the "god of the
philosophers." While Heidegger's diatribe against Christianity is feral,
so the argument goes, he was targeting only a certain version of
Christianity, a metaphysical, inauthentic Christianity. His critique, therefore, simply does not hold with regards to a non-metaphysical
Christianity. Heidegger, for example, rebukes the relation to the onto-
technological god as a form of non-relation. "Man can neither pray nor
sacrifice to this God," he maintains. "Before the *causa sui*, man can
neither fall to his knees in awe nor can he play music and dance before
God."[105] Does this not gesture toward the sacramentality of a non-
Hellenized, authentic God of the Christian Gospel? Does not his rejection
of the ontotheological God of philosophers lead him to the proximity of
the living God of Abraham? Does not Heidegger's condemnation of the
abstract in favor of the concrete, the a-temporal in favor of the historical,
the static in favor of the transient, the eternal in favor of the finite, and the
celestial in favor of the worldly, mean that it is more appropriate to situate
his thought on the side of Jerusalem rather than of Athens? Is the biblical
world not an originary mode of being-in-the-world uncontaminated by
Greek metaphysics? When, in the *Der Spiegel* interview, Heidegger projects that perhaps the old traditions of thought in Russia or China will free
thinking from the bondage of the technological, would not the biblical
world be a legitimate possible source as well?

The question of Heidegger's compatibility with Christianity is the
subject of an ongoing scholarly debate and is unlikely to be resolved

[104] *GA* 11, 77/Heidegger, *Identity and Difference*, 72.   [105] Ibid.

anytime soon.[106] Generally, his attitude toward it is marked by a deeply polemical objective. Heidegger's knowledge of Christian thought cannot be questioned, but he represents it in an overly generalized way which cannot be said to qualify as a serious engagement. It is clear, however, that while he was, in his own way, a God seeker his entire life, the God he was seeking was decidedly not the Christian God as he understood it. Not only the metaphysics of Christian Scholasticism, but also the non-metaphysical "living God of Abraham" of a Christianity that "rejects philosophy as the work of the devil" operates within the determinations of philosophy and is therefore ontotheological. "Theologians," Heidegger postulates in "Nietzsche's Word 'God is Dead,'" "talk of the beingmost of all beings [*das Seiendste alles Seienden*], without ever letting it occur to them to think about being itself."[107] In two entries in the *Black Notebooks* from around 1947–1948, he directly addresses these matters. In the first entry, entitled "On the Doctrine of Gods," he writes of the biblical God:

Jehovah is the god who presumed to make himself the chosen god, and not to tolerate any other gods beside himself. Only the fewest people can guess that this god, even so, and necessarily so, must count himself among the gods; how else could he set himself apart? That is how he could become the one, only god, apart from whom (*praeter quem*) there was no other. What is a god who raises himself up against the others to become the chosen one? In any case, he is never "the" God pure and simple, if what this means could ever be divine. What if the divinity of a god lay in the great calm from which he recognizes the other gods? "God is" – speaking this way is thoughtlessness, and a veiling of thoughtlessness to boot, not to mention the presumption that such idle talk reveals, if it is supposed to be the talk of a thinking person at all. Anxiety in the face of the divine flees to "God," who neither is *a* god, nor can be "the" god; or else one flees to mere theology.[108]

In the second entry, Heidegger reflects on the Pascalian distinction between the "God of the philosophers" and the "God of Abraham":

What if the god of the philosophers were still more divine than the god of Abraham, who tolerated no others of his kind aside from himself, and whose son Jesus sent all who did not love him to Hell and let them roast there? What sort of god is it who denies divinity, and who has none of the generosity of pure joy at his kind and at their inexhaustible richness? (A note on Pascal).[109]

---

[106] See, for example, Haar, "Heidegger and the God of Hölderlin." For the view that Heidegger and Christianity are compatible see for example Hemming, *Heidegger's Atheism* 21 where he claims "Heidegger's methodological atheism allows the question of God to reappear"; Armitage, "Heidegger's God: Against Caputo, Kearney, and Marion."

[107] Heidegger, *Off the Beaten Track*, 194.   [108] GA 97, 369. Translation by Richard Polt.

[109] GA 97, 409. Translation by Richard Polt.

It cannot be said that these passages constitute a very thoughtful critique of biblical monotheism, but they do aptly convey Heidegger's negative stance on the matter. From his perspective, Christianity, together with metaphysical philosophy (and Judaism), are a thought gone astray, an impoverished and nihilistic manner of thinking, utterly oblivious to the urgency of thought. Concerning the option of escaping technology to Christian faith, Heidegger quips, "is this not like fleeing the cold by going to the North Pole?"[110]

In the 1955 Cerisy Colloquium in France, Heidegger makes a dismissive gesture toward "the Hebraic cluster" when Paul Ricoeur confronted him with the following question:

> What has often astonished me about Heidegger is that he would have system-atically eluded, it seems, the confrontation with the block of Hebraic thought. He sometimes reflected on the basis of the Gospels and of Christian theology, but always avoided the Hebraic cluster, which is the absolute stranger of Greek discourse ... Does the task of rethinking the Christian tradition by way of a "step backward" not require that one recognize the radically Hebraic dimension of Christianity, which is first rooted in Judaism and only afterward in the Greek tradition? Why reflect only on Hölderlin and not on the Psalms, on Jeremiah? There lies my question.[111]

Heidegger responds that Ricoeur is touching on "what I have called the 'onto-theological' character of metaphysics" and that the uncovering and recovering of the pre-metaphysical Greek teaching in his thought "bears no relation to biblical dogmatics."[112] On the face of it, Heidegger seems to be either genuinely or deliberately misunderstanding that Ricoeur's point is that the biblical tradition is precisely *removed* from ontotheology and metaphysics. The point insinuated in Ricoeur's question that Heidegger seems to miss is that had the "Hebraic cluster" not been avoided, Heidegger would have discovered that it holds conceptual solidarity with his project. Unsurprisingly, perhaps, Heidegger is not open to this manner of thinking. Personal biases and his overall reductionist approach toward Judaism neutralized the possibility of a productive encounter with this tradition, together with the fact that his distinction between

---

[110] *GA* 97, 238.
[111] Quoted in Zarader, *The Unthought Debt*, 9. In this work Zarader develops the provo-cative thesis that while Heidegger avoids what she calls the "Hebraic heritage," a comparative examination of key features of the Hebraic tradition and his thought reveals many similarities, and that this tradition can be seen as Heidegger's "unthought."
[112] Ibid., 187.

philosophy and theology places the biblical tradition as a whole outside the realm of thought.[113] It would seem, however, that Heidegger's rejection of the biblical tradition goes beyond mere biases and reductionism and pertains to issues of content as well. We have seen this with respect to the notion of creation and the creator God, and we shall see shortly that he opposed the very definition of human in relation to an independent "God" as overly anthropological and metaphysical. For him, there is a co-responsiveness between Dasein and gods and there is no external and ultimate reference point that can offer a stable ground to human existence and history beyond the ecstatically temporal dynamic of concealment and disclosure of being that emits transcendence from within.

As is the case with his earlier thought, and notwithstanding his overt and repeated repudiation of Christianity and metaphysics, a subtle ambiguity with regards to his philosophical and theological upbringing still remains. In his later writings, too, Heidegger occasionally expresses the recognition that despite his efforts, his own facticity, language, and path of thinking are still stamped by the very traditions he seeks to emancipate himself from. In a letter from August 6, 1949, Karl Jaspers wrote to Heidegger about his "Letter on Humanism," noting that "Your 'being', the 'clearing of being', your reversal of our relation to being into a relation to being to us, being itself remaining residual – I believe something similar has been perceived in Asia." Heidegger was indeed fascinated with Eastern thinking from early on, and a few years prior, in 1946, he had even attempted to translate the *Daodejing* together with the Chinese scholar Paul Shih-yi Hsiao. But his response to Jaspers is telling:

I remain sceptical when I am not at home in a language; I feel this even more with Chinese, translating Laozi with my own words, themselves informed by Christian theology and philosophy; through questioning I first experienced how essentially strange the whole of language is to us; so we have given up the attempt.[114]

---

[113] In his grand comparative work on Heidegger and Kabbalah, Wolfson writes on this point: "these affinities [between Heidegger and Kabbalah] disrupt his own adverse characterization of Jewish thought as irrefutably metaphysical. Heidegger could have found in the Jewish esoteric lore a precedent to his inceptual thinking, a counternarrative to the story he tells of Western philosophy as the tale of a depreciating forgetfulness of beyng, the philosophical equivalent to the theological account of the fall from grace. Of course, this was demonstrably not the case, as Heidegger was either steadfastly ignorant of or deliberately hid any indebtedness to Jewish thought, let alone the most recondite part of that literary-cultural heritage." Wolfson, *Heidegger and Kabbalah*, 112.

[114] Quoted in Pöggeler, *The Paths of Heidegger's Life and Thought*, 67–68.

In a similar manner, in his 1959 "A Dialogue on Language" he confesses
to the complicated relation his philosophy holds with his Christian
upbringing and early theological reflections: "Without this theological
start, I would never have come onto the path of thought. But origin always
remains future [*Herkunft aber bleibt stets Zukunft*]."[115] These statements
bear witness to Heidegger's acknowledgment that Christianity is an una-
lienable part of his "having-been" and thus continues in some sense to
mark his philosophical efforts with its baggage. The difficulty of achieving
what he sets out to do is underscored in his Nietzsche lectures, where he
asserts that even the effort to counter Christianity is conducted within the
terms of Christian discourse. Commentating on Nietzsche's remark that
the "feast is paganism par excellence," Heidegger contends that "the feast
of thinking never takes place in Christianity. That is to say, there is no
Christian philosophy. There is no true philosophy that could be determined anywhere else than from within itself. For the same reason there is
no pagan philosophy, inasmuch as anything 'pagan' is always still something Christian – the counter Christian."[116] Expressing a similar point in
a 1938 entry from the *Black Notebooks*, he affirms:

Even all doctrines of humanity (e.g. the Christian-Jewish doctrine) that define man
immediately on the basis of his relation to a "God" are anthropological – which is
why, in non-Christian anthropology and in those that would like to be it and cannot,
it is precisely *Christian* anthropology and its body of doctrine that must play an
essential role, if only in its mere reversal.[117]

It can be seen that Heidegger was well aware of the prospects and constraints
implicit to his task of thinking. On the one hand, he attempts to develop
a philosophy that is neither Christian nor "pagan" but beyond the
Christian–pagan distinction, which addressed the issue of the holy and
divinity solely from within itself. On the other hand, he also knows that
the difficulty of becoming liberated from metaphysics and Christianity is not
only rooted in the nature of these traditions but also in the fact that his own
language and manner of thinking are conditioned by them. In a letter to his
student Karl Löwith from 1921, Heidegger described himself as a Christian
theologian. "I work concretely and factically out of my 'I am,'" he discloses,
"out of my intellectual and wholly factic origin, milieu, life-contexts, and
whatever is available to me from these as a vital experience in which
I live."[118] Heidegger's thought had, no doubt, advanced greatly since these

[115] *GA* 12, 91/ Heidegger, *On the Way to Language*, 10.
[116] Heidegger, *Nietzsche*, vol. 1, 5.   [117] *GA* 94, 475–476.
[118] Kisiel, *The Genesis of Heidegger's Being and Time*, 78.

early years and he most certainly no longer identified with the faith of his youth. But he did not lose sight of the enduring and inevitable constraints on his thinking bequeathed by his facticity. Perhaps it is for this reason that in "On Time and Being" he states that the metaphysical tradition of thought binds us in such a way that the very act of overcoming it inherently participates in a metaphysical discourse, hence preserving it. "Metaphysics cannot be abolished like an opinion. One can by no means leave it behind as a doctrine no longer believed and represented."[119] Rather than perpetuating that which is being exited, metaphysics should therefore be accepted as an endowment of our thrownness and "left alone."[120]

GREECE AND GERMANY

Driving Heidegger's desire to overcome this impasse and reintroduce a new attunement to the holy, an "other beginning" to thought, is the following narrative: Plato absolutized the unconcealment of the propositional conception of truth as "correctness," taking philosophy "on an erroneous and fateful course,"[121] and Aristotle prioritized the restricted understanding of being as presence. Setting a non-metaphysical thinking into motion requires therefore a retreat to the primordial Greek thought of the pre-Socratics, obscured and concealed by the Platonic and Aristotelian breakthroughs. In his investigations into the inception of thought by the early Greeks, Heidegger attempts to make overt what the ancient Greeks only tacitly recognized, namely, being as a happening of coming-into-presence, unconcealment from concealment, the anonymous event of being "showing-up" and its relation to temporality and cultural orderings. Heidegger's appeal to ancient Greek thought adheres to a well-established tradition of German Philhellenism, from Johann Joachim Winckelmann through luminaries such as Kant, Hegel, Schiller, Humboldt, Lessing, Herder, Hölderlin, and von Harnack. Yet his return to the pre-Socratics does not reflect a naïve desire for historical and theoretical "better times," nor is it a simplistic retreat to "breathe life" into lost or forgotten ideas – these would mean approaching time metaphysically. The "other beginning," as Heidegger envisions it, is a restorative and creative *confrontation* with the first inception of thought in ancient Greece.[122] First and foremost continuous, but

---

[119] Heidegger, "Kant's Thesis about Being," 85.
[120] Heidegger, *On Time and Being*, 70.   [121] *GA* 34, 17.
[122] One of the best analyses on this theme is still Fell, "Heidegger's Notion of Two Beginnings." See also White, "Heidegger and the Greeks"; Bambach, *Heidegger's Roots*.

also discontinuous, the "first" and "other" beginnings are interlinked; the first beginning, as an *Ursprung*, an originary origin, rather than merely a starting point (*Beginn*), "endures." The "other beginning" does not cancel the past nor does it revive it. It consists, rather, of a new appropriation of what is already, a new encounter with, and retrieval of, past possibilities in the present. Advancing out of the beginning, Heidegger states in his lectures on Nietzsche, does not necessitate abandoning the beginning.

Heidegger explains the relationship of Hölderlin's later poetry to Greece in a way that seems to reflects his own position: "The new relationship to Greece is not a turning away, but rather a more essential turning toward Greece and a pressing for a more originary confrontation, without of course seeking in Greece the origin and ground of the proper [*Grund des Eigenen*]."[123] For Heidegger, ancient Greece and Germany are intimately intertwined. The historical-spiritual mission of preparing for the advent of the "second beginning" is endowed by being to the German *Volk*. His enthusiastic welcoming of National Socialism is intrinsically tied to this philosophical-historical-eschatological persuasion. As he makes clear in his rectorial address on the occasion of his Nazi-sponsored inauguration as the rector of the Freiburg University, the German university will achieve its unique scientific vision:

> Only when we submit to the power of the *beginning* of our spiritual-historical being [*Dasein*]. This beginning is the breakout [*Aufbruch*] of Greek philosophy. That is when, from the culture of one Volk and by the power of that Volk's language, Western man rises up for the first time against *the totality of what is* and questions it and comprehends it as the being that it is.[124]

In the 1933–1934 lecture course *Vom Wesen der Wahrheit* Heidegger clarifies that the need to confront ancient Greece is not "in order to bring to completion a Greek world [*ein Griechentum*] but, on the contrary, in order to draw out the fundamental possibilities of the proto-Germanic ethnic essence and bring them to power."[125] Heidegger's relatively speedy disillusionment with the National Socialist Party (he left the rector position in 1934 but remained a member of the Party until 1945) and overall distancing from the political is rooted in his recognition that the Party was deepening, rather than offering an alternative to, the technological

[123] *GA* 52, 141.
[124] Heidegger, "The Self-Assertion of the German University," in Wolin, *The Heidegger Controversy: A Critical Reader*, 31. Translation amended.
[125] *GA* 36–37, 89.

perversion of modernity.[126] It, too, was a manifestation of the historical unfolding of the destructive drive of the technological "will to power" and blind "will to will" that was threatening to nullify the world. At times, Heidegger relates that the eventual deliverance from the quicksand-like framework of technological calculativity and efficiency will occur apocalyptically, by means of the self-annihilation of the technology. Most often, however, he articulates the idea, inspired by Hölderlin's verse "But where danger is, grows/ the saving power also," that the "saving power" from the technological grip resides in technology itself. Focusing and pondering on its nature as a mode of disclosure can assist humans to cultivate a receptivity to the mystery of revealing. Later on, Heidegger develops the idea that a comportment of *Gelassenheit*, a "renouncing of willing," constitutes a preparatory anticipation of a future redemptive intervention that may usher in a non-technological, poetic mode of revealing.[127] Nevertheless, his vision of language and thought unencumbered by metaphysics remains an unpredictable possibility, not an inevitability.

If we recall the wide-spanning trajectory of Heidegger's thought, it is suggestive that at first he searches for a remedy for Greek metaphysics outside the Greek tradition, in the early Christian texts. The possibility of "Jerusalem" offering a genuine avenue of thought from a philosophical standpoint is at first entertained, but it is then conclusively closed off. Instead, Heidegger decides to delve *deeper* into the Greeks to retrieve a primordial and more genuinely "Greek" manner of thinking. In the *Black Notebooks* he writes:

From here one can assess what the remembrance of the first beginning in Greece – a beginning that remains outside of Judaism, and that means outside of Christianity – signifies for thinking into the concealed inceptual essence of the history of the West.[128]

SOME EARLY CHRISTIAN RECEPTIONS OF HEIDEGGER

From the very beginning, the early readership of *Sein und Zeit* was attuned to its theological resonances and read it as a paragon of *Existenzphilosophie*. Husserl, after finally studying the work, attributes

[126] On Heidegger's philosophical developments during the 1930s, in particular as they relate to "the political," see Polt, *Time and Trauma*. Polt captures Heidegger's attitude nicely when he notes that "although his criticisms of Nazism are substantial, these are the grumblings of a disappointed lover" (p. 154).
[127] An excellent study of this topic is Davis, *Heidegger and the Will*.   [128] GA 97, 30.

his student's diversion from his own ideal of phenomenology as rigorous science to Heidegger "never having freed himself completely from his theological prejudices."[129] Hinting at the unresolved role of theology in this work, the young Sidney Hook, who published his observations from a year of studying philosophy in Germany, writes: "one closes the book with a feeling that it could only have been written by a pagan philosopher with a Christian's sense of original sin."[130] Max Scheler also inquires of *Sein und Zeit*: "Aren't these the gloomy old theologoumena of Calvinist origin (cf. also 'thrownness'), which are here translated into an apparently pure ontological language?" He also points out that the concentration on human "dread" is deeply conditioned by the definition of man as put forth by "Christianity and Judaism" – "and furthermore that this dread has emerged in a very peculiar and strong way in Protestantism."[131] Also Werner Brock, Heidegger's Jewish assistant, lists in 1935 "the Christian experience of thinkers like Augustine and Kierkegaard" as among the central influences on Heidegger's thought, and likens Heidegger's approach to the history of philosophy to "the way in which an independent and thoughtful, though devout, Christian might read the Bible."[132] In his survey of contemporary philosophy at the time, the Jewish intellectual Fritz Heinemann, a student of Hermann Cohen and Paul Natorp, notes the uniquely Protestant heritage that is present in Heidegger's work. He identifies the overall religious under-tones of *Existenzphilosophie*, which draw upon "the entire framework of Pauline Christianity, Paul himself, Augustine, Luther" to develop the themes of individualism, interiority, and conscience, and points out that Kierkegaard's framework "develops in the fullness of its historical-religious concretion the deepest wellspring that nourishes the Heideggerian view of existence and his anthropology."[133] Likewise, Heinemann judges that Heidegger's portrayal of Dasein is the outcome of an integration of a secularized Kierkegaard and Dilthey, wherein "the Pauline-Kierkegaardian suffering sinful, guilty, human living in fear and trembling becomes a historical being fixed in time and not separate from it."[134] Yet unlike Kierkegaard, for Heidegger the main question is not "how can a person become a Christian again, but: how can a human become a human again?"[135] Heidegger's anthropology is secularized, and thus

---

[129] Cairns, *Conversation with Husserl and Fink*, 9.
[130] Hook, "A Personal Impression of Contemporary German Philosophy," 155.
[131] Scheler, "Reality and Resistance," 135, 143.
[132] Brock, *An Introduction to Contemporary German Philosophy*, 109–111.
[133] Heinemann, *Neue Wege der Philosophie*, 373.   [134] Ibid., 374.   [135] Ibid., 373.

"the major problem is that man is not understood out of nature as he was by the Greeks, nor out of God, as in the middle ages, but out of himself."[136] Similarly, Siegfried Marck's account of present-day philosophical trends confirms that *Existenzphilosophie* "reaches its highpoint and receives its comprehensive formulation" in Heidegger's scheme, which "erupts as a religious or political system."[137]

It is of little surprise, therefore, that almost immediately *Sein und Zeit* elicited great interest and provoked debates among its religiously minded readers.[138] Central moments in these debates pertained to the significance and weight of its residual secularized theological notions, to the godlessness of the portrayal of Dasein, to the theological ramifications of Heidegger's methodological a-theism, and to the relationship between philosophy and theology more generally. Our survey below touches on all these themes succinctly, but in order to best prepare us for the discussion of Heidegger's Jewish reception, our main concern will be the following question: is his ontology prior to and independent of theological assumptions, or does it implicitly reflect and promote a theological program? Does the fact that references to Dasein's possible being-from or - toward God are nowhere to be found mean that Dasein's world is *de facto* godless?

It is best to begin with Rudolf Bultmann, an associate of the dialectical theology circle, a friend and colleague of Heidegger's at Marburg, and a key figure in the latter's early Christian reception.[139] It is sometimes debated whether Bultmann naïvely appropriated Heidegger's philosophy for the development of an existentialist theology, but one thing is clear: he accepts the philosopher's claim for theological neutrality and the ontic/ontological distinction undergirding it. The analysis of Dasein, Bultmann agrees, is purely formal – it "has neither *weltanschauliche* nor theological intentions."[140] As such, its fruitfulness for theology is to be judged according to the merit of its analysis of human existence. And since, according to Bultmann, "all of the basic Christian concepts have content that can be determined ontologically prior to faith," then one finds in Heidegger "approaches that are useful for an ontological foundation of

[136] Ibid., 375   [137] Marck, *Die Dialektik in der Philosophie der Gegenwart*, 144.
[138] On Heidegger's early Christian reception, see Wolfe, *Heidegger and Theology*, 151–208; Baring, *Converts to the Real*, 211–240; Williams, *Martin Heidegger's Philosophy of Religion*; Schaeffler, *Frömmigkeit des Denkens*.
[139] Dennison, *The Young Bultmann*, 132–140; Gadamer, "The Marburg Theology," 29–43.
[140] Bultmann, "Heidegger, Martin," 1687–1688.

Christian theology as a science."[141] This allows one to see that the ontic Christian notions of sin, love, and creatureliness are factual instances, acknowledged within faith, of the Heideggerian ontological notions of guilt, care, and thrownness, respectively. Likewise, the authentic/ inauthentic structure of Dasein's being informs the Christian existential task of salvation. The existential modification from a fallen and lost being to authenticity is the ontological preunderstanding (*Vorverständnis*) of the transition, made possible by the advent of Christ, from *Welt-bleiben*, a sinful existence fallen away from God, to the authenticity of life in faith, *Nicht-Welt-Sein*. Implementing Heidegger's "existential" terminology to the "*existentiell*" call to faith, Bultmann asserts that receptivity to the message of Christ is engendered by the terror of awareness of finitude. The acknowledgment of temporality brings about the inner transmutation of rebirth – represented by the cross and resurrection – that enables the departure from a sinful life to a life of faith. Bultmann, who adheres to a philosophically informed theology whose autonomy as the language of faith is nevertheless safeguarded, is quoted as saying: "I learned from [Heidegger] not what theology has to say but how it has to say it."[142] Bultmann was, of course, well aware of Heidegger's background in theology and the Christian sources of some of his categories. Indeed, he claims that "Heidegger's existentialist analysis of the ontological structure of being would seem to be no more than a secularized, philosophical version of the New Testament view of human life."[143] However, conceding that Heidegger outlines the underlying pre-Christian ontological foundation of existence, Bultmann maintains that "one should be startled that the philosophers are saying the same thing as the New Testament and saying it quite independently."[144] We shall return to this Bultmannian link between Heideggerian existential analysis and biblical hermeneutics, as it is latently taken up and debated in Jewish responses to Heidegger.

The basis of Bultmann's constructive engagement with Heidegger's philosophy is the acceptance of its formal character. Yet the fact that Bultmann is fiercely rebuked by many of his fellow contemporary theologians for utilizing Heidegger for the sake of faith demonstrates how controversial this assumption is. Unlike Bultmann, many Christian theologians at the time, Protestant and Catholic alike, read *Sein und Zeit* as a secularized program reflecting and made possible by particular

---

[141] Bultmann, "The Historicity of Faith," 96.   [142] Thiselton, *The Two Horizons*, 28.
[143] Bultmann, "New Testament and Mythology," 23.
[144] Ibid., 25. Translation slightly amended.

theological traditions. According to some Protestant readings, the god-lessness of Dasein, whose existential possibilities are confined to the insurmountable immanent horizon of facticity and finitude, depicts the human being *before* revelation. Accordingly, the entire analysis of Dasein amounts to a snapshot of a godforsaken existence. Since divine revelation alone is the condition of possibility of existential redemption, Heidegger's program as a whole is situated within the realm of inauthenticity. For some, this godforsaken depiction gives philosophical voice to the present-day resurgence of theological attitudes accentuating the breach between the radically transcendent God and the fallen, sinful world. Heidegger's bracketing of God and resulting godless world corresponds, from the perspective of philosophy, to the position of *Deus absconditus* looming large over the theological scene in the Weimar period. This position found its quintessential articulation in Karl Barth's exegesis of Paul's *Römerbrief* (1919, 1922), which spurred the consolidation of the most impactful (if short-lived) theological movement in 1920s Germany, dialectical theology. Hans-Georg Gadamer and Karl Löwith both report that in the years when *Sein und Zeit* was being written, Heidegger voiced his great respect toward dialectical theology.[145] Indeed, in the introduction to *Sein und Zeit*, listing the various disciplines that were currently undergoing crises and reflecting "freshly awakened tendencies to put research on new foundations," he likely refers to Bultmann and Barth when he writes:

Theology is seeking a more primordial interpretation of man's Being towards God, prescribed by the meaning of faith itself and remaining within it. Theology is slowly beginning to understand again Luther's insight that its system of dogma rests on a "foundation" that does not stem from a questioning in which faith is primary and whose conceptual apparatus is not only insufficient for the range of problems in theology but rather covers them up and distorts them.[146]

To be sure, there is much that divides Heidegger the philosopher and Barth the theologian, yet their shared Protestant heritage and the important mark of Kierkegaard's "infinite qualitative difference" on both men generated the view that Heidegger's philosophical a-theism is in truth closer to Barth's theological theism than may first appear (the Jewish perspective on the Heidegger–Barth connection will be taken up in Chapter 3).[147] One propagator of the claim that dialectical theology and

---

[145] Gadamer, "The Marburg Theology," 198–212. Löwith, *My Life in Germany*, 31.
[146] *SZ* 10/*BT* 8.
[147] As Safranski put it, "Heidegger's 'bracketed-in' God probably resembled Karl Barth's God." Safranski, *Martin Heidegger*, 111. See also Bambach, *Heidegger, Dilthey, and the*

Heidegger's philosophy are not oppositions but share a continuum is Löwith himself, whose interpretation of Heidegger as a secularized, post-Christian thinker has been immensely influential. Löwith advanced the view that there is a "concrete 'relation' between existential ontology and dialectical theology."[148] For him, Heidegger's atheism is not alien to the tenets of Protestantism, but rather derives from implicit secular impulses within that very tradition.

Most theologians firmly rejected both Heidegger's philosophy and its purported affiliation with the Barthian project.[149] For them, inasmuch as a strict separation between theology and philosophy is upheld and revelation provides all that is worth knowing about human existence, philosophy as such, and especially one so deeply mired in history and human experience as Heidegger's, is at best of no interest and at worst perilous. In Heidegger's atheistic portrayal, Dasein's lack of being-toward-God reflects not only its ignorance of revelation as an eruptive existential event, but its fundamental impenetrability to the novelties of revelation. Heidegger offers not the structure of a pre-faithful person, but of a unfaithful person. Barth's mindful avoidance of Heidegger is the flip side of other theologians' vocal critique of the philosopher.[150] While Bultmann links the Heideggerian authentic/inauthentic distinction to the distinction between graced and ungraced existence, claiming the former distinction is the ontological precondition of the latter, Barth rejects Heidegger's framework as a whole in favor of Christian faith. To add to Heidegger's inadequacies, the ontological nature of his thought exhibits problematic residues of natural theology. Heidegger's a-theism, then, is hardly neutral, and his program should be rejected "not only because it is atheistic," as Emil Brunner warns, "but also because it is secretly theological."[151]

Also in Heidegger's early Catholic reception there is a dominant strand concerned with unmasking the theological presuppositions and

Crisis of Historicism, 189–203. On the debates over the nature and extent of Kierkegaard's influence on Barth, see Lee C. Barrett, "Karl Barth: The Dialectic of Attraction and Repulsion."

[148] Löwith, "Grundzüge der Entwicklung der Phänomenologie," 36; and Löwith, "Phänomenologische Ontologie und protestantische Theologie."

[149] Barth, "Ontologie und Idealismus," 511–512; Kuhlmann, "Zum theologischen Problem der Existenz," 32. This essay was directed against Bultmann's theological appropriation of Heidegger.

[150] Barth's silence regarding Heidegger characterizes at least this early stage of his thought. He later equates Heidegger and Sartre as two atheist existentialists in *Church Dogmatics* vol. III, 3, 334–349.

[151] Brunner, "Theologie und Ontologie," 122.

implications of his work. Initially, for some of his Catholic readers, Heidegger's preoccupation with ontology and its traditional categories of "essence" and "existence" was perceived as bearing thematic and methodological semblance to Scholastic philosophy, thereby purportedly affirming the much-needed return to "traditional" philosophy after Kant's fatal attack on ontology. That the monograph on Duns Scotus (Thomas of Erfurt) was Heidegger's only published work to date fostered the expectation that *Sein und Zeit* would continue the Scholastic path.[152] But this expectation was not destined to be realized, and from the Catholic perspective, the Protestant assumptions that were identified in Heidegger's ontology made it woefully flawed. In its implicit repudiation of the account of the human being as *imago Dei*, the presence of Luther was seen as detrimentally hovering over Heidegger's philosophy. In a manner predating Jean-Luc Marion's claim that the "suspension of God" in Heidegger's methodological atheism generates "idolatry," early Catholic readers insist that the aspiration to delineate the conditions of possibility of human existence without direct reference to God will unavoidably result in distortion.[153] From the neo-Scholastic perspective, while Heidegger contends that his approach is prior to theism, atheism, or agnosticism, from an operative perspective, in methodological a-theism God is absent from the horizon of the interpretation of human existence, which is approached from the worldly perspective of immanence. Thus, while lauding the reappearance of "the Aristotelian-Thomist doctrine of Being as foundational *prima philosophia*" as a positive return to a traditional-Scholastic way of philosophizing, the Jesuit philosopher Erich Przywara makes clear that unlike in this tradition, "being" in Heidegger's scheme remains planted in the immanent world and does not point to transcendence.[154] Heidegger is occupied with *Leben-Sein* and *Existenz-Sein*, which is more "an Aristotelianization of Dilthey" than an actual "revival of Aristotle." In his untraditional return to tradition, Heidegger "frames the concept of being in such a way that ... the inner-worldly is closed and locked in on itself, since being as being is in its essence 'in the world.' At the same time, the supra-worldly falls away by itself or at least must be traced back to the immanent." Heidegger thus

---

[152] Wolfe, *Heidegger and Theology*, 174; Baring, *Converts to the Real*, 85–115.

[153] Marion, *God Without Being*, 43.

[154] Przywara, "Drei Richtungen der Phänomenologie," 252. Przywara here echoes a view already expressed by Heidegger's student Oscar Becker, who perceived Heidegger's turn to being as "a new Scholasticization." See Pöggeler, *Philosophie und hermeneutische Theologie*, 77.

advances a covert theological position, one that establishes a perilous dualism between God and world, divine transcendence and human imma- nence. In his 1934 *Augustinus*, Przywara speaks of Heidegger in terms of Gnostic Manichaeanism.[155] The dualism characteristic of Protestant theology as a whole and radicalized recently by Karl Barth, he proclaims, is guilty of driving God completely out of human sphere. Elsewhere Przywara equates Barth and Heidegger for promoting an either/or para- digm between heaven and earth, when the one-sided transcendence offered by the former and the one-sided immanence offered by the latter are two sides of the same coin.[156] Both, like Nietzsche's atheism, manifest the logical outcome of Lutheranism – "the most refined form of worldli- ness and paganism."[157] Alongside his critique, Przywara develops a theological corrective to Heidegger by formulating an analysis of Dasein's being-toward-God, drawing on Patristic and Scholastic ontology.[158] By emphasizing the creatureliness of the human being and the existential openness toward God, he seeks to arrive at an account of a religious Dasein who leads a life in which the transcendent divine is "in us and above us" ("*Gott in uns und über uns*").[159]

The stark polarity between God and the finite man, argues Przywara, spawns a tragic form of existence. What surfaces from Heidegger's phi- losophy is the urgency of the human's ultimate decision between Nothingness, upon which Heidegger's structure is founded, and God.[160] Developing this point, the Jesuit theologian Alfred Delp opines that Dasein's authentic resolve is "heroism of Nothing," courageously but tragically established on an abyss.[161] Heidegger, according to Delp, offers a distorted account of *analogia attributionis* in which not God but Nothingness serves as the *analogans* of man's being. This tragic heroism is self-contradictory, because by claiming that meaning and transcendence are derived from the finite spirit of Dasein, Heidegger commits the all-too- modern sin of ascribing secularized quasi-divine attributions to the human being. Just like God, whose essence and existence are identical – *Deus, cuius essential est ipsummet suum esse*, in Aquinas's formulation – Heidegger writes of Dasein: "The 'essence' of Dasein lies in its

---

[155] Przywara, *Augustinus*, 72–97.   [156] Przywara, *Das Geheimnis Kierkegaards*, 30.
[157] Ibid., 71.
[158] Cf. his "Der Mensch des Adgrundes"; Pryzwara, "Theologische Motive im Werk Martin Heideggers," 55ff.
[159] Cf. for instance Przywara, "Gott in uns und über uns?"
[160] Przywara, "Wende zum Menschen."
[161] Delp, *Tragische Existenz*. See also his "Sein als Existenz."

existence."[162] In Heidegger, a banished God is replaced by a deified Dasein, generating a pagan, immanent ontology. In the end, Delp grieves, "the tragedy of this ethos of our day is that this courage is ultimately just a big illusion, without ground and content."[163]

It is important to stress again that Heidegger completely opposes these confessional readings of his thought. In a letter to Elisabeth Blochmann he explicitly objects to Löwith's claims that his philosophy is a "disguised theology [*verkappte Theologie*]."[164] What emerges from this survey, at any rate, is that Heidegger's complicated relation to Christianity and theology is integral to the way in which the first generation of his Christian readers approached *Sein und Zeit* and that, notwithstanding Bultmann's endorsement, many Protestant and Catholic theologians alike find Heidegger's system to be theologically inflected, both in its presuppositions and its ramifications.

We have examined some early Christian reactions to *Sein und Zeit* because many of the issues raised in this discourse are taken up and debated by Heidegger's Jewish readers, albeit from their own particular perspective, and with special attention to its intersections with Christianity. These included, as we have seen, matters regarding the interface between transcendence and immanence, Gnosticism, nihilism, creatureliness, and secularization. As we turn now to Heidegger's Jewish reception, it will become clear that the conceptual terms of this reception are set up in the philosophical, theological, and political climate of interwar Germany, and that like their contemporary Christian counterparts, many of Heidegger's twentieth-century Jewish readers reject his claims for neutrality and identify in his thought a religiously charged program.

---

[162] *SZ* 42/*BT* 67.   [163] Delp, *Tragische Existenz*, 83.
[164] Storck, ed., *Martin Heidegger, Elisabeth Blochmann, Briefwechsel*, 103.

2

Kant's Legacy and New Thinking: Heidegger, Cassirer, and Rosenzweig

INTRODUCTION

When *Sein und Zeit* appeared, it was hardly an isolated work of philosophy. Self-consciously rebellious, it operated within a highly charged set of assumptions, values, and views in a crisis-laden cultural context in which philosophy, theology, and politics were tensely intertwined. As noted in the introduction, the world this work rebelled against was, inter alia, represented by the philosophical idealism of the neo-Kantian schools that had increasingly lost their appeal in the minds of many younger students. From the perspective of the younger generation of Jewish intellectuals who sought to shake off the devitalizing legacy of the Enlightenment and embrace a more existential and expressive mode of thinking, Heidegger's framework would be, potentially, an ally in their effort of revitalizing Jewish existence. However, while it is figures from this rebellious generation of German Jews who are often taken to represent the Weimarian intellectual and aesthetical world in the narrative of twentieth-century European intellectual history – Scholem, Benjamin, Arendt, Rosenzweig, Buber, Adorno, Horkheimer, and others – it is important to remember that the majority of German Jews at the time generally adhered to the very worldview *challenged* by Heidegger and his philosophy. For them, Heidegger represented the crisis of the Enlightenment's liberal and humanist values which they saw as their own.

The present chapter sketches out the contours of early Jewish responses to the emergence of Heidegger onto the intellectual scene through the prism of the divided cultural and intellectual landscape of interwar Germany. Our point of departure will be the battle raging at the time over the legacy of Immanuel Kant. By analyzing the famous Davos encounter between Ernst Cassirer and Heidegger, we shall attend to specific political and theological resonances of the encounter with respect to the heated debate over the ties between *Judentum* and *Deutschtum*. Particular attention will be given to Cassirer's interpretation of Heidegger as a propagator of myth and enemy of the liberal order, as this response, I suggest, can be taken as representative of the general perspective of the majority of German Jews at the time. The chapter then shifts to discuss Franz Rosenzweig, a representative of the younger generation, who proposes a controversial interpretation of Davos by announcing Heidegger's outlook to be akin to his own "new thinking." Following this, we will chart some of the response to Rosenzweig's discomforting affiliation with Heidegger and trace the tendency to repudiate it.

DAVOS AND THE QUARREL OVER KANT

Martin Heidegger and Ernst Cassirer, arguably Germany's two most prominent philosophers at the time, met and debated each other at an annual conference on Kant at the picturesque Swiss resort in Davos in 1929.[1] On the face of it, their discussion – which drew on their sustained and diverging philosophical outlooks – revolved around rather technical issues pertaining to the basic structures of human understanding according to Kant's *Critique of Pure Reason*. However, behind the veneer of a debate over philosophical minutiae was, in fact, an intellectual clash over the essence of human being and the nature of philosophy. Since the main aim of this chapter is not the philosophical intricacies of the Davos encounter itself, which has been explored in enviable detail and depth by others, but rather the light it sheds on Heidegger's early Jewish reception, I will touch on what directly pertains to the discussion that follows and not even attempt a comprehensive interpretation of the debate.[2] As is well known, Kant strictly distinguishes between the mind's receptive passive

---

[1] Prior to their meeting in Davos, Heidegger had already mentioned Cassirer's *The Philosophy of Symbolic Forms* in his 1925 lecture series and had written a review of the second volume of that work in 1928. Cassirer referred to *Sein und Zeit* in the third volume of his aforementioned work. He also reviewed Heidegger's Kant book in 1931 and engaged philosophically with Heidegger's political agenda in his posthumous 1946 *The Myth of the State*.

[2] The two most extensive works in English are Gordon, *Continental Divide* and Friedman, *A Parting of the Ways*. See also Carman, "Heidegger's Anti-Neo-Kantianism"; Schalow, "Thinking at Cross Purpose with Kant"; Schrag, "Heidegger and Cassirer on Kant"; Lynch, "Ernst Cassirer and Martin Heidegger"; Cristaudo, "Heidegger and Cassirer"; Meyer, *Ernst Cassirer*.

capacity of sensibility (intuition) and the spontaneous active capacity of understanding (concepts). Both, Kant claims, are needed for objects of empirical experience to be given the phenomenal and logical form of entities. "Thoughts without content are empty, intuitions without concepts are blind," as he famously puts it.[3] Yet this dualism was often criticized for presupposing an unprovable and metaphysically independent thing-in-itself that is intuited. Cassirer, representing the steadily declining Marburg neo-Kantian school, follows Cohen's interpretation of downplaying the role of intuition and highlighting the spontaneity of human understanding. On his account, Kant provides a vision of the human subject as a free and creative agent whose spontaneity allows it to construct reality. Heidegger's reading of the First Critique, on the other hand, stresses the receptive and utterly temporal character of human cognition. "Finite knowledge is non-creative intuition," he asserts.[4] "In order to understand the Critique of Pure Reason," Heidegger writes in *Kant and the Problem of Metaphysics*, published immediately after the Davos debate, "this point must be hammered in, so to speak: knowing is primarily intuiting [and] the new interpretation of knowledge as judging (thinking) violates the decisive sense of the Kantian problem. All thinking is merely in the service of intuition."[5]

The epistemological question regarding the primacy of intuition or understanding partakes in a more general question about the human condition as such. Cassirer, rather clearly, offers an optimistic account of selfhood marked by autonomy, sovereignty, and independence, while Heidegger puts forth a model of subjectivity predicated on the primacy of intuition, and thus on receptivity, dependence, and limitedness. On this more pessimistic account, human beings, in their everydayness in-the-world and *Geworfenheit*, are inextricably bound to, and fatefully determined by, the confines of the context into which they have been thrown. This dispute, in turn, is closely related to questions regarding temporality and truth. For on Cassirer's account, the Kantian rationalistic subject possesses unrestricted creative intellectual power and therefore also the ability to overcome the limitations of its finitude and arrive at objective knowledge which is not time-bound. One of Heidegger's most provocative exegetical moments, on the other hand, is his claim to expose the insight that "transcendental imagination" is the mysterious "common root" of understanding and sensibility that Kant hinted at in the

---

[3] Kant, *Critique of Pure Reason*, 93.
[4] GA 3, 25–26/Heidegger, *Kant and the Problem of Metaphysics*, 18.   [5] Ibid., 15.

Critique's "A" edition, before he backtracked in the "B" edition. "[T]he power of imagination," Heidegger writes, "is also and precisely a faculty of intuition, i.e., of receptivity." The ramification of reading Kant in this manner is not only elevating the primacy of sensitivity over understanding, but also emphasizing the role of temporality, a fundamental feature of sensitivity, for understanding, previously defined by Kant as free of time and causality. In other words, it maintains that originally, Kant found temporality to be the condition of all knowledge.

From Heidegger's perspective, the intrinsically finite character of human existence and knowledge reveals neo-Kantian (and Husserlian) projections of atemporal knowledge and ego to be suffused with illicit traditional theology and metaphysics. "Does not the finite creature become infinite through its 'creative' behavior?," he asks, only to then respond: "Absolutely not."[6] By taking Kant's insistence on the essential limitation of human thought seriously, one arrives at "the destruction of the former foundation of Western metaphysics (spirit, logos, reason)" which he himself is carrying out in his fundamental ontology.[7] Thus Heidegger announces that the great Prussian philosopher was less concerned with scientific knowledge than with outlining the foundations for a metaphysical ontology. By reading Kant against the grain – while claiming to be recovering a lost Kantian insight – Heidegger can position himself as continuing Kant's project in his own work. The transvaluation of Kant is completed when Heidegger pushes further and claims that the receptivity and primordial temporality implied in *Geworfenheit* is deeper than the Kantian distinction between sensuous passivity and conceptual spontaneity. Undergirding them but also suppressed by them, it denotes that we are fundamentally "overwhelmed" by or delivered over to the factical world that presses upon us. Not our cognitive faculties but rather unreflective moods and attunements – equiprimordial with what he terms "understanding" and "discourse" – are our most basic affordances toward being. Reflecting the overarching pessimistic atmosphere of the time, Heidegger powerfully diminishes the force of human freedom, spontaneity, and reason that is in the center of Cassirer's interpretation of Kant, and instead underscores human dependency, receptivity, and limitedness.

Within its historical context, the Davos encounter unfolded as a quarrel between the "old" neo-Kantianism and the "new" *Existenz* thinking.

---

[6] Ibid, 88.   [7] Ibid, 171.

Indeed, Heidegger explicitly attacked Cohen's neo-Kantianism through Cassirer, Cohen's student. This is understandable, though matters are somewhat more complicated. Notwithstanding the enduring impact the Marburg school had on him, Cassirer was not an orthodox neo-Kantian. He departed from the standard Marburgian scientific "critique of reason" with his occupation with an expanded "critique of culture" that included independent, prescientific, primitive "symbolic forms," and he unstitched Kant's "productive synthesis" of the transcendental schematism of understanding by distinguishing between the symbolic forms of scientific knowledge and everyday sensory perceptions.[8] In fact, he agreed with Heidegger that the anthropological as well as the fundamental hermeneutic problem of meaning are of profound philosophical importance.[9] Nevertheless, the reason the Davos debate is engraved in the memory of twentieth-century intellectual history, and the reason it is discussed in the present study, is because it was never solely over philosophical minutiae. Embodying some of the generational, cultural, and political clashes, the conflict over Kant was perceived from the very beginning as a momentous event of symbolic import. Hermann Herrigel, reporting at the time for the *Frankfurter Zeitung*, presents the event as a watershed moment, encapsulating "not merely an academic struggle of the professors" but "a confrontation between representative figures of the two epochs."[10] Echoing this testimony, Emmanuel Levinas, who was present in Davos, recalls decades later that "for a young student, the impression was of being present at the creation and the end of the world."[11] As it was generally agreed that Heidegger emerged triumphant, the Davos encounter came to exemplify the twilight of neo-Kantian idealism and the rise of *Neues Denken* and *Existenzphilosophie*. By extension, it was taken to reflect the dusk of philosophical rationalism and the dawn of a more subjective and experiential mode of philosophizing.[12] It has also been identified as the moment of birth of the so-called analytical and continental philosophical divide.[13] In what follows, I wish to add (yet another) interpretive

[8] Friedman, *A Parting of the Ways*, 108. See also Kaufmann, "Cassirer, Neo-Kantianism, and Phenomenology."

[9] In *Sein und Zeit* (*SZ* 51 n6/*BT* 490) Heidegger recalls a meeting with Cassirer in 1923 in Hamburg where they agreed on the necessity of "an existential analytic."

[10] Herrigel, "Denken dieser Zeit," 4.   [11] Levinas, *Is It Righteous to Be?*, 35.

[12] Gordon, *Continental Divide*, 50; Meyer, *Zwischen Philosophie und Gesetz*, 234–272.

[13] Friedman, *A Parting of the Ways*. In his thorough analysis of the confrontation, Friedman discusses a third figure, Rudolf Carnap, who will be absent from the present chapter's discussion.

lens though which the Davos encounter can be considered, and propose that the confrontation between Cassirer and Heidegger can be seen as representing the termination of a specific German-Jewish vision, pertaining to a general conflation of Judaism with the values of the Enlightenment and to the possibility of forming an enlightened and rational society inspired by the Jewish spirit of ethical monotheism in which Jews are treated as equals. Without reducing its philosophical character to either a political or theological confrontation, I suggest that a fuller understanding of the resonances of the debate for Jews at the time must take these aspects into account as well.[14]

THE DAVOS DEBATE: THEOLOGICAL ANGLES

One of Cassirer's prevailing intellectual concerns is the phenomenon of myth as a cultural and philosophical category. In his three-volume masterpiece, *The Philosophy of Symbolic Forms,* he expands Kant's critique of reason to a full-fledged critique of culture, adding to the original Kantian a priori representations of space, time, and the categories also symbolic forms by which the transcendental consciousness produces reality. Building on the Kantian legacy of the spontaneity of consciousness governed by its own internal principles, Cassirer records a Hegelian narrative of a progressive and synthetic development of human consciousness from its primitive mythical stage to its most advanced stage in the Enlightenment model of autonomous human subjectivity.[15] While Cassirer rejects the Hegelian idea of the identity

---

[14] My interpretation of the Davos encounter is indebted to Gordon's work, particularly in focusing on the notion of "throwness" and receptivity as encompassing the philosophers' main point of contention, as well as his useful analysis of the lectures by Cassirer and Heidegger in Davos (chapters 3 and 4 of his book). I also agree with David Nirenburg, who suggests contextualizing the Davos encounter and reading Heidegger's responses to Cassirer in light of, and as intertwined with, a German political and philosophical anti-Jewish legacy. See Nirenburg, "When Philosophy Mattered," 39–43. Complementing Nirenburg, who contextualizes the debate with some derogatory post-Kantian renditions of "Judaism," I offer the more immediate context of the political, anti-Jewish connotations of the early-twentieth-century debates over Kant. Some important background for this can be found in chapter 6 of Gordon's book. A thoroughly politicized interpretation of the Davos debate is offered by Bourdieu, *The Political Ontology of Martin Heidegger.* In order to avoid interpreting this moment in light of what took place afterwards, I draw primarily on texts written before Hitler's seize of power and before Heidegger puts in place the overt link between Judaism and technology that is exhibited in various entries of the *Black Notebooks* throughout the 1930s and 1940s.

[15] Cassirer, *The Philosophy of Symbolic Forms*, vol. II, "Mystical Thought."

of reality and thought, he does focus on concrete, cultural manifestations of symbolic forms and depicts the mythical consciousness as
advancing by way of Hegelian *Aufhebung* – negation, preservation,
and self-overcoming – to the expression of more developed symbolic
forms, such as religion, art, historiography, and ultimately, rational
science.[16] As he explains in the second volume, dedicated to "Mythical
Thought," while profoundly undeveloped, myth is a form of expression
by which "consciousness frees itself from the passive capacity in sensory impression and creates a world of its own in accordance with
a spiritual principle."[17] Myth is a form of objectification of spirit,
a tool for organizing reality, and hence situated within the domain of
rationality. And yet, it lacks self-reflection and transparency; it
bespeaks the creative and autonomous capacities of the human spirit
by imposing a symbolic form on reality while perceiving itself overwhelmed by and absolutely receptive to the surrounding world. It also
does not distinguish between its mythological symbolism and the non-
mythical world it symbolizes. Religious consciousness is only slightly
more developed, according to Cassirer. It successfully differentiates
between sign and meaning, but the two are still closely interrelated,
identical in content though not in form. "If we attempt to isolate and
remove the basic mythical components from religious belief," Cassirer
argues, "we no longer have religion in its real, objectively historical
manifestation; all that remains is a shadow of it, an empty
abstraction."[18]

Overcoming the mythical and religious consciousness amounts to its
subordination to the rule of reason and self-transparency. Thus, the
demythologized scientific mind "knows that the symbols it employs are
symbols and comprehends them as such."[19] For Cassirer, ascending the
ladder of symbolic forms is tantamount to the increase of freedom,
which he understands as the spontaneous ability to form symbolic
images in consciousness. "Human culture taken as a whole," he writes,
"may be described as the process of man's progressive self-liberation."[20]
In his portrayal of the evolution of human spirit from the most basic
expressive type of symbolic meaning, through the *representative* symbolic meaning and finally to the *significative* function of symbolic meaning, Cassirer demonstrates his faith in an overarching Enlightenment

---

[16] On Cassirer's debt to Hegel, see Verne, "Kant, Hegel, and Cassirer."
[17] Cassirer, *The Philosophy of Symbolic Forms*, vol. II, "Mystical Thought," 14.
[18] Ibid., 239.   [19] Ibid., 26.   [20] Cassirer, *An Essay on Man*, 228.

narrative of progress (though situating the analysis of myth and religion in this threefold outline is hardly straightforward). While it is true that Cassirer presents a "centrifugal" structure in which developments spring from a common core and center, it is still the case that for him consciousness and history progress internally and teleologically from the juvenile mythical thinking toward the mature scientific thinking.[21] Driving his philosophical vision is the *Bildung* ideal of cultivation of knowledge and skill and above all the improvement of one's character. Cassirer's program, thus, is predicated on the development of human spirit from an illusion of receptivity, passivity, and myth, to the veneration of creative spontaneity, agency, and reason, and on the principle that driving this narrative of progression is the need to overcome myth and religion.

When considering this account in the context of the Davos debate over Kant, it becomes clear that for Cassirer, Heidegger's emphasis on the receptivity of Dasein's thrownness resembles the primitive mythical consciousness that ought to be overcome. Indeed, the critical distinction between the mythical and disenchanted mind corresponds to the crux of his dispute with Heidegger over the role of spontaneity and receptivity in Kant. As Cassirer writes: "while logical reflection tends . . . to resolve all receptivity into spontaneity, mythic conception shows exactly the opposite tendency, namely, to regard all spontaneous action as something receptive, and all human achievement as something merely bestowed."[22] For him, Heidegger's insistence on the centrality of the preconceptual and the prescientific for the meaning of our existence is strikingly similar to the primitive mythical and religious mind. While acknowledging that Heidegger's philosophy is not a religious program, Cassirer stresses that its content is nevertheless *secularized*, that is, determined by its repressed religious origin and as such detrimentally continues to bear its weight. This point is made in the lectures Cassirer delivered at Davos before the conversation with Heidegger, where he calls attention to Heidegger's "Christian-religious" image of the individual Dasein, in its "world-fallenness" (*Weltverfallenheit*) and confined to its own finitude.[23] In other notes, published only recently, he returns to this theme, observing that Heidegger "comes . . . from the philosophy of religion." The perspective of *Existenzphilosophie* as a whole emulates religious structures, and in Heidegger this is blatantly so: the

---

[21] Richter, "Symbol, Mythos, Religion."   [22] Cassirer, *Language and Myth*, 60.
[23] Gordon, *Continental Divide*, 118.

general world of *das Man* and the modality of inauthenticity are portrayed as "a kind of 'fall from grace,'" and the emphasis on historicality
is "always a religious-individualistic comprehension of history."[24]
Cassirer also participates in the then-widespread interpretive trend of
reading Heidegger as a secularized Kierkegaard, which figured prominently in Jewish and non-Jewish circles throughout the century.[25] He
states, for example, that in *Sein und Zeit* "all temporality has its roots in
the 'present moment' [*Augenblick*] seen in a religious sense – for it is
constituted through 'Sorge' and through the basic religious phenomenon of death – and 'Angst' (cf. Kierkegaard)."[26] In Heidegger's analysis of anxiety and finitude "a genuine religious tone becomes audible, as
with Kierkegaard."[27] Perceptively, Cassirer also counts Luther alongside the Danish thinker as a core theoretical source from which the
"power and depth" of Heidegger's "religious purposes" is gained. He
even compares Heidegger's "deeply religious, especially Protestant"
tone with a sermon by Luther on death.[28]

Cassirer's problem with Heidegger drawing on Luther and Kierkegaard
for a philosophical system pertains both to content and methodology. In
terms of content, it evokes an individualized and subjectivist tradition
instead of a universalist, intersubjective perspective. Voicing what will be
one of the most common critiques leveled against Heidegger, Cassirer
charges that Heidegger's philosophical anthropology paints a radically
individualistic image of human existence, which as such is sealed off from
intersubjective ethics and truths. In terms of methodology, the problem for
Cassirer is that these Christian thinkers are utilized while their theological
commitments are ignored. Unlike Kierkegaard, Cassirer observes,

with Heidegger, the problem seems to cut more deeply, insofar as his posing of the
question was wholly determined by theological considerations . . . , but the theological solution to the problem is rejected. He does not allow anxiety, as man-
kind's basic state of mind, to be pacified through either theological metaphysics or
a religious Gospel of salvation.[29]

---

[24] Cassirer, *The Philosophy of Symbolic Forms*, vol. IV, 202. The materials in the fourth
volume were written around 1928 and 1940.
[25] Baring, *Converts to the Real*, 211–240; Herskowitz, "Heidegger as a Secularized
Kierkegaard," 155–174 (many of the findings of this article have been absorbed into
Chapters 3 and 4 of the present study). Theodor Adorno interprets Heidegger along these
lines in his *The Jargon of Authenticity*, 1. On Heidegger and Adorno, see Gordon,
Adorno and Existence. See also Taubes, *The Political Theology of Paul*, 68.
[26] Cassirer, *The Philosophy of Symbolic Forms*, vol. IV, 200–201.   [27] Ibid., 206.
[28] Quoted in Skidelsky, *Ernst Cassirer*, 212.
[29] Cassirer, *The Philosophy of Symbolic Forms*, vol. IV, 206.

Heidegger is still beholden to religious provenance, Cassirer maintains. His analysis of death, for example, is "religious" and hence not "authentically philosophical."

One can say that a central impulse in Cassirer's thinking is the affirmation of what Hans Blumenberg calls "the legitimacy of the modern age."[30] Indeed, he no doubt identifies with the view of the Enlightenment thinkers which he describes in a later work thusly: "between myth and philosophy there could be no point of contact. Myth ends where philosophy begins – as darkness gives way to the rising sun."[31] Yet there is good reason to question both the portrayal of his own position and that of modernity as simply non- or a-theological. Insofar as Cassirer offers a model of *Aufhebung*, it follows that his liberated modern consciousness is both superior to and at the same time indebted to previous mythical and religious forms. According to this logic, myth and religion are overcome but not dispensed with.[32] Moreover, Cassirer's account of selfhood as intelligent, spontaneous, free, infinitely creative, and atemporal echoes familiar divine attributes and is depicted precisely in the same way that Kant himself thinks about God.[33] This very point came up in the Davos encounter itself, and Cassirer has no problem with equating the human capacity for spontaneous creation of forms to God's way of knowing.[34]

Indeed, the religious reverberations of the debate as a whole are easily comprehended, for the dispute over the dependency or agency of human existence is a steadfast theological theme. Appropriately, it has been suggested that we understand the Davos quarrel over Kant with reference to both the conflict between Luther and Erasmus and the rivalry between Augustinianism and Pelagianism.[35] In both cases, the nature of the human being is debated: are humans completely dependent on divine grace, or does human agency have an active role in the process of salvation? Cassirer's optimistic view of human potentiality situates him alongside the "humanism" of Pelagius and Erasmus, while Heidegger's pessimism regarding the fallen and dependent character of human existence parallels with the 'anti-humanism' of Augustine and Luther.

The debate approximates the theological on another point as well: the question of transcendence and prospect of the human spirit's strive for

---

[30] Freundenthal, "The Hero of Enlightenment," 189–213.
[31] Cassirer, *The Myth of the State*, 182–183.
[32] Bongardt, "Must Religion Be Overcome?"   [33] Cooke, "Kant's Godlike Self."
[34] Gordon, *Continental Divide*, 182–187.
[35] Krois, "Cassirer's Unpublished Critique of Heidegger"; Moyn and Yadin-Israel, "The Creaturely Limits of Knowledge," 123–144.

infinitude as its *terminus ad quem*. For Cassirer, this striving is episte-mological and moral, not theological. Human spirit can transcend the constrictions of its finitude through the universality of moral action and the symbolic objectification of culture. Heidegger too insists on a theologically free manner of philosophizing, although he denies Cassirer's ability to attain that goal. For him, the striving for a fictional atemporality contradicts the fact that any disclosure of Dasein and its world is grounded in the fundamental temporality and finitude of its being-in-the-world, which no historical development can overcome. "The idea of an infinite thinking," Heidegger proclaims, "is an absurdity."[36]

In Davos, arguing against Cassirer's interpretation of the Kantian categorical imperative as a moment in which the finite human can break out into the infinite, Heidegger declares:

[I]n the Categorical Imperative we have something which goes beyond the finite creature. But precisely the concept of the Imperative as such shows the inner reference to a finite creature. Also, this going-beyond to something higher is always just a going-beyond to the finite creature, to one which is created (angel). This transcendence too still remains within the creatureliness [*Geschöpflichkeit*] and finitude.[37]

In Heidegger's view, Cassirer does not draw the radical conclusions of Dasein's "creatureliness." For even had we been able to transcend our fallen state and become angels, we would still have done so as "creatures," as temporal and finite. In noting the creatureliness and dependency of Dasein, Heidegger deliberately opposes the Enlightenment's self-created and autonomous self promulgated by Cassirer – a position he associates with the theologically flavored negative trait of "pride."[38] Indeed, his insistence on the immanence and ultimate finitude of Dasein's transcen-dence aims to do away with the optimistic neo-Kantian possibility of infinitude as an operative concept. "Thought as such ... is in itself the seal of finitude," he writes in his Kant book. His overarching philosophi-cal concern at this time is to come clean of the essentially theological tendency of thinking of time in relation to eternity and to understand time through time (*die Zeit aus der Zeit*). Even the temporal modality of divine infinitude is derivative of Dasein's originary temporality. Crucial to this effort is breaking with the long-standing philosophical and theological

---

[36] GA 3, 272/Heidegger, *Kant and the Problem of Metaphysics*, 170.
[37] Gordon, *Continental Divide*, 162.
[38] Heidegger, *Kant and the Problem of Metaphysics*, 88.

tradition that perceives the "now" as the truth of time. At the same time, the rhetoric, logic, and horizon of theology continues to reverberate, and Heidegger's contestation with Cassirer's neo-Kantian anthropology could be seen as a continuation of his youthful attack on the theology of glory from the perspective of the theology of the cross, couched in secular philosophical idiom. A pattern thus emerges, whereby both thinkers see themselves as overcoming a religiously informed manner of philosophizing, while seeing their interlocutor as still burdened and impoverished by it. For Heidegger, Cassirer's *philosophia perennis* is defective; for Cassirer, the flaw lies in Heidegger's religiously stamped *Existenzphilosophie*. What is disclosed, at any rate, is the subcurrent of theological entanglement in the discussion. This is not to say that the philosophical encounter between Cassirer and Heidegger should be reformulated theologically, but rather, that both seem to recognize that the theological is present in it.

KANT BETWEEN DEUTSCHTUM AND JUDENTUM

As almost everything else in the tumultuous period between the wars, the philosophical discourse too was deeply political. Disputes over the interpretation of Kant were a particularly charged political matter, as the heated debate over the belongingness of *Judentum* and *Deutschtum* was projected onto it. The most outspoken advocate of the harmonizing position was of course Hermann Cohen, whose patriotic *Deutschtum und Judentum* (1916), as well as other essays, championed the philosophical and political alignment of Judaism, Kantianism, and Germanism. In a response to it, Bruno Bauch, one of the editors of the prestigious journal *Kantstudien* and an established neo-Kantian philosopher, offered an analysis of the concept of the German nation, defined as the "*Gemeinschaft der 'Mitgeborenen,'*" intentionally aiming to exclude the Jews, who were considered *fremdvölkisch*.[39] With the backdrop of the failing war effort and the increasing suspicion of Jewish loyalty, Bauch specifically denounced the "Jewification" (*Verjudung*) of German philosophy by the foreign influences of Jewish thinkers. Sympathetic to an earlier attack on Cohen by the journalist Lenore Ripke-Kühne and echoing her claim, Bauch also singled out Cohen in an ensuing explanatory letter, challenging "the Jewish thinker's" ability to understand "the German philosopher" Kant. According to Bauch, Jews could only produce a "Jewish Kant,"

---

[39] Bauch, "Vom Begriff der Nation"; Bauch, "Leserbrief."

while "real" Germans alone are capable of aptly understanding the great philosopher. "Not even a Jew of Cohen's intellectual rank" can be included into the exalted tradition of German idealism. Tainted by "Jewish formalism," Cohen and Marburg neo-Kantianism as a whole pose a threat to genuine German philosophy. Notwithstanding the vulgarity of Bauch's letter, there was, to a certain extent, a split between German and Jewish Kantianism that allowed him to generalize from Cohen to the entire Marburg school, whose major adherents were Jews. In his memoir, Löwith somewhat dismissively called the Marburg school a "Jewish liberal affair."[40] In response to Bauch's anti-Semitic pronouncements, Cohen and Cassirer resigned from the *Kant Gesellschaft*, and when the idea of conducting a debate on the matter in the pages of the *Kantstudien* journal was suggested, Bauch resigned from its editorial board, claiming it was "Judaized" (*verjudet*).[41]

Around the same time, Cohen's claim for the "inner affinity" (*innere Beziehung*) between Kantianism and Judaism came under further attack by another prominent German intellectual, Ernst Troeltsch. This time, the controversy revolved around the question of the parochiality or universality of the biblical prophets' message. Cohen argued that in terms of content, there was absolutely no difference between "the religion of the prophets and the ethics of Kant."[42] Troeltsch, on the other hand, set up a barrier between Judaism and Kant by historicizing and hence confining the significance of the prophets to the limited context of the ancient Hebrews. Here, too, Troeltsch claimed that between himself, the Protestant German, and Cohen, the Jew, lay a fundamental gap that prevented the possibility of their mutual understanding. In effect, Cohen's philosophy was opposed to what is essentially German.[43] What is demonstrated by the Bauch and Troeltsch polemics is that around the First World War, the deepening social wedge between Germans and Jews was paralleled in, and at the same time drew on, matters of spirit. Indeed, many among the intelligentsia perceived the war to be not a mere military or political event, but a spiritual one. What was at stake was not only state borders or political institutions, but the very civilization, values, and philosophical ideas embodied in these institutions; that is, the German

[40] Löwith, *My Life in Germany*, 105.
[41] The "'Bauch affair' affair" is nicely presented in Sieg, "Deutsche Kulturgeschichte und Jüdischer Geist"; see also Hoeres, *Krieg der Philosophen*, 232–238; Sluga, *Heidegger's Crisis*, 82–85.
[42] Cohen, "Deutschtum und Judentum I–II," 237–301, 302–318.
[43] Troeltsch, "Glaube und Ethos der hebräischen Propheten," 34–64, 820, 821.

spirit as such. The enemy, accordingly, was not merely a political and military force; it was a threatening metaphysical power. There were two fronts in the German struggle, in the trenches and in spirit. But the former derived from the latter: philosophy was the true front.

Interestingly, it was not Cohen who responded to Bauch and Ripke-Kühne, but Cassirer. In a defense that remained unpublished until recently, Cassirer argues against the "dogmatic naturalism" expressed in Bauch's tirade, noting that philosophical concepts transcend ethnic boundaries.[44] As to the mutual exclusivism through which Bauch frames the "spiritual-national relationship" between Germans and Jews, Cassirer notes that Germany is indeed the native land of its Jews as well, and that it is solely the result of an external and simplistic confrontational framing that people like Bauch use to neutralize the possibility of true encounter and relation, "for everything that could ground such a relationship is denied to the Jew."[45]

Of course, the harmonized portrayal of German-Jewish spirit fell on deaf German ears, and the debacle in the trenches only intensified the duty to prevail in the philosophical war. Indeed, the urgency around matters philosophical and specifically the chauvinism informing the dispute over Kant continued also after the Treaty of Versailles. A few weeks before the encounter in Davos, Othmar Spann, a Nazi thinker, delivered a lecture in Munich, attended by Hitler, on the "contemporary cultural crisis." In a report of the lecture it is stated that Spann discussed neo-Kantianism, bemoaning that "it was sad that the German people should have to be reminded of their own Kantian philosophy by foreigners [*Fremden*]." The names of Cohen and Cassirer were explicitly mentioned as such foreigners.[46]

While on a personal level Heidegger and Cassirer conducted relatively cordial exchanges, it is more than likely that these political connotations were present in the Davos encounter, not least because Heidegger shared Bauch's fears of the Jewish threat to *Deutschheit*.[47] Heidegger, like Bauch, proves to be caught up in the "Myth of Judaization" that was an integral element of the way in which the *Judenfrage* was discussed in Weimar Germany.[48] According to this perception, the "Jewish Spirit" was taking

[44] Cassirer, "Zum Begriff der Nation," 42.   [45] Ibid., 47.

[46] Krois, "Why Did Cassirer and Heidegger Not Debate in Davos?"

[47] Toni Cassirer, wife of Ernst, noted in a later occasion that those present at the conference in Davos "were not unaware of Heidegger's antisemitism." Cassirer, *Aus meinem Leben mit Ernst Cassirer*, 165.

[48] On this theme see Aschheim, "'The Jew Within': The Myth of 'Judaization' in Germany."

over and undermining the German destinal march. Heidegger's desire to overcome what he took to be the "Jewish" worldlessness and machination of being, as discussed in Chapter 1, is an idiosyncratic version of the effort for *Entjudung*. In a letter from late 1929, only a short while after Davos, Heidegger writes: "We are faced with a choice, either to provide our *German* intellectual life once more with real talents and educators rooted in our own soil [*bodenständige*], or to hand over that intellectual life once and for all to the growing Jewification [*Verjudung*] in the broad and narrow sense."[49] Evidently, this was a steadfast view of Heidegger, who already in 1916 considered "Jewification" to be a "frightening" threat to "our culture and universities."[50] It is also interesting that in *Sein und Zeit*, when discussing what he considers the debased interpretation of Kant in his analysis of the ontological structure of "conscience," he assembles together the Kantian "idea of moral law" and what he disparagingly calls "Pharisaism" (*Pharisäismus*) as mistakenly perceiving Dasein's conscience as oriented and orienting toward a practicality governed by "calculative maxims," instead of what "calls it forth to its factical potentiality-of-being -a-self."[51] In 1933, in a letter denouncing the neo-Kantian philosopher of Jewish origin Richard Hönigswald, Heidegger antagonistically associates neo-Kantianism with liberalism and implies its foreignness to true Germanism. There he argues that "under the seemingly strict [*streng*] scientific philosophical grounds, the neo-Kantian view of man obscures his historical rootedness and his *völkisch* belonging to his origin from soil and blood [*Herkunft aus Boden und Blut*]."[52]

Manifestly, Heidegger objects to the entire theoretical "package" of neo-Kantianism and liberal universalism that Cohen and Cassirer represent. Their idealism and liberalism betray an adherence to modern subjectivism and metaphysics, and these, together with the groundlessness (*Bodenlosigkeit*) of their universalism, reflect their inconsistency with that which is authentically German. In his mind, their Jewishness was not disconnected. There is little evidence that Heidegger was interested in diversifying his conception of Judaism or Jewishness. Nor was he intent on complicating the image of its alliance with liberalism and universalism and taking serious note, for example, of the expansion of Jewish nationalism at the time. His sporadic (and critical) references from this time to Martin Buber, one of the most prominent and well-known Zionists

---

[49] Sieg, "Die Verjudung des deutschen Geistes."
[50] Gertrud Heidegger, *"Mein liebes Seelchen!"*, 91.   [51] *SZ*, 294/*BT*, 341.
[52] *GA* 16, 132–133.

working in Germany at the time, are strictly philosophical and do not mention Buber's public activities.[53] He was certainly at least vaguely aware of the Zionist movement, because in a letter to his wife from 1932 he mentions reading some issues of the *Jüdische Rundschau*, the twice-weekly organ of the Zionist Federation of Germany (*Zionistische Vereinigung für Deutschland*).[54] Some of the relevant letters are missing, but it is rather clear that his compliment of its "outstanding layout and standard [*ausgezeichnet orientiert u. Niveau*]" does not represent his thoughts on its content. That the periodical issues were ordered to him by Alfred Baeumler, the Nazi philosopher, together with the fact that on one occasion, he notes in agreement with his wife, who was an open anti-Semite and Nazi sympathizer, that "one cannot be too distrustful here,"[55] may suggest that his views of Zionism were not positive either.

Few of Heidegger's political remarks and practical involvement can be understood outside the paradigm of the need for a German spiritual mobilization.[56] As demonstrated in his rectorial address and on many other occasions, he was among those who perceived the 1933 revolution to be a continuation and corrective to what the spiritual German revolution of 1914 was supposed to be. In 1934, for instance, he declares that "the Great War comes over us *only now*," but that this war is philosophical, and hence "the Great War must now be *spiritually* conquered by us, i.e., the battle will become the *innermost law* of our existence [*Daseins*]."[57] Thus, while the philosophical tastes of Bauch, Spann, Troeltsch, and Heidegger are in many ways conflicted, they stand united in perceiving themselves as fighting Germany's philosophical war and in viewing the Jews as at odds with what is German. Evidently – and with respect to Heidegger, perhaps also consequentially – they also concur in their objection to Cohen's and Cassirer's understanding of Kant.

Likewise, Cassirer himself was certainly aware that the political tensions around the "Jewish" interpretation of Kant were as heated now as they had been around 1914. It is perhaps for this reason that he chooses to begin his critical but graceful review-essay of Heidegger's Kant book in 1931 by recalling Kant's 1772 letter to Marcus Herz, the Jewish physician, about his breakthrough concerning the vital role of "the transcendental

[53] Heidegger, *The Metaphysical Foundations of Logic*, 187–190; *Phenomenological Interpretation of Kant's* Critique of Pure Reason, 214; *The Basic Problems of Phenomenology*, 297.
[54] Heidegger, *Letters to His Wife, 1915–1970*, 176.   [55] Ibid., 134, 137.
[56] Flasch, *Die geistige Mobilmachung*.   [57] GA 16, 280, 283.

object" to metaphysics, a letter illustrating the possibility of a productive philosophical conversation between Germans and German Jews.[58] Yet an acknowledgment that these times have passed can be seen in a later letter he wrote on November 26, 1938 to Albert Görland, a former colleague who had become a Nazi supporter. Rebuking Görland for allowing his unbridled ambition to lead him to betray his teachers, friends, and beliefs, Cassirer exclaims, with bitter irony:

> You knew what Jews and Judaism are; you knew all about the corruptive influence of Judaism on German philosophy. Because you knew and understood the accomplishment of Hermann Cohen and knew about yourself that you would not have written a single line of your own books without it. Was it really necessary to throw all this away?[59]

Indeed, while never entirely central, one cannot deny a certain political flavor in Cassirer's philosophical work as a whole.[60] His occupation with myth aimed in part to conceptualize and combat what he considered to be the reemergence of prescientific, narrow-minded, and harmful forces taking over Germany – of which Heidegger was a proponent.

It is thus unsurprising that the political accent of the Heidegger–Cassirer encounter was registered, and indeed amplified after the former joined Hitler's ranks. Through a deeply fragile conceptualization according to which philosophical irrationalism is intrinsically prone to reactionary political views, Heidegger's rejection of rationalism served as an explanation for his support of National Socialism, and Cassirer's adherence to reason was tied to his political liberalism. This conceptualization matched the political penchants of these two philosophers, but it cannot be said to reflect the larger political and philosophical landscape. In fact, it is easily refuted when one considers that not all who huddled under the umbrella-term of neo-Kantianism leaned to the political left. Many who pledged alliance to the new regime, from inside and outside the academia, believed in reason and science and fervently rejected the conceptual framework of Heidegger and his ilk.[61] It should be stressed, moreover, that approaching their point of contestation through the rational/irrational distinction is counterproductive, for Heidegger was not against the

---

[58] Cassirer, "Kant und das Problem der Metaphysik." This perceptive point is made by Gordon, *Continental Divide*, 269.

[59] Cassirer, *Aus meinem Leben*, 242.

[60] On some of the political dimensions of Cassirer's thought see Skidelsky, *Ernst Cassirer*, 220–238; Barash, "Ernst Cassirer's Theory of Myth."

[61] Amongst these, Sluga lists Rickert, Frege, Bauch, Hartmann, and Gehlen. Sluga, *Heidegger's Crisis*, 7, 99–100.

intellect and science, but rather against intellectualism and scientism, seeking to dethrone reason from its pretense of ultimacy rather than reject it altogether.

But while inaccurate, this politicized interpretation was dominant, and it was particularly appealing in Jewish circles. Like most acculturated and progressive-leaning Jewish *Bildungsbürgertum*, Cassirer had confidence in the power of reason to organize and improve society. And it is no coincidence that the autonomous, self-governing, and rational Kantian notion of self he championed bears the identical features of the citizen of the liberal society he wished to realize. In this respect, Cassirer, who in 1929 became the first Jew elected as a rector of a German university and who offered a passionate defense of Weimar's liberal constitution at his university's celebration for the Republic's tenth anniversary in 1928, was *pars pro toto* for liberal German Jews. No one embraced so enthusiastically the interlacing of emancipation from myth and political emancipation as the Jews, who hoped it would dismantle the deep-seated religious prejudices and fictitious superstitions that continued to thwart the realization of their hope for true equality. And nowhere was the unfulfilled promise of modernity experienced more acutely than in Weimar, when its liberal constitution granted Jews *de jure* the equal rights they so coveted for the first time, while *de facto*, amid rising tides of political reactionaryism and anti-Semitism, they were increasingly perceived as outsiders.

HEIDEGGER, REASON, AND JUDAISM: ORTHODOX AND LIBERAL PERSPECTIVES

As noted, it would be a mistake to reduce the battle over Kant to the political or to the theological, but it was never a decontextualized, purely philosophical engagement. In both orthodox and liberal Jewish discourses, these political and theological resonances did not go unnoticed. In a review of Julius Kraft's 1932 *Von Husserl zu Heidegger: Kritik der phänomenologischen Philosophie*, Ludwig Feuchtwanger, an esteemed journalist and publisher in the Jewish intellectual scene in Germany and the editor of the *Bayerischen Israelitische Gemeindezeitung*, applauds Kraft for brilliantly carrying out a "productive critique of Heidegger's pseudo-philosophy" in which "bombastic descriptions of trivial everyday wisdom" grant a misleading "appearance of philosophical profundity." Feuchtwanger had attended some of Heidegger's lectures and recognized the philosopher's talents – a month earlier he had written to the Jewish scholar Ernst Simon: "I could really use a good Heideggerian essay.

Heidegger is the leader of National Socialism and is committed [*verschrie-ben*] to the party in his seminar, root and branch [*Haut u. Haar*]."[62] Yet his review gives voice to a deep disapproval of Heidegger's non-rationalistic tendencies and methodology. Indeed, Feuchtwanger approves of Kraft's view that phenomenology is an intuitionalist and irrational endeavor, and hence associated with authoritarian politics and nihilism. "Heidegger's philosophy-en-vogue," Feuchtwanger writes, "had to provide the euphemistic 'ideal' garb for our whole 'intellectual' National Socialism and Noble-Anti-Semitism in which the most brutal nihilism exempts oneself impressively and truly 'intellectually.'" Making an early connection between Heidegger and Carl Schmitt, he continues: "This existence philosophy is also the foundation of the new theories concerning suspending the state-law."[63] Framing Kraft's work within its broader intellectual context, Feuchtwanger pairs Kraft's critique of Heidegger with Cassirer's aforementioned critique of Heidegger's inter-pretation of Kant. In both cases, Heidegger's anti-rationalism is indicted from the standpoint of reason. That very year Cassirer published his monograph *The Philosophy of the Enlightenment*, which was likewise enthusiastically welcomed by Feuchtwanger. In a review of the work, he claims it is a worthy defense of the values of the Enlightenment that alone can lead human sciences to overcome "the false lights of *Seins- und Lebensphilosophie*, whether drawn from Klages or Heidegger." According to Feuchtwanger's rationalistic worldview, Judaism, too, is a religion of reason, and Heidegger's opposition to reason situates him as an enemy of the foundations of Judaism as well.

A similar and more direct identification between reason and Judaism, together with an overt contrast to Heidegger's non-rationalism and Nazism, is made by Joseph Soloveitchik. Later to become the towering rabbinical figure of postwar modern orthodoxy in America, Soloveitchik wrote his philosophy dissertation on Cohen's epistemology in Berlin around the time of the publication of *Sein und Zeit*.[64] In his work

---

[62] Quoted in Meyer, *Zwischen Philosophie und Gesetz*, 285. The letter is found in the Ernst Simon archive file 332, 4 letters b/w 1932–1937, in the Israel National Library in Jerusalem.

[63] Feuchtwanger, "Review of Julius Kraft," 298–299.

[64] On Soloveitchik's acquaintance with Heidegger's philosophy, see Herskowitz, "Rabbi Joseph B. Soloveitchik's Endorsement and Critique of Volkish Thought"; Herskowitz, "The Moment and the Future." Soloveitchik shared a room with his fellow philosophy student Alexander Altmann, who was occupied with applying Heidegger's philosophical insights to Jewish theology (see Chapter 3). One of Soloveitchik's students records the

Halakhic Man (1941), a spiritual portrait of an idealized modern orthodox Jew, Heidegger is subjected to fierce diatribe.[65] Soloveitchik includes
"the phenomenological, existential and antiscientific school of Heidegger
and his coterie" together with the likes of Bergson, Nietzsche, Spengler,
and Klages as a manifestation of "the entire Romantic aspiration to escape
from the domain of knowledge, the rebellion against the authority of
objective, scientific cognition." Drawing what he sees as its direct political
outcome, Soloveitchik announces that these irrational tendencies

have brought complete chaos and human depravity to the world. And let the
events of the present era be proof! The individual who frees himself from the
rational principle and who casts off the yoke of objective thought will in the end
turn destructive and lay waste the entire created order.

Warning against the penetration of the dangerous worldview associated
with Heidegger into Judaism, he advocates for a religion of reason.

It is preferable that religion should ally itself with the forces of clear, logical
cognition ... rather than pledge its troth to beclouded, mysterious ideologies
that grope in the dark corners of existence, unaided by the shining light of
objective knowledge, and believe that they have penetrated to the secret core of
the world.[66]

Later in this work, "[the] development from 'inauthentic existence'
[*uneigentliches Sein*] to 'authentic existence' [*eingentliches Dasein*] in
the philosophy of Heidegger (as expressed in *Being and Time*)" is
charged for secularizing and corrupting the notion "of the obligatory
nature of the creative gesture, of self-creation as an ethical norm," which
Soloveitchik claims finds its "pure and holy" origin in Judaism.[67] This is
a telling point, not only because Soloveitchik sees the existential ideal of
authenticity as a corruption of the *Bildung* ideal of self-creation, which
he attributes originally to Maimonides, but because he presents
Heidegger as secularizing not a Christian, but a fundamentally Jewish
notion.

following testimony, purportedly stated by Soloveitchik himself: "I was in Heidegger's
class. I was a good student. He continually spoke about human destiny, spiritual perceptions, and the events of that time." Rakeffet-Rothkoff, *The Rav*, 195. Given the pithy
information provided in this testimony, its reliability is difficult to assess. Another
testimony is provided by Zev Gotthold, who claims that Soloveitchik commented to
him on the difficulty of Heidegger's *Sein und Zeit*. See Johnston, *Engagement and
Dialogue*, 119–124, 126–31. On Heidegger and Soloveitchik see also Wolfson,
"Eternal Duration and Temporal Comprescence."
[65] Soloveitchik, *The Halakhic Man.*   [66] Ibid., 141n4.   [67] Ibid., 164n163.

Soloveitchik mentions Heidegger alongside Kierkegaard, Ibsen, and Scheler in a broad polemic; nothing close to an elaborate discussion of Heidegger's position or his charged terminology is offered.[68] It is clear, however, that for Soloveitchik, uncorrupted existentialism, that is, the ideal of moral self-creation and cultivation, emerges from Judaism. Whether the corrupted character of modern existentialism reflects any theological biases and whether the rejection of reason is itself an outcome of a theological bias, remains unclear. Its corruption, however, results in barbaric ethical and political ramifications, for "the longing for creation was perverted into the desire for brutal and murderous domination. Such views have brought chaos and disaster to our world, which is drowning in blood."[69] Echoing this point again in 1944 in *The Halakhic Mind* and following Kraft's critical approach toward phenomenology as such, Soloveitchik considers "modern existential philosophy" to be a "mystical tren[d]." He identifies this program's roots in the *strenge Wissenschaft* of Husserl's intuitionism that recedes from the "'public' critical reason" to "a 'private' distorted subjective experience," and in this regard, Heidegger is a true student of Husserl. "It is no mere coincidence that the most celebrated philosophers of the third Reich were outstanding disciples of Husserl," he explains.

Husserl's intuitionism (*Wesensschau*), which Husserl, a trained mathematician, strived to keep on the level of mathematical intuition, was transposed into emotional approach to reality. When reason surrenders its supremacy to dark, equivocal emotions, no dam is able to stem the rising tide of the effective stream.

The contrast between "intellectual morality" and "mystic wisdom," Soloveitchik announces, "was the philosophical Armageddon of our age."[70]

It should be noted that while never retracting his damning judgment of Heidegger, Soloveitchik's perspective later veers toward a more subjectivist and non-rational existentialism, and indeed one finds in some of his writings a more "Heideggerian" tune.[71] Claiming now that existentialism is an ally to Judaism, Soloveitchik stresses the thrown and anxiously finite nature of human existence. "Man is in exile," he muses. "Man is a homeless being ... Judaism says that not only the Jew is in exile, but

[68] Though the thought of Scheler left a clear mark on Soloveitchik. See Ozar, "The Emergence of Max Scheler."
[69] Soloveitchik, *Halakhic Man*, 164n147.   [70] Soloveitchik, *The Halakhic Mind*, 51, 53.
[71] For example, Soloveitchik, "The Lonely Man of Faith," 5–67. And see Possen, "J. B. Soloveitchik."

that man as such, man in general, leads an exilic existence … Man was cursed by the Almighty and expelled from Paradise and became a homeless being."[72] In a Bultmannian manner, Soloveitchik now both accepts the existential idea of the *unheimlich* character of existence and implicitly reclaims it as an originally biblical-theological precept. Nowhere, however, does he explain how his emigration from the rationalistic perspective to a more existentially oriented perspective evades the political and ethical pitfalls he previously associated with Heidegger with such ferocity.

When Feuchtwanger and Soloveitchik consider Heidegger's assault on reason to be a threat on Judaism, they envision orthodox Judaism. Yet the clearest articulation of the affiliation of reason, Judaism, and morality in contrast to irrationality, Nazism, and Heidegger, is presented by Cassirer himself, who unlike Feuchtwanger and Soloveitchik, better represented the majority of the German Jews at the time. While never entirely out of sight, Cassirer's Jewishness became increasingly important to him after the Nazi takeover and his subsequent exile – first to Oxford in England, then to Sweden, and eventually to the United States.[73] Already in the second volume of *The Philosophy of Symbolic Forms*, he crowns the emergence of the idea of pure monotheistic prophetic Judaism as the turning point in the religious consciousness. It is here that it breaks loose from its mythical foundations and transitions toward philosophical idealism. "The classical example of this great transformation," he declares, "will always be the form of religious consciousness in the Prophetic books of the Old Testament."[74] In volume IV of *The Philosophy of Symbolic Forms*, he contrasts this conception of religion with Heidegger's framework:

In opposition to [Heidegger's philosophy], we uphold, despite everything, the broader, more universal, *idealistic* meaning of religion and the idealistic meaning of history. In it we behold liberation and deliverance from the "anxiety" which is the signature, the basic "state-of-mind" of finite Dasein. But this anxiety signifies only the beginning, not the final, inevitable constraint on our finite Dasein.[75]

---

[72] Soloveitchik, "The Synagogue as an Institution and as an Idea," 326.
[73] Mali, "Ernst Cassirer's Interpretation of Judaism," 187–215. See also Meyer's suggestively titled essay, "Ernst Cassirer, Judentum aus dem Geist der universalistischen Vernunft"; Schwarzschild, "Judaism in the Life and World of Ernst Cassirer"; Hertzberg, "A Reminiscence of Ernst Cassirer."
[74] Cassirer, *The Philosophy of Symbolic Forms*, vol. II, "Mystical Thought," 240.
[75] Cassirer, *The Philosophy of Symbolic Forms*, vol. IV, "The Metaphysics of Symbolic Form," 203–204.

In "Judaism and the Modern Political Myths" (1944), written a decade
and a half after the Davos encounter, Cassirer continues this line of
thought in his attempt to make sense of the present-day political context.
He explicitly identifies the religion of "universal, idealistic meaning" with
prophetic Judaism and describes the tormented present situation as
a manifestation of a spiritual combat between it and its antithesis, the
new tribal modern myth espoused by Nazism. Historically and conceptually, it is Judaism that "first made the decisive step that led from
a mythical to an ethical religion."[76] Nowhere is the war of ethical religion
against myth more apparent than in the biblical commandment forbid-
ding the making of "a graven image" and in the Hebrew prophets' ethos of
replacing sacrifices with "the fundamental religious and ethical duties."
Both, he claims, challenge poetic imagery and anthropomorphism, the
very core of mythical idolatry. This argument exemplifies Cassirer's logic
of idealism, whereby pure idea is superior to materiality, and physical rites
progress to moral ideals. On this account, the ritualistic element in
Judaism is superseded by a spiritualized ethical impulse. In unequivocal
Kantian language, he considers this the universal calling of Judaism, one
that induces the "ideal of perpetual peace."[77] While in some respects
Cassirer disassociated himself from what he saw as the limited philosophical perspective of Marburg neo-Kantianism, his depiction of Judaism
follows in the footsteps of Cohen, promulgating an ethical monotheism
from the sources of Judaism and Kant.[78] From Cassirer's perspective, the
model of moral Judaism is the bulwark against the nihilism promoted by
Heidegger.

  It would be wise, at this point, to clarify what would appear as an
inconsistency in Cassirer's stance on religion. On the one hand, he suggests in this essay that only religion – Judaism – can combat the myth of
totalitarian politics, and on the other hand, in *The Philosophy of Symbolic
Forms* he argues that religion and myth are closely comparable and that
they are transcended by reason; and moreover, that religion must overcome myth in the name of rationalism, idealism, and morality. This
inconsistency, however, only arises if one ignores Cassirer's Cohenian
perception of Judaism as a religion aligned with philosophical idealism
and Kantian morality. Historical Judaism, as it is depicted in the Hebrew
Bible, embodies the spiritual development of human consciousness from

---

[76] Cassirer, "Judaism and the Modern Political Myths," 115.   [77] Ibid., 123.
[78] Compare Cassirer's "Judaism and the Modern Political Myths" to his essay "Cohen's
    Philosophy of Religion," 101.

mythical religion to idealism, with its development from rites and ritual to the universal ethics of the prophets. Judaism gives itself to enlightened idealism because it in important respects anticipated and embodied it. One difficulty with this view is that it would seem that crafting the image of Judaism as the force prompting the advancement of spirit toward the scientific, universal, and ethical consciousness yields to the very secularized model Cassirer denounces in Heidegger. Nevertheless, if we consider Cassirer's critique of the Protestant remnants in Heidegger's philosophy side by side with his unapologetic advocacy for Judaism as a philosophical position, we can come to recognize the covert Jewish polemic against Christianity that is inscribed in Cassirer's celebratory philosophical narrative of the progression of human spirit.

Cassirer continues to reflect on these themes in his analysis of myth and its function in the history of Western philosophy in *The Myth of the State* (1946). Best seen as an intellectual response to the travesty in Germany and as a counterprogram to the lionization of the mythical by political theorists such as Georges Sorel, Carl Schmitt, and Alfred Bäumler, this work is an attempt to explain the rehabilitation of the mythical in modern political thought. The third part of his analysis is dedicated to tracing the main intellectual sources of twentieth-century political myth. At one point he claims that the political leader of the modern totalitarian state serves the equivalent role to that of the magician in primitive societies. This is interpreted as a de-secularization of politics, for "the *homo magus* is, at the same time, the *homo divinans*."[79] Notably, he recognizes Oswald Spengler – "a prophet of evil" – and Heidegger, with their rejection of scientific causation and promotion of the fatalistic force of destiny, as chief contributors to the "new art of divination" in politics. As before, Cassirer focuses on the notion of *Geworfenheit* as encompassing the core of Heidegger's philosophical deficiencies. In his earlier reproach of Heidegger, he claimed that the fallacy of this notion is that it does away with the ideal of eternal truth.[80] To this he now adds the charge of fatalism, for "we cannot change" the general conditions into which we are thrown, a charge culminating with an ethical and political accusation:

A theory that sees in the *Geworfenheit* of man one of his principal characters [has] given up all hopes of an active share in the construction and reconstruction of man's cultural life. Such philosophy renounces its own fundamental theoretical

---

[79] Cassirer, *The Myth of the State*, 288.
[80] Cassirer, *The Philosophy of Symbolic Forms*, vol. IV, 205–206.

and ethical ideals. It can be used, then, as a pliable instrument in the hands of the political leaders.[81]

For the *Aufklärer* and humanist Cassirer, as for the many who marched under the banner of reason and liberalism, this Heideggerian notion encapsulates the dangers of irrationalism and constitutes an assault on what they held most dear: freedom, ethics, and the capacity to reach the truth.

In his essay "Judaism and the Modern Political Myths," Judaism is depicted as the anti-mythical force of universal ethics and reason, offered as the antithesis to Heideggerian philosophy and as the sole cure to Western civilization after its "open and solemn enthronement of myth."[82] With this, Cassirer voices a common modern Jewish position pertaining to the "contribution" of Judaism to the general society. Bearing a message to the nations, the import of Judaism transcends the limits of its national and confessional constituents and holds the salvific key to remedy society's ills. For Cassirer, like David Neumark, Abraham Geiger, Leo Baeck, Hermann Cohen and others, Judaism was *mythosfrei*, and it is this message that is its most urgent contribution.

Tellingly, while acknowledging the unprecedented horror that is presently taking place, Cassirer still voices what can be seen as a manifesto of nineteenth-century liberal Judaism in 1944:

What the modern Jew had to defend in this combat [against Nazism] was not only his physical existence or the preservation of the Jewish race . . . We had to represent all those ethical ideals that had been brought into being by Judaism and found their way into general human culture, into the life of all civilized nations . . . these ideals are not destroyed and cannot be destroyed. They have stood their ground in these critical days. If Judaism has contributed to break the power of the modern political myths, it has done its duty, having once more fulfilled its historical and religious mission.[83]

The almost improperly triumphant tone of this passage notwithstanding, Cassirer's depiction of Judaism as the ethical monotheism of the biblical prophets demonstrates a lack of the self-transparency that he so highly esteems. For like Cohen, he presents a deeply spiritualized Judaism that is modeled according to the salient tenets of nineteenth-century *Kulturprotestantismus* and defined by the epistemological and ethical significations of Kantianism.

---

[81] Cassirer, *The Myth of the State*, 293.
[82] Cassirer, "Judaism and the Modern Political Myths," 234.   [83] Ibid., 241.

In addition, in his grand vision of the development of human spirit, Cassirer is not so much overcoming mythical thinking as cultivating an alternative myth buttressing his own vision of rational liberalism. His demythization is conducted through mythization. By framing contemporary world events as a war waged between logos and mythos, Cassirer presents his own version of the common mythical motif of *Chaoskampf*. It is therefore ironic, if also fitting, that he concludes *The Myth of the State* by resorting to the Babylonian myth of the clash between the highest god Marduk and the dragon Tiamat, representing the battle between the forces of order and chaos. In order to illustrate the conflict between enlightenment and myth, Cassirer inadvertently reveals the mythical features of his own thought. Hardly the anti-mythical force it is championed to be, it becomes apparent that Judaism is itself a player in a broader mythical clash. In fact, Cassirer does not only resort to Babylonian mythology, he also corrects it and in so doing presents a new myth. For according to the legend of Marduk and Tiamat, as Cassirer writes, "the cosmic order arose from the primeval chaos, and it will be preserved for all times." In his new adaptation, however, "the mythical monsters . . . still survive in this universe" and maintaining the order of creation demands constant subduing of the powers of chaos with countering forces of humanism. Otherwise, chaos will once again irrupt, as it had at his time of writing.[84] The correction to the myth implies that in Cassirer's model of historical development, the negation of the lower stage that fuels progress is not final and can be revisited on a higher plane. Hence it is a constant battle against, or negation of, earlier and more primitive symbolic forms. It can be seen, therefore, that his critique of political myth draws out the implicit logic of his critique of culture in that it no longer employs a narrative of progress. Not *telos* but *polemos* characterizes Cassirer's updated narrative of history. Religion does not dissolve into a higher stage of consciousness; a perpetual war wages between Judaism and the mythical forces of irrationality that ceaselessly threaten the very foundations of society.

In this late work, Cassirer comes to recognize that Nazism is not a mere return to primitivism, but a "regulated and organized" modern phenomenon, synthetic and indeed rationalized. Still, he does not go as far as the Frankfurt school philosophers Max Horkheimer and Theodor Adorno, who in their 1947 study *Dialectic of Enlightenment* proposed that the violence of fascism is internal to the Enlightenment itself and that the

[84] Cassirer, *Myth of the State*, 297–298.

dichotomies between reason and violence, enlightenment and totalitarianism are in fact false. But Cassirer's belated liberal Jewish manifesto
raises the following point: at this crucial moment, after staging and losing
the mythical struggle between reason and myth, he continues to claim that
his Jewish ethical monotheism is the only remedy for the present situation,
without explaining why his version of rationality is still able to reform
society after it had so tragically failed to do so.

I have thus far proposed that the Heidegger–Cassirer debate can be
perceived as the symbolic intellectual moment of the breakdown of the
German-Jewish liberal faith in the political-theological framework
undergirding the modern promise of emancipation and equality. For
Cassirer, representing the dominant German-Jewish perspective at the
time, the battle over Kant stages the clash between enlightened Jewish-
German values and reactionary promulgation of myth. As the ideal of
the *Bildungsliberalismus* and Kantianism represents the height of the
Jewish spirit, Heidegger is not merely offering a competitive interpretation of the philosopher from Königsberg; he is orchestrating an assault
on the very soul of Judaism, its message, and the identity of German
Jews.

There is no doubt that the mythical structure of the battle between
Judaism and Heidegger is powerful. Indeed, it is employed by Cassirer *and*
Heidegger. As we shall see, this image is repeated by other thinkers
discussed in this study, who regardless of their disapproval of liberal
Judaism, frame their encounter with Heidegger as a spiritual war between
a perilous position rooted in a perverse religious tradition and the universal message of Judaism – however constructed.

FRANZ ROSENZWEIG'S "EXCHANGED FRONTS"

One Jewish thinker who was not impressed by the liberal dream of
demythologization or by its dichotomizing position vis-à-vis Heidegger
was Franz Rosenzweig. In what may have been his last essay before his
premature death in 1929, Rosenzweig pens an enthusiastic reaction to the
Davos debate, where he finds a deep kinship between Heidegger's thought
and his own. In this short essay, entitled "Vertauschte Fronten," he points
to what he identifies as the reciprocal significance of two juxtaposed
events: the publication of the second edition of Hermann Cohen's posthumous book *Religion der Vernunft aus den Quellen des Judentums* and
the conference in Davos. Both events, he believes, announce the philosophical transition from "old" to "new" thinking. As he explains in the

introduction to *The Star of Redemption*, "old" thinking denotes philosophy animated by conceptual abstractions and the desire to gain "knowledge of the All [*Allheit*]" through the reduction of plurality to one single principle.[85] This tendency is as old as philosophy itself, beginning with the pre-Socratics and climaxing in Hegel – from "Ionia to Jena." In contrast, "new" thinking is instigated with the defiance of the factical, historical "I" against its nullification by reduction to the All. It takes its cue from the experiential being prior to conceptualization and does not pay heed to the false promises of overcoming temporality offered by idealism. As Rosenzweig identifies these features in Heidegger's Dasein, he announces that Heidegger's existential ontology is "a philosophical position [that is] precisely our position, that of the new thinking."[86]

In a somewhat puzzling analysis, Rosenzweig portrays the late Cohen, Heidegger, and himself as promulgators of a shared vein of thought. In an unlikely link, Heidegger, a known nemesis of neo-Kantianism, and Cohen are paired up against Cassirer, Cohen's Marburgian affiliate. This connection is made possible by Rosenzweig's controversial reading of Cohen's posthumous book. As he explains in his introduction to the collection of Cohen's essays on Judaism, *Jüdische Schriften* (1924), for the Cohen of the early works, religion was not independent vis-à-vis reason, as he regarded it a transitional stage in the moral development of humanity.[87] In his *Ethik des reinen Willens* (1904), Cohen develops the idea that religion is tied to ethics in that God is a precondition and guarantee of morality – "God signifies that nature has stability so that morality is eternal."[88] Ethics addresses the individual as an instantiation of the *Allheit* of humanity, and the idea of God is the "guarantor of humanity." In this stage in Cohen's thought, religion is firmly bound to the limits of the system of philosophy. However, Rosenzweig continues, toward the end of his life, in *Religion of Reason from the Sources of Judaism*, when he was deeply engrossed in Judaism, Cohen came to understand that his earlier system was unable to account for the historical "I." This "I," he discovered, is found in religion, as God is concerned with each individual and her personal task of moral advancement. This specific feature is highlighted in the notion of sin, as articulated by the biblical prophet Ezekiel, representing the individual's moral deficiency and the

---

[85] Rosenzweig, *The Star of Redemption*.
[86] Rosenzweig, "Vertauschte Fronten," 85–87. In English: Rosenzweig, "Transposed Fronts," 150.
[87] Rosenzweig, "Einleitung," 299–350.   [88] Cohen, *Ethik des reinen Willens*, 446.

notion of atonement through which the individual's unique self is constituted before God. Resorting to religion as an indispensable and independent framework with respect to philosophy, Cohen's earlier abstract
account of the individual gives way to the concrete person.

In "Vertauschte Fronten" Rosenzweig finds affinities between "what
[Heidegger] called Dasein" and what enables the "leap into Dasein," and
the Cohenian concept of "correlation" that gave rise to his own "new
thinking" as well. This notion denotes the mutual relationship between
God and man, wherein both attain their actuality through this non-
mediating bond. The correlation between God and human, according to
Rosenzweig, is what enables Cohen to account for the concrete individual
person not as an anonymous representative of humanity, but as
a particular "you." Through this notion, Cohen reveals that religion can
accomplish what ethics and philosophy cannot, namely, the establishment
of an actual, living, and finite individual. At first, Cohen represented for
Rosenzweig the idealism of old thinking and its desire to grasp the All
through concepts and cognition. As Rosenzweig put it, Cohen was a "new
Hegel." But his later work initiated the understanding that the basic
idealistic principle of the absolute sovereignty of cognition must be for-
feited to release God and man from the fetters of their functional roles and
comprehend them as separate-in-relation. In so doing, the "pagan" philosopher Cohen became a philosopher of faith and ultimately anticipated
new thinking's overcoming of idealism. According to Rosenzweig,
Heidegger's thought holds surprising affinities with the breakthrough
accomplished by the later Cohen, because "Heidegger gives philosophy
the task of revealing to man, the 'specifically finite being,' his own 'nothingness in all freedom.'"[89] In this manner, by maintaining that late in his
life Cohen shifts from Kantian idealism toward philosophy of existence,
Rosenzweig can proclaim Heidegger, not Cassirer, as Cohen's true inheritor and ally to his own "new" thinking.

Rosenzweig's intellectual narrative and interpretation of Cohen is
highly controversial. His dichotomized reading of Cohen has since been
challenged, and alternative interpretations stressing continuities between
Cohen's earlier critical philosophy and his later philosophy of religion
have been put forth.[90] It appears that the reading of the development in

[89] Rosenzweig, "Transposed Fronts," 150. This is a quote from Hermann Herrigel's report
of the Davos debate.
[90] Altmann, "Hermann Cohens Begriff der Korrelation"; Poma, *The Critical Philosophy of
Hermann Cohen*, 158–202; Gordon, *Rosenzweig and Heidegger*, 58–74; Weiss, *Paradox*

Cohen's thought probably better reflects Rosenzweig's own theoretical itinerary than an impartial interpretation of Cohen's writing. "Vertauschte Fronten" thus offers an invaluable insight into the manner in which Rosenzweig, on his deathbed, situates his own thinking within the philosophical horizon of the day. But it is important to notice that in this case, the competition over Cohen's legacy is also a competition between two models of Judaism and Jewish identity. In the second volume of his work on symbolic forms, Cassirer appeals to Cohen's notion of "correlation" and his account of prophetic Judaism's spiritualization of mythical thinking to buttresses his vision of liberal Judaism:

This ethical-social pathos of the Prophetic religion preserves the I through the emphatic opposition of its counterpart, the "thou," through which alone the I truly finds and asserts itself. A purely ethical correlation is established between I and thou, and an equally strict reciprocal bond between man and God. In characterizing the basic idea of the Prophetic religion Hermann Cohen writes: "it is not before the sacrifice or before the priest that man stands to obtain purity ... The correlation is ordained and concluded between man and God, and no other link may be interpolate in it ... Any participation by another destroys the uniqueness of God, which is more necessary for redemption than for Creation."[91]

From the other side, Rosenzweig grounds his rebellion against this very liberal vision in his understanding of the "late" Cohen of *Religion of Reason*. By affiliating Cohen and Heidegger and drawing them into the orbit of his own thought, Rosenzweig latently gathers philosophical support for his own perspective of existential and experiential Judaism.

In terms of its exposition of Rosenzweig's commonalities with Heidegger, however, it must be admitted that "Vertauschte Fronten" offers an all-too-general, brief, and cursory argument. It is unclear whether the Jewish thinker, whose physical condition had drastically deteriorated by 1927, is at all familiar with *Sein und Zeit*, or whether the main sources of his information about Heidegger are the newspaper report on Davos by Hermann Herrigel, which he cites, and Leo Strauss, who visited him after the debate. It is therefore difficult to determine how much one should read into the essay. Rosenzweig's perspective of *Existenz* is blind to the phenomenological and ontological nature of Heidegger's project, and for our purposes, it is noteworthy that there is nothing in the

---

and the Prophets; Rashkover, *Revelation and Theopolitics*, 9–53; Adelmann, *Einheit des Bewußtseins als Grundproblem der Philosophie Hermann Cohens*; Gibbs, *Correlations in Rosenzweig and Levinas*.

[91] Cassirer, *The Philosophy of Symbolic Forms*, vol. II, 225–226. The quote from Cohen is from *Religion der Vernunft*, 236.

essay regarding the religious bearings of Heidegger's scheme – a theme picked up by many of its Christian and Jewish readers at the time.[92] The absence of this theme in the dealings with Heidegger by a thinker who thought as much about Judaism and Christianity as Rosenzweig may suggest that he had at best a superficial familiarity with Heidegger's masterpiece.

BREAKING THE BOND: THE RECEPTION OF THE ROSENZWEIG–HEIDEGGER AFFILIATION

Notwithstanding the question of the depth of Rosenzweig's familiarity with Heidegger's philosophy, recent comparative studies of the two thinkers have fleshed out their association in much detail.[93] However, it is important to point out that the link between Rosenzweig and Heidegger was hardly discovered lately. It is, in fact, a persistent and recurring theme in the Jewish reception of Heidegger. The novelty of the aforementioned scholarly trend resides in the fact that it is disposed to highlight the commonalities between the two thinkers, whereas throughout the twentieth century the inclination has been to emphasize their divergences. Hans Liebeschütz, the prominent German-Jewish historian and former colleague of Cassirer in the University of Hamburg, openly expressed what seemingly remained unstated by many others when he wrote that although Rosenzweig could not have known in 1929 of Heidegger's future political undertakings, his philosophical "solidarity" with Heidegger, "the descendent of Black Forest farmers and a representative of a certain atheistic philosophy," is worrisome. For insofar as there is a direct connection between Heidegger's philosophical and political stances, then particularly for "the Jewish reader who experienced 1933 in Germany," Rosenzweig's suggestion is "somewhat horrifying."[94] Alongside the political reason for this, Liebeschütz's mention of Heidegger's "atheistic philosophy" is significant, for it touches upon a further implicit claim underlying the attempt to dispute Rosenzweig's self-proclaimed affinity with Heidegger: that had Rosenzweig been attentive to the theological charge

---

[92] I find no evidence in "Vertauschte Fronten" that "Rosenzweig sensed the religious urgency in Heidegger's thought" as claimed in Gordon, *Rosenzweig and Heidegger*, 233.

[93] The scholarship juxtaposing the two is rapidly accumulating. A considerably updated bibliography on this theme can be found in Wolfson, *Giving Beyond the Gift*, 303–304n20.

[94] Liebeschütz, *Von Georg Simmel zu Franz Rosenzweig*, 170–172.

of Heidegger's philosophy, he would have recognized that their philosophical anthropologies are in deep discordance.

Already with the publication of *Sein und Zeit*, some of the early readers of *The Star* recognized similarities between the two programs, though some found it difficult to square Rosenzweig's theistic thought with the ambiguous traces of religion in Heidegger. The first extensive study of Rosenzweig thought, Else Freund's published dissertation *Die Existenzphilosophie Franz Rosenzweigs: Ein Beitrag Zur Analyse Seines Werkes: "Der Stern Der Erlösung"* (1933), perceives Rosenzweig's thought as participating in the philosophical horizon of *Existenzphilosophie* with which Heidegger was often associated.[95] Written before Heidegger's political misconduct, her monograph points to various moments of comparison between the two thinkers. Among these are the shared renunciation of German idealism's conception of the "I," the emphasis on temporal existence, the recognition of the philosophical force of death and nothingness, the acknowledgment of the finite scope of the philosophical undertaking, and the understanding of the partial nature of truth. According to Freund, the link between the two thinkers is grounded in the implicit ties between *Existenzphilosophie* and theology. "The human being in the solitude and uncertainty of his actual existence, in the distress of his life and in his dilemma of conscience, has always been the subject of theology," she maintains. "Both *Existenzphilosophie* and theology occupy themselves with the 'center of life of the human being.'"[96] This common feature can explain "the great interest which present-day theology takes in Heidegger's philosophy." Moreover, "Heidegger's theologically-hued expressions, such as guilt and consciousness, being-toward-death, being-fallen can be explained in terms of the identity of the subject matter." Making use of explicit religious categories, Heidegger's thought is clearly nourished from the springs of theology, but "the explicit reference to God is missing in his work and his position regarding theology is not yet clear." According to Freund, Heidegger's philosophy is ambiguously secularized, for "tentatively, when [Heidegger] speaks of the transcendence of existence in his philosophy, this transcendence merely marks the spot at which God could

---

[95] Freund, *Die Existenzphilosophie Franz Rosenzweig*. A slightly revised edition of this work was published in 1972 in Hebrew, and then in 1979 in English as *Franz Rosenzweig's Philosophy of Existence*. Reference and citation here are from the English edition with occasional amendments.

[96] Freund, *Franz Rosenzweig's Philosophy of Existence*, 8.

find a place."[97] And while Rosenzweig's philosophy of existence is not theology per se, it is nevertheless solidly fastened to it. Insofar as "the distinction between authentic and unauthentic existence is peculiar" to theology, then Rosenzweig's thinking "almost of necessity trespasses on the realm of theology."[98] Thus, while Rosenzweig and Heidegger correspond in vital moments, the former overtly embraces the theological connotation implicit to his existential perspective, while the latter's secularized system seems both to depend on it and turn a blind eye to it.

For a long time, the most elaborate and influential analysis of Heidegger and Rosenzweig was Karl Löwith's essay "M. Heidegger and F. Rosenzweig or Temporality and Eternity" (1942).[99] As we have seen in Chapter 1, Löwith is a key figure in the early confessional readings of Heidegger in the 1930s, and his analysis of the conceptual continuity between Protestant theology and Heidegger's godless world proved impactful. In his 1942 essay, Löwith follows this line of thought in approaching Heidegger's potential ties with the Jewish thought of Rosenzweig. By focusing on the theme of temporality and eternity, he sets out to dispute Rosenzweig's association with Heidegger and show that despite their apparent affinities, these are in final analysis negligible, as their diverging theological commitments lead them in opposing directions.

Löwith begins by commenting on Rosenzweig's "Vertauschte Fronten," explaining that Rosenzweig's employment of eternity as an operative concept situates him closer to Cohen, the neo-Kantian master, than to Heidegger. Cohen cannot be considered Heidegger's philosophical godfather, for his retreat to the actual human person is exercised within his idealistic system where the infinitude of knowledge is the overarching aim. In contrast, for Heidegger, who addresses Dasein from within the finitude of its temporality, the idea of eternity is completely empty. Rosenzweig's narrative, Löwith determines, is misconceived. To be sure, Rosenzweig's reconstrues the idealistic "eternity" into an existential-religious category. But for Löwith, the epistemological and the theological are not detached. The neo-Kantian strive for infinitude is "the religious idealism of the *homo noumenon*," and Heidegger's rejection of eternity reflects a theological stance as well. Löwith admits that this does not mean that Rosenzweig was completely off the mark in his identification with

[97] Freund, *Die Existenzphilosophie Franz Rosenzweig*, 113.
[98] Freund, *Franz Rosenzweig's Philosophy of Existence*, 8.
[99] Löwith, "M. Heidegger and F. Rosenzweig."

some salient themes in Heidegger's program, such as the departure point of human facticity. But their differences immediately surface: On the one side, Rosenzweig celebrates eternity, and on the other, Heidegger puts forth a "radical temporalization of truth and existence." Rosenzweig puts divine revelation at the heart of his thinking, while Heidegger construes it as *a-letheia* – the primordial happening of truth where the being of a being is unconcealed as what it is – and thus "empties the concept of revelation of its theological sense." For Rosenzweig, the temporal coordinates of past-present-future are mapped onto creation-revelation-redemption, while Heidegger's world is bereft of transcendence and anchored in being-toward-death. The former seeks to de-secularize the world, while the latter seeks to de-theologize it.

The vacancy of God in Heidegger's scheme has crucial moral ramifications for Löwith, because for him divine transcendence is the condition of possibility for human self-transcendence toward the other person. In this reading, Heidegger's horizontal transcendence excludes the vertical transcendence of the divine, an exclusion testified to in the secularization of the notions of transcendence and revelation in his work. Yet in actuality, these two modes of transcendence coalesce – there is no having one without the other. Without the vertical divine transcendence, horizontal transcendence toward the other person is neutralized. Thus Löwith claims that the notion of selfhood advanced by Heidegger is enclosed within itself, "within a *circulus*," unable to move beyond "the first person's being" and treat the "other person" as a "second person," a "rightly conceived thou." In other words, Heidegger's solipsistic monism is godless and at odds with Rosenzweig's religious dialogicalism. In this analysis there are strong echoes of Martin Buber's discussion of Heidegger in his *Who Is Man?* (which will be examined more closely in Chapter 4). Löwith basically follows Buber's dialogical logic and echoes the religious basis of his criticisms of Heidegger. This is no wonder, as Löwith makes use of Buber's sociality of I–Thou already in his 1928 *Habilitationsschrift*, entitled *Das Individuum in der Rolle des Mitmenschen*, which he wrote under Heidegger. There he develops the notion of *Miteinandersein*, a corrective to Heidegger's *Mitsein*, which he sensed does not succeed in breaking out of Dasein's solipsism.[100] From Löwith's perspective, therefore, the radical immanence of Heidegger's world is a theological but also a social and ethical deficiency. Without

[100] Löwith, *Das Individuum in der Rolle des Mitmenschen*.

revelation, Heidegger's Dasein possesses a "deaf-blind selfhood" and
lacks intersubjectivity.[101] Heidegger's radical temporalism is bound to
his immanentism and is ultimately nihilistic, which explains his resolute
seizure of the "decisive 'instant'" to support the Nazis.[102]

While not explicitly stating so, Löwith strongly indicates that
Heidegger's Dasein is best equated to the pagan Greek hero delineated
by Rosenzweig in *The Star*. In book III of part I, entitled "Man and His
Self, or Metaethics," Rosenzweig begins to reconstruct human selfhood
from the point of infinitesimal nothingness. The first stage is called
"personality" (*Personlichkeit*), denoting the everyday self lacking individuation and determined by social roles and conceptions. The following stage of the self is "Character" (*Charakter*), that is, radical
inwardness, which is "metaethical" because the individual does not
participate in any universal genus or category. The metaethical person
is configured as the Greek tragic hero, "mute as a marble" and shut off
from fellow humans and God.[103] Soul (*Seele*), the final stage of the self's
development, is introduced by the event of revelation as speech, which
shatters the hermetic world of the Greek hero. In Rosenzweig's depiction, revelation is the bridge between self-enclosed personhood and the
relationality with one's fellow person. It is a moment of fusion of
vertical and horizontal transcendence. Subjectivity and intersubjectivity fully emerge in revelation, as it brings about the discovery of dialogue and love, and the command to love God and the neighbor.
Accordingly, in this reading Heidegger is a pagan, and hence between
the three irreducible elements of God, man, and world that Rosenzweig
posits in his *magnum opus*, the affiliation with Heidegger pertains to
the element of man alone.

This reading has some strengths to it: it identifies a reference point in
Rosenzweig's thought that appears to accommodate Heidegger's position, and also prepares for its overcoming. It also echoes the common
labeling of Heidegger as pagan and grounds his ethical and political
shortcomings in a philosophico-theological moment. Nevertheless, this
reading is misguided in binding Heidegger's ontological concerns with
regards to Dasein and the meaning of being to Rosenweig's ontic concern
over the relations between God, world, and man. Yet even from within the
perspective of *Existenzphilosophie*, the difficulty with interpreting Dasein

---

[101] Löwith, "M. Heidegger and F. Rosenzweig," 59.
[102] Löwith, "My Last Meeting with Heidegger in Rome, 1936," 140–143.
[103] Rosenzweig, *The Star*, 207.

as Rosenzweig's pagan hero is that Rosenzweig's pagan is a pre-revelation person, while the depiction of *Dasein* in Löwith's influential reading is the result of the secularization of a particular Protestant legacy. To put it in the language of Heidegger's early Christian reception, Rosenzweig's pagan hero is *vorglauben*, while Heidegger's Dasein, as interpreted by Löwith himself, is *unglauben*.

This is a crucial point, for according to Löwith, Heidegger is a "godless theologian" and his hybrid program betrays a "fundamentally anti-Christian and altogether irreligious purport" which at the same time "though inexplicitly, living on the Christian 'saeculum' and failing to dechristanize it."[104] Dasein's "entanglement of death, guilt, and conscience in an existence responsible only to itself means, it is true, an eradication of these concepts from their Christian sphere of origin, but on this very account they are still related to it."[105] This is the interpretation Löwith popularized in a variety of texts: Heidegger is "a theologian by tradition, and an atheist as a scholar" whose program offers a post-Christian alternative to theism:[106]

The basis that serves as the background for everything said by Heidegger ... is something unsaid: the religious motive, which has surely detached itself from Christian faith, but which precisely on account of its dogmatically unattached indeterminacy appeals all the more to those who are no longer faithful Christians but who nonetheless would like to be religious.[107]

Yet Heidegger's secularized program is to his deficit, Löwith makes clear, for not only is his objection to eternity nihilistic, his inability to thoroughly release himself from his Christian legacy makes his project impractical. He attempts to achieve a goal with a set of concepts that will inevitably resist and pull in the opposite direction.

In contrast to Heidegger's secularized Christianity, Löwith attributes Rosenzweig's "happy position of being able to hold up David's star of eternal truth in the midst of time" to his Jewish inheritance.[108] Rosenzweig's view of eternity-in-the-world as exhibited in Jewish self-perpetuation through procreation is faithfully presented and situated between the "Greek and Christian tradition," wherein "true being was set in the Eternal or 'always present'" and human temporality is discredited, and Heidegger's wholesale temporalization of existence and

---

[104] Löwith, "M. Heidegger and F. Rosenzweig," 67, 64.   [105] Ibid., 68.
[106] Löwith, *My Life in Germany*, 47.
[107] Löwith, *Martin Heidegger and European Nihilism*, 9.
[108] Löwith, "M. Heidegger and F. Rosenzweig," 75–76.

animosity toward eternity.[109] Löwith thus depicts Rosenzweig as presenting a post-metaphysical Jewish philosophy that is absorbed in the concrete
temporal world without succumbing to the paganism and nihilism of
Heidegger's secularized Christianity.

By encapsulating the differences between Heidegger and Rosenzweig in
the distinction between religious eternity and secularized temporality, as
Löwith does, it would appear that Heidegger is a secularized Rosenzweig
or Rosenzweig a theologized Heidegger, and revelation is what separates
them. But this cannot be the case, for Löwith emphasizes Heidegger's
secularized Christianity and celebrates Rosenzweig's Jewish perspective.
And if, as Löwith claimed earlier, there is an intrinsic tendency toward
secularization in Protestantism that is typified in Heidegger – a tendency
to which Rosenzweig's Jewish outlook appears to be immune – then it
follows that their differences do not pertain solely to revelation, as Löwith
maintains, but rather stem from deeper theological impulses that are
played out in both thinkers.

Inserting another relevant figure into the discussion, the Swiss theologian
Karl Barth, can demonstrate that the focus on eternity and revelation is
insufficient to account for the differences between Heidegger and
Rosenzweig, even when observed from Löwith's perspective. In many
respects, these three thinkers are products of the discontent from nineteenth-
century philosophical liberalism, neo-Kantianism, and historicism, and
they all formed innovative works of thought that were associated at the
time with the perspective of *Existenzphilosophie*. Löwith even mentions
Barth's name briefly in a footnote explaining "new thinking," illustrating the shared theoretical context of the three thinkers. But beyond this,
Barth and his parallels with Rosenzweig are out of Löwith's sight in this
essay. This is at least somewhat curious, for some of the fundamental
presumptions he admits Heidegger and Rosenzweig share and which
make their existential breakthrough possible are precisely the points
Löwith himself had identified as grounded in Protestant theology and
that link dialectical theology to Heidegger. As noted in the previous
chapter, Barth's specific theological commitments in his early
Römerbrief period bear some resemblances to those of Heidegger, and
indeed they were frequently read together – first and foremost, by Löwith
himself. There are strong parallels between Rosenzweig and Barth, as

---

[109] Löwith does not attribute to Rosenzweig the metaphysical concept of eternity, and hence
by no means forces him back into "the dogmas of Platonic idealism he wished to escape,"
as claimed by Gordon, *Rosenzweig and Heidegger*, 20.

both channel their critique of nineteenth-century liberal theology to produce a theocentric theology stressing divine otherness and a robust account of revelation. They, too, are recurrently compared.[110]

This is certainly a charged intellectual triangle. Rosenzweig was sympathetic to Heidegger's perspective but fiercely critical of Barth's. Heidegger expressed early appreciation for Barth (as reported by Löwith) but it quickly dwindled. Barth disapproved of Heidegger's entire philosophical project and admits to having a merely perfunctory familiarity with the Jewish thinker's work.[111] Heidegger did not hear of Rosenzweig until much later. But considering Barth alongside Heidegger and Rosenzweig allows us to see that the heart of the matter is not merely the acceptance of eternity and revelation. To recall, Heidegger does not reject revelation per se; he situates it in the domain of faith, outside the domain entrusted to philosophy. In this respect at least, while coming from opposite sides, Heidegger and (early) Barth are in agreement. But while there is no exaggerating the centrality of "the offensive idea of revelation," as Rosenzweig called it in his early 1914 essay "Atheistische Theologie," to his system as a whole, he becomes critical of the Protestant theological trend he openly associates with Barth for overstating the "offensiveness" of revelation and attributing to it exclusive theological significance.[112] "The Barthian colossal negations," as Rosenzweig terms it, is a deprived theology unworthy of Christianity and ultimately amounts to Gnosticism and Marcionism. Indeed, he expressly perceives himself a "missionary" against the recent prominence of these perspectives.[113] Moreover, for him dialectical theology's strict divorce of faith and reason disregards the fact that "there is only one truth."[114] Importantly, these critiques would be applicable to Heidegger as well. In Chapter 3 we will have occasion to expand on Jewish readings of the Heidegger–Barth bond, but for now, our discussion aims to demonstrate that from Rosenzweig's point of view, the main issue is not only eternity and revelation, but

---

[110] Rashkover, *Revelation and Theopolitics*; Myers, *Resisting History*, 94–100; Moyn, *Origins of the Other*, 113–163; Busch, *Barth – ein Porträt in Dialogen*, 151–169.

[111] Barth, *Letters 1961–1968*, 262. Barth and Rosenzweig shared early ties to the Patmos group. See Busch, *Barth – ein Porträt in Dialogen*, 158–166.

[112] Rosenzweig, "Atheistische Theologie," 697. In English: Rosenzweig, *Philosophical and Theological Writings*, 10–24. On Rosenzweig's reading of Barth see Herskowitz, "Franz Rosenzweig and Karl Barth."

[113] Letter to Buber, *Briefe und Tagebücher* II, 876; Letter to Buber 29.7.1925, ibid., 1055–1056. For a reading of *The Star* as a theological rejoinder to the contemporary rise of "Gnosticism," see Pollock, *Franz Rosenzweig's Conversions*.

[114] Quoted in Glatzer, *Franz Rosenzweig*, 209f.

a cluster of theological premises pertaining to the co-belonging of philosophy and theology, revelation and creation, and reason and faith.
Heidegger and Barth, from reverse directions, both hold a separationist
position whereby God has no place in the philosophical discourse, while
Rosenzweig believes that philosophy has something to learn from theology. Unlike Barth and Heidegger, Rosenzweig espouses a God who is *Der
Fern-Und-Nahe* and advocates an anti-compartmentalized, harmonizing
position of *gläubiges Wissen*, which overcomes the clefts between philosophy and theology and offers a schematization of their mutuality.[115]
   This crucial difference notwithstanding, it is also true that Löwith's
chiseled distinction between Rosenzweig's Judaism and Heidegger's secularized Christianity is oversimplified and overlooks the decisive mark of
Protestant theology on the Jewish thinker. And note: in his earlier essays
on the Christian origins of Heidegger's philosophy, Löwith stresses the
shared departure points and presuppositions of Protestant theology and
fundamental ontology, despite the secularized character of the latter. With
respect to Rosenzweig, on the other hand, he acknowledges the shared
departure point with Heidegger, but then quickly moves on to underscore
the discrepancies in their final destinations, thereby allowing him to
announce that they are fundamentally opposing. In both cases, the logic
at play is the same, but in his early essay, the motivation is to affiliate,
while in his later essay, it is to divorce. Why this is so is subject to
speculation, but it is not unlikely that the desire to distance Rosenzweig
from Heidegger is grounded in a symbolic binary of German versus Jew
and driven by extra-philosophical motivations, such as Löwith's personal
animus toward Heidegger after 1933.
   For a long time, Löwith's essay had set the tone for the scholarly
discussion of these two thinkers. This is true especially, though not exclusively, of Jewish thinkers who were happy to disassociate Rosenzweig,
who had quickly cultivated a heliographic status in the Jewish imagination, from Heidegger, the Nazi collaborator. A case in point in this regard
is Else Freund's aforementioned study. As stated, in the German edition,
written before Heidegger publicly supported Hitler, she readily points to
the two men's resemblances and explains them through their shared
participation in *Existenzphilosophie* and its conceptual affinity to theology. At this point, she admits that Heidegger's relation to theology "is not
yet clear." In the subsequent 1972 Hebrew edition and the 1979 English

[115] Rosenzweig, "Jehuda Halevi," 68–71. In English: Galli, *Franz Rosenzweig and Judah
Halevi*, 204–206.

edition, this passage is revised. Explicitly mentioning Löwith's essay and repeating its argument, Freund now claims that Heidegger's stance regarding theology and God is definitive: "human existence in the case of Heidegger remains closed in finiteness and temporality and has no relationship to a human Thou, to the world or to God," she writes, placing him in contrast to Rosenzweig.[116] Also Hans Liebeschütz, whose contestation to Rosenzweig's affiliation with Heidegger was noted above, cites Löwith's essay, as does Julius Guttmann in the expanded English edition of his impactful study *Philosophies of Judaism*, where he writes: "Löwith sets the atheistic existentialism of Heidegger against the believing existentialism of Rosenzweig and proves that Heidegger remains within the sphere of temporality, while Rosenzweig transcends it and points toward eternity."[117] Likewise, Nathan Rotenstreich, the prominent Israeli philosopher and scholar, attends to the comparison between Rosenzweig and Heidegger.[118] Also mentioning Löwith, he contends that despite superficial affinities between the two thinkers, when perceived through the perspective of their stance toward transcendence, it becomes clear that not Heidegger but Karl Jaspers would be a more appropriate comparison with Rosenzweig. Jaspers constructs an *Existenzphilosophie* focused on the experience of freedom marked by what he calls limit-situations (*Grenzsituationen*). In these critical situations we become aware of our limited subjectivity and historicity and direct ourselves beyond the limited immanence of our existence toward transcendence. Rotenstreich judges that "the affinity between Rosenzweig and Jaspers should be stressed more than that between Rosenzweig and Heidegger, because the unique aspect of Jasper's account is seeing the relation to transcendence as a relation that determines the existential quality of man."[119] Like Rosenzweig but unlike Heidegger, Jaspers includes in the constitution of human existence the possibility of "leaping-out of immanence, a leap made by man in his way from the world to God." Rotenstreich avers that "it is obvious that this point," shared by Jaspers and Rosenzweig, "can anchor conclusions of faith." The two philosophers differ, he notes, in that Jaspers speaks of a unilateral leap into transcendence while Rosenzweig describes a dialogical communication between God and human. In contrast to them, Heidegger's framework is

---

[116] Freund, *Franz Rosenzweig's Philosophy of Existence*, 145–146.
[117] Guttmann, *Philosophies of Judaism*, 527–528.
[118] Rotenstreich, *Jewish Thought in the Modern Era*, vol. II, 205–206 (Hebrew).
[119] Ibid.

confined to the boundaries of immanence and finitude. The distinction presented here is simple: Rosenzweig and Jaspers accommodate transcendence, while Heidegger does not.

Also following Löwith in disputing Rosenzweig's association with Heidegger is Martin Buber, who supports his critique of Heidegger's monological account of language in his "The Word that is Spoken," a paper presented in a conference he organized with Heidegger, by making the point stressed by Löwith that in Rosenzweig divine revelation enables human speech (see Chapter 4).[120] A similar dynamic is discernible in Emmanuel Levinas as well. Levinas's first major work, *Totality and Infinity*, is an assault on Heidegger's ground rule that "ontology is first philosophy." In the introduction to this work he writes that "we were impressed by the opposition to the idea of totality in Franz Rosenzweig's *Stern der Erlösung*, a work too often present in this book to be cited."[121] While the accuracy of Levinas's interpretation of both Rosenzweig and Heidegger is a matter of dispute, two points can be drawn out of this statement. First, that he parallels his attempt to overcome what he sees as Heidegger's totalitarian philosophy with Rosenzweig's attempt to overcome what he sees as Hegel's totalitarian philosophy. It follows from this analogy that Heidegger, like Hegel, espouses the logic of representation, reductionism, and the ingrained violence of "old thinking." This is contrary to Rosenzweig's view, which effectively positions Heidegger *against* Hegel. Second, that instead of associating Rosenzweig and Heidegger, Levinas pits them against each other. As we shall see, a central element of Levinas's philosophical effort is confronting a lesson he learned from Rosenzweig, that "Jewish existence is a category of being," with what he calls the Heideggerian pagan category of being (see Chapter 7).[122] It should be added that a key impulse in Emil Fackenheim's main work of post-Holocaust theology, *To Mend the World: Foundations of Post-Holocaust Jewish Thought* (1982), builds on Löwith's analysis of Rosenzweig and Heidegger. With respect to the possibility of their grappling with what he considers the rapturous *Ereignis* of our time, the Holocaust, Fackenheim writes:

Rosenzweig dies prior to the advent of the Nazi regime; Heidegger survived it long enough to have all the leisure necessary to ponder it. Rosenzweig's

[120] Buber writes: "It is through God's addressing man – Franz Rosenzweig's *Stern der Erlösung* teaches us – that He established man in speech." Buber, "The Word that Is Spoken," 105.

[121] Levinas, *Totality and Infinity*, 28.

[122] Levinas, "Between Two Worlds (The Way of Franz Rosenzweig)," 183.

thought, though situated in history, rose above it, and hence also above the evil that is part of it; Heidegger's thought in both its earlier and later periods remains in history, unable to rise above it. Yet it is Heidegger's thought that cannot confront the Holocaust; and it is Rosenzweig's thought that – had the thinker lived long enough – would have found a confrontation with the *Ereignis* inescapable.[123]

As these examples illustrate, until recently the overarching aim has been to disassociate Heidegger from Rosenzweig. This is at variance with the Jewish thinker's self-professed affiliation, but it is driven by the implied assumption that his ignorance of important theological and political elements in Heidegger's philosophy and life explain, and excuse, his misjudgment.

One important exception to this rule is Leo Strauss in the 1965 "Preface to the English Translation" to his book on Spinoza. In this quasi-autobiographical introduction, which will be discussed in Chapter 5, Strauss begins by coupling the two thinkers and highlighting the weighty difference between them: Rosenzweig represents a new thinking based on the experience of God, while Heidegger rejects revelation and does not experience God. He even references Löwith's essay in this context. Interestingly, however, while noting their apparent divergences, Strauss's conclusion is that Rosenzweig and Heidegger in fact share a religious horizon and are thus in agreement with respect to fundamental theoretical assumptions. It should be noticed, however, that even in Strauss's "heterodox" reading of the Rosenzweig–Heidegger bond, the matter is approached through a religious prism and their main difference, at least prima facie, is located in their respective theological attitudes.

Closing this discussion, it is crucial to recognize that the general apprehension with regards to Heidegger is more than post-traumatism, and what is at stake is more than the accuracy of Rosenzweig's testament. What is at stake, rather, is the promises and perils of post-metaphysical Jewish thought. Does the crisis of reason hold in store Heideggerian nihilism and totalitarianism? Is intersubjectivity, morality, and humanism possible after the plunge into history and temporality? Is God possible at all after the jettisoning of eternal truths? Does the rejection of metaphysics require or resist secularization? One might phrase the animating concern as follows: Can one begin with Rosenzweig without necessarily ending up with Heidegger?

---

[123] Fackenheim, *To Mend the World*, 320, see also 149–200.

CONCLUSION

We have seen how the divided intellectual landscape of Weimar played itself out in the early Jewish receptions of Heidegger. The decline of the worldview represented by neo-Kantianism and the rise of the worldview represented by Heidegger was taken as either an attack on what is most valuable in Judaism or as an opportunity to develop an authentic Judaism. Serving as the "ideal types" of this split, as we have seen, are Cassirer and Rosenzweig. That Cassirer referred to Heidegger as a foe to his vision of philosophy and Judaism should come as no surprise. Yet the resistance to Rosenzweig's endorsement of Heidegger exhibits not only the diverse stances that existed within the seemingly solidified perspective of "new thinking," but also the confrontational structure between Judaism and Heidegger's philosophy that will often mark this encounter as a whole. Central to the confrontational structure is the sense that Heidegger's philosophy is both grounded in, and itself grounds, a religious picture, and that at the heart of his philosophical and personal deficiencies lay a theological fault. This point will be picked up in the following chapter, where we explore a recurring early Jewish reading of *Sein und Zeit*, according to which Heidegger does not detail the existential structures of Dasein as such, but rather that of a specific secularized Christian or Protestant Dasein, and which therefore has little bearing on being-Jewish.

3

A Christian Anthropology? Early Jewish Readings of *Sein und Zeit*

INTRODUCTION

INTRODUCTION

In this chapter we will explore early Jewish interpretations of Heidegger's philosophy that understood it as exhibiting specific Christian presuppositions regarding human existence. As we have seen in Chapter 1, the question of the significance and role of the theological undertones in Heidegger's Dasein analytic is central to its early Christian reception. From a common Jewish standpoint, insofar as Jewish thought seeks to stay clear of Christian influences, the question of whether or not Heidegger's thought harbors layers of Christian tradition has ramifications for the possibility of its productivity for Jewish expression. Accordingly, one way to display its inappropriateness for Jewish thought is to uncover its Christian resonances, and conversely, establishing its potential suitability for Jewish thought would require reading it as a theologically neutral portrayal of human existence. Either way, the question of secularization must be confronted: if the existential analysis of Dasein involves de-theologization and ontologization of Christian notions, is the result universally valid and neutral structures which can potentially illuminate being-Jewish? Or is something of their origin inevitably preserved, so that regardless of the absence of any explicit Christian message, Heidegger's system is stamped by a foreign doctrine and as such at odds with Judaism? Is secularization liberating or constraining? As we shall see, the Jewish reactions to Heidegger reflect on broader issues concerning the potentially theological charge of modern secularism. Is the main impulse of modern secularism anti-Christian, or is it in fact a particularly Christian phenomenon? What is the stand of Judaism with regards to secularism? Can secularism offer a basis for Jewish-Christian exchanges? Does it have political ramifications? As will become clear, the Jewish grappling with Heidegger between the wars takes place within the wider discourse of the polemic against Christianity, reflecting a moment in the Jewish understanding of the Jewish-Christian difference.

SEIN UND ZEIT: A CHRISTIAN ANTHROPOLOGY?

As noted, the publication *Sein und Zeit* turned Heidegger into a leading voice of the European philosophical scene almost overnight, and Jewish intellectuals immediately took notice of his thought and explored the appropriateness of its terms to the Jewish case. For example, a dispute in the 1930s over the place and role of the Jew in non-Jewish German society is formulated in clear Heideggerian idiom when Alexander Altmann, the young Orthodox and Zionist rabbi and scholar, opposes the liberal rabbi Ignaz Maybaum's "theology of the Diaspora," according to which the spiritual goal of the Jews is to remain in the diaspora. Altmann explains Maybaum's "central formula," namely, that "the Jew's being-in-the-world" is to be understood as "being a Jew *amidst* the peoples of the world." The most important "Jewish question" for Maybaum does not regard faith or practice, but "what shall be the Jew's relation to the Christian and pagan world?" Since, Altmann continues, "it is clear that Maybaum's method of phenomenology of religion, i.e., the determination of the character of Jewish being through structural comparison with Christianity and paganism, is realized in this centralization of being-in-the-world," then ultimately, his non-Zionist view is that "being-in-the-world, as the Jewish task, means being-in-Exile [*das in-der-Welt-Sein als jüdische Aufgabe heißt im-Exil-Sein*]."[1] Maybaum's position is explicated by drawing on the dual sense of the term "world," understood both as the Heideggerian notion employed in the context of the existential meaning of being-Jewish and in its literal sense as a geographical designation. With this double entendre, one of the contemporary German-Jewish predicaments is captured: is Jewish nationalism, outside Germany, the path to secure the future of Jewish existence, or is it liberal Judaism within Germany? That Heidegger was a point of reference in the Jewish intellectual and cultural discourse of the time can also be seen in a book on the famed Jewish poet Chajjim Nachman Bialik's life and work, where its author, Ernst Simon, associates Bialik's "ambiguity of poetic words" and "the void of nothingness, in the fear of the lonely, in the loquacious fear of death" from which they emerge, with "the existential thinking of Kierkegaard,

---

[1] Altmann, "Um das Erbe Franz Rosenzweigs," 6.

Heidegger and Rosenzweig."[2] Likewise, in a review of the German-Jewish rabbi and thinker Max Wiener's *Jüdische Religion im Zeitalter der Emanzipation*, Simon identifies Heidegger's mark in its description of a particular experience of modern Jewish existence.[3] In this work, Wiener presents an analysis of the vicissitudes of modern perceptions of Jewishness after the decreasing role of Jewish law as the traditional "system of existence" (*Daseinssystem*) in the wake of emancipation. After analyzing Reform Judaism, the Wissenschaft des Judentums movement, Neo-Orthodoxy, Zechariah Frankel's Historical School and other almost-exclusively German movements and thinkers, in the concluding chapter Wiener offers an additional category through which modern Jewishness can be perceived: *Judentum als Stimmung*. Rejecting historical attempts to regulate Jewishness through "rational" principles, Wiener finds the category of "mood" – irrational, vital, and experiential, albeit difficultly elucidated – to be well suited for the Jewish case, and specifically to express its national modality, for him the most promising path for Jewish rejuvenation. While there is no trail of references to Heidegger, and "mood" was an important concept in the Romantic world-picture and discussed by various thinkers, Simon identifies the German philosopher's mark when he praises Weiner's "important discovery of the notion of 'Jewish mood' [*heleḥ -ruaḥ Yehudi*] (that Heidegger has fashioned)."[4] Also the renowned German rabbi Leo Baeck evokes Heidegger in a 1935 lecture, "Die Existenz des Juden," where he claims that the current "existentiellen Denken," according to which thinking comes after existence and is never independent of it, is basically Jewish. For "Jewish thinking," he states, "is precisely the thinking in which the human being is enclosed, which concerns him, him, in his definite, concrete reality, in the definite, concrete hour in which he is now." This is precisely the view he identifies in Heidegger. Baeck writes:

The philosopher Heidegger has – intentionally or unintentionally – expressed a biblical thought by saying … : "Dasein, that is not a being present-at-hand [*Vorhandensein*], but a being ready-to-hand [*Zuhandensein*], something that is laid down before the human, something he forms, makes, shapes." This is Jewish thinking.[5]

[2] Simon, *Chajjim Nachman Bialik*, 109.
[3] Wiener, *Jüdische Religion im Zeitalter der Emanzipation*. On Wiener see Luz, "Max Wiener as a Historian of Jewish Religion in the Emancipation Period"; Schine, *Jewish Thought Adrift: Max Wiener (1882–1950)*.
[4] Simon, "Hadat Shel Ha'Ratzionalismus," 110–113 (Hebrew).
[5] Baeck, "Die Existenz des Juden," 245–253. I wish to thank Yaniv Feller for informing me of this source.

Baeck is clearly paraphrasing; no such statement exists in *Sein und Zeit*, and Heidegger does not think Dasein is ready to hand. Baeck may have in mind a passage from §31: "Dasein is not something present-at-hand [*Vorhandenes*] that has the added value of being able to do something, but is primarily Being-possible."[6] His point, however, is this: striking similarities exist between existential thinking, and Heidegger's at that, and Jewish thinking.

From early on, then, Heidegger's philosophy was drawn into the orbit of Jewish intellectual, cultural, and political discourses. For many, however, the possible theistic residues in his work did not go unnoticed. One of the early detailed Jewish engagements with Heidegger's philosophy is offered by Raphael Seligmann in an article entitled "Sein oder Nichtsein: Zu Heideggers Existenzphilosophie" (1932).[7] Lauding *Sein und Zeit* as a "notable" and "serious" work, Seligmann outlines an organized and at times critical elucidation of some fundamental notions of Heidegger's thought. Throughout his philosophical analysis, Seligmann acknowledges some Christian undertones present in the work. He contends, for example, that one of the central sources of the exposition of Dasein's existence is "the original sin." "This idea," he writes, "reverberates essentially in Heidegger's concept of guilt [*Schuld*]: I am already sinful from the very moment of my birth, and I am already guilty from the very moment of my thrownness"; indeed, "the idea of the Original Sin is the *spiritus rector* of this philosophy of existence."[8] By pointing to this Christian debt, Seligmann indicates that Heidegger's account of Dasein's existence is conditioned by a Christian belief in the inherent sinfulness of human existence. This becomes more evident in another essay composed in Hebrew around 1934, where Seligmann interprets Heidegger's notion of thrownness and guilt in terms of "sin and transgression." Dasein's guilt does not surface in light of transgression or moral deficiency, since for him "sin precedes morality." One is always already guilty and sinful, and the birth of morality is the moment one is awakened to this fact.[9] Yet these assumptions "are wrong," Seligmann claims. Ontologically, Dasein is *not* always already sinful, and guilt is not implicit to Dasein's existence; one becomes guilty only in light of one's actions. Guilt and sin are existential

---

[6] *SZ*, 144/*BT*, 183. Translation amended.
[7] Seligmann, "Sein oder Nichtsein." Seligmann penned additional articles dedicated exclusively to Heidegger, as well as other pieces of personal musing attesting to Heideggerian influences. See his short essay "The Antinomies of Being," 232–235 (Hebrew).
[8] Seligmann, "Sein oder Nichtsein," 437.   [9] Seligmann, "Heidegger," 135–142.

possibilities open to any person, but they are outcomes of deeds rather than fundamental ontological features of our being-in-the-world. Heidegger, of course, warns against precisely a reading of "being-guilty" that makes "basic the derivative conception of guilt in the sense of an indebtedness which has 'arisen' through some deed done or left undone,"[10] for the ontic guilt that is the result of misdeeds is only possible on the basis of "a primordial Being-guilty."[11] Seligmann may simply be offering an uninformed reading of Heidegger, though it may also reflect a certain Jewish polemic against Christianity, for his philosophical critique is highly reminiscent of the common Jewish charge against the idea of Original Sin, according to which humans are guilty prior to any of their actions.

This brief acknowledgment of theological layers at play in Heidegger is picked up and developed by Hugo Shmuel Bergmann. Bergmann had already left Europe for Palestine in 1920, but his intellectual pulse remained closely attuned to the European scene. Geographically removed from the furor around the publication of *Sein und Zeit*, Bergmann was nevertheless fairly up-to-date philosophically. A file in his archives entitled "Heidegger, Sein u. Zeit" holds handwritten comments and thoughts on Heidegger dating back to at least August 1931. In the academic year of 1931/1932 he delivered a lecture course on "Existentialism" at the newly founded Hebrew University, consisting of five lectures on Kierkegaard, two on Dilthey, and seven on Heidegger.[12] This is a widely unknown historical fact: the newly established Hebrew University in Palestine is one of the first places in the world where Heidegger's thought was taught in an academic setting as a significant philosophical milestone.

In Bergmann's work on contemporary philosophers, *Hogey Ha'Dor* (1935), the chapter dedicated to Heidegger is the lengthiest and most elaborate. Labeled as "typifying the younger school of thought in Germany today," Heidegger's philosophy – paradigmatically existentialist – is said to be animated by a deeply secularized religiosity.[13] "The gates of the heavens are not open for this kind of religiosity," Bergmann states, "The painful spur of religion drives it, yet it does not accept religion's consolations." Bergmann offers an overview of central themes in *Sein und Zeit* which is sensitive to the de-theologized vocabulary in Heidegger's

---

[10] *SZ*, 287/ *BT*, 333.   [11] *SZ*, 284/*BT*, 329.

[12] A typed English version of these lectures is found in the Shmuel Hugo Bergmann Archive, 4*1502 04 101b, Israel National Library, Jerusalem.

[13] Bergmann, *Hogay Ha'Dor*, 122.

existential analysis and its general religious ambiance. He interprets, for example, Dasein's quest for existential meaning as an unattainable religious desire for transcendence in a technical, godless, and ultimately finite world, where "the gates of the heavens are locked shut, no path leads upwards." Dasein's thrownness also reflects the godlessness of Heidegger's world, according to Bergmann. "Who threw him into this world and what is found beyond his birth and death? To this question there is no answer, and the question is not even asked in the first place."[14] Heidegger's "call of consciousness" is understood as a form of existential repentance; it calls Dasein for *Teshuva*, to return to itself from within the alienating idle talk of *das Man*. To highlight its religious connotations, Bergmann illustrates its affinity to the revelatory call in the Bible by relating it to God's call to Abraham and to Samuel. He is aware that these overtones notwithstanding, it is a mistake to explain the call through recourse to "divine forces or theological explanations." This is not a call "coming from another world" or a "divine epiphany [*bat kol*]," he clarifies; the bursting call of consciousness is voiceless and empty, emerging from within, not from without. It is thus a circular, short-circuiting, secularized call wherein Dasein calls upon itself. The notion of guilt is likewise interpreted as a de-theologized existential sin. Inauthentic Dasein "can err," Bergmann writes, "but it is unworthy of sin." Conversely, "only whoever resolves its authentic being can also bear sin ... Sin is the testimony for the ability of Dasein's being-itself."[15] Like Seligmann, Bergmann points out that according to Heidegger, existential "sin does not originate in a particular action or lack thereof." Unrelated to the believer's being-toward-God, to divine law, or to any specific deed, Heidegger's notion of existential sin "is an existential predicate pertaining to the very root of existence, because existence in its foundation is knotted in negation. The 'no' is an inseparable element of man."[16]

As secularized, the view of the overarching negation looming over Dasein's finite and fallen existence is hardly neutral. Bergmann makes clear that "the Christian teaching, and in particular the Protestant Christian idea of original sin that is bequeathed from Adam finds its philosophical expression here. Man is sinful in his essence."[17] Indeed, he explicitly flags the mark of "Kierkegaard and Protestant religion in general" on Heidegger's early work.[18] Following the interpretive trend we have already encountered previously, Bergmann singles out the

---

[14] Ibid., 122–123.   [15] Ibid., 152.   [16] Ibid., 153.   [17] Ibid.   [18] Ibid., 123.

secularization of Kierkegaard's notions of Repetition (*Gjentagelsen*) and the Moment (*Øieblikket*) in Heidegger's *Wiederholung* and *Augenblick* to demonstrate the similarities and differences between the two thinkers.[19] "Kierkegaard's thought is entirely fastened to faith," he determines, "while Heidegger constructs his system without a God."[20] If divine grace within a life of faith offers an outlet to existential salvation in the Kierkegaardian scheme, the godlessness of Dasein's resoluteness "cannot brighten the dark element and passive root of our existence, and does not eliminate the *nothing*, the negation, for we have been *thrown* into life."[21] By juxtaposing Heidegger with Kierkegaard, Bergmann allows for the former's Christian heritage and lack of theological neutrality, as well as the secularized, godless character of his philosophy to come to light. "The profound seriousness of this system is due to this religiosity," though what it promotes is a "religiosity without God."[22]

It is clear that in Bergmann's understanding, Heidegger's godless religiosity is rooted in, and only explained by, his Christian-Protestant legacy. For him, as it is for Cassirer and others, Heidegger's framework is constituted by an adoption of the negative moments of Protestant anthropology – the fallen, sinful, guilty, finite, and anxiety-fraught human existence – without its complementing affirmative moments of glory and redemption in divine eternity. While doing away with faith's redemptive aspects, Heidegger retains, in a philosophical register, this tradition's account of Original Sin and the overarching "no" marking human existence. In the final analysis, the theological ambiguity marking Heidegger's secularized formulations betrays the post-Nietzschean spiritual crisis. The Dasein of *Sein und Zeit* is a de-Christianized Dasein, and Heidegger's account of resoluteness is an updated form of Nietzsche's atheistic ideal of *amor fati* wherein one's fate is chosen resolutely.

Bergmann's understanding of Heidegger's religiously grounded anthropology is embedded throughout his lengthy explication of Heidegger's philosophy. But the full import of his reading of *Sein und Zeit* comes to light when the structure of his book is taken into account. The chapters of *Hogey Ha'Dor* are dedicated to various philosophical attempts to address the crisis of objectivity and subjectivity bequeathed by Kant. Within this outline, *Sein und Zeit* is addressed as one serious but ultimately flawed post-Kantian existential stance. Significantly, it becomes evident from the concluding chapter of the book that

[19] Herskowitz, "Heidegger as a Secularized Kierkegaard," 155–174.
[20] Bergmann, *Hogay Ha'Dor*, 155.   [21] Ibid.   [22] Ibid., 165.

Bergmann believes that the Kantian problematic has in fact found a suitable solution in Cohen's notion of the "correlation" between the human and the divine, as presented in his late Jewish work. "The problem of knowing, that is, of according the world and our reason," he explains Cohen's view, "can be solved only by the view that the world and human reason were both created by divine reason. We can know the world and reason because the world was created, and we were created in the image of God."[23] Thanks to Cohen's later philosophical innovations the Kantian schism has been overcome – and for Bergmann there is no question these developments are profoundly linked to Cohen's personal return to Judaism. He specifically stresses the "Jewishness" of Cohen's philosophical proposal by stating that not the younger Cohen, engulfed by Kant's anti-religious idealism, but only "the elderly Cohen, who returned to his Judaism," would have dared to recognize the God–human correlation which upholds divine transcendence and at the same time promulgates an account of human existence that is not inextricably marred by negativity. The Kantian schism between man and world is overcome through the Jewish teaching of their shared divine origin. Thus, when we take the overarching structure of Bergmann's book into account, it becomes clear that pointing to the Christian layers in Heidegger's framework plays an additional role to merely uncovering the various theoretical influences on his work – it constitutes part of the argument against it. Ultimately, Heidegger's secularized Christian anthropology is rejected in the stead of (a Rosenzweigian reading of) Cohen's philosophical contribution "from the sources of Judaism," which, Bergmann proclaims, exhibits that Judaism "still bears a message to the entire world."[24]

HEIDEGGER AND DIALECTICAL THEOLOGY: A JEWISH PERSPECTIVE

Reading Heidegger as a secular version of Kierkegaard, as Bergmann does, was hardly uncommon at the time. Juxtaposing Heidegger and Barth – who too was taken by the Danish philosopher – was similarly a prevalent trope. Despite the fact that in many respects they depart from different premises and lead dramatically dissimilar paths – for the one anthropocentrism, for the other theocentrism, here philosophy, there theology, here

---

[23] Ibid., 11.
[24] Ibid., 224. Bergmann continues to explore the religious ambiance of Heidegger's later work in both published and private writings.

von oben, there *von unten* – many understood the bracketing of God in Heidegger's scheme and subsequent depiction of a godless world to correspond, from the perspective of philosophy, with the position of *Deus absconditus* exhibited in Barth's radical theology. Indeed, not only were the ties between the philosophical project of *Existenzphilosophie* and Protestant theology acknowledged by many, but the very term *Existenzphilosophie* labeled both Heidegger's perspective and dialectical theology.[25]

Reading these two thinkers side by side is a central feature of Heidegger's early general reception, and it figures in his Jewish reception as well. One such example is Albert Lewkowitz, a liberal rabbi and philosophy lecturer in the Breslau Jewish Theological Seminar. In his 1936 essay "Vom Sinn des Sein: zum Existenzphilosophie Heideggers" he offers an elaborate interpretation of Heidegger's philosophy, reflecting on its ties to Christianity, dialectical theology, and secularism.[26] Lewkowitz is typical of the younger Jewish generation's critical stance on the amalgamation of Kantianism and Judaism. While he believed that a turn to metaphysical and ontological categories was the way to restore authentic Jewish spirituality, he refused to follow Heidegger's path to do so. In this essay, he situates Heidegger's fundamental ontology within an apparent contrast between Nietzsche's nihilistic and atheistic will to power on the one side, and dialectical theology, associated with Kierkegaard, Barth, and Friedrich Gogarten, on the other. This contrast, certainly commonplace, is based on the apparent distinction between Christian authors and an avowed atheist. However, Lewkowitz contends, this is in fact deceptive, for both sides share a denial of the human ability to know the truth and both demand irrationality and submission. In ostensible contrast to them, "the existential philosophy [*Existenzphilosophie*] of Heidegger" reinforces human capacity for truth, as it "sees its fundamental task in the ontological illumination of the being of beings." Heidegger is inserted into a discussion with an overtly religious theme, positioned between Nietzsche's atheism and Barth's theism. And indeed, Lewkowitz points to the theological terminology grounding the analysis of Dasein as well as to Heidegger's

---

[25] Baring, "Anxiety in Translation." Walter Benjamin, for example, observes with regards to Barthian theology, "at their outer limits the waves of this theological movement make contact with the concentric circles set in motion by Heidegger's existential philosophy." Benjamin, "Kierkegaard," 703.

[26] Lewkowitz, "Vom Sinn des Seins."

connection to Kierkegaard: "The terms care, anxiety, guilt, conscience, *Augenblick*, remembrance, repetition, in which Heidegger records the essence of existence are central concepts for Kierkegaard and through them a deep influence of Kierkegaard on Heidegger is recognized."[27] Moreover, "as it is in Christian theology," he notes, "also for Heidegger death, guilt and conscience are deeply intertwined."[28] The manifest Christian stamp notwithstanding, Lewkowitz is well aware of the secularized setting within which these terms are invoked. "It cannot be overlooked," he observes, "that in Heidegger these concepts are completely rescinded of the atmosphere of Pauline theology which permeates Kierkegaard."[29] Like Protestant theology, Heidegger's system offers an all-encompassing framework that presents both Dasein's existential predicament and its path to existential salvation, using similar categories. Unlike its theistic source, however, for Heidegger, "not the theological teaching of salvation shows man his guilt and the way to overcome it, but rather the resoluteness of anxiety in face of the nothing brings man to the truth of his awareness of being." Fixed in immanence, the path to salvation proposed by the German philosopher "is not over-worldly, other-worldly, religious, but rather the free affirmation of fateful destiny." Heidegger's thought, therefore, is "a secularized Protestant style of theology."[30] Establishing the constitutive role of this theological legacy in Heidegger's philosophy allows Lewkowitz to argue that while seemingly offering a distinct position, Heidegger is in fact one with dialectic theology and Nietzsche. From his perspective, the unbridgeable distant God of dialectical theology, Nietzsche's "dead" God, and Heidegger's secularized description of human godforsakenness are one and the same.

Having established that the dichotomy set out in the beginning of the essay does not stand, Lewkowitz arrives at his main point: the moral ramifications of a worldview lacking a transcendent anchor and compass in God. Like others, he too turns to the notion of the "call of conscience" to illustrate the locked immanence of the Heideggerian Dasein. Since this call does not erupt from without but rather is Dasein's call to itself, and since Dasein's being-toward-death solidifies its solitude, then "no ray of the idea of moral being [*sittlichen Seins*]" can penetrate its impenetrable existence. "Heidegger seeks to yield a phenomenological analysis of human existence that would lead human beings to meaningful freedom. But without the realm of value upon which human beings are based in all concreteness of values and human existence, human beings are left in

27 Ibid., 193.   28 Ibid., 194.   29 Ibid., 193.   30 Ibid.

darkness."[31] Morality, he suggests, is impossible in the world depicted by Heidegger. In final analysis, Kierkegaard, Barth, Gogarten, Nietzsche, and Heidegger are all cut from the same cloth, and all effectively bespeak a nihilistic account of human forsakenness. Heidegger is unable to offer a spiritual antidote to the ills of modernity. In fact, he perpetuates the crisis of the times because his philosophy stems from the same nihilistic assumptions of Protestantism's radical externality of God and leads to the same nihilistic outcomes. The leading theological systems and the secular philosophies are both rooted in this tradition's enterprise.

The moral bankruptcy of this position has political ramifications as well. Unlike Bergmann, whose strictly philosophical discussion made only a brief mention of Heidegger's ties to the "German revolution of 1933," for Lewkowitz Heidegger's endorsement of extreme German nationalism exhibits the dire ethical pitfalls that the absence of a divine compass has in store. Making the connection between Heidegger's philosophy and politics, he marshals Heidegger's rectorial address as evidence for the moral deficiency of his thought.[32] Since, as he reads him, Heidegger barricades transcendent values and meaning out of Dasein's existence, then "heroic nationalism ... is for Heidegger life's last meaning." Lewkowitz continues: "This barrier against the realm of values and its transcendent roots in God threatens to naturalize National Socialism. Have we not returned to Nietzsche's Productive Nihilism?" Reading Heidegger's philosophy as a secularized Christianity impervious to the possibility of morality and linking his politics to this theological legacy suggests a connection between Christianity, modern secularism, and the nihilism manifested in the Nazi ideology. We shall see that this argument, identifying a causal relation between the immanence of Heidegger's worldview and his politics, is repeated time and again. It is commonplace, but its flimsy logic and minimal explanatory power must be laid bare: while it may seem to explain the specific case of Heidegger – and this in itself is highly questionable – it has too many counterexamples and it does not explain why some who held a similar position rejected Hitler, and why others who held the opposite position embraced him. Simply put, one's view about the interface between immanence and transcendence is not a reliable indicator of one's receptivity to totalitarian politics. It appears, rather, that the argument linking Heidegger's politics to the immanence of

---

[31] Ibid., 194.
[32] On the reception of Heidegger's rectorial address, see Zaborowski, "Die Heidegger-Rezeption in Deutschland zwischen 1933 und 1945."

his philosophy sheds more light on the polemical and apologetical motivations of those who voice it than on the actual speculative motives behind Heidegger's Nazism.

In contrast to Heidegger and his theologically grounded nihilism, Lewkowitz posits the Jewish message of "the concrete substantiality of an enlightened moral idea and its fulfilling spiritual life. 'The human's spirit is the candle of God.'"[33] In Heidegger's view, as Lewkowitz interprets it, the meaning of true being is attained through memento mori, and this is contrasted to "the moral interpretation of Being through Judaism," according to which "the knowledge of the good, the knowledge of God" is the path to "true being, true life." For Lewkowitz, regardless of their diverging assumptions and methods, the Bible and the Midrash, as well as medieval and modern Jewish philosophy all unite around one fundamental message, namely, the necessity "to understand and shape the world out of God."[34] With these concluding remarks, Lewkowitz situates Judaism as a corrective to Heidegger's de-Christianized philosophy. "The philosophy of existence will become the true philosophy of human existence only if it accentuates the meaningful relatedness of human spirit to the realm of values." This statement is to be read as an imploration for a "Jewish" corrective to German philosophy and in particular to Heidegger, but it also serves as a warning against the extreme nationalism and the moral pitfalls that shall befall Germany if it does away with this Jewish principle. Even in the mid-1930s, and even after turning his back on the rationalism of liberal Judaism, Lewkowitz expresses his belief that the Jewish message, as he interprets it, holds the spiritual remedy for the nihilism-infected German culture.

Lewkowitz's argument against Heidegger and reference to Pauline theology and Barthianism is best understood in the context of the Jewish reactions to the emergence of views that at the time were collected under the blanket terms of Gnosticism or Marcionism.[35] A recurring theme in this polemical encounter is the claim that counteracting the Gnostic rift between God and the world is the "Jewish" position that upholds divine

---

[33] Proverbs 20:27.

[34] Lewkowitz, "Vom Sinn des Seins," 195. See also his "Religion und Philosophie im jüdischen Denken der Gegenwart."

[35] These terms were taken to be interchangeable, although this has been contested ever since. See for instance Williams, *Rethinking "Gnosticism."* An early discussion of the difficulty of making sense of the dualisms at play in Heidegger's otherwise monistic framework is offered by Marck, *Die Dialektik in der Philosophie der Gegenwart*, 160–165. Seligmann draws on and develops Marck's discussion.

transcendence without forfeiting its connection with immanence. This is evident in Lewkowitz's essay and is a recurring rejoinder to the theologies of Barth and Gogarten. In the interwar political and cultural climate, the anti-Judaism of the Marcionite tradition paired up with the swelling popularity of antisemitism. The theological dimension of the link, staked out by Lewkowitz, between Heidegger's philosophy and his notorious political affiliation, is merely one instantiation of this theoretical pattern.

The so-called "Gnostic" ambiance in Heidegger and Barth was of much concern to Hans Jonas, who composed a philosophical analysis of Gnosticism for his doctorate dissertation, written under Heidegger's supervision.[36] Unlike prior scholarship on the theme of late antiquity, Jonas's philosophical investigation treats Gnosticism as an attitude or stance of human existence (*Daseinshaltung*) in the world. In his analysis he draws substantially on the Heideggerian philosophical lexicon to articulate what he construed as the pessimistic existential features of the Gnostic cosmic dualism, according to which the world is a dark and fallen realm, completely abandoned by a far-removed God. Jonas openly writes in the introduction that "our undertaking will draw to a large extent on an already crafted ontology of Dasein" as put forth by Heidegger "especially in the work *Sein und Zeit*."[37] The human being, in Jonas's Heideggerian delineation of the early Gnostic view, is thrown into an uncanny and dreadful world from which the sole path to redemption is by means of *Gnosis*, the secret knowledge that liberates the soul from the world. Alongside thrownness (*Geworfenheit*), Jonas also offers the notions fallenness (*Verfallenheit*), dread (*Angst*), and being-abandoned (*Verlorensein*) as hermeneutical keys to express the fallen and alienated state of human existence in a devalued world radically detached from divine transcendence.[38]

---

[36] Jonas published his dissertation in 1930 and then *Gnosis und spätantiker Geist. Teil I. Die mythologische Gnosis* in 1934. The second part, entitled *Von der Mythologie zur mystischen Philosophie*, was published by the same publishing house in 1954. The 1958 English translation of these works, *The Gnostic Religion: The Message of the Alien God and the Beginning of Christianity* is an abridged version that lacks the deep-seated Heideggerian inflection of the original German. On Jonas's time in Marburg and his relation to Heidegger, see Jonas, *Erinnerungen*, 108–128; Wiese, *The Life and Thought of Hans Jonas*; Wasserstorm, "Hans Jonas in Marburg, 1928," 39–72.

[37] Jonas, *Gnosis und spätantiker Geist*, 9.

[38] Jonas's influential construct of Gnosticism has since come under attack. See, for instance, Williams, *Rethinking "Gnosticism"*; Waldstein, "Hans Jonas' Construct of 'Gnosticism'"; King, "Translating History: Reframing Gnosticism in Postmodernity," 264–277.

Alongside the details of his existential analysis of the Gnostic Dasein, Jonas intervenes in the raging, and deeply political, debate over the origins of Gnostic theology.[39] Between the different options suggested by scholars at the time – Hellenic, Christian, Persian-Iranian, and Jewish – Jonas finds the latter option to be incomprehensible. His reason is conceptual: the defining Gnostic devaluation of the world (*Entweltlichung*) is a direct offense against Judaism and the biblical God. "The infallible testimony of [the Gnostic] revolutionary character," he writes, is that "it positioned itself in open opposition" to Judaism and it "unleashed on the Jewish God of the world all its accumulated resentment."[40] Jonas, who claims to have felt "especially drawn to the 'biblical word'" from a young age and who found early interest in the thought of Leo Baeck and Hermann Cohen, admits that it may appear at first that the radically transcendent Gnostic God is consonant with the Jewish God of the Bible.[41] "In itself," he notes, "it would have to be conceivable that in this God – transcendent and, since the prophets, detached from the natural religion, could more likely be a starting point for the Gnostic God of transcendence, rather than its anti-type."[42] Yet in reality this is far from being the case. "Even though it was a transcendent [*überweltlicher*] God," he explains, "it was in no way a world-negating [*gegenweltlicher*] God." This position is reproduced in Jonas's famous tirade against the use of Heidegger for Christian theology in his 1964 lecture "Heidegger and Theology." In this later piece, "the profoundly pagan character" of the deification of the world and de-divinization of God that he identifies in Heidegger's later thought is contrasted to a Christianity true to itself and, also, to Judaism. There Jonas asserts: "theology should guard the radical transcendence of God, whose voice comes not out of Being but breaks into the kingdom of Being from without."[43] That the far-removed biblical God exercises a relation to the world constitutes a non-Gnostic ontology, whereby the world is valued and thus the existential abandonment and desire to escape are

[39] See on this Brenner, "Gnosis and History: Polemics of German-Jewish Identity from Graetz to Scholem."

[40] Jonas, *Gnosis und spätantiker Geist*, 228.

[41] Interestingly, amid an overall Heideggerian analysis, Cassirer's imprint is discernable as well. Cf. the section "Gnostische Bildwelt und symbolische Sprache."

[42] Jonas, *Gnosis und spätantiker Geist*, 228.

[43] In claiming that Jonas is generally consistent between his earlier and later engagements with Heidegger, I am in disagreement with Lazier, *God Interrupted*, 37–48, and closer in certain aspects to Cahana, "A Gnostic Critic of Modernity." For two then-contemporary responses to Jonas's piece, one philosophical and one more theological, see Scott, "Heidegger Reconsidered"; Richardson, "Heidegger and God – and Professor Jonas."

irrelevant. Primarily through the notion of "creation," the biblical position posits radical divine transcendence while undermining cosmic dualism. The affirmative relation of the biblical God to the world stands in
marked contrast to the Gnostic conception of the divine. It is therefore
little surprise that Gnosticism identifies the God of the Hebrew Bible with
the evil deity of creation – a view most sharply articulated by Marcion of
Sinope. "The revolutionary culmination of the gnostic development" in
Marcion recognizes "the world-God (=God of creation=God of
justice=God of Law) = God of the Jews as the truly and metaphysically
pure condensed counter-principle to the otherworldly God."[44]

According to Jonas, the abandonment of the world by an unreachable
God makes the Gnostic concept of God "a nihilist concept."[45] The
negativity of the Gnostic God "was conceived as a springboard for
absolutely denying all positivity of the world, the entire claim of the
world's existence, all worth and definitive value of existing being [*das
Seiende*] as such."[46] This pessimistic position stands in strict opposition
to the optimism of the biblical worldview. For by "overseeing the world
through creation and providence," the biblical God "bound[s] the entire
person on worldly probation by his *Law*, or, what is the same, issued His
moral interpretation in the givenness of creation under a positive
norm."[47] By rejecting the notions of creation, providence, and divine
law, Gnosticism is categorized as "decidedly a-moral." Dualism is nihilism; a radically divorced God generates fallen human existence in
a devalued world. In Jonas's depiction, then, Gnosticism is a rebellion
against the Jewish notion of a created, and therefore good, world governed by God. For the Gnostic tradition, "the mighty figure of the Old
Testament God" was always perceived "as the only worthy symbol of
the contrast: principle of the world, of temporality, and of positive
morality."[48]

It should be noticed that two out of these three features defining
Judaism – worldliness and temporality – are consonant with Heidegger's
conceptions, which are utilized for portraying the Gnostic worldview but
also aptly describe its Jewish antithesis. But this will soon change. In the
1930s Jonas does not yet openly deduce from what he finds to be the
striking effectivity of Heidegger's perspective to approaching the Gnostic
phenomenon that the two are analogous. Only after Heidegger's infamous
Rektoratsrede does Jonas recognize that his mentor's philosophy and

---

[44] Jonas, *Gnosis und spätantiker Geist*, 230–231.   [45] Ibid., 145.   [46] Ibid., 248.
[47] Ibid., 228.   [48] Ibid., 231.

politics are intertwined and that they are of a nihilist character.[49] Although he recognizes this in the 1930s, only two decades later, in the 1952 article "Gnosticism and Modern Nihilism," and then in further publications, does he finally articulate a philosophical critique of Heidegger along these lines.[50] At the heart of his critique, which is itself indebted to his Heideggerian reading of Gnosticism, is that the phenomenon of Gnosticism helps us to see that modern secular existentialism, of which Heidegger's *Sein und Zeit* is "the most profound and still most important manifesto," is nihilistic.[51] The modern secular existence, the terminus of the philosophical tradition emerging from the modern scientific revolution, can be illuminated by comparison to the ancient Gnostic myth, whereby dualism collapses into monism: "what is the thrown without the thrower, and without a beyond whence it started?"[52] Drawing the conclusions from his early assessments, Jonas resolves that the reason Heidegger's terminology was so instructive for the examination of the phenomenon of Gnosticism is because it itself exhibits similar features and is animated by similar impulses. Jonas continues to hold the notion of creation as the key *philosophical* contribution of Judaism to Western thought in his later works. In his article "Jewish and Christian Elements in Philosophy: Their Share in the Emergence of the Modern Mind," he summarizes what he takes to be some key ideas of the "Old Testament tradition" that are at variance with the Gnostic and Heideggerian worldview: that the world is created by God, that God saw his creation as good, that man in created in God's image, and that man is expected to do "the good."[53]

Jonas's early engagement with Heidegger is conducted as part of his general grappling with the predominance of contemporary Marcionism, which he found above all in Barth's theology. His first published book, *Augustin und das paulinische Freiheitsproblem* (1930), set out to provide a Jewish counter-position to the anti-Jewish Gnostic approach he,

---

[49] Jonas, "Heidegger's Resoluteness and Resolve," 197–203.

[50] Jonas, "Gnosticism and Modern Nihilism." See also Taubes, "The Gnostic Foundations of Heidegger." Susan Taubes's account of Heidegger's Gnosticism is developed in her correspondence with her then-husband, Jacob. Interestingly, Taubes reports that Arendt found Jonas's thesis "very suspicious," Taubes, *Die Korrespondenz*, vol. II, 206.

[51] Jonas, *The Gnostic Religion*, 335.

[52] Ibid., 339. Also Günther Anders uses the example of *Geworfenheit* without a thrower in his critique of Heidegger's secularized philosophy. Stern (Anders), "On the Pseudo-Concreteness of Heidegger's Philosophy," 357.

[53] In Jonas, *Philosophical Essays*, 21–44, 168–182.

following Barth's influential reading, found in Paul.[54] The exploration of Gnosticism through a Heideggerian lens is in many respects a continuation of this first work. By the time he embarked on his doctoral study, Jonas was already involved in Jewish and Zionist activities, and he would later observe that "my dissertation topic of 'gnosis' was potentially a thousand times more political than Hannah Arendt's work on 'The Concept of Love in Augustine,'" due to its defiant Jewish stand against the prevailing Marcionism.[55]

That Jonas finds Heidegger's conceptuality conducive to a description of the Gnostic *Entweltlichung*, the world-negating desire to overcome temporality and transcend immanent existence, is tightly linked to his association of Heidegger with Barth's early dualistic agenda. His later outspoken critique of Heidegger is linked to his objection to the exaggerated radical transcendence of Barth's theology and its opposition to the Jewish standpoint. For Heidegger, to be sure, there is no transcending temporal existence and values are not grounded in an external source. Such a view is paradigmatically nihilistic; *eigentliche Existenz* means embracing, rather than evading Dasein's factical historicity. Furthermore, Heidegger perceives his own philosophical project as an overcoming of metaphysical dualisms – be they Platonic, Cartesian, or Christian. But for Jonas, the monism of Heidegger's secular existentialism is the other side of the coin of nihilistic dualism. Thus, while it would seem that the characterization of Judaism as upholding this-worldliness and temporal existence is equally suiting of Heidegger, Jonas would fiercely resist this equation. For him, Heidegger's radical immanence is made possible by the paradigm of *Deus absconditus*, which is, as he later exclaims, "a profoundly un-Jewish conception."[56] Already the young Jonas makes note of the theological biases at play in Heidegger's existential meditations when, in an unpublished text from the early 1920s, presumably written in the context of a seminar by Heidegger, he points out that Heidegger's decision to phenomenologically bracket out the question of God is not neutral but rather a theologically charged decision against God's role in the constitution of human existence. The operative outcome of this a-theistic methodology is that *eo ipso* the horizon of the interpretation of human existence is godless.[57] Similarly, he notes that

---

[54] Jonas, *Augustin und das paulinische Freiheitsproblem*.   [55] Jonas, *Erinnerungen*, 124.
[56] Jonas, "The Concept of God after Auschwitz: A Jewish Voice," 140.
[57] I would like to thank Elad Lapidot for providing me with a scanned version of this unpublished text.

Heidegger's notion of *Geworfenheit*, which is exploited to describe the Gnostic soul's experience of being-thrown into the fallen world, "secularizes [*säkularisieren*] the reclaiming of a theological tradition that started out from that epoch."[58]

The Heidegger–Barth connection is frequently employed in the Jewish construals of the theological echoes of Heidegger's "pessimistic" philosophical anthropology. But Shlomo Zemach, the Zionist agronomist and literary figure who would be the first to translate a work by Heidegger into Hebrew, inserts a somewhat unexpected philosophical figure into the discussion on the purported relations between Heidegger and Judaism: Arthur Schopenhauer. In an article "Nazism, Jewish-hatred, and Schopenhauer" (1940), Zemach offers a telling analogy between Schopenhauer's philosophical pessimism and anti-Judaism, and Heidegger's philosophy and support of Nazism.[59] As he explains, Schopenhauer divides world religions according to their "optimism" or "pessimism," himself clearly siding with the latter. Pessimistic and "world denying" are New Testament Christianity, Brahmanism, and Buddhism, while optimistic and world affirming are paganism, pantheism, and above all, Judaism. For Schopenhauer, the Jewish doctrine that has woefully left its mark on philosophy is "the doctrine that the world has its existence from a supremely eminent personal being and hence is also a delightful thing."[60] Zemach singles out Schopenhauer's philosophical antisemitism not only for what he terms its near-religious fanaticism, but for its being "a philosophical, moral, spiritual, anthropological, and legal basis for aggressive and murderous anti-Semitic madness, that is one with the raging anti-Semitism of the racist third Reich!"[61] Explicitly referring to Heidegger, the philosopher-prophet of Nazi antisemitism, Zemach brings the two German philosophers together.

If Martin Heidegger pokes reed in the sandbank of the "naught" and melancholy, if he is determined to renew a religiosity, as Dr. Hugo Bergmann has nicely put it, that the heavens are shut to it, a religiosity without a God – so then this doctrine too bears something from the depth of hell. And from the Schopenhauerean plane it draws the roar of the predatory beast, which is its voice.[62]

---

[58] Jonas, *Gnosis und spätantiker Geist*, 106.

[59] Zemach, "Nazism, Sin'at Hayehudim, ve'Schopenhauer." Almost three decades later, Zemach translated Heidegger's essay *Origin of the Work of Art* to Hebrew. On the emergence and reception of this translation in post-Holocaust Israel, see Herskowitz, "Heidegger in Hebrew." See also Michael Roubach, "Die Rezeption Heideggers in Israel"; Kenaan, Rottem, and Barnea, "Heidegger in Jerusalem" (Hebrew).

[60] Schopenhauer, *Parerga and Paralipomena*, 192.

[61] Zemach, "Nazism, Sin'at Hayehudim, ve'Schopenhauer," 242.   [62] Ibid., 247.

Heidegger's focus on nothingness, angst, and the overall bleak understanding of existence are likened to Schopenhauer's pessimism, and both
are contrasted to the optimism of Judaism. Their pessimistic worldview, in
Zemach's explication, is rooted in a theological position regarding the
forsakenness and negation of the world, which is conceptually tied to
antisemitism and anti-Judaism. The problem with Heidegger, in this reading, is the irrationality and dark passions that animate his philosophy, but
also the theological view regarding the absence of a relational God to
which Judaism bears witness.

Interestingly, the theologically grounded "pessimism" in Heidegger's
thought to which Zemach draws attention is evoked slightly after as part
of the ideological justification of the Socialist *kibbutzim* movement in pre-
state Palestine. In an essay published in the socialist newspaper *Al
Ha'mishmar* newspaper – the motto of which was "For Zionism – For
Socialism – and For the Brotherhood of Nations" – the author, Tzvi Rody,
criticizes the existentialism put forth by Heidegger and, more contem-
porarily, by Sartre. In his interpretation, the embedded pessimism of the
Heideggerian notions of *Verfallenheit*, *Angst*, and *Sorge* are existential
reflections of the decadence and depression of the capitalist society:

> The pessimism that accompanies this doctrine was fitting for the capitalist Western
> European society between the wars, consumed by despair and doubt. Heidegger
> taught that being should be conceived as fallen [*nechshelet*] in essence and the
> entire world should be seen as hopelessly drenched in sin (why? He does not say),
> and the essence of existence and being is concern.[63]

Rody also calls attention to the dependence on a certain version of Christian
anthropology in Heidegger's pessimistic portrayal of human existence.
"Heidegger clings to the story of the Original Sin (Adam and Eve) as a last
anchor," he writes, "yet the Original Sin is for him a psychosis of 'concern
and fear,' and the ultimate melody of this then-fashionable philosophy is:
fear." The Christian legacy at play in Heidegger is best understood as
a secularized appropriation of Kierkegaard. "It should be reminded," he
continues, "that Heidegger fully appropriates the principles of his great
predecessor and spiritual guide . . . the tragic, surly, sorrowful and depressive
Dane Søren Kierkegaard, with regards to the doctrine of dread infused with
consciousness of sin."[64] By revealing the covert capitalistic and Christian
overtones in Heidegger and Sartre, Rody indicates to his Jewish socialist

---

[63] Rody, "Nazi Metaphysics (Or: Thoughts on Existentialism)," 4.   [64] Ibid.

comrades that contemporary existentialism is antithetical to real socialism and should be dismissed.

A similar self-distancing from what is seen as problematic ideological undercurrents in Heidegger is echoed by Lea Goldberg, who would later become one of the most celebrated Israeli poets. Having studied in Germany in the early 1930s and experienced firsthand the degradation of German culture with the rise of Nazism, Goldberg dedicates a number of journalistic essays to the German intellectual scene over this period.[65] In an article entitled "The German Intellectuals and Nazi Germany," published in 1943 in the same socialist newspaper, she discusses the disturbing relationship between German intellectuals and the Nazi party. Goldberg claims that the betrayal of the intellectuals and intellectualism can be attested in the "linguistic process" of "Aryanization" in the German world of literature and philosophy. Instead of taking the obvious example of the "barbaric, brute, untethered language of the Nazi press," she takes "a very mild example from German philosophy," namely, "the "Aryanization" of the terms in Heidegger's masterpiece '*Sein und Zeit*,' 'Being and Time.'" What Goldberg claims is the linguistic feature in this work that reflects the collapse of the German spirit is the infatuation with *Sein*:

> Here the entire system is dependent on the usage of the verb "Being," without which no idea can be expressed in the Indo-Germanic languages (that is: the Aryan languages). Everything is determined by this auxiliary verb … Only in the "Aryan" way of thought, as it were, does this absurdity exists, that no determination can begin without the word *est* or *ist*, which is not the case in eastern languages and, for instance, the Semitic way of thinking. Thus, the style of the philosopher inadvertently exhibits the spirit of the segregation and arrogance of this period. The wise reader cannot ignore this, indeed German intellectuals could not ignore it either.[66]

Anticipating a critique that would been voiced much later by Richard Rorty, Goldberg maintains that Heidegger's entire philosophical scheme is predicated on an exclusively German linguistic feature, and this reflects the contemporary German nationalistic exclusivism and demonstrates the alignment of German thought with its totalitarian regime.

In this 1943 article, Goldberg stresses the essential antithesis between Heidegger's German exclusivist philosophy and "the Semitic way of

---

[65] On her years in Germany, see Weiss, *Lea Goldberg*.
[66] Goldberg, "The German Intellectuals and Nazi Germany," 5 (Hebrew).

thinking." But in an earlier article, from the end of 1935, one can detect the uneasy recognition of the bearings of Heidegger's nationalism on the contemporary Jewish situation.[67] In this piece she focuses on the case of Heidegger in her attempt to come to terms with the question of how intellectuals, paragons of culture, could possibly join hands with the barbarism and anti-culturalism of fascist and totalitarian movements. How could it be, she asks, that Heidegger, the philosophy professor, took "the path of the uncivilized and unaware masses in Germany and join[ed] from the very beginning of National Socialism, this organized group of ignoramuses?" Her response is that his "nationalistic senti-ments," his "connection" to and even "love" of his "community, lan-guage, and the air of his homeland" is what led him to sacrifice his conscience and join the Nazis. By underscoring the appeal that philistine and destructive forms of nationalism can have on anyone – even on *intellectuals* – Goldberg offers a concealed call for self-reflection to her fellow Zionists: nationalism is a double-edged sword, and the case of Heidegger, among others, illustrates that even education and "culture" do not guarantee morality and humanism.

HEIDEGGER, BARTH, AND THE CONSTRUCTION OF JEWISH THEOLOGY

So far, we have examined various cases in which Heidegger's thought is interpreted as indebted to specific theological presuppositions within the orbit of Christian tradition. Often, this led to the juxtaposition of Barth and Heidegger as two thinkers whose schemes, while ostensibly distinct, are in fact comparable to each other, but are equally dissimilar to Jewish thought. One interesting case in which this juxtaposition is denied is Hans Joachim Schoeps's book, *Jüdischer Glaube in dieser Zeit. Prolegomena zur Grundlegung einer systematischen Theologie des Judentums* (1932), an audacious attempt to establish a new sys-tematic Jewish theology, grounded in Barth's doctrine and spotted with vocabulary borrowed from *Existenzphilosophie*. In this work, where the traversing of the traditional boundaries between Judaism and Christianity is overt, Schoeps elaborates on a Protestant understanding of revelation as "an experience of grace in which God opens up a possibility of salvation to the fallen ones," situated in a Jewish

---

[67] Goldberg (Log), "Ha'Orchidea Mul Ha'Totach," 9. "Log" is Goldberg's pseudonym. See Kenaan, Rottem, and Barnea, "Heidegger in Jerusalem" (Hebrew).

setting.[68] With recognizably Heideggerian locution, he declares that the task of contemporary Jewish theology is to identify the ontic character of contemporary existence and enhance it with a complementarily faithful understanding, preached as dogma. To do so, the Jewish theologian must recognize that a long process of apostasy and secularization has left the modern Jew existentially godless. Schoeps diagnoses his fellow German Jews (and Christians, who share a similar crisis of faith) as having completely appropriated the "western history of fallenness" characterized by "the practical and theoretical elimination of God-consciousness."[69] Due to this "so secularized and terribly perverted consciousness," being-Jewish has become meaningless and void of content. Against this Schoeps presents a theological formulation that urgently implores Jews to abandon their godless existence and return to a Jewish life of obedience based on the ever-present event of the Word of God.

The "unbinding sketch" of the foundations of doctrines of faith which he presents as a model for a "systematic theology of Judaism" consists of the doctrines of the uniqueness of God, creation *ex nihilo*, which Schoeps stressed in particular, revelation of the law of salvation, and divine retribution. Discussing the last doctrine, which he characterizes as "Retribution as God's Rule over History and the Return of the Fallen," Schoeps maintains that "Heidegger's fundamental ontology can be the base for our task of the historical-theological exploration of contemporary understanding of existence," as it articulates the spiritual condition of the time. Portraying the existential makeup of a person alienated from the redeeming revealed Word of God, Schoeps perceives Heidegger as delineating the Dasein who is "always already determined as not-being-for-itself, as 'inauthentic,' 'not-at-home,' so that it must call itself out from the 'fallen being of *das Man*' to its authenticity."[70] Yet for Schoeps the existential transition from inauthenticity to authenticity is not to be equated with the transition from a sinful existence to an existence in God. Heidegger's framework *en tout* is situated within the hermetic worldview of modern secularism, because Dasein lacks the possibility of projecting toward a transcendence external to its world. Heidegger's

---

[68] Schoeps, *Jüdischer Glaube in dieser Zeit*, 73. Schoeps would later reflect that his own "entire existential structure has always been a Protestant and Lutheran one." Schoeps, *Ja-Nein-und Trotzdem*, 138. On Schoeps see Lease, *"Odd Fellows" in the Politics of Religion*, 191–231; Brumlik, *Preussisch, konservative, Jüdisch.*

[69] Schoeps, *Jüdischer Glaube in dieser Zeit*, 63–64, 84.   [70] Ibid., 86.

immanent analysis of Dasein "had destroyed … the greatness of the philosophical approach of the created nature of Dasein."[71] God is completely absent from the portrayal of Dasein's existential conditions, according to Schoeps; Heidegger "always swings the human Dasein back to where it is ultimately fastened, in its self." The only condition of possibility for authenticity is Dasein's self-grounding through its being-toward-death, wherein not God but "death becomes the only actuality."[72]

From Schoeps's perspective, the godless existential notions offered in *Sein und Zeit* reflect the spiritual constitution of the modern fallen existence: "Heidegger's fundamental ontology has revealed 'thrownness,' 'Angst' and 'Concern' as the mood of today's Dasein, who recognizes in the 'threatening nature of Being-in-the-world' of his existential condition and in the 'worldliness of the world' the final ontic ground."[73] Noticeably, with this claim Schoeps relativizes the scope of Heidegger's Dasein analysis from its claimed designation as the portrayal of human existence as such to merely its modern, secularized mode of existence. Indeed, Schoeps insists that "the basic mode of such a mood can also be viewed as nothing other than the being-thrown into the naked finitude of the world."[74] The immanent worldliness of Dasein cannot ground itself or provide salvific paths, as it reveals itself as "the nothingness of the nothing," directed toward death rather than toward "rest in God, the Lord." Taken from the perspective of faith, Schoeps claims, "the suffering in torturous meaninglessness" of the godforsaken existence articulated by Heidegger is in fact a form of divine retaliation that the modern person cannot even see as such due to their imperviousness to revelation. More than anything, Heidegger's system expresses the prevalent "radical rigidification of immanence" plaguing the modern consciousness.[75]

In Schoeps's view, what is dubious about Heidegger's philosophy is not its possible Christian roots or undertones, but its utterly secular character. Unlike those who couple Barth and Heidegger, Schoeps sees them as fundamentally disjoined. And since Schoeps by and large conflates Barthianism and Judaism, it follows that Heidegger is negated to Judaism. Following Barth, he rejects Heidegger's authentic/inauthentic distinction in favor of a distinction between graced and ungraced existence, and in line with the radical perspective of dialectical theology, he sees Heidegger's philosophy to be situated outside the realm of theology altogether and in opposition to it. And yet evidently, Heidegger is incorporated into Schoeps's theological program, albeit negatively: Dasein

---

[71] Ibid., 85.   [72] Ibid., 86.   [73] Ibid.   [74] Ibid.   [75] Ibid.

portrays the existential model of the sinner, the heathen, the fallen person, before revelation.

As a result, Heidegger's philosophy provides Schoeps with a language for articulating his concern for the present and future of Jewish faith. In his peculiar Jewish Barthianism, the overall Heideggerian, that is, secular state of modern Judaism is manifested in the prevalent Jewish denominations in Germany. These are, according to Schoeps, either subjugated to the Enlightenment's historicism and liberalism, to the spiritless legalism of rabbinical orthodoxy, or, worst of all, to the assimilationist impulses of Zionism. Albeit differently, all lack the openness and attentiveness to hear the Divine Word in its absolute concreteness, which alone permits the constitution of "the single possible, genuine, true relationship" between God and human.[76] Schoeps's appeal to the Jewish people to divest themselves of their secular consciousness and return to a genuine relationship with God that constitutes a meaningful and authentic existence could be formulized as an appeal to move from Heidegger to Barth – which in his program means, from secularism to true Judaism.[77]

This indirect incorporation of Heidegger for theological purposes would likely be strongly disapproved of by Barth, for whom even the

---

[76] Cf. Schoeps, "Secessio Judaica-Israel in Ewigkeit," written in 1934, republished in *Bereit für Deutschland*, 285, as well as his "Zur jüdisch-religiösen Gegenwartssituation," 98–104.

[77] A related case that, due to space limitations, will not be discussed in the present study, is Michael Wyschogrod (1928–2015). In a forthcoming essay I examine Wyschogrod's relation to both Barth and Heidegger in his outlining of the features of Jewish existence and the divine-Israel relationship as it is disclosed in the Hebrew biblical text. Wyschogrod's main work is *The Body of Faith: God in the People Israel* (1996). See also Wyschogrod, "Heidegger's Tragedy" and his "Heidegger: The Limits of Philosophy."

It should be noted that to his theological scheme Schoeps adds a conservative reactionary political plan whereby the Jewish and Prussian nationalistic-spiritual missions are coalesced in the effort to restore the monarchy in Germany. These theologico-political convictions led him to establish an anti-liberal, fervently patriotic movement called "Der deutsche Vortrupp. Gefolgschaft deutscher Juden," a vanguard that was to spearhead the actualization of his views of the necessary spiritual revolution and that was committed to the unified cause of German patriotism and Jewish religion. Schoeps welcomed the rise of the National Socialist party as a promising opportunity for the restoration of a traditional and conservative German monarchy. This support spurred repeated attempts, beginning in 1933, for rapprochement with the new power. As there was little the Nazis detested more than 'racially inferior' Jews who insisted upon their Germanness, this attempt failed miserably. Schoeps's extreme views and political activism made him target of the harshest of critiques from fellow Jews, before and especially after the war. He was accused, for example, of being a "Heil Hitler Jew," a "Jewish Nazi," or undergoing "swastika assimilation."

description of the fallen person is to be made through the language of faith, with no need to resort to philosophy. A few years later Schoeps seems to have aligned himself with this Barthian vision, and in a review of Delp's aforementioned *Tragische Existenz*, he approves of Delp's view that "Heidegger's method is anything but presuppositionless" and "everything but 'ontically neutral.'"[78] Delp notes "very correctly" that Heidegger's philosophy "works like a 'theology' without a 'theos,'" but this form of secularism is irredeemable: its immanent worldview cannot accommodate a genuine theological position. By positing death as the ultimate end of being human, it "has disabled the possibility of the presence of a higher authority from the very beginning." After lauding the study, Schoeps contends that its only weakness is that despite its critique of Heidegger, the Jesuit author mistakenly "wants to hear a 'good and useful message' from this philosophy for the people of our day."[79] For Schoeps, however, Heidegger's secular system bears absolutely no potential productivity for theology. "There is no accommodation between a truly present ontological philosophy which does not allow real transcending, and dogmatic theology."[80]

Schoeps's heavy dependence on Christian theology and his chauvinistic and reactionary theologico-political scheme drew fervent opposition from his Jewish contemporaries.[81] Here we will only touch upon the instances in which these reactions shed light on Jewish understandings of Heidegger. For Ludwig Feuchtwanger, for example, the Barthian tone dominating Schoeps's work manifests an overall Christian impact hampering his attempt to produce an authentic Jewish theology. Restating his aversion to phenomenology and non-rationalism, he bemoans: "Nowadays, inside and outside our university, Kant and Schleiermacher are pushed to the margins through the celebrated positive teachings of phenomenology from Husserl over to Scheler and Heidegger."[82] Also Eduard Strauß disapproves of what he called Schoeps's "theological assimilation" wherein he attempts to draw into the Jewish conceptual orbit inappropriate sources such as the "new 'theology of crisis'" expounded by Karl Barth's circle, "with its very Christian-eschatological character" and "perhaps Heidegger's

---

[78] Schoeps, "Tragische Existenz: Bemerkungen zu einem Buch über die Philosophie Martin Heideggers," 142–145.
[79] Ibid., 144. [80] Ibid., 145.
[81] I discuss this in Herskowitz, "An Impossible Possibility? Jewish Barthianism in Interwar Germany."
[82] Feuchtwanger, "Jüdischer Glaube in dieser Zeit," 167.

philosophy as well."[83] Neither Feuchtwanger nor Strauß elaborate on their disapproval of Heidegger, but it is clear that both find him an illegitimately "foreign" source inappropriate for Jewish purposes.

Perhaps the most intriguing protest against Schoeps's theology for our concern comes from Alexander Altmann, who has already been mentioned earlier in this chapter. Altmann objects not only to the alleged suitability of dialectical theology for Jewish theology, but also to Schoeps's approach toward Heidegger's thought and to its bearing on contemporary Judaism.[84] Before becoming one of the preeminent scholars of Jewish studies of the previous century, the young Altmann ventured into constructive theology in an attempt to establish orthodox Judaism on firm philosophical grounds and to present it as a viable option for the modern Jew.[85] As part of this endeavor, he draws inspiration from dialectic theology while at the same time emphatically ruling against its application in a Jewish framework. Coming to terms with recent attempts to incorporate Barthian themes into Jewish theology by Schoeps and Max Wiener, Altmann targets in a 1933 essay the either/or conception of selfhood undergirding both dialectical theology and Schoeps's attempt at Jewish Barthianism.[86] According to this "Christian" conception, one is either a heathen or a Christian, and openness to and acceptance of the revealed Word of God constitutes the brink differentiating between the two states. Schoeps, following Barth, asserts that by opening oneself to revelation, the apostate contemporary Jew can move from a heathen's existence to a pious one. "For Schoeps," Altmann maintains, "the apostate Jew is identical with the existential type sketched in Heidegger's anthropology," which, he admits, is "wholly valid philosophically."[87] Heidegger provides Schoeps with a portrait of the sinful existential state of the Jew, a portrayal of "the person divested of all that is specifically Jewish, [who] is to be called upon to hear the Sinaitic revelation." But this view presupposes a uniform existential structure between Christians and Jews, while the existence of the secular Jew, Altmann insists, still betrays a specifically Jewish (albeit ontic) mark, and hence makes them dissimilar to the general Western (Christian) person. The correct structure through which Jewish existential transformation should be comprehended is not

---

[83] Strauß, "Eine jüdische Theologie?" 313.
[84] Published in three parts in the issues of *Der Israelit* on June 15 and 22, and July 6, 1933.
[85] Meyer, *Zwischen Philosophie und Gesetz*, 107–165.
[86] Altmann, "Was ist Jüdische Theologie?" An expanded version was republished later that year. In English: Altmann, "What Is Jewish Theology?" 40–56.
[87] Ibid., 53.

"either/or," but that of return – *Teshuvah*, or "always already." Over
against Schoeps's Christian *heutigen Daseinsverständnis*, Altmann
polemically particularizes Schoeps's efforts and formulates "the Jewish-
historical understanding of existence." He thus attempts to establish an
alternative "specifically Jewish" theology, centering on the particularistic
character of Jewish revelation and peoplehood (*Volkstum*), in his view the
two fundamental elements of a Jewish theology. In Altmann's particularistic account, *halakha*, Jewish law, is the content of Jewish revelation and
the Jewish people are its subject – "a very specific law seeks its very special
bearer and shaper."[88]

To counter Schoeps's diagnosis of the spiritual situation of contemporary Jews, Altmann too draws on Heidegger's analysis of Dasein in his
outline of the "existential possibilities" of Jews seeking to return to "the
organic attitude of authentic Jewish theological thought."[89] He, however,
understands the place and role of the theological in Heidegger's scheme
differently. Altmann equates Schoeps's theological reading of Heidegger
to Erich Przywara's, according to which "Heidegger's metaphysics of
finitude   as   the   defiant   will   to   a   'closed,   tragic-heroic
innerworldliness.'"[90] In this reading, Dasein is confined to the rigidification of immanence and the divine is found only outside the Heideggerian
framework and the modes of existence it portrays. Altmann is willing to
concur that the world of the "Heideggerian man" is one of immanence
and that "Heidegger himself does not discuss whether and how 'man's
being-toward-God' is compatible with the existence of being-in-the-
world";[91] however, he invokes the ontological/ontic distinction to claim
that the immanent Dasein can carry out a "leap ... into a theological
sphere in which his ontological structures (anxiety, decline, conscience,
guilt, temporality etc.) experience a theological translation." In a manner
resembling Bultmann's reading, Altmann holds that Heidegger's ontology
allows a translation or application of its existential conditions to the
vocabulary of faith. There is no need to overcome Heidegger's framework
in order to arrive at authentic Judaism; it can, in fact, enrich its appreciation. Altmann favorably mentions Friedrich Traub's interpretation of
authentic being-toward-death whereby "man, in his consciousness of
finitude, yearns for an infinite God" as an example for the possibility of
implementing Heidegger's ontology in the sphere of theology.[92] In this
way, one can delineate an appropriate construal of ontic religious

[88] Ibid., 50.   [89] Ibid., 53.   [90] Ibid., 53–54.   [91] Ibid., 53.
[92] Traub, "Heidegger und die Theologie."

authenticity from Heidegger's ontological terminology. The possible relation between Heidegger's ontology and theology thus understood provides a "bridge from a radically secularized conscious attitude to
a theological one. Or better, the 'leap' from exclusive worldliness to the
turning toward God, born out of yearning, seems today entirely possible
and meaningful precisely for modern man's existential condition."[93]

   Altmann suggests to apply Heidegger's ontological preconditions to the
ontic case of Jewish particularity, wherein the "special feature of the ontic
character of Jewish existence is present even if in his outer existence the
Jew is not made to feel this specialness in some way."[94] In search for
existential notions that specifically illuminate the ontic Jewish case and
concur with his account of Jewish theology as a particular process of
halakhic decision making, Altmann finds that "most likely the existential
moments, adduced by Heidegger, of 'heritage' and 'fate' could prove to be
decisive for an understanding of Jewish existence."[95] In *Sein und Zeit* §74
Heidegger explains that Dasein's resoluteness entails a shift in the self-
understanding of its historicity and temporality. Appropriating its
thrownness, Dasein comes to see its historical facticity and past as "heritage": "The resoluteness in which Dasein comes back to itself, discloses
current factical possibilities of authentic existing, and discloses them in
terms of the Heritage which that resoluteness, as thrown, takes over."[96]
This consists of seeing its historical situation as well as its being-toward-
death as "fate": "Once one has grasped the finitude of one's existence, it
snatches back from the endless multiplicity of possibilities which offer
themselves as closest to one . . . and brings Dasein into the simplicity of its
fate."[97] In Heidegger's employment, "fate" does not denote predestina-
tion or subjugation to a definitive higher force, but rather an acceptance
and a focusing of Dasein's possibilities in light of its finitude and heritage.
Dasein's owning up to its finitude has an individualizing effect which
detaches it from the conformity of *das Man*, but this does not imply
solipsism or solitude. For Heidegger, heritage is always contextualized
in a historical community (*Gemeinschaft*) of a specific people (*Volk*).
Authenticity therefore involves taking over inherited possibilities in the
present within a shared communal setting. As such, it acts as a catalyst for
a community "to become authentically bound together."[98] Importantly,
the appropriation of heritage does not mean a restraining commitment of
obedience to a forsaken past. Rather, putting to use a term bequeathed

[93] Altmann, "What Is Jewish Theology?" 54.   [94] Ibid., 54.   [95] Ibid.
[96] *SZ*, 383/*BT*, 435.   [97] *SZ*, 383/*BT*, 435.   [98] *SZ*, 122/*BT*, 159.

from Kierkegaard, it is accomplished as repetition (*Wiederholung*), a process of creative interpretation and realization of past possibilities in light of the present. Since resolute Dasein is always already part of a community, fate is integrated into the historical destiny (*Geschick*) of its community, and "its historizing is a co-historizing and is determinative for it as *destiny*."[99]

From Altmann's point of view, an ontic application of the ontological notions of §74 adequately articulate the peculiarities of Jewish existence, for "it is characteristic of the Jewish people that they are conscious of their heritage, as well as of their destiny, believing that they are always being addressed anew by God in the course of history … it is the actuality of the 'Hear O Israel.'"[100] *Volk*, in this understanding, is the Jewish peoplehood, "heritage" is the Torah and the *halakha*, and "destiny" is the Jewish mission of unfolding the Word of God in history. Translating the ontological conditions extended by Heidegger to apply to "the Jewish case," Altmann states that "these concepts display a very conscious turning toward the transcendent moment of divine revelation." Schoeps, Altmann implies, overlooks the fact that this particular destiny of the Jews can find fertile ground in Heidegger because he denies both the particularistic nature of Jewish existence and the theological possibilities embedded in Heidegger.

Altmann's application of Heidegger's philosophy for a particularistic Jewish theology is founded upon the premise of its theological neutrality, which allows him to break the perceived connection between Barth and Heidegger and endorse the latter while rejecting the former. In fact, Altmann asserts that Heidegger's formal vocabulary gives itself to describing Jewish existence in particular. Conveying a view held by Barth and Rosenzweig as well, Altmann contends that volkish language is inadequate for the Christian faith, which is established on the theological construct of the Church. Judaism, on the other hand, is founded upon its *Volk*, and thus it can boast an actuality and "organic growth" lacking in Christianity: "The ever new way in which God addresses Israel is the Jewish destiny, which … legitimizes the heritage of the Torah in its totality. Christianity is not able to possess this category of destiny as a theological category of, say, the ecclesiastical collectivity."[101] The usage of Heidegger's terminology of *Volk* and destiny therefore better suits Judaism than Christianity. This is a striking claim, because with it Altmann opposes the dominant reading of the existential portrayal in *Sein*

---

[99] *SZ*, 384/*BT*, 436.   [100] Ibid., 54–55.   [101] Ibid., 55.

und Zeit as inflected by Christian presuppositions. By accepting Heidegger's self-proclaimed neutrality, Altmann can identify in Heidegger a portrayal of the existential notions of the Jewish person, and thus utilize *Sein und Zeit*'s vocabulary for the formulation of a Jewish theology.

Composed in 1933, the echoes of the recent Nazi *Machtergreifung* and the deteriorating reality of the Jews in Germany resonate clearly in Altmann's essay. Indeed, his theological appeal to Heidegger distinctly reflects the contemporary German-Jewish situation. Not only does it constitute an attempt to categorically distinguish Judaism from Christianity in the wake of Schoeps's extensive appropriation of Christian frameworks, it also highlights the volkish character of the Jews and distinguishes them from the German *Volk*. Ironically, it is Heidegger who is culled to substantiate Altmann's proposed national and religious Jewish revival in the wake of Hitler. Drawing on his philosophical terminology, Altmann articulates that Jews do not share a spiritual vocation with Germany but rather constitute a distinct *Volk* with a heritage, fate, and destiny of its own. It is significant that the Heideggerian notions to which Altmann turns are not those that bear the resonances of Christian tradition, but rather the volkish lexicon that as a religious Zionist he believes express the Jewish situation best.

Admittedly, Heidegger's notion of the *Volk* is introduced abruptly in *Sein und Zeit*, in a rather unwarranted fashion, and remains woefully undeveloped.[102] That Altmann picks up on this terminology nonetheless and appropriates it affirmatively into his own scheme displays an important point that is often overlooked in the debates about the conceptual ties between Heidegger's philosophy and his politics: until Heidegger legitimized the bond between §74 and radical German nationalism by joining the Nazi party in 1933, there was actually nothing necessarily alarming in the employment of terms such as *Volk*, *Gemeinschaft*, *Geschick*, *Schicksal*, and even *Kampf* in his philosophy. These terms were common and used by diverse, even opposing, social and political groups in the ideological clashes of the day. They were, of course, employed by advocates of political chauvinism, antisemitism, and racism, but at the time they did not necessarily denote these things. Not only could one employ these terms in a manner detached from Nazi ideology – consider, for example, Franz Rosenzweig's usage of volkish language to speak of the non-Zionist rooted unrootedness

---

[102] Pöggeler writes of "the *coup de main* of the immediate introduction of the concept of *Volk*." Pöggeler, *Martin Heidegger's Path of Thinking*, 251n32.

of Jewish diasporic existence, or Gustav Landauer's volkish expressions in his anarchic socialism, among many examples – but even in the context of Heidegger's philosophy, they were not taken as necessarily incriminatory until 1933.[103] In a late radio interview by Jonas, he reflects on 1933, when "Heidegger came out of his hiding place. Until then, he had never expressed any political affinities or even sympathies," although "a certain 'Blood-and-Soil' point of view was always there" and "certain remarks ... showed a sort of (how should I say it?) primitive nationalism" – but this only assumed significance in hindsight.[104] Also the Catholic theologian Max Müller, noting the shudder that befell his fellow students upon hearing of their teacher's open support of Hitler, affirmed that "None of his students thought about politics at the time. Not a single political word was uttered in these seminars." Müller specified, when speaking of Heidegger, that "the word *national* [volkish] was very close to him. He did not connect it to any political party."[105] Indeed, as was the case among the general population, volkish terminology was pervasive in German-Jewish discourses at the time as well, where one of the pressing questions was – to *which Volk* did the Jews belong? Were they Germans by nationality and Jews by descent or confession and therefore part and parcel of the German *Volk*, as many liberal Jews saw themselves to be? Or were they an independent *Volk*, the Jewish *Volk*, as many Zionist Jews believed? Altmann's essay is but one instantiation of the investment of Jews in volkish thought and vocabulary and serves as an important reminder of the diverse uses and connotations of the volkish notions that appear in §74.[106]

---

[103] I demonstrate the pervasiveness of the volkish outlook and point to some of Heidegger's Jewish readers who *identified* with the volkish strands in his philosophy in Herskowitz, "Between Exclusion and Intersection: Heidegger's Philosophy and Jewish Volkism." It is for this reason, among others, that the direct and almost teleological line from §74 to National Socialism that is sketched by Emmanuel Faye cannot be defended. Faye claims, in what seems to be hindsight bias, that in this section "the ideas that are at the very foundation of National Socialist doctrine are already present – namely, those of a community of destiny and of a community of the people: the Gemeinschaft understood as *Schicksalsgemeinschaft* and *Volksgemeinschaft*." Faye, *Heidegger: The Introduction of Nazism to Philosophy*, 16. A noteworthy response to Faye's book that stimulated much discussion is Sheehan, "Emmanuel Faye." See also Fried, "A Letter to Emmanuel Faye"; Fritsche, "Absence of Soil, Historicity, and Goethe in Heidegger's Being and Time: Sheehan on Faye."

[104] Jonas, "Heidegger's Resoluteness and Resolve," 199–200.

[105] Max Müller, "Martin Heidegger," 178.

[106] Martina Urban argues that the terminology of §74 was also employed by Nachum Glatzer and Ludwig Strauss for the purpose of affirming Jewish dignity and heritage in the wake of the rising tide of anti-Jewish sentiment. It is most likely that Glatzer and

The question worth asking here is why, out of the rich and varied tradition of volkish thought, does Altmann turn specifically to Heidegger? The immediate answer to this is that his recourse to Heidegger is made in the context of Altmann's dispute with Schoeps over Jewish theology, and more specifically, over his damning judgment of the potentiality in Heidegger's thought for Judaism. It should not go unnoticed, however, that Heidegger proves to be remarkably fitting for Altmann's religious-Zionistic purposes. For example, the understanding that there is no grouping of individuals but rather an individuation within the "always already" established commonality of being-with is precisely an antithesis to Schoeps's "Christian" either/or structure that Altmann finds amiss. Likewise, the underlying meaning of Jewish history in Altmann's approach as an evolving hermeneutic process of ontological import conforms to Heidegger's understanding of history as not merely a process of sequential events, but as *Geschichtlichkeit*, a temporal-hermeneutical happening that determines who we are.[107]

Comparing Heidegger's Volk to other available volkish notions at the time, like those of Buber and Rosenzweig, can shed further light on this question. Buber, for example, spoke passionately of a historical Jewish *Volk*, but for him, the inclination of the Jewish *Volk* is to eventually transcend its initial particularistic character and encompass all humanity. Furthermore, he does not perceive the past as a normative heritage that has claims on the present. The ek-static temporal structure that underlies Dasein's communal historicizing is also at odds with Buber's rendition of the I–Thou encounter as totally present, isolated from the past and the future. For him, Jewish law – which is situated in the sphere of It – is not an ongoing task demanding continuous commitment but rather a fossilized impediment on religiosity. Also Rosenzweig's conception of Jewish *Volk* would be ill-suited for Altmann's aims. Unlike Buber's universalized *Volk*, for Rosenzweig

Strauss and Heidegger were all making use of prevalent volkish vocabulary. Urban, "Persecution and the Art of Representation," 153–179.

[107] On some parallels between Heidegger's volkism and Jewish conceptions of peoplehood, see Fagenblat, "'Heidegger' and the Jews," 145–168; Fagenblat, "Of Dwelling Prophetically," 245–267. The shared volkish framework of Rosenzweig and Heidegger is the foundation of the in-depth analysis of Jewish "uprootedness" and exilic existence in Wolfson, *The Duplicity of Philosophy's Shadow*, 1–32. See also Schwarzschild, "Franz Rosenzweig and Martin Heidegger: The German and the Jewish Turn to Ethnicism," 887–889.

the Jewish *Volk* is indeed particularistic. Yet the spiritual task to be unfolded in history is ascribed in *The Star* to Christianity, while the Jewish *Volk* subsists in its a-historical existence. Rosenzweig also famously differs from Buber in his positive attitude toward *halakha* as commandment (*Gebot*). While Rosenzweig's perspective toward law is primarily focused on the individual, it is nevertheless also communal, generational, and even trans-generational. In this respect he is close to Altmann. Yet Rosenzweig's approach does not explicate on the process of development of *halakha* – the only development accounted for is the individual's gradual existential progress toward accepting more *halakhot* as personally commanded. In comparison to these, Heidegger's notion of *Volk* is more operative for Altmann, for it enables him to speak ontically and constructively of a particularistic, historical, nationalist, and traditionally focused Jewish community, whose identity is illuminated through a process of hermeneutics. It accounts for the person as both an individual and a member of a community whose authenticity is based on a resolute rejuvenation in the present of past normative traditions perceived as heritage, as the destiny of a trans-generational *Volk*. Implicitly, Heidegger's conceptuality also assists Altmann to resist the accusation of formal legalism often directed toward Jewish orthodoxy by certain Christian stances and by liberal Judaism. For according to Altmann, *halakha* is not a form of dry, external legalism, but rather the Jewish resolution and fate, a manifestation of its authenticity.

Altmann's essay was published in three segments on June 15 and 22, and July 6, 1933 – in other words, *immediately after* Heidegger's rectoral address, the event where his championing of Hitler became public. This is noteworthy, though it is probable that the essay was written beforehand, and in any event it is hard to believe that Altmann was aware of Heidegger's political endorsement at the time of its composition. It is perhaps indicative that he immediately ceased to develop a Heidegger-informed Jewish theology and refrained from dealing with Heidegger altogether. He fled Germany soon after, settling first in England and then in the United States, and after an illustrious rabbinic and academic career, resumed dealing with Heidegger only at the very end of his life. In one of the last papers he wrote, he returns to Heidegger and identifies in his call for non-propositional language a possible avenue by which the God of religion and the God of philosophy can be reconciled. Altmann does this while acknowledging Heidegger's distinction between theology and philosophy and that "Heidegger preferred to be silent rather than name the mystery" that religion calls God. However, Altmann also points out that "there is now a growing recognition of Heidegger as an essentially religious thinker."[108]

At the time, however, Altmann would have no way of knowing how history would unfold in Germany or of the role volkish terminology would play in Heidegger's philosophy soon after, as part of this historical unfolding. In the ensuing years, especially throughout the 1930s and beginning of the 1940s, the invocation of volkish terms in Heidegger's writings increases significantly. Over this period, he develops more openly his understanding of the reciprocal relation between the question of the *Volk* and the question of being. The task of preparing for and opening up the *Seinsfrage*, which he thought of in terms of a "homecoming" to "the Fatherland" – "The "Fatherland" is beyng [*das Seyn*] itself," he proclaims in the 1934–1935 lecture course on Hölderlin's hymns "Germania" and "The Rhine" – is a task endowed particularly, perhaps exclusively, to the German *Volk*.[109] The *Volk*, like the *Seinsfrage*, is not present but futural; it is currently an absence, a not-yet, a challenge contingent on the most urgent existential decision. For this reason, Heidegger quickly came to object to the notions of *Volk* that were dominant at the time in Germany. These accounts treated the *Volk* as a present-at-hand technological entity, a collective of individuals that has more in common with liberalism and modern subjectivism than with the metaphysical essence of Germany.[110] His critique of the biological reductionism of the German *völkische Bewegung* and of the Nazi party is rooted precisely in this conviction.[111] For him, the decisive question is not so much whether one belongs to a certain "line of descent," but "*how* one does belong, i.e., whether one merely gives 'expression' to the common and familiar qualities of the line of descent or rather, through one's course of life and achievement, sets forth undeveloped tasks and new possibilities."[112]

It seems that the fact that volkish terms appear only briefly and in an undeveloped manner in *Sein und Zeit* is what allowed Altmann to draw

[108] Altmann, "The God of Religion, the God of Metaphysics and Wittgenstein's 'Language-Games,'" 304–305. Cf. Wolfson, *Giving Beyond the Gift*, 290n37.
[109] Heidegger, *Hölderlin's Hymn "Germania" and "The Rhine,"* 109.
[110] Though in the 1933–1934 lecture course *Vom Wesen der Wahrheit* (*On the Essence of Truth*), his rejection of this mode of volkish thinking is more modest: "Blood and soil are certainly powerful and necessary, but they are not a sufficient condition for the Dasein of the people" (GA 36/37, 263).
[111] GA 38, 61/Heidegger, *Logic as the Question Concerning the Essence of Language*, 53.
[112] GA 94, 350/Heidegger, *Ponderings II–VI*, 255.

on them and apply them to the Jewish case. Nevertheless, Altmann would perhaps agree that authentic participation in the *Volk* is grounded in the manner in which the gift of its heritage is appropriated and how one's decisions determine one's being through action. He would also agree that this appropriation is a challenge, a future. Yet Altmann's Jewish *Volk*, while not reduced to biology, is based, at least in part, on lineage and descent, and its destiny does not correspond to the question of being but to a commitment to divine commandments and to the people of Israel. Altmann's reliance on Heidegger for the construction of a religious Zionist theology therefore appears to be based on the tentative nature of the volkish terminology in *Sein und Zeit*.

Altmann's 1933 essay is not the first time he approached Heidegger for theological assistance. He draws on Heidegger's philosophy as a legitimate source for Jewish thinking already in an earlier essay, "Metaphysics and Religion."[113] Here Altmann takes to Heidegger's "What is Metaphysics?" to reestablish the possibility of absoluteness in religion after its denial in metaphysics by Kant. Altmann explains that Heidegger succeeds in resurrecting metaphysics as a philosophically respectable field by designating its basic task to the inquiry into the question of the Nothing as revealed in Dasein's experience of dread, which undergirds and leads to the question of being. According to Altmann, the Heideggerian wonder that there is something rather than Nothing at all constitutes a consequential moment in post-Kantian philosophy because it denotes an absolutization of being that is ultimately "directed towards immanence." By breaking the Kantian deadlock in philosophy Heidegger opens the door to a revival in theology as well. Equipped with Heidegger's phenomenological vocabulary of moods and the ontological positivity he attributes to Nothing, Altmann seeks "to lay bare the supratranscendental real givenness of the divine, appearing in a certain mode of experience."[114] Leaping beyond immanence can be attained when the metaphysician's experience of wonder (*Staunen*), which is content with that which *is* and does not seek beyond the given, is replaced with the devout person's experience of reverence (*Ehrfurcht*) and its intentionality toward the beyond. This attitude "presupposes the metaphysical experience of Nothing being given," yet the "reverence

---

[113] Altmann, "Metaphysik und Religion," 321–347. In English: Altmann, "Metaphysics and Religion," 1–15.

[114] Ibid., 10.

points not toward the immanence of the object but in the direction of the transcendent without wanting to grasp this transcendent in any way."[115] With this, Altmann consciously locates himself within the tradition of *docta ignorantia* of Plotinus, Arabic, and Christian Scholasticism, but "it is Jewish philosophy" – particularly Maimonides' doctrine of negative attributes – "that has held fast to this thought most emphatically and has elevated it to the cardinal tenet of its theological conviction."[116] Thus, according to Altmann's reasoning, the key to overcoming Kant and crowning the Maimonidean outlook as a legitimate post-Kantian position resides in Heidegger. Consistent with his above reading of Heidegger, in this piece too Altmann recognizes the possibility of grounding theological claims in Heidegger's neutral ontology and applies its insights to the case of Jewish thought.

Altmann's constructive engagement with Heidegger is interesting from a speculative point of view, but it is also instructive from an historical point of view. For not only does it demonstrate how original Jewish thought was conducted at the time through the conceptual frameworks that were available and found compelling – including, indeed, Heidegger's philosophy – it also boasts a straightforwardness about the constructive potentiality of the Jewish encounter with Heidegger that would immediately be made impossible by the historical and political travesties that ensued.

CONCLUSION

As for many of *Sein und Zeit*'s early readers, the question regarding the theological independence of its program is raised in Jewish circles as well. Many, as we have seen, contest the veneer of neutrality of Heidegger's ontology and highlight its theological presuppositions; specifically, its Christianity-inflected secularized anthropology and Dasein's godless world. With the backdrop of the desire for self-assertion in the face of Christianity and modern secularism, many of the Jewish intellectuals discussed in this chapter conclude that insofar as Heidegger's philosophy is bound up in foreign theological assumptions, the fruitfulness of his program for addressing the existential situation of the Jewish person is precluded. As such, their judgment of *Sein und Zeit* participates in the effort of outlining and upholding the Jewish-Christian difference. And since part of the assessment pertains to its secularized categories, they

---

[115] Ibid., 11, 12.   [116] Ibid., 13.

implicitly touch on the question of secularization and its relations to both traditions.

It is at this point that we must inquire: should it at all matter whether Heidegger's philosophy is rooted in, or bears the mark of, Christian tradition? Would this not be committing a genetic fallacy of rejecting a position because of its origin? Should the question not center on whether or not Heidegger offers a compelling account of human existence, *regardless* of the sources he draws on? On the one hand, taking into account the historical context and the desire for Jewish self-assertion, any remnants of a Christian legacy in Heidegger's philosophy may be undesirable *as such*. To be sure, reducing Heidegger's thought to various theological residues found in it does not only simplify the complex and tension-filled character of his work with regards to Christianity, but also misunderstands the phenomenological task he set out to achieve. On the other hand, this does not necessarily mean that the charge of a genetic fallacy is justified. For exposing residues of a certain particularistic heritage in a philosophical account that claims for universality could have the consequence of delimiting its overall cogency. If Heidegger's exposition of the ontological features of human existence is indebted to, or in some way based on, a specific legacy with specific assumptions about what it means to be human that are otherwise open to debate, then its universality and neutrality is curtailed. It is worthy of emphasis here that in the various interpretations and responses to Heidegger that were discussed in this chapter, we do not find the argument that being-Jewish is an ontologically distinct category. This will be Emmanuel Levinas's claim, and it will be discussed in Chapter 7. Rather, the implied argument is that Heidegger's philosophy provides an inadequate existential portrait of Dasein because it relies on a specific and biased tradition of what it means to be human, and for this reason, it is at odds with the ontic instantiation of the Jewish Dasein. At the same time, often in the Jewish reactions to Heidegger, the response to a perceived particularity flaunting as universality is itself a particularity flaunting as universality. The crucial matter then becomes the nature of the particularity vouching for universality rather than the fact of particularity. Nevertheless, in a time of Jewish disenfranchisement and ostracization from German culture, not only was what was seen as Heidegger's secularized Christian anthropology taken as an obstacle from many Jewish points of view, his support of Nazism added a political dimension to this mismatch. In the next chapter, we shall see that Martin Buber's long-standing philosophical dispute with Heidegger plays out through the prism of intersubjectivity and dialogue, which bears theological and political layers as well.

4

Dwelling Prophetically: Martin Buber's Response to Heidegger

Martin Buber's critique of Heidegger is centered on what he takes to be the latter's neglect of the dialogical principle in human existence. This critique is one instance of a reading of *Sein und Zeit* that interprets Dasein as a solipsistic entity impervious to intersubjective relations. We have encountered this interpretation in Chapter 2, in Cassirer's criticism against the individualistic theological traditions Heidegger draws on, and in Löwith's claim that Heidegger cannot account for the "second person" in the context of his analysis of Rosenzweig and Heidegger. This was not an uncommon reading of Heidegger: Ernst Simon voiced a similar view, as did Eugen Rosenstock-Huessy, who recalled that the editors of the *Die Kreature* journal "were aware that Martin Heidegger's 'thrown man' certainly exists, but it is dumb. They were aware that we only speak if others are there; that others speak because we are there."[1] Karl Jaspers repeats this claim in his *Notizen zu Martin Heidegger*, and Max Scheler likewise wrote that "what I reject in Heidegger is the solipsism of existence which he takes as his *point of departure*. It represents a pure *reversal* of the Cartesian 'cogito ergo sum' into a 'sum ergo cogito.'"[2] To this list we can add Friedrich Gogarten, who reproached Heidegger for his lack of attention to interhuman love and friendship, and Hannah Arendt, who wrote of Heidegger's notion of Self: "the essential character of the Self is its absolute Self-ness, its radical

---

[1] Simon, "Zwiesprache mit Martin Buber," 314; Rosenstock, "Rückblick auf Die Kreature," 209.
[2] Jaspers, *Notizen zu Martin Heidegger*, 33–34, 147, 197, 247; Scheler, "Reality and Resistance," 135.

separation from all its fellows."[3] Levinas's response to Heidegger, which will be dealt with in Chapter 7, is an elaboration on this perspective.

While previous research has primarily focused on the relation between Buber's I–Thou and Heidegger's *mit-Sein*, in this chapter I argue that Buber's continuous engagement with Heidegger's early and later works demands a wider critical examination. I suggest that Buber framed his discord with Heidegger as a confrontation between a generally "Greek" monological philosophy and a "Jewish" dialogical alternative, and that he counters the Heideggerian call to "dwell poetically" with a biblical alternative which I shall call "dwelling prophetically."[4]

When Buber published his short work *Ich und Du* in 1923, he was already a well-known intellectual in both Jewish and non-Jewish circles, recognized for his writings on Hasidism and mysticism, his editorial work for the journal *Der Jude*, his activities with Jewish adult education, and Zionism. But the publication of this treatise, with its expressive articulation of the dual relationality of human existence of I–It and I–Thou, secured his role as major organ of the "new thinking" and *Existenzphilosophie*. Indeed, from early on he was read alongside Heidegger as participating in a common philosophical trajectory.[5] This is not entirely incorrect: any assessment of Buber's readings of Heidegger must begin with acknowledging some of their shared philosophical assumptions.[6] These include the dethroning of reason as the primary characteristic of being human; the shared legacy of *Lebensphilosophie* and the departure point of human facticity; a rejection of the traditional modern subject and its replacement with the temporal and concrete self; an acknowledgment of the determining role of social relations in the world; an emphasis on existence and immediacy; a belief in the impediment that the technological modern world imposes on the ability to reach authenticity; and a fascination with language and Eastern thought, among

[3] Arendt, "What Is Existential Philosophy?" 181. For a more recent critique of Heidegger's non-relational notion of conscience, see Critchley, "Original Inauthenticity – on Heidegger's *Sein und Zeit*," 145–147.

[4] Fagenblat harnesses Heidegger's statements about the uprootedness of the Jews to construct a Jewish political theology in a Levinasian key in his essay "Of Dwelling Prophetically." Here I make use of this designation as I believe it captures the core of Buber's response to Heidegger.

[5] Heinemann, *Neue Wege*, 390.

[6] The most elaborate comparison between Buber and Heidegger is Siegfried, *Abkehr vom Subjekt*. See also Gordon, *The Heidegger-Buber Controversy*; Ward, *Barth, Derrida and the Language of Theology*, 126–146; Wood, *Martin Buber's Ontology*, 71, 82, 101, 120; Theunissen, *Der Andere. Studien zur Sozialontologie der Gegenwart*, 266–273.

others. Alongside these important affinities, some fundamental differences call for our attention as well. A case in point is raised by Buber himself in a remark regarding Heidegger's project as a whole: "I shall only confess," he writes, "that for me a concept of being that means anything other than the inherent fact of all existing being, namely, that it exists, remains insurmountably empty [*unüberwindlich leer*]."[7] With respect to Heidegger's assertion that "Being is the nearest thing," Buber comments:

if by the last sentence, however, something other is meant than that I myself am, and not indeed as the subject of a *cogito*, but as my total person, then the concept of being loses for me the character of genuine conceivability that obviously it eminently possesses for Heidegger.[8]

These statements set the stage for what can only be termed, in Buber's vocabulary, his mismeeting (*Vergegnung*) with Heidegger.[9] Insofar as Buber dismisses Heidegger's approach towards being in its entirety and associates being with human existence, then he is, largely, talking past Heidegger, for whom Buber's discussion as a whole is conducted on what he would consider an ancillary, ontic philosophical plane. It is only fitting that when Heidegger was asked about his position toward Buber's thought, he "did not really know what to answer," adding that "Buber probably did not address himself to his, Heidegger's, basic question of Being . . . but that he was not sure."[10]

SECULARIZING KIERKEGAARD: BUBER ON HEIDEGGER'S GNOSTIC MONOLOGISM

Later in his life, Buber intimates that reaching the heart of his philosophical differences with Heidegger would necessitate a "religious dialogue."[11] This statement can be elucidated if we consider the theological

[7] Buber, *Eclipse of God*, 73.
[8] Ibid., 74. Cf. Heidegger, "Letter on Humanism," *Pathways*, 234.
[9] This is how Paul Mendes-Flohr, borrowing the term from Buber, describes the Buber–Heidegger encounter. I take this characterization to be apt, but in contradistinction to Mendes-Flohr, I argue that for the most part this intellectual mismeeting is rooted in *Buber's* inability to truly "encounter" Heidegger's thought. See Mendes-Flohr's study, "Martin Buber and Martin Heidegger in Dialogue." See also Mendes-Flohr, *Martin Buber: A Life of Faith and Dissent*, 286; Goldstein, "Buber's Misunderstanding of Heidegger: Being and the Living God"; Rotenstreich, "The Right and the Limitations of Buber's Dialogical Thought," 127.
[10] Letter from Hans A. Fischer-Barnicol to Buber, dated November 3, 1964, in Glatzer and Mendes-Flohr, eds., *The Letters of Martin Buber*, 663.
[11] Fischer-Barnicol, "Spiegelungen-Vermittlungen," 92.

ramifications of his programmatic insight that Heidegger portrays a "monological" world. To do so, it is best to begin with the lecture series "What Is Man?," which, somewhat belatedly, constitutes Buber's first extended encounter with Heidegger.[12]

The historical context and geographical location of these lectures are important to keep in mind. The year is 1938, and Buber, after continuous attempts of persuasion by his friends, has finally agreed to leave Nazi Germany and move to Jerusalem to take up a chair at the Hebrew University in Palestine, where these lectures are delivered. This lecture series takes its cue from Kant's famous fourth question of anthropology from the introduction to his lectures on logic – "What is man?" It surveys what Buber sees as the history of failed attempts at formulating a satisfying philosophical anthropology, from ancient times to modernity. Heidegger, the only living philosopher addressed in "What Is Man?," occupies a significant place in its general outline. Alongside the chapter dedicated to his thought – the longest and most detailed in the entire lecture series – Heidegger's interpretation of Kant is presented in the introduction and he figures importantly in the expositions of Kierkegaard and Scheler as well. Interestingly, Heidegger's political affiliation goes unmentioned in this lecture series, where only a few vague indications of the stormy political situation can be found. Buber seems to have tried to guarantee their pure philosophical nature, but perhaps the fact that he published the analysis of Heidegger immediately, in 1938, five years before the rest of the lecture series, hints to his intention that it be read in light of contemporary events.[13]

Buber's interpretation of the Dasein analytic is based on the sense that Heidegger's focus on the ontological rather than the ontic is guilty of abstraction. He believes that the distinction between "existential" and "existentiell" is overly beholden to the metaphysical distinction between universal and particular, and therefore falls short of its proclaimed objective. The analysis of Dasein in *Sein und Zeit*, he maintains, does not deal with concrete human existence in its wholeness and actuality, as it is still bound up with the abstract tradition of idealism's notion of subjectivity. This critique should be understood against the general view that Heidegger's speculative revolution consists in offering the much-needed concrete philosophy that addresses everyday, actual existence. This was part of the great appeal of his philosophy. Herbert Marcuse, for example, described the initial reaction to the publication of *Sein und Zeit*: "To me

---

[12] Buber, "What Is Man?" 118–205.   [13] Buber, "Die Verwirklichung des Menschen."

and my friends, Heidegger's work appeared as a new beginning: we experienced his book ... as, at long last, a *concrete* philosophy: here there was talk of existence, of *our* existence, of fear and care and boredom, and so forth."[14] Like others, however, including Max Horkheimer, Löwith, Adorno, Arendt, and Günter Anders, Marcuse's enthusiasm quickly dwindled. In a late interview, he recalls:

But I soon realized that Heidegger's concreteness was to a great extent a phony, a false concreteness, and that in fact his philosophy was just as abstract and just as removed from reality, even avoiding reality, as the philosophies which at the time had dominated German universities, namely a rather dry brand of neo-Kantianism, neo-Hegelianism, neo-idealism, but also positivism.[15]

Buber is to be added to this list of esteemed thinkers who find that Heidegger's concentration on the ontological left the concrete and ontic behind. In "What Is Man?," this line of reasoning leads Buber to anticipate another common charge, often associated with Maurice Merleau-Ponty, regarding Heidegger's neglect of the body. In *Sein und Zeit* Heidegger curiously avoids direct engagement with the question of Dasein's embodied character. He mentions "Dasein's spatialization in its 'bodily nature,'" though he immediately adds that "this bodily nature hides a whole problematic of its own, though we shall not treat it here."[16] Pointing to the insufficient account of Dasein's corporeality, Buber harnesses what he claims to be the abstract features of the Dasein analytic to claim that it "yields only the concept and outline of an almost ghostly spiritual being, that possesses, indeed, bodily contents of its basic sensations ... yet possesses even these in a way that has nothing to do with the body."[17] Unlike Marcuse, Merleau-Ponty, and others, Buber directs the critique of the abstractness of Heidegger's philosophical anthropology toward his own interests in the relationality of human existence. For him, the abstractness of Heidegger's analysis proves that it is unable to account for the concrete truism that "the fundamental fact of human existence is man with man."[18] Dasein's existence is solipsistic.

Buber, in truth, is aware that his portrayal of Dasein as an isolated being "seems to be contradicted by Heidegger's statement that man's being is by nature *in the world*." He also lists the notions of *Fürsorge*

---

[14] Quoted in Wolin, "Introduction: What Is Heideggerian Marxism?" 191n3.
[15] Marcuse, "Heidegger's Politics," 96.   [16] *SZ*, 108/*BT*, 143.
[17] Buber, "What Is Man?" 180–181. On Buber's embodied theology, see Shonkoff, "Sacramental Existence and Embodied Theology."
[18] Buber, "What Is Man?" 203.

and *mit-Sein* as indicating that "Heidegger fully knew and acknowledged that a relation to others is essential."[19] The reference here is to Heidegger's discussion of Dasein's *mit-Sein* in §26, where he outlines two structures: concern (*Besorgen*) and solicitude (*Fürsorge*). The latter includes two positive "extreme" modes: the first "take[s] away 'care' from the Other and put[s] itself in his position in concern: it can *leap in* for him."[20] The second "*leap*[s] *ahead* of him in his existentiell potentiality-for-Being ... This kind of solicitude ... helps the Other to become transparent to himself *in* his care and to become *free for* it." It is clear that Heidegger considers the latter, "authentic" concern, to be preferable to the former, "inauthentic" one. From Buber's perspective, however, these distinctions are meaningless: Heidegger's "solicitous" (*Fürsorge*) human relations are not 'essential' but utilitarian and non-mutual relations – a distinction corresponding to the I–It and I–Thou relations. By paralleling Heidegger's *Fürsorge* with I–It, Buber implies that both authentic and inauthentic modalities of Dasein are situated in the I–It sphere. Real authenticity, that is, the moment of mutual dialogue and openness, has no place in *Sein und Zeit*'s system. "In Heidegger's world there is ... no true Thou."[21] Any intersubjective relation in Heidegger's scheme would fall under the category of "monologue disguised as dialogue."[22]

Buber's critique, thus, is directed at what he considers the deficiency in Heidegger's description of Dasein's existential constitution. This philosophical critique is also an ethical critique, because intersubjective responsibility (*Verantwortung*) is grounded in the I–Thou meeting, which Heidegger, Buber insists, cannot account for. But grasping Buber's critique of Heidegger's early thinking remains incomplete if we overlook its theological foundation. To lay bare the difference between Heidegger's solipsism and his own view of relational existence, Buber contrasts Dasein's self-relating internal "call of consciousness" and primal guilt with the biblically resonant external call of "'Where art thou?' [*Ayequa*]," to which the reply is "'Here am I' [*Hineni*]."[23] By invoking the *Ayequa* call, Buber implies that in Heidegger's construal of Dasein, the exaggerated weight put on *Sein* leads to insufficient attendance to the actuality and specificity of *Da*. For him, only when I encounter – with all my being – the presence of someone who is not myself, "only then am I 'really' there: I am there [*Ich bin da*] if I am *there* [*da*], and where this

[19] Ibid., 169.   [20] *BT*, 159/*SZ*, 122.   [21] Ibid., 172.   [22] Buber, "Dialogue," 19.
[23] Buber, "What Is Man?" 166.

'there' is, is always determined less by myself than by the presence of this being which changed its form and its appearance."²⁴ Buber here covertly appropriates Heidegger's terminology by replacing Dasein's call with the biblical call. One's "there-ness" and existential guilt are inherently relational and constituted by others. In other words, Buber insinuates that only the relational I in its encounter with a Thou should be rightly termed "Dasein."²⁵ Heidegger's category, abstract and subjectivist as it is, simply does not make the cut. We can say therefore that Buber takes an anti-Bultmannian position, according to which the Heideggerian portrayal of Dasein is at odds with the dialogical depiction of human existence that is found in the Bible. To be sure, countering Heidegger's ontological notion of guilt, which is a fundamental and permanent constituent of one's being-in-the-world, with an existential guilt that dissolves in genuine dialogue exhibits the typically ontic vantage point from which Buber reproaches Heidegger. For Buber, the question to Dasein's *da*, "*Where* art thou?," is answered by "I am *here*"; this here-ness is not, as it is for Heidegger, the thrownness into a world within which Dasein's being receives its import, but an actual responsiveness, from within a situation, to the call of another. What is clear, however, is that Buber believes that his own biblically attuned dialogical framework is better equipped to account for the actual nature of human existence than Heidegger's philosophy.

It is one thing to protest the limited elaboration on genuine human interrelations in Heidegger's analytic as Buber does. After all, right after Heidegger lays out the two positive modes of *Fürsorge*, he remarks that Dasein's being-with-one-another maintains itself between them, bringing "numerous mixed forms to maturity," but "to describe these and classify them would take us beyond the limits of this investigation." While suggestive, there is no doubt that the analysis offered in *Sein und Zeit* falls short of a satisfactory account of interhuman relations – a deficiency

²⁴ Ibid.
²⁵ Novak points attention to Buber and Rosenzweig's idiosyncratic rendering of the name of God "Ehyeh" and the formulation "Ehyeh asher Ehyeh" (Exod 3:14) as, respectively, "Ich bin Da" and "Ich werde dasein als der ich dasein werde," noting that "the fact that this use of Dasein was made after the publication of *Sein und Zeit* is not to be overlooked." Novak, "Buber's Critique of Heidegger," 138. We shall return to this formulation below. As will be seen, my interpretation of Buber's critique of Heidegger differs significantly from that of Novak, who lauds Buber for "how deeply he had penetrated to the core of Heidegger's thought" and calls Buber's critique "a true confrontation between a Jewish thinker and a German thinker, each representing and incorporating respectively different world views." I argue that often Buber misconstrued Heidegger's view and that their worldviews overlap in many important ways.

Heidegger never actually rectifies. But it is quite another thing to claim, as Buber does as well, that Dasein is fundamentally *impervious* to genuine interrelations. To understand the conceptual framework that makes this argument possible, we must turn to Buber's reading of Kierkegaard.

In Buber's rendition, Kierkegaard holds that being a Single One (*der Einzelne*) is the ultimate realization of the Christian individual's existence before God. "Kierkegaard's anthropology is … a theological anthropology," for he reflects on "guilt, fear, despair, decision, the prospect of one's own death and the prospect of salvation" as "elements of an existence 'before God.'"[26] Importantly, the goal of becoming a Single One is "the entry into a relation."[27] But while Buber affirms Kierkegaard's acknowledgment of human relationality, he also determines that this self-transcending relationality is exclusivist, for the bond with the absolute must come at the expense of human relations. The Kierkegaardian Single One "stand[s] alone before God." According to Buber, for whom God resides in and through the meeting with the other person, distinguishing between the two relations, that is, in Kierkegaardian terminology, between the religious and the ethical, and granting one superiority over the other, as found in Kierkegaard, is utterly mistaken. For him, Kierkegaard typifies an enduring Gnostic propensity animating Christianity from the days of Paul through Augustine and onward, wherein the genuine relation to God ultimately entails "renunciation of every essential relation to anything else, to the world, to community, to the individual man."[28]

Buber's interpretation of Kierkegaard, both appraised and rebuked, stands in the background of the discussion of Heidegger in "What Is Man?" For Buber claims that Heidegger has "taken over Kierkegaard's mode of thinking," but in so doing, he also "secularizes [*säkularisiert*]" him.[29] By this Buber means that "he severs the relation to the absolute for which Kierkegaard's man becomes a Single One."[30] Approaching the matter through the prism of relationality, Buber is most concerned with the fact that the human's relation to God "is completely lacking in Heidegger."[31] In Heidegger's adaptation of Kierkegaard, the existential composure of the solitary individual standing in the face of God is not

---

[26] Buber, "What Is Man?" 162–163.   [27] Buber, "The Question of the Single One," 50.
[28] Buber, "What Is Man?" 178.
[29] See also Herskowitz, "Heidegger as a Secularized Kierkegaard." A good overview of Buber's reading of Kierkegaard is Šajda, "Martin Buber." And see also Perkins, "Buber and Kierkegaard"; Perkins, "The Politics of Existence."
[30] Buber, "What Is Man?" 174.   [31] Ibid., 178.

directed toward God but inward, toward Dasein's absolutized self. And insofar as Kierkegaard advocates warding off human relations, then Dasein suffers a double privation: it is solipsistically closed upon itself and blockaded from relationality to either God or man.

Buber's conceptualization of Heidegger as a secularized Kierkegaard touches on the question of the relation between I–Thou and I–Eternal Thou, which gets to the heart of the theological layer of his critique. Buber offers two complementing assertions in this regard: that his philosophical anthropology avoids "saying anything independent of man," and that "when I seek to explain the fact of man, I can not leave out of consideration that he, man, lives over against God."[32] In other words, Buber's philosophical anthropology entails a theological anthropology. In his mind, there is a unison of horizontal and vertical transcendence – the encounter with the human Thou and the Eternal Thou are concomitant. As he says in *Ich und Du*: "By means of every particular Thou the primary word addresses the eternal Thou."[33] It follows, then, that the Kierkegaardian decoupling of the coexistence of the interhuman and human–God encounter is in fact detrimental to both. Thus, in accordance with Buber's assumptions, it can be suggested that Heidegger's position is the logical outcome – and the inversion – of Kierkegaard. "When the man who has become solitary can no longer say 'Thou' to the 'dead' known God," Buber writes, "everything depends on whether he can still say it to the living unknown God by saying 'thou' with all his being to another living and known man."[34] If this is not the case, as it is in Heidegger's analysis of Dasein, "as man he is lost." The world depicted in *Sein und Zeit*, Buber concludes, is one in which Dasein is a solipsistic monad who is incapable of self-transcendence and whose absolutized immanent world hinges on nothingness.

It is significant that throughout the analysis of Dasein's godlessness, Buber is careful not to attribute to Heidegger atheism, which he considers a lesser spiritual threat than Gnosticism.[35] And while never outright dubbing him a Gnostic, Buber conceptualizes the early Heidegger as a proponent of Gnosticism, wherein the transcendent is so utterly extraneous and detached that the immanent is absolutized and no human–divine dialogue is possible.[36] Buber even finds in Heidegger's covert

[32] Sydney and Beatrice Rome, eds., "Martin Buber," 76–78; Buber, "Replies to My Critics," 690.
[33] Buber, *I and Thou*, 75.   [34] Buber, "What Is Man?" 168.
[35] Buber, "Supplement: Reply to C. G. Jung," 136.
[36] Brague, "How to Be in the World," 133–147; Feller, "From Aher to Marcion"; Erlewine, *Judaism and the West*, 78–104.

imperative to regain Dasein's self from its absorption in *das Man* "a gnostic concept by which the gnostics meant the concentration and salvation of the soul which is lost in the world."[37] For him, the Pauline–Gnostic attitude is a poignant manifestation of a monological worldview, which defines the modern age in general and is particularly evident in the resurgence of Marcionism in Germany in the early decades of the twentieth century.[38] On various personal and intellectual fronts, including his famous translation of the Bible with Rosenzweig, Buber confronts this spiritual and cultural force and its antisemitic associations. In Buber's mind, his discovery of the dialogical situation, to which the biblical-prophetic worldview attests more than any other faith, can counter this impoverished and perilous spiritual condition.

ECLIPSING HEIDEGGER'S GODS

Throughout the 1950s, after a long hiatus in which the World War II, the Holocaust, and the establishment of the State of Israel took place, Buber returns to deal with Heidegger's philosophy. It is over this period that he develops more clearly his dialogical thought and what I shall call the notion of "prophetic dwelling" as an alternative to Heidegger and his idea of "poetic dwelling."

To be sure, Buber continues to refer to Heidegger's earlier work in this period. He remarks, for example, in an address that Goethe "anticipates what in our time has been defined as 'thrownness' [*Geworfenheit*]" and discursively contrasts "all beings in nature" which "are indeed placed in a being-with-others" to the human being, who is alone "*the* being that is over against."[39] Primarily, however, it is Heidegger's later thinking that occupies now the center of Buber's concern. Evidence for Buber's familiarity with Heidegger's later writings can be found, for example, in a folder entitled "Heidegger" in Buber's archive, which holds a draft of a sixteen-page-long review of Heidegger's lecture "The Question Concerning Technology," offering an attempt at a constructive engagement between Buber and the later Heidegger, written by the Catholic theologian Richard Schaeffler.[40] Schaeffler sent it to Buber, who read it

---

[37] Buber, "What Is Man?" 174.
[38] Mendes-Flohr, "Buber and the Metaphysics of Contempt," 221.
[39] Buber, "Remarks on Goethe's Concept of Humanity," 227–233; Buber, "A Tentative Answer," 35.
[40] It was delivered as a lecture as part of a series on the topic "The Arts in the Technological Age" that took place between November 16 and 20, 1953 in Munich, organized by the

carefully and jotted down handwritten comments, inquiries, and even corrections to Schaeffler's presentation of Heidegger's position. Indeed, there is no doubt that Buber was remarkably up-to-date with Heidegger's ongoing publications. In the footnotes to his 1952 essay "Religion and Modern Thinking," he references the following post-*Sein und Zeit* works: Heidegger's 1928 work *Vom Wesen des Grundes*, the 1933 rectorial address, the commentary on Hölderlin's poetry, the 1947 publication "Brief über den Humanismus," and "Nietzsches Wort 'Gott ist tot'" from *Holzwege* (1950). As we shall see, Buber remained informed about Heidegger's subsequent publications as well, attended his lectures, and even met him personally as part of the preparation for a conference on "language" they organized together.

There is an interesting feature of the 1950s engagement to which I wish to call attention: Hölderlin's poetry often serves as the battleground upon which Buber attacks Heidegger. Heidegger's engagement with Hölderlin goes back at least to the first decade of the twentieth century, but his publications between 1933 and 1945 are chiefly dedicated to the poet. This has evidently caught the attention of Buber, who himself, like many others at the time – including Scholem, Schmitt, Benjamin, Adorno, Rilke, Ludwig Strauss, and Celan – was an avid reader of Hölderlin.[41] As we shall see, Buber's philosophical alternative to Heidegger is presented, inter alia, by putting forth a counterinterpretation of Hölderlin, portrayed not as "the poet – the founder – of the German beyng," as he is for Heidegger, but as a proponent of dialogical existence, a modern version of the biblical prophets of old. Through this poetic dispute, especially with respect to the poems "Patmos" and "Hyperion," a crucial difference between the two thinkers, one pertaining to their competing visions regarding the agreement between the biblical tradition and Western thought, is crystallized: for Buber, the European humanistic tradition at its best is aligned with the dialogical message of the Hebrew Bible. This is evident, he believes, when Hölderlin is interpreted correctly. And it is precisely this unified tradition, committed to universal humanism and dialogue, that is currently threatened by the philosophical and theological currents with which Heidegger is associated. For Heidegger, on the other hand, the salvation of the West

---

Bayerischen Akademie der schönen Künste, and titled appropriately, "Rezension zu M. Heideggers Vortrag über: 'Die Frage nach der Technik.'" It was published in 1955 by the *Zeitschrift für Philosophische Forschung*. I would like to thank Paul Mendes-Flohr for his assistance with this archival item.

[41] A comprehensive study of the role of Hölderlin in twentieth-century Jewish thought is a desideratum.

depends on overcoming the concerted humanistic-biblical tradition of which Buber is a mouthpiece, and the poet who can lead the way is Hölderlin. Here, then, is a clash over the theological-political charge of the contemporary world that is projected onto, and performed through, a clash over literary exegesis.

Buber's renewed encounter with Heidegger's philosophy is part of his larger project of addressing the present spiritual situation he terms the "eclipse of God" (*Likuy Ha'or Ha'elohi, Gottesfinsternis*). "Eclipse" here does not denote the death or disappearance of God, but the existence of an obstacle impeding the divine–human relationship. Nietzsche's "God is dead" is the epithet of the spiritual condition of modernity, according to Buber, but he interprets it not as Heidegger does, as announcing the end of the fantasy of a metaphysical supersensory realm in which God is the primal being, but rather to mean that "man has become incapable of apprehending a reality absolutely independent of himself and having a relation with it."[42] In the aforementioned 1952 essay, Buber levels an expansive critique of the religious currents of leading contemporary thinkers: Sartre, Heidegger, and Carl Jung. In a similar manner to his response to *Sein und Zeit*, Buber thinks that also the later works of Heidegger, "who undoubtedly belongs to the historical rank of philosophers in the proper sense of the term," are to be approached through a religious prism.[43] Nietzsche's "God is dead" is the departure point for Heidegger's general effort to think beyond "the absolute" in metaphysics and religion. This does not mean he is an atheist, Buber reminds, alluding to Heidegger's complaint in "Letter on Humanism" against those who claim he is an atheist or indifferent to the God question. Rather, even more clearly than before, Heidegger's later thinking undertakes one of the most important attempts to "to fill the horizon that has been declared empty."[44]

Focusing on Heidegger's "theses about the divine," Buber explains that not unlike him, Heidegger too pronounces this hour to be an hour of night, and he too projects a spiritual reorientation that will prepare the grounds for an ontological turning point that will allow for the return of the divine, "the appearing of God and the gods," in unprecedented forms. Buber, however, finds Heidegger's scheme to be deeply faulty. For one, he finds most disquieting the hardly accidental "coupling of an

---

[42] Buber, "Religion and Reality," *Eclipse*, 14.
[43] Buber, "Religion and Modern Thinking," *Eclipse*, 70.
[44] Buber, "Religion and Reality," 21.

absolute singular with an iridescent plural" of God and the gods in Heidegger's Hölderlinean inspired writings. As he observes in an over-looked response to Shmuel Hugo Bergmann's critical review of *Eclipse*, with respect to "the extreme phenomenological promise of Heidegger, who prophesized a turn in thinking which will bring about the renewal of 'the appearance of the God and the gods'" – "the plural language here empties the singular language that preceded it of all content of true being."[45] By calling out Heidegger's misreading of Hölderlin's "gods," Buber charges what he takes to be the polytheistic impulse in Heidegger's thought.

Perhaps the main deficiency in Heidegger's scheme, however, pertains to how he conceives preparing the ground for the reappearance of the gods. The most urgent task for thought, according to Buber's interpreta-tion of Heidegger, is "the thinking through of the basic religious concepts, the cognitive clarification of the meaning of words such as God or the holy."[46] The reference here is to Heidegger's passage from "Letter on Humanism," cited already in Chapter 1:

> Only from the truth of being can the essence of the holy be thought. Only from the essence of the holy is the essence of divinity to be thought. Only in the light of the essence of divinity can it be thought or said what the word "God" is to signify. Or should we not first be able to hear and understand all these words carefully if we are to be permitted as human beings, that is, as eksistent creatures, to experience a relation of God to human beings?

Buber takes this passage to indicate that Heidegger holds the view that humans could conjure (*beschwören*) the gods to appear as objects of thought. While he is aware of Heidegger's insistence that "it is not for man to decide whether and how the divine will reappear," for this takes place "only through the fate of being itself," Buber ultimately interprets him contrarily.[47] His line of reasoning is as follows: insofar as the "fate of being" will bring about the advent of the gods, and "it is precisely in human thought about truth that being becomes illuminated," then humans have an active role in the reappearance of the gods. According to Buber, the view that the gods do not come independently of humans, that the gods can be conjured by humans, is characteristic of magic. Buber interprets Heidegger's aforementioned urge to "hear and understand these words carefully" according to the logic of sympathetic magic. In this form of magic, knowledge of the "word" or "name" of an object

---

[45] Buber, "Between Religion and Philosophy," 3 (Hebrew).
[46] Buber, "Religion and Modern Thinking," 71–72.   [47] Ibid, 72.

reflects its essence, and through correct denotation of the lingual sign, a link between language and reality is established and access and control of the object is made possible. It is likely, moreover, that Buber interpreted Heidegger's Hölderlinian-inspired idea of "naming the gods" (*Nennen der Götter*), which frequently appears in *Elucidations* and particularly in the passages to which Buber is reacting, in a literal sense, as evoking the name of the gods in order to conjure them.

As Buber explains, magic is as an all-around distorted human–divine interaction in which neither side is independent: humans need the gods' "bundle of powers" and the gods are conjured to appear. True religiosity, that is, human–divine encounter, is founded on the independence and relationality of both sides. "God does not let himself be conjured," Buber affirms, "but He also will not compel. He is of Himself, and He allows that which exists to be of itself. Both of these facts distinguish divine from demonic powers."[48] Heidegger's gods, on the other hands, are treated as instruments or forces to be conjured, controlled, and utilized through "man's mysterious knowledge and might." Moreover, those which Heidegger designates as gods are knowable and subsumed under the immanence of being. However, Buber posits, not only does cognitive clarification of concepts or "words" hamper the immediacy of divine presence, but throughout human history "those who have been named by this word have been transcendent beings."[49] Heidegger's gods, then, cannot be God: "He who confines God within the immanent," Buber announces, "means something other than Him."[50] God is "wholly Other" and at the same time "the wholly Same, the wholly Present." We know nothing about God, though we can intensely sense his presence in a holy, noumenal dialogical encounter Buber calls revelation. If, as Buber defines it, God is that which is always a Thou and never an It, then Heidegger's gods, in contradistinction, are never a Thou and only an It. Heidegger may talk *about* the gods, but never *to* God; he will never *encounter* him.

It should not go unrecognized that despite his insistence on their immanence and knowability, Buber refuses to term Heidegger's gods "mythical." This is because he sees myth as a positive spiritual force, one which is "the nurturing source of all genuine religiosity," and "fundamental to Jewish religiosity, and central to Jewish monotheism."[51] Buber holds an apophatic theological position and, at the same time, attributes

---

[48] Ibid., 75.   [49] Ibid., 74.   [50] Buber, "Religion and Reality," 28.
[51] Buber, "Myth in Judaism," 105.

positive religious quality to concrete mythical representations of the
divine, insofar as they bear witness to the intimate encounter with the
living and unknown God and recognize that every image of the utterly
unrepresentational God conceals just as much as it reveals. According to
Buber, "[t]he religious reality of the meeting with the Meeter, who shines
through all forms and is Himself formless" is a fundamental truism of the
prophetic worldview.[52] But this cannot be said of Heidegger; the possibility that Heidegger's invocation of the gods marks a positive spiritual
development of mythic revival is invalidated due to the simple fact that
it does not stem from a mutual encounter. "Without the truth of the
encounter," he states, "all images are illusions and self-deception."[53] It
is, rather, part of a coerced encounter and the apparatus of thought.[54]

It is noteworthy that despite his polemical motivations, Buber identifies
some loose invocations of the dialogical principle in Heidegger's commentary on Hölderlin. For example, in "Hölderlin and the Essence of Poetry"
Heidegger reflects on the line from Hölderlin's poem "Hyperion": "Since
we are a conversation" (*Seit ein Gespräch wir Sind*): "The gods can only
enter the Word if they themselves address us and place their demand upon
us. The Word that names the gods is always an answer to this demand".[55]
Buber too is fond of this line and repeatedly invokes it in his polemic over
Hölderlin. Heidegger's reflections on this line, Buber states, are "pregnant
seeds" that are ultimately "destroyed" in his ensuing work. His conjurable
polytheistic gods are conceptually linked to his monologism, that is, to his
confinement within the immanent It-world that denudes the possibility of
divinely grounded dialogue.

In Buber's view, Heidegger's preparation for the new advent of the
divine necessitates the discarding of all past encounters with God.
Heidegger, as he puts it, "summons all of the power of his thought and
words in order to distinguish him, the 'Coming One,' from all that has
been."[56] In order to remain fixed on a future advent, "a belief in the
entirely new," Heidegger rejects all existing forms of religiosity and
demands a complete detachment from the past. His denial of dialogue
leads to a radical futurism that is a threat to "religion" generally. "[B]ut in

[52] Buber, "Religion and Philosophy," 45; cf. Wolfson, *Giving Beyond the Gift*, 25–29.
[53] Buber, "Religion and Reality," 23.
[54] Susan Taubes makes a similar observation: "Heidegger's Seinsdenken and naming of the
holy remains an empty form on paper. Let him come out dancing from his cubiculum and
then I'll believe him." Taubes, *Die Korrespondenz*, vol. II, 129.
[55] Heidegger, *Elucidations of Hölderlin's Poetry*, 76.
[56] Buber, "Religion and Modern Thinking," 76.

particular," Buber continues, Heidegger is "against the prophetic principle in the Judeo-Christian meaning."[57] To support this statement, Buber
quotes (slightly inaccurately) a passage from Heidegger's attack on the
biblical prophets in his elucidations of Hölderlin: "the 'prophets' of these
religions do not begin by foretelling the word of the Holy. They announce
immediately the God upon whom the certainty of salvation in
a supernatural blessedness reckons." The context of this statement is
a passage where Heidegger clarifies the distinction, indeed opposition,
between the "prophetic" according to the Judeo-Christian tradition and
the "prophetic" character of the Hölderlinian poet. He writes:

The poets are, if they stand in their essence, *prophetic*. They are not, however,
"prophets" according to the Judeo-Christian sense of the term. The "prophets" of
these religions do not only utter in advance the primordial word of the holy. At the
same time they prophesy the God on whom they count for the security of their
salvation in celestial blissfulness. Let one not disfigure Hölderlin's poetry by "the
religious element" [*das Religiöse*] of a "religion" which expresses the Roman
interpretation of the relation between men and gods. Let one not overburden the
essence of this poetic calling by making the poet into a "seer" in the sense of
soothsayer. The holy which is foretold poetically merely opens the time for an
appearing of the gods, and points into the location of the dwelling of historical
man upon this earth. The being of this poet must not be thought in correspondence
to those of "prophets": rather, the "prophetic" element of this poetry must be
grasped in terms of the being of the poetic foretelling.[58]

This passage targets two traditions Heidegger associates with technology:
the Judeo-Christian tradition and the Roman culture. Heidegger's accusation, that the message of the biblical prophets focuses on the escape from
insecurity and the quest for serenity and stability, is a development of his
early kairological readings of Paul and his critique of Augustine. The
biblical prophets offer strategies of comfort through the God of religion
and refuse to risk the uncertainty of attentiveness to what he calls the word
of the holy. The prophetic call on an accustomed God amounts to settling
for the familiar and the safe, thereby frustrating the genuine preparation
for the holy. In other words, it calls on a technological god who, operating
according to a utilitarian exchange, can offer security and stability. We
have mentioned previously that Heidegger typically singles out the notion
of creation and the monotheistic notion of creator God as the chief
theological reflection of the technological modality of truth. But his anti-

---

[57] Ibid., 77. Translation amended.
[58] Heidegger, *Elucidations of Hölderlin's Poetry*, 136–137. On the background for this
passage see Bernasconi, "Poets as Prophets and as Painters," 146–162.

monotheistic ire extends to biblical prophecy as well. In his mind, the two
are bound up with each other in their technological urge for control and will
to power. While he lists, later on, "the godly [*Göttlichen*] in Greek culture,
in prophetic Judaism [*Prophetisch-Jüdischen*], in the preaching of Jesus" as
examples of divinities that are the "beckoning messengers" who bear out
the presence of the gods,[59] Heidegger also highlights, contemporaneously
with his Hölderlinian commentaries, the Jewish-technological root of biblical prophecy: "Prophecy," he notes, "is a technique of defence against
what is destinal in history. It is an instrument of the will to power. That the
great prophets are Jews is a fact whose secret has still not been considered."
And he continues: "'prophecy' is forward-looking history and therefore the
technological perfection of the Wesen of history."[60]

Alongside the monotheistic tradition, Heidegger also tends to contrast
the pre-Platonic Greek world with the Roman culture. Like Hegel and
others in this German tradition, Heidegger judges the Roman culture to be
inferior to the Greeks'. He particularly despises this culture because he
believes everything in it was approached in terms of utility and by an
imposition of a preconceived and systematic set of assumptions and conceptions. It was, in Heideggerian terminology, a culture marked by an
impoverished notion of *technē*. In the late 1930s he attributes technology
to the "*Roman-Romanic*-modern spirit," characterizing it as "most deeply Un-German."[61] Technology also marks the inappropriate conception
of the human–gods interaction in the Roman world, which he terms,
disparagingly, "religion." In contrast to the Romans, he notes, "The
Greeks had no 'religion,' because they were and still are those who are
under the gaze of the gods."[62] In "Aufenthalte" (1962) he writes: "The
Greek relation to the divinity of the god and the gods was neither a faith
nor a religion in the Roman sense of *religio*,"[63] and in "Zu den Inseln der
Ägäis" (1967), this view is repeated: "the possibility of interpreting the
relation to the gods according to the manner of the Roman *religio* and of
speaking of a 'religiosity' of the Greeks and their faith, disappears."[64]

Responding to Heidegger's attack on the biblical prophets in
Elucidations, Buber charges:

I have never in our time encountered on a high philosophical plane such a far-
reaching misunderstanding of the prophets of Israel. The prophets of Israel have
never announced a God upon whom their hearer's striving for security reckoned.

---

[59] GA 7, 185/Heidegger, *Poetry, Language, Thought*, 182.   [60] GA 97, 159.
[61] GA 95, 323.   [62] Heidegger, *Introduction to Philosophy – Thinking and Poetizing*, 18.
[63] GA 75, 241.   [64] Ibid., 260.

They have always aimed to shatter all security and to proclaim in the opened abyss of the final insecurity the unwished-for god who demands that His human creatures become real, they become human, and confounds all who imagine that they can take refuge in the certainty that the temple of God is in their midst. This is the God of the historical demand as the prophets of Israel held Him. The primal reality of these prophecies does not allow itself to be tossed into the attic of "religions": it is as living and actual in this historical hour as ever.[65]

From Buber's perspective, Heidegger is not only mistaking the poets for the prophets, he is also misunderstanding the meaning of the prophetic. Heidegger attributes to the biblical prophets features of I–It modality, such as stability, predictability, and control, while for Buber the prophets exemplify the exact opposite: the unmediated contact with the flux, indeterminacy, and instability of the dialogical life. The spiritual value of "holy insecurity" is a recurrent motif in Buber's writings, present since at least his work *Daniel* (1913). Taking note of a specific biblical allusion inserted in this paragraph can illuminate the full meaning and severity of Buber's response. By associating Heidegger with those who take "refuge in the certainty that the temple of God is in their midst," Buber alludes to the prophet Jeremiah, who vilifies his fellow Jerusalemites for their unfounded dogmatic security in the indestructability of the temple: "Do not trust deceptive words and say 'This is the temple of the Lord, the temple of the Lord, the temple of the Lord'" (Jeremiah 7:4). Buber thus pushes back not only against what he sees as Heidegger's misinformed identification of I–It religiosity with biblical propheticism that stands in contrast to the prophetic message; he also accuses him of promoting the very same depraved form of religiosity. What Leo Strauss saw as the competition between Heidegger and Buber in which "he wins who offers the smallest security and the greatest terror," captures how Buber understands the different application of their otherwise shared standards and assumptions.[66] Heidegger's radical rejection of security means for Buber a denunciation of the past and past religiosity as such, including the biblical-prophetic message, while the very same rejection of security leads Buber to the God of the biblical prophets, who is, as he claims, by definition never familiar or a source of complacency.

The association of Heidegger with magic seems counterintuitive, even odd. A brief overview of Buber's writings shows that the category "magic" carries specific import for him and that the accusatory

---

[65] Buber, "Religion and Modern Thinking," 73.
[66] Strauss, "Preface to the English Translation," 11.

association of Heidegger with it is not accidental. For Buber, "magic" is almost a technical term, specifying a coercive and instrumental appeal to the divine. It involves manipulation and power, and as such is antithetical to dialogical religiosity. The conceptual opposition between "proper" religiosity and the spiritual perversion of magic is consistent in Buber's writing from the moment he centers on the exploration of the dialogical situation of human existence.[67] Buber opposes magic to the human–God encounter in *I and Thou* where he distinguishes "sacrifice [*Opfer*] and prayer [*Gebet*] from all magic [*Magie*]." While the former two are set "in the consummation of the holy primary word that means mutual action," magic "desires to obtain its effects without entering into relation, and practices its tricks in the void."[68] A similar distinction is made around the same time in a correspondence with Rosenzweig, where he insists that "Magic does *not* belong to the 'religious' life; it is the impediment, the countering, oppositional element."[69] In the 1928 lecture "The Faith of Judaism," Buber declares with regards to magic: "he who thinks he can conjure [*beschwören*] [the mystery, God] and utilize [*benützen*] it, is unfit for the venture of true mutuality."[70] This verdict is repeated in a more developed manner in his work of biblical exegetics *Moses* (1945) where he interprets the theophany of the Burning Bush as the revelation in which "religion is demagicized."[71] In the reading offered in this work, Moses' request for God's name is understood in terms of sympathetic magic, wherein obtaining a deity's name allows the appealer to get hold of the deity and evoke and control his manifestation. God's response to Moses' request is directed against this logic – the enigmatic doubled "*Ehyeh asher ehyeh*" is interpreted as follows: "If the first part of the statement says: 'I do not need to be conjured for I am always with you,'" then "the second adds: 'but it is impossible to conjure me.'"[72] That Buber associates this coercive mode of human–divine interaction with Heidegger is confirmed by his statement in "Religion and Modern Thinking" that the god of magic "had become for man a bundle of powers of which man's mysterious knowledge and might could dispose." Accordingly, any appeal to the

---

[67] In his pre-dialogical writings, like in *Daniel: Dialogues on Realization* (1913) and "The Spirit of the Orient and Judaism" (1916), Buber uses the term "magic" affirmatively in the context of the celebrated moment of "decision."
[68] Buber, *I and Thou*, 109.
[69] Glatzer and Mendes-Flohr, *The Letters of Martin Buber*, 272–276.
[70] Buber, "Der Glaube des Judentums," 194–195. In English: Buber, "The Faith of Judaism," 21–22.
[71] Buber, *Moses*, 59–60.   [72] Ibid., 52–53.

divine that includes conjuring, that is, an appeal dictated by power, utility, and predictability, is antithetical to the mutuality of the human–divine dialogue.

We saw earlier that Buber discursively links Heidegger's early work to Gnosticism by presenting him as a "secularized Kierkegaard." While Buber identified some important continuities between Heidegger's "early" and "late" writings, he judges that in terms of affiliated spiritual tendencies, Heidegger's later writings betray the faults of magic more than those of Gnosticism – though, it is important to stress, from the perspective of the possibility of dialogue, the two are closely related. For Buber, both magic and Gnosis are not spiritual forces limited to a specific historical era or people – they are sustained spiritual tendencies that present a constant threat to the possibility of dialogue. Ancient Egypt, Augustine, medieval Kabbalah, and Heidegger all instantiate these perverse spiritual frameworks that ought to be surmounted in order for the human–divine meeting to be realized. By linking later Heidegger to magic, it is implied that his philosophy advances a framework in which the human–divine interaction is fraught with interest, manipulation, and control. It becomes clear, then, that for Buber, Heidegger's later philosophy, too, instantiates a spiritual illness to which his own dialogical thought can serve as a remedy.

EVALUATING BUBER'S CRITIQUE OF HEIDEGGER

Turning now to evaluate Buber's analysis of Heidegger, some serious misinterpretations and misrepresentations come to the fore. Some of these can be explained by Buber having access to a more limited overview of Heidegger's work than that which we enjoy now, but others are rooted in the conceptual molds through which he approaches Heidegger.[73] Attending to these misinterpretations can help us to appreciate better the details of this intellectual mismeeting.

We shall begin with the "gods." This is one of the most enigmatic themes in Heidegger's thinking, but some things can be asserted with some level of certainty. First of all, the rendition of the "gods" is not an advocacy for polytheism. In *Contributions to Philosophy* Heidegger

---

[73] Walter Kaufmann notes that Buber's "discussion of the thought of Nietzsche, Heidegger, and Sartre – to give only three examples – are open to objections. At important points he seems to be mistaken in his views of their views." For some reason, however, Kaufmann decides that "this is unimportant." Kaufmann, "Buber's Religious Significance," 667.

openly states that "the talk of 'gods' here does not indicate the decided assertion on the exactness of a plurality over against a singular but is rather meant as the allusion to the undecidability of the being of gods, whether one single god or of many gods."[74] The gods (or god), moreover, are decidedly not the God of faith. They are not universal or eternal, either: the gods are always the gods of a people in a historical epoch. "The gods only as those of a people," Heidegger writes in his private notebooks, "no common god for everyone, which means for no one."[75] The gods are not entities – they cannot be simply said to "be," as this may destroy their divinity.[76] They are, however, in some way, subordinated to being[77] and finite.[78] They are in need of being as being is in need of them.[79] What Heidegger is after is the *Entgegnung*, the countering and encountering of the gods and the mortals through which the gods open up a world for humans and orient them toward new orders of arrangements of entities, significances, and commitments. "To bring the world into world-ing as a world is: to venture the gods once more."[80] This is the process of interaction that presences or names the gods. The gods, then, are fundamental to one's being-in-the-world, signaling an attunement toward the elevated and the holy.

This means that the affiliation of Heidegger's gods with magic is wildly off the mark.[81] Just as Heidegger does not perceive the gods as ontic entities, he does not think their reappearance involves conjuring or manipulation. In the lecture course *Parmenides* he makes clear that the gods are not invoked by humans by contrasting "the low-German word '*Got*'" signifying "a being humans invoke and hence is the invoked one," with the Greek term for God, which is "something essentially different." The Greek terms, *theos-theaôn* and *daimon-daiôn*, "are not seen from the standpoint of humans, as invoked by humans."[82] Humans cannot bring about the arrival of the gods; all that can be done is to anticipate and prepare. This, indeed, is a fundamental theme that is constantly repeated

---

[74] GA 65, 437/Heidegger, *Contributions to Philosophy*, 345.   [75] GA 94, 214.

[76] GA 65, 263, 437/ Heidegger, *Contributions to Philosophy*, 207, 345

[77] GA 4, 59/Heidegger, *Elucidations of Hölderlin's Poetry*, 82; *Pathmarks*, 258, 294.

[78] Heidegger, *Contributions to Philosophy*, 8–10, 191–192, 324–330.

[79] Cf. Polt, *The Emergency of Being*, 204–213. Wrathall and Lambeth, "Heidegger's Last God," offer a formalized interpretation of Heidegger's gods. Cf. Wolfson, "*Gottwesen* and the De-Divinization of the Last God." See also Welte, "God in Heidegger's Thought."

[80] GA 94, 209.

[81] I argue this in fuller detail in Herskowitz, "Everything Is Under Control."

[82] GA 54, 164–165/Heidegger, *Parmenides*, 111–112. Translation altered.

in Heidegger's later writings. The poets, whose words stand in the center of this ontological drama, have a preparatory role. As it is stated in the passage attacked by Buber, "The holy which is foretold poetically merely opens the time for an appearing of the gods, and points into the location of the dwelling of historical man upon this earth." The poets foretell, open the time, and point, but they do not conjure and do not attempt to control. The reappearance of the gods, rather, is linked to achieving a special vicinity to being. This is the role of the poet, who must "remain near to the god's absence, and wait long enough in this prepared nearness to the absence till out of the nearness to the absent god there is granted an originative word to name the high one."[83] In a similar manner, in the lecture "Bauen Wohnen Denken," while developing the idea of the "fourfold," Heidegger *defines* the "mortals" as those who await the gods:

Mortals dwell in that they await the divinities as divinities. In hope they hold up to the divinities what is unhoped for. They wait for the intimations of their coming and do not mistake the signs of their absence. They do not make their gods for themselves and do not worship idols.[84]

Heidegger makes this point in the *Der Spiegel* interview as well: "I see the only possibility of salvation in the process of preparing a readiness, through thinking and poetizing, for the appearance of the god or for the absence of the god in the decline."[85] Seemingly, an earlier statement by Buber himself equally reflects Heidegger's view on the matter: "We know that it will come; we do not know how it will come. We can only be prepared. To be prepared, however, does not mean to wait immovably ... to be prepared is to prepare."[86]

Heidegger's insistence on preparation and anticipation also contests the affiliation of his program with attitudes of utility and manipulation that are inherent in Buber's accusation of magic. Indeed, such a position seems utterly misplaced in the case of Heidegger, whose reflections on "the essence of technology" constitute a powerful disavowal of the ideas of manipulation, utility, and control. His critique of technology focuses precisely on its manifestation of the "will to power" and the challenge or demand (*Herausforderung*) it brings forth in terms of calculative efficiency and exploitation of being.[87] As we have seen, Heidegger associates

---

[83] Heidegger, *Elucidations of Hölderlin's Poetry*, 46–47.
[84] Heidegger, *Poetry, Language, Thought*, 148/GA 7, 152.
[85] Heidegger, "Only a God Can Save Us," 197/GA 16, 671.
[86] Buber, "Renewal of Judaism," 55.
[87] Dallmayr, "Heidegger on *Macht* and *Machenschaft*."

this overarching framework with the Judeo-Christian and Roman traditions. Heidegger's notion of the anticipated "return of the gods" is
intended to represent the exact opposite of this modality, namely, the
cultivation of a new receptivity and unprescribed attunement to the over-
abundance of possibilities of being's showing up, marked by gratitude to
the mystery and indeterminacy of being. The arrival of this poetic dwelling
is predicated on the demise of the technological enframing of
a manipulative, power-laden response to being's disclosure – a demise
that direct human activity cannot accelerate. Indeed, magic itself, with its
techniques of power, strict calculative formulas, conception of necessary
causality, and demand for efficacy, appears to betray precisely the attitude
of machination that Heidegger so detests.

Moreover, the reappearance of the gods is not governed by a mechanistic,
cause-and-effect rule tied to evocation of language. Throughout the 1930s,
especially in *Contributions*, *Besinnung*, and his readings of Hölderlin, after
Heidegger comes to acknowledge that *Sein und Zeit* prioritizes Dasein in its
relation to being by insinuating that being is in some way dependent on
Dasein, he begins to develop the idea that there is a co-responding,
a simultaneity between the two. It is arguable whether Heidegger manages
to offer a satisfactory account of precisely how this simultaneous relation is
played out, but it is clear that he now sees Dasein as a *response* to the gift of
being, as a co-participant in its creative "world-play" (*Weltspiel*). At
a certain point, he adds a hyphen to the designation Dasein – "Da-sein" –
to call attention to its correlation and co-belonging with *Sein* (*Die
Zugehörigkeit von Dasein zum Sein*). As he writes in *Elucidations*:

> But again it is important to see that the presence of the gods and the appearance of
> the world are not merely a consequence of the occurrence of language; rather, they
> are simultaneous with it. And this to the extent that it is precisely in the naming of
> the gods and in the world becoming word that authentic conversation, which we
> ourselves are, consists.[88]

This ontological mutuality takes place in the *between* (*Zwischen*) of
humans and gods. "Neither do the gods create humans, nor do humans
invent the gods," he writes in *Besinnung*. "The truth of be-ing decides 'on'
both but not by ruling over them, but by appropriatively occurring between
them and thus they themselves first come into an en-counter."[89] In this
updated scheme, the poet is defined as "the one who has been cast out – out

---

[88] Heidegger, *Elucidations of Hölderlin's Poetry*, 57–58.
[89] Heidegger, *Mindfulness*, 208/GA 66, 235. Translation amended.

into the *between*, between gods and men."⁹⁰ With respect to the accusation of magic, therefore, it can be judged that Jean Wahl's claim that "it seems at least that Buber has exaggerated Heidegger's involvement in what Buber calls 'modern magic'" is an acute understatement.⁹¹

In order to articulate his critique of Heidegger, Buber draws on the conceptual reservoir through which he is accustomed to justify and legitimize his dialogical position. In "Religion and Modern Thinking" he correlates the three spiritual tendencies he frequently employs in his polemics with three prominent contemporary thinkers: atheism with Sartre's existentialism, magic with Heidegger's later thinking, and Gnosticism with Carl Jung's psychology. Yet at least when relating to Heidegger, Buber's established framing is deeply inadequate for the task. Attributing to Heidegger the position of magic amounts to a misrepresentation of his views on virtually all fronts (we shall see below that the correlation of language and being in play in magic is foreign to Heidegger as well). It seems difficult to avoid the conclusion that the unfounded attribution of magic to Heidegger has less to do with Heidegger's actual position than it does with the ideational framework through which Buber theorizes.

PROPHETICISM AND APOCALYPTICISM

That Buber approaches Heidegger through predetermined structures is further apparent in another steadfast conceptual subcurrent operating in his thought: the binary of propheticism and apocalypticism.⁹² As we have seen, Buber attributes to Heidegger a radical futurism that eschews the familiar for the sake of the utterly not-yet. This is a fundamental feature of the apocalyptic consciousness according to Buber. For him, apocalypticism and Gnosticism are conceptually interlinked: a radical rift lies between God and the unredeemable world and no dialogue or relation is possible between the two. Both hold that the present world is so fallen that redemption is projected into the future and is *from*, not *of* the world. For Buber, these allied outlooks encompass a cluster of derived ideas, including the lack of historical alternatives to the overcoming of the present world and the advent of a future; the depreciation of human decision;

⁹⁰ GA 4, 47/Heidegger, *Elucidations of Hölderlin's Poetry*, 64.
⁹¹ Wahl, "Martin Buber and the Philosophies of Existence," 499.
⁹² For example, Buber, "Prophecy, Apocalyptic, and the Historical Hour," 192–207; "The Two Foci of the Jewish Soul," 36–37.

a subsequent sense of existential stability and predictability; and an emphasis on individual rather than collective salvation. It is only fitting, thus, that Buber classifies apocalypticism and Gnosticism as a Hellenistic rather than Jewish phenomenon.[93] Controversially, he also considers Pauline Christianity, with its conception of faith as *pistis*, a believing *that* (*Glauben dass*), as bearing Gnosticist and apocalyptic tendencies. *Pistis* as agreement to proposition implies not mutuality but concession and abstraction, and hence monologue and lack of immediacy with God. This account of faith, Buber maintains, led to a dogmatic Christian history of salvation.

Against this general outlook, Buber posits what he takes to be the anti-apocalyptic prophetic worldview, driven by the following conviction: "that God dwells in His creation and that God will redeem it are also one and the same thing."[94] Redemption on this account consists not in overcoming the world but in hallowing it. This is affected dialogically – everyday historical life and concrete human existence are the platforms of this effort. "The prophetic faith," Buber writes, "involves the faith in the *factual* character of human existence, as existence that factually meets transcendence."[95] Since the prophet speaks in an "actual historical-biographical situation," the focus is ultimately not on the future but on the present hour, the enacting moment of decision to turn to God. The core teaching of the prophetic experience of history, Buber emphasizes, is its openness to alternatives. It follows that the prophetic message possesses an inherent element of distress, uncertainty, and instability. In contrast to *pistis*, what informs the prophetic worldview is *emunah*, that is, faith, truthfulness, trust *in* (*Vertrauen*), which for Buber amounts to an openness to the indeterminacy of an abiding dialogical intimacy and immediacy with the divine.

Here, too, the animating conceptual subcurrents of Buber's program are applied inappropriately to Heidegger's thought. Contrasting the features Buber attributes to the prophetic outlook to Heidegger is unsound, and the association to apocalypticism is at the very least misleading, if it is understood as a destruction or negation of the world. Heidegger's thinking can indeed be considered apocalyptic, given that it is first clarified

---

[93] Buber, *Two Types of Faith*, 9–12ff; Cf. Buber, "Spinoza, Sabbatai Zevi, and Baalshem," 95–116, 123.

[94] Buber, "Spinoza," 105. The major milestones in Buber's counter-history are the prophets, the Essenes and Jesus, Hasidism, and his own dialogical thought.

[95] Buber, "Prophecy, Apocalyptic, and the Historical Hour," 198.

what he means by this label. Especially in the 1930s, and mainly though not exclusively in his private notes, Heidegger deals with the theme of apocalypse (the word *apocalypsis*, literally "unveiling," is a close parallel to *Unverborgenheit*).[96] During this time Heidegger tends to think of being as happening or emerging at inceptive, "apocalyptic" moments of urgency and emergency (*Not*). There is, he maintains, a fundamentally "catastrophic" quality to being, because the extremity of the first inception, in which an epoch of essencing emerged, will ultimately collapse in a great downfall – the word *Untergang* is used often – and give way to the emergence of a new inception. This does not mean a destructive cosmological "end of times" in which the world is judged and the worthy are spared, but a collapse or ending of a certain manner of being's essencing, a necessary destinal event in the history of being, which can serve as the condition for another inception. "The great begins great, sustains itself only through the free recurrence of greatness, and if it is great, also comes to an end in greatness," Heidegger declares in *Introduction to Metaphysics*. "... Only the everyday understanding and the small man imagine that the great must endure forever, a duration which he then goes on to equate with the eternal."[97] At more pessimistic moments, it is true, Heidegger expresses a vision of the *Selbstvernichtung* of the conditioning of technology, which, he projects, will reach its end only by eventually challenging itself and bringing about its own destruction. Most often, however, as noted in Chapter 1, Heidegger is wedded to the view inspired by Hölderlin's "But where danger is, grows/ the saving power also": redemption from technology is found *in* technology as a mode of disclosure. This, indeed, is certainly the view expressed in the texts to which Buber is responding.

But Buber is not mistaken in claiming that Heidegger seeks a departure from the traditions of the past. This can be seen, for example, in the preface to the section of *Contributions* entitled "the Last God," consisting of one sentence: "The god wholly other than past one and especially other than the Christian one."[98] This departure, however, is not a disowning. The preparation he wishes to cultivate does not necessitate a deletion of the past. Indeed, Heidegger is strongly against a simplistic invalidation of the past. In *Sein und Zeit* he explains that authentic historicizing involves

---

[96] I thank Richard Polt for this observation.
[97] GA 40, 18/Heidegger, *Introduction to Metaphysics*, 17. Cf. in particular Polt, *The Emergency of Being, passim*; Polt, *Time and Trauma*, 144–145.
[98] GA 65, 403/ Heidegger, *Contributions to Philosophy*, 319.

a retrieval and repetition of Dasein's heritage in light of a projected future. "There is need for a rethinking which is to be carried out with the help of the European tradition and of a new appropriation of that tradition," Heidegger says in his famous 1966 *Der Spiegel* interview. "Everything essential and everything great originated from the fact that man ... was rooted in a tradition."[99] In "The Principle of Identity" (1957) he maintains:

> Whatever and however we attempt to think, we are thinking within the sphere of tradition. Tradition prevails when it frees us from thinking back to a thinking forward, which is no longer planning. Only when we turn thoughtfully toward what has already been thought, will we be turned to use for what must still be thought.[100]

Liquidating the past institutes an inauthentic disowning of Dasein's ecstatic temporal structure, a position which better reflects Buber's own perception of the temporally autonomous present moment of I–Thou. Buber misinterprets Heidegger in disconnecting the "unaccustomed," the "unlike," and the "different" in Heidegger's analysis of Hölderlin's *Andenken* from the re-membering, re-thinking, and retrieval mentioned in that very analysis. The advent of new gods, according to Heidegger, will not prompt the radical disassociation with the familiar, but rather the unconcealment of new possibilities and forms of ordering from within a familiarity that was thought to have been exhausted.

   With this in mind, it becomes clear that while Buber sees himself as putting forth an account opposing the limitedness of the I–It encounter and in favor of an openness to the undecidability and multiplicity of the encounter with the world and God as Thou, this undecidability and multiplicity is framed from the very outset by a monotheistic affirmation. Buber's claim that "When Israel confesses (Deut. vi. 4) that JHVH is its Lord, JHVH the One, it does not mean that there is not more than *one* God – this does not need to be confessed at all," or his rhetorical exhortation with regards to Heidegger, "who would dare ... to juxtapose God and the gods on the plane of the real encounter?" reveal a monotheistic presupposition regarding the necessary nature of the encounter with the divine.[101] With this departure point, Buber's critique of Heidegger in terms of the lack of complete open-endedness in the human encounter with the divine is severely weakened.

---

[99] Heidegger, "Only a God Can Save Us," 113.
[100] GA 11, 34/Heidegger, *Identity and Difference*, 41.
[101] Buber, *Two Types of Faith*, 130–131.

BUBER'S THEOPOLITICS AND HEIDEGGER'S NAZISM

Buber's schematization of propheticism versus apocalypticism is not without difficulties, as is the covert conflation of his debate with Heidegger on this schematization. But it is significant that for Buber, Heidegger's theoretical flaws are interlinked with his immoral theologico-political identification. Buber's conviction that apocalypticism is the political outcome of a monologistic worldview illuminates his analysis of the theological underpinning of Heidegger's alliance with Nazism. From a theoretical standpoint, Buber's philosophical attack on Heidegger's politics is an extension of his critique of Hegel, in particular, the Hegelian notions of totality, the immanent identity of being and Idea (God), and the ultimacy of the state. As he explains, Heidegger is nourished by the Hegelian absolutization of history, itself a modern heir of the Pauline dualistic conception of history that collapses into immanence.[102] "The existentialism of Heidegger is also rooted in Hegel's thought," Buber writes, "but in a deeper, indeed the deepest possible, level. For Hegel world history is the absolute process in which the spirit attains to consciousness of itself; so for Heidegger historical existence is the illumination of being itself."[103] In a rare appearance of the notion of "divine judgment" in Buber's *oeuvre*, he claims that Heidegger's immanentist framework leaves no room "for a supra-historical reality that sees history and judges it." This, for Buber, explains Heidegger's apocalyptic embrace of National Socialism:

If historical time and history are absolutized, it can easily occur that in the midst of present historical events the time-bound thinker ascribes to the state's current drive to power the character of an absolute and in this sense the determination of the future.[104]

The tacit analogy made here is that between Hegel's enthusiasm for Napoleon and Heidegger's embrace of Adolf Hitler.[105] Buber, like other thinkers discussed in this study, expresses the view that Heidegger's political travesty is tied to the radical immanence of his philosophy. By affirming his own hour, marked by Hitler's rise to power, as an elevated and absolutized "historical" moment in which "the essence of truth is

---

[102] Cf. Taubes, "Buber and Philosophy of History," 451–468.
[103] Buber, "The Validity and Limitation of the Political Principle," 215.   [104] Ibid.
[105] Consider also Buber's conversation with Werner Kraft from January 12, 1941, where Buber says that "Hitler is only the caricature of Napoleon." After revealing he does not like the "cold" Stendhal, he continues: "Stendhal's last development is Heidegger." To this Kraft responds: "behind Stendhal is Napoleon, behind Heidegger is Hitler." Kraft, *Gespräche mit Martin Buber*, 13.

originally decided," Buber proclaims, Heidegger "has bound his thought to his hour as no other philosopher has done."[106] Lacking the contact with the "One who does not dwell in time but only appears in it," Heidegger's immanent account of history can only absolutize moments within itself. And as it lacks a supra-historical purview and standard, his immanent account is susceptible to absolutizing problematic historical moments. "Heidegger," Buber concludes, "creates a concept of a rebirth of God out of the thought of truth which falls into the enticing nets of historical time."[107] It should be noted that the analysis of the theological link between Heidegger and Nazism is the mirror image of Buber's critique of Carl Schmitt's political theology.[108] Buber disapproves of Schmitt's instrumentalization of theological conceptions in the service of the authoritarian state, while his claim against Heidegger is that his *denial* of divine power is harnessed to the services of the authoritarian state. Of course, it can be said that Buber himself absolutizes the biblical-prophetic moment as an elevated and ever-valid model of human existence. Yet he holds history to be under the judgment of God, and this absolutized moment confirms the reality of the boundary between right and wrong, justice and injustice. It is, therefore, not absolute in the same sense as Heidegger's conception of history is said to be.

But there is more to the dispute between Buber and Heidegger than the difference between purportedly religious and secular conceptions of history. For while Buber believes that the model of prophetic-dialogical existence should and could be revived here and now, Heidegger considers the simplistic "flight to the Greek gods" to be a "self-deception," and that resurrecting the glory of Greece is a "childish" wish.[109] In his view, the poets – and for Heidegger, this means above all Hölderlin – are able to identify and create space for unexposed potentialities within the past. What surfaces here is a political inflection to the crucial difference between Buber's conception of time as presence and Heidegger's ecstatic conception of time.

Against this overall theologico-political view associated with Hegel and Heidegger, Buber sets forth a theopolitics founded on what he takes as the prophetic call to resist the claim for human sovereignty and crown God as absolute king. This political vision is developed in Germany and Palestine

---

[106] Buber, "Religion and Modern Thinking," 77.   [107] Ibid., 78.
[108] See on this Schmidt, "Die theopolitische Stunde"; Lebovic, "The Jerusalem School: The Theopolitical Hour."
[109] GA 53, 66/Heidegger, *Hölderlin's Hymn "The Ister,"* 53.

in the 1930s and 1940s, in the wake of and as a response to the rise of Nazism and totalitarianism.[110] The embodiment of this anarcho-theopolitics is the narrative in which Gideon declines kingship in the book of Judges chapter 8. For Buber, Gideon's refusal is a representative statement of Israel's recognition that no human can truly rule because God is already the king. Resisting kingship and curtailing the power of human leadership in the name of the absolute sovereignty of God is the main political teaching of the biblical prophets as well. Confirmation that Buber perceives Heidegger's theology of history to be anti-prophetic is found in an insinuation to the opportunism embedded in Heidegger's political lapse while discussing his absolutized account of history: "[A]fter all," Buber remarks, "the goblin called success, convulsively grinning, may occupy for a while the divine seat of authority."[111] The motif of "historical success" appears in Buber's works as part of his anti-Hegelian polemic against the criterion of historical success as the marker for meaning. In contrast to world history, wherein "what determines the importance of events is achievement and success," Buber claims the biblical conception of history "attaches no particular importance to achievement or success."[112] According to this account, "the real history of the world is covert, or hidden history." The desire for historical success characterizes false prophets, while "this glorification of failure culminates in the long line of prophets whose existence is failure through and through."[113] For Buber's perspective, the indictment of Heidegger's political affiliation is rooted in his godless, monological, absolutized account of history, and is mapped on the differing theo-political forms of propheticism and apocalypticism.

Nevertheless, it is important to clarify that unlike what is suggested by Buber's explication, it is now clear that Heidegger develops his thoughts about the coming of the gods in the wake of what he saw to be the *failure* of the Nazi party, and his subsequent political estrangement. Although Heidegger remained a member of the Nazi party until 1945, his writings testify to a self-distancing from his initial identification of Hitler as a Germanic savior approximately a decade before. In this respect, Buber is reading Heidegger backwards: he explains Heidegger's political actions through the philosophical developments that emerge from Heidegger's

---

[110] The best and most extensive account of Buber's account of theopolitics is Brody, *Buber's Theopolitics*.
[111] Buber, "The Validity and Limitation of the Political Principle," 215.
[112] Buber, "Biblical Leadership," 142.   [113] Ibid., 143.

retreat from politics. Of course, this retreat was not caused by moral con-
foundment by the Nazi horrors, but by Heidegger's disappointment at what
he saw as the party's betrayal of its destiny to instigate the Greco-German
"new beginning." Yet Heidegger also continues to speak of the truth,
destiny, homecoming, language, and historical being of the German *Volk*
after his distancing from the Nazi party. Indeed, Heidegger's disassociation
from National Socialism was decidedly not a disassociation from his idiosyncratic volkish ideology, which led him to the party in the first place. This
fact may explain Buber's historico-political concretization of the elusive
Kommende in Heidegger's writings from this time as referring to Hitler.

   Another noteworthy point in this context is that the publication of
Heidegger's *Black Notebooks* divulges that after his disillusionment
with National Socialism, he too interprets the essence of the party
along politico-theological lines.[114] The political manifestation of the
technological and metaphysical perception of being which he ties to
biblical monotheism culminates in the violent domination of National
Socialism. "The modern systems of total dictatorship stem from Jewish-
Christian monotheism," Heidegger maintains. "In the timeframe of the
Christian West, that is, of metaphysics," he notoriously urges, "Judaism
[*Die Judenschaft*] is the principle of destruction."[115] Continuing this
point, he offers one of his most abominable formulations, implying that
the persecution of the Jews by the Nazis is an internally technological
confrontation, an event of Jewish self-destruction: "When the essentially
'Jewish' in the metaphysical sense comes to combat the Jewish, the highpoint of self-annihilation in history has arrived – supposing that the
'Jewish' has everywhere completely seized mastery for itself, so that
even the fight against 'the Jewish,' and it above all, becomes subject to
it." The Jewish principle of technology, the destructive drive of power
and manipulation, has turned against itself, and the drive for destruction
becomes a drive toward self-annihilation.

   Both thinkers thus come to see the Nazi regime as an apocalyptical
power, but Heidegger interprets it as the outcome of conceptual frameworks associated with Judaism, while for Buber it is the political manifestation of deep-seated anti-Jewish forces.[116] Once again, we witness

---

[114] A detailed account of Heidegger's political theology is Schmidt, "Monotheism as
a Metapolitical Problem."
[115] *GA* 97, 20.
[116] A comparison between the two thinkers' onto-political stances is Hadad, "Fruits of
Forgetfulness."

how the two men's shared suppositions run in parallel and are applied differently. Both thinkers seek to reestablish a sense of sacredness, transcendence, and belonging in a world impoverished by technological culture, metaphysical conceptuality, and totalitarian politics. Both find comparable features of the present to be problematic, and they attribute eschatological quality to the recovering of an obfuscated attunement to the world. But the speculative traditions they identify with the disease and the proposed remedy are crisscrossed, and in both cases, their analyses are formulized by monolithic, oversimplified, and self-serving construction of Jewish (or Judeo-Christian) and Greek (or Greco-Germanic) traditions. For Buber, Heidegger's ontological program perpetuates a monological way of life that denudes the possibility of experiencing divine presence and is tied to totalitarianism. For Heidegger, the biblical-monotheistic framework to which Buber self-ascribes participates in a violent technological tradition limiting the possibilities of being's showing up and correlates to the destructiveness of the totalitarian state. At this point, it is worth citing the critical reaction of a close reader of both thinkers, Jacob Taubes, who noted the similarity – and fruitlessness – of their shared search for hallowed origins: "I have no patience," he announces in one of his many throwaway remarks in his lecture series on Paul's political theology, "neither with respect to Heidegger nor with respect to Buber, for this apotheosis of the early. Why the early should be better than the later I simply don't understand."[117]

BUBER'S ONTOLOGY OF THE BETWEEN AS A RESPONSE TO HEIDEGGER

Alongside his critique, in a number of essays composed throughout the 1950s, the aging Buber set himself the task of formulating an ontology of "the between" which, in part, is to serve as an alternative to Heidegger's ontology. Already in 1948, in a short lecture "On the Situation of Philosophy," Buber proposes that the philosophical anthropology so urgently needed after loss of faith in metaphysical truth – and after the devastations of the war – should take as its departure point Heidegger's claim that truth is "an inherent property of Being" rather than just "the agreement of the representation with the object."[118] We indicated above, however, that what Buber understands by "being" differs significantly

---

[117] Taubes, *The Political Theology of Paul*, 7.
[118] Buber, "On the Situation of Philosophy," 136–137.

from Heidegger's understanding of that term. That Heidegger is a covert interlocutor throughout this entire period can be said to betray Buber's negotiation between the attraction and repulsion of Heidegger's fertilizing philosophy.[119] Supporting this assessment is Werner Kraft, the German-Jewish scholar and friend of Buber, who reports a conversation he held with Buber at the time: "Buber then said: 'Heidegger's central idea is a sham [*Fälschung*],' but I have the impression that he – like Löwith – cannot free himself from Heidegger."[120]

In the essay "Distance and Relation" (1951), Buber explores "the principle of human life" by considering "the category of being [*Seinskategorie*] characterized by the name of man."[121] He begins to work out a relational ontology of "the between" by positing the twofold movement of originary distance (*Urdistanz*) and relation. This twofold dynamic involves making an object independent of human determinations, in order to then enter into a relation with it. "Man turns to the withdrawn [*abgerückten*] being [*Seiende*] and enters into a relation with it."[122] This dynamic of self-distancing and recognition creates the world: "Only when a being [*Seienden*] is independently over against a being [*Seiende*], an independent opposite [*selbständiges Gegenüber*], does a world exist [*ist Welt*]."[123] One does not only encounter the world, but rather *sets up* the encounter through which the world emerges. Being the endower of distance and relation is a unique feature of human existence: "The human is like this because he is the creature [*Wesen*] that through its being its beingness becomes detached from it [*durch dessen Sein das Seiende von ihm abgerückt*] and recognized for itself."[124] Typically, Buber's ontology is concerned with beings and is clearly anthropocentric: the setting of things into independence is accomplished by humans and for the sake of human activity: "when and to the extent to which a world exists, there exists the man who conditions it."[125] The unified movement of "distance" and "relation" can be seen as a Buberian alternative to the disclosive character of Dasein, as well as to the relationship between truth and freedom in Heidegger, whereby beings manifest themselves as what they are once they are freed to be themselves. This is Buber's concretized,

[119] Buber to Friedman, letter from August 11, 1951, *Briefwechsel* vol. III, 291.
[120] Kraft, *Gespräche mit Martin Buber*, 22.   [121] Buber, "Distance and Relation," 49.
[122] Ibid., 52.
[123] Ibid., 51. Ronald Gregor Smith obscures the likely rejoinder to Heidegger by translating *Seiende* as "structure of being" or "living being" rather than the more immediate rendition of "[a] being." The quotations below have been amended accordingly.
[124] Ibid. Translation amended.   [125] Ibid., 52. Translation amended.

ontic corrective, from his dialogical perspective, to what he took to be Heidegger's overly abstract ontology. As he later tells Werner Kraft: "Particularly important minds today built a world above which does not accord with reality, and that is a dangerous game; one sees it in Heidegger."[126]

Another tacit challenge to Heidegger can be found in Buber's resort to Heraclitus amid a discussion of Taoist, Hindu, and modern mystical approaches in the 1958 essay "What is Common to All."[127] In 1954, Heidegger published an analysis of Heraclitus' fragment 50, which he renders: "Habt ihr nicht mich, sondern den Sinn vernommen, so ist es weise, im gleichen Sinn zu sagen: *Eins* ist Alles" – "When you have listened not to me but to the Meaning, it is wise within the same Meaning to say: *One* is All."[128] The main insight Heidegger draws from this is the notion of logos as "gathering-laying together." Logos is that which "lets things lie together before us" in a relational coherent unity, so that they are disclosed as what they are – "the *presencing* of that which lies before us into unconcealment."[129] This insight is built upon Heidegger's notion of truth as *a-letheia*, which is equated to logos: "Logos is in itself both unconcealment and concealment. Logos is the A-letheia." In his 1958 essay, Buber, who confesses that "ich halte Heideggers Heraklit-Interpretation für absolut falsch," appeals to the pre-Socratic sage in support of his own dialogical ontology, and in so doing implicitly counters Heidegger's reading.[130] Upon examination, it can be confirmed that what Gadamer said of Heidegger, that what he found in ancient Greek texts "was certainly himself," applies to Buber as well. For Buber utilizes Heraclitus' fragment 88, "the waking have a single cosmos in common," and fragment 2, "one must follow that which is common," in order to pronounce the uniting common sphere opened up by human sociability and relationality: "'the common' is the sustaining category for Heraclitus. It enables him . . . to grasp and confirm as a spiritual reality [human] being-with-another [*Miteinandersein*], the full mutuality of human being."[131] Through Heraclitus' fragments, Buber attempts to explicate ontologically the expanded I–Thou relation of the togetherness of We – a notion which in *What Is Man?* was said to be unanchorable in Heidegger's

[126] Kraft, *Gespräche mit Martin Buber*, 36.
[127] Buber, "What Is Common to All," 79–99.
[128] *GA* 7, 213/Heidegger, *The Metaphysical Foundations of Logic*, 59.
[129] Ibid., 62, 63; Cf. *SZ* §7. B.
[130] Buber to Friedmann, 11 August 1951, *Briefwechsel* vol. III, 291.
[131] Buber, "What Is Common to All," 80. Translation amended.

individualistic framework. Repeating this judgment, Buber explicitly contrasts his teaching of We with "what Kierkegaard designates as the 'crowd' and Heidegger designates as 'das Man'" – although for some reason the reference to Heidegger is omitted in the English translation.[132] This common We, the genuine communion of fellow humans within which being is bound up, is what is expressed in Heraclitus' cryptic proclamations. With an eye to Heidegger, Buber relates that "Heraclitus' teaching accepts the being of beings [*das Sein des Seienden*] in all its manifoldness and knows no other harmony than that which arises out of its tensions," but nevertheless "he finds the meaning of being [*den Sinn des Seins*] not in the ground of separateness but in what is common to all."[133] In Buber's appropriation, the unsurmountable *polemos* between concealment and unconcealment that Heidegger finds expressed in Heraclitus gives way to an underlying common logos enacted in the live moment of essential dialogue. In this moment, the manifoldness of being is exposed in its ultimate unified nature.[134]

Both Buber's and Heidegger's notions of logos seek to account for the surplus of meaning of being, and there is no doubt that both also aim to ward off the established Christian legacy of *Logos Christi*. But the disparity between the ontological and the anthropological interests once again comes to the fore, as do the diverging perspectives on the possibility of ontological presence and ultimate synthesis. Heidegger's Heraclitus brings into focus the juncture of revealing and concealing in the event of being which takes hold over humans, while for Buber it is the togetherness of fellow humans in their determination of being's meaning that is betrayed by the enigmatic Greek thinker.

It should be recalled that Heidegger's reading of Heraclitus is anchored in two convictions. The first, that language is a repository of previously undetected meanings that can be revealed through a rather idiosyncratic technique of exegesis. The second, that the pre-Socratics had an originary attentiveness to being uncontaminated by the history of metaphysics, and that while they are, at the same time, part of that history, they present themselves as particularly valuable sources for thinking beyond metaphysics. Buber shares neither of these presuppositions, and thus his resort to Heraclitus demands clarification. His attraction to the pre-Socratic thinker around this time is linked to the idea of "the common" that he seeks to

---

[132] Ibid., 96.   [133] Ibid., 93. Translation amended.
[134] *Introduction to Metaphysics*, 64–66.

develop. When Maurice Friedman tells Buber of affinities he identifies between his dialogical thinking and Heidegger, Buber objects to "bringing my thought closer to Heidegger, to whom I stand in opposition more than ever." He adds: "although I feel myself as in the days of my youth, and even more, near to Heraclitus whom he treats as his father."[135] Notwithstanding the pull to Heraclitus, purporting to resurrect the prophetic and Hasidic attitude is quite different from emulating Heidegger in reclaiming a Greek thinker as a moment of originary thinking – especially given the fact that elsewhere he posits the Greek account of logos *as presented by Heraclitus* and taken up as the Word by the "Hellenizing Gospel of John," *in contrast* to the Hebrew Bible's account.[135] Seemingly aware of this, Buber discursively links Heraclitus to "the Israelite prophets" and claims that the pre-Socratic too "arose from the heart of the East." He also justifies the appeal to Heraclitus by noting that it "is for the sake of a specific need of our time," which is, above all, confronting the self-glorified and absolutized individualism – a likely allusion to Heidegger.[137] Also problematic, as Buber himself points out, is looking for ontological grounding in Heraclitus' self-contained cosmos where "there is no real transcendence."[138] Alluding to Deuteronomy, Buber admits: "No salvation is in sight for us, however, if we are not able again 'to stand before the face of God' in all reality as a We – as it is written in that faithful speech that once from Israel . . . started on its way." To fill the lack of theological a priori, Buber turns once again to Hölderlin and interprets him in contrast to Heidegger: "In our age," he exclaims, "this We standing before the divine countenance has attained its highest expression through the poet, through Friedrich Hölderlin."[139] While the polemic against Heidegger is implicit in this article, it is telling that Buber buttresses his vision of the ontology of the We by drawing on two steadfast sources of the German philosopher.

Perhaps the most critical engagement with Heidegger takes place in the essay "The Word that Is Spoken" (presented 1959, published 1960). In this piece, written as a late contribution to a conference he organized

---

[135] Buber to Friedman, *Briefwechsel, vol. III*, 291.
[136] Buber, "Biblical Humanism," 215. Here Buber contrasts the Heraclitian and Johnian meaning of logos as an eternal, preexisting "word" with the understanding of the Hebrew Bible, according to which the "word" "comes to be, it is spoken . . . there is no word that is not spoken; the only being of a word resides in its being spoken." As we shall immediately see, this anticipates his debate with Heidegger over the essence of language.
[137] Buber, "What Is Common to All," 87.   [138] Ibid., 99.   [139] Ibid.

together with Heidegger, Buber develops a theory of language as a concealed response to Heidegger.[140] Underlying this effort is a covert reissuing of the confrontation between the Heideggerian poet and the biblical prophet. Buber approaches the nature of language in "The Word that Is Spoken" through the intersubjective realm of "the between" by focusing on the actual occurrence of language, that is, "its spokenness, or rather being spoken – the word that is spoken." In this context, the emphasis on the spokennes of language is brought as a response to Heidegger's point that not humans but rather *"Die Sprache spricht."* Buber counters the "monological primal character of language" advanced by Heidegger by claiming that language is primarily address, actual dialogue between people in a situation. Dialogue thus holds ontological primacy over monologue: "language never existed before address; it could become monologue only after dialogue broke off or broke down."[141] As part of his effort to distinguish between his account of the nature of language and Heideggerian monologism, Buber develops a dialogical conception of poetry. In his commentaries on Hölderlin, which, as we have seen, Buber is familiar with, Heidegger writes: "poetry itself first makes language possible. Poetry is the primal language of a historical people. Thus the essence of language must be understood out of the essence of poetry."[142] Poetry reveals language in its radical nearness and complete otherness and draws attention to the happening of language itself. "The primary language is poetry as the founding of being," he writes.[143] The poet, aware of the force and limitation of language, can prompt others to have an experience with language and its working. With Heidegger's position no doubt in mind, Buber posits poetry as the manifestation of genuine language, understood as dialogue: "The poem is spokenness," he declares, "spokenness to the Thou, wherever this partner might be."[144] Also in the essay "Man and his Image-Work," itself an attempt to formulate an alternative to Heidegger's reflections on art from his dialogical perspective, Buber underscores the preeminence of poetry:

---

[140] Heidegger's lecture in this conference, "On the Way to Language" ("Der Weg zur Sprache") indirectly addresses Buber and will be discussed below. On this episode see Mendes-Flohr, "Martin Buber and Martin Heidegger." My interpretation of the implicit Buber–Heidegger exchange over "language" differs greatly from the one presented by Mendes-Flohr.

[140] Buber, "The Word that Is Spoken," 105.

[142] *GA* 4, 42/Heidegger, *Elucidations of Hölderlin's Poetry*, 60.   [143] Ibid, 61.

[144] Ibid., 108.

Poetry does not originate from one of the senses' standing over against the world, but from the primal structure of man as man ... poetry is not obedient to anything other than language, whether it calls and praises, narrates, or allows the happening between men to unfold in dialogue.[145]

In "The Word that Is Spoken," the Heideggerian poet comes under tacit reproof for overlooking the "personal texture of speech" at the heart of language, its location in "the between" of the speakers. "Were there no more genuine dialogue, there would also be no more poetry."[146] On the other hand, Heidegger's anonymous and monological account of language lacks "the ontological basic presupposition of conversation" and hence lacks "the otherness, or more concretely, the moment of surprise" that exists in dialogue. Similarly hinting to Heidegger and putting his vocabulary into use, Buber makes the point that

many modern – and that means often de-Socratizing – philosophers have fallen, with the totality of their thought world, into a monologizing hubris, something which rarely happens to a poet. But this monologism, which, to be sure, is well acquainted with the existential but not with the existentiell, means in all its conjuring force the starkest menace of disintegration.[147]

This critique is directed in part against what Buber sees as Heidegger's general neglect of the ontic and concrete "existentiell," which generates an overly abstract character to his ontology. It is also a reproach of Heidegger's style of philosophizing. It appears that Buber senses that Heidegger perceives himself as the poet bringing forth the destiny of being. The "monologizing hubris" demonstrated when Heidegger violently imposes his views on the thinkers with which he is engaged in "dialogue" is "something which rarely happens to a poet." Heidegger, to be sure, did not see himself as a poet, and in *Contributions* he expresses his envy of "poets, who manage to capture the essential in a single, surveyable form."[148] But Buber here puts his finger on a controversial issue with respect to Heidegger's hermeneutics: his "violent" readings of thinkers of the past aiming at exposing their "unthought." This point is hinted at in the essay "Man and His Image-Work" as well, where Buber charges Heidegger's hermeneutics for being "so grandiose a deed of violence."[149] This common critique underlies Buber's general assessment of Heidegger's interpretations of Hölderlin: the German poet simply does not say what Heidegger claims he does. In

---

[145] Buber, "Man and His Image-Work," 155.
[146] Buber, "The Word that Is Spoken," 101.   [147] Ibid., 103.
[148] Heidegger, *Contributions to Philosophy*, 47–48.
[149] Buber, "Man and His Image-Work," 142–143.

the context of this critique, it is worth mentioning that on May 8, 1962, Ludwig Binswanger, a psychiatrist who developed a psychotherapy based on Heidegger's analysis of Dasein, wrote to Buber in protest against the accusation that Heidegger is involved in "monologizing hubris." To the contrary, Binswanger confirms, Heidegger is deeply committed to a "permanent dialogue" with the great thinkers of the past, as demonstrated for example in his study of Nietzsche. On May 14, Buber replies that "I cannot regard what you call 'permanent dialogue' *in concreto* as a dialogue at all. Dialogue in my sense implies of necessity the unforeseen, and its basic element is surprise, the surprising mutuality."[150] One can certainly be sympathetic to Buber's objection to the hermeneutical intensity, even arbitrariness, with which Heidegger conducts his philosophical investigations. But the analysis in the present chapter shows that the same accusation of "monological hubris" must be directed at Buber's interpretation of Heidegger as well. For his judgment of Heidegger is determined from the outset by the limitations of his own set of paradigms and hermeneutical lens, and lacks the dialogical openness to listen to what Heidegger is actually saying.

Buber's reflections on poetry offer him the opportunity to respond to Heidegger's idea of the co-belongingness of the truth and untruth. Recounting an ancient Indian myth about the blending of truth and falsehood, Buber explains that falsehood concerns the ambiguity of language, while truth emerges with the transparency of the spoken word. Dialogue, then, is the event of arrival at full clarity of language in its spokenness with another, that is, the establishment of truth. Yet Buber makes clear that by "truth" he means his biblically anchored *emuna*, in contrast to Heidegger's "Greek" idea of *aletheia*:

The truth that is concerned in this fashion is not the sublime "unconcealment" [*Unverborgenheit*] suitable to Being itself, the *aletheia* of the Greeks; it is the simple conception of truth of the Hebrew Bible, whose etymon means "faithfulness" [*Treue*], the faithfulness of man or the faithfulness of God.[151]

Echoing his earlier distinction between *pistis* and *emunah*, Buber unmistakably contrasts Heidegger's account of truth with his own biblically construed understanding. Dialogue, on his account, is not based on the disclosure of being in and through language, but on the biblical notion of

---

[150] Letters from May 8 and 14, 1962, Glatzer and Mendes-Flohr, *The Letters of Martin Buber*, 646–647.

[151] Buber, "The Word that Is Spoken," 110.

emunah, of *getreue Wahrheit*, enacted in the dialogical immediacy of interhuman and human–divine embrace. Language springs from actual, live situations. This understanding of language is emblematically reflected and crystalized in the prophetic utterance, which is proclaimed in an actual living situation. "Not things but situations are primary," Buber announces. "And if Stefan Georg's saying that no thing exists for which the word is wanting ['*Kein ding sei, wo das wort gebricht*'] may hold true for things, it is inapplicable to the situations that man is given to know before he comes to know the things."[152] The contrast between "situations" and "things" with allusion to Stefan Georg in the context of a polemic against Heidegger is a covert reference to a lecture by Heidegger on Georg's poem "Das Wort" from *Das Neue Reich*, which Buber attended.[153]

In dialogue, moreover, there is a convergence of the achievement of clarity and truth in language and the attainment of authenticity and truth of human existence. "The relation between meaning and saying," Buber professes, "points us to the relation between the intended unity of meaning and saying, on the one side, and that between meaning and saying and the personal existence, on the other side."[154] The transition from ambiguity to transparency in dialogue is concomitant to the existential fulfillment achieved by ascending from the I–It to the I–Thou encounter. "Genuine dialogue," he states elsewhere, "is an ontological sphere which is constituted by the authenticity of being."[155] The ontological stakes of this moment are obviously high, for "the fate of being is determined through the speaking of the word."[156] But for Buber, "being" is above all human existence, and thus, once again contesting Heidegger's reading of Hölderlin, he stresses: "We *are* a dialogue" – "Hölderlin says not 'since we are in dialogue'; he says and means: since we are a dialogue. The explanation 'since the gods bring us into the dialogue' (Heidegger) is simply not what is said. We ourselves are dialogue: we are spoken . . . Our being-spoken is our Dasein."[157] Human existence is poetic inasmuch as it

---

[152] Ibid., 106.

[153] Kraft, *Gespräche mit Martin Buber*, 80; GA 12, 147–204/ Heidegger, *On the Way to Language*, 57–108.

[154] Buber, "The Word that Is Spoken," 109. A similar exposition of the crystalization of the language–being correspondence in the notion of logos is found in "What Is Common to All."

[155] Buber, "Elements of the Interhuman," 76.

[156] Buber, "The Word that Is Spoken," 119.

[157] This line from Hölderlin's *Hyperion* concludes the original German version of "What Is Common to All" but is absent from the English version. Buber, "Seit ein Gespräch wir sind," 83–85.

cultivates a mode of being marked by an openness to the dialogical encounter in "the faithfulness of man or the faithfulness of God."[158] Humans are thus truthful – authentic – when they dwell poetically, that is, prophetically, that is, dialogically.

Buber's conception of language is illuminated by Heidegger's "Way to Language,"[159] which is itself, in part, a response to "The Word that Is Spoken." Setting the tone for the entire discussion is a quote from Novalis's *Monologue*, with which the essay begins. Heidegger interprets Novalis's title to mean "language speaks solely with itself." Signaling toward a very different understanding than Buber's of what language is, Heidegger asserts that language must be approached mindfully, due to a particular hermeneutical tangle. Language is not something that can be looked at from the outside, from a position beyond language; "We human beings remain committed to and within the being of language." This is not merely because we speak of language by means of language, that is, through words, sentences, and so forth, but because "[t]he essence of language cannot be anything linguistic," as he affirms elsewhere.[160] For Heidegger, language is not "a stock of words and rules" but an ontological structure, a prelinguistic, originary, world-disclosive feature, orienting us toward things that emerge as an organized setting within which their meaning and importance is obtained.[161] Through a dynamic of disclosure and concealment, it gathers and lays out references into a coherent, unified context, stabilizing meaning and relations in such a way that things can be made known. Language is the "house of being," as he famously puts it in "Letter on Humanism," as it provides the underlying structure of meanings that allow beings to be intelligible to us as what they are. In the "soundless voice" of language's monologue, certain things and possibilities stand out as salient, relevant, and meaningful, while others recede, and others still lack the opening to be disclosed and remain concealed altogether.

It is for this reason that Heidegger cannot agree that the fact that language could be used dialogically between people means that dialogue

---

[158] Buber, "The Word that is Spoken," 110.
[159] GA 12, 241–257/Heidegger, *On the Way to Language*, 111–136.
[160] GA 12, 108/Heidegger, *On the Way to Language*, 30.
[161] See Wrathall, *Heidegger and Unconcealment*, 119–155. Wrathall argues, I believe convincingly, that Heidegger does not hold an account of "linguistic constitutionalism" as argued, for example, by Lafont, *Heidegger, Language, and World Disclosure*, 7. See also Gregory, *Heidegger's Path to Language*; Powell, "The Way to Heidegger's 'Way to Language,'" 180–200; Ziarek, "Giving Its Word: Event (as) Language."

is the essence of language. In Buber's view, human dialogue has ontological priority because humans *have* language; they guide it along through the "between" of their encounter. Language as dialogue is a response, from within, to human encounter. For Heidegger, however, the dialogue of which Buber speaks is only possible because language is the "saying" or "showing" that essences and lets things appear as something about which humans can conduct a dialogue. For us to speak, Heidegger insists, we must first listen; not to the other person, but to language itself. Responding to Buber and echoing his phrasing, Heidegger states: "Every spoken word is already an answer: counter-saying, coming to the encounter, listening to Saying."[162] In this respect, language is "the foundation of human being,"[163] leading humans along in its monological self-saying. "We do not merely speak *the* language," Heidegger points out, "we speak *from out of it*."[164] This is possible only because as humans, we already belong to and within language: "We hear Saying only because we belong within it." As such, language can be said to be a monologue of two, or a dialogue of one: it is the wellspring that "precedes" our ordinary language. In "Hebel – der Hausfreund" (1957) Heidegger conveys this line of thought: "it is language, not man, which genuinely speaks. Man speaks only to the extent that he in each case co-responds to language."[165]

In "On the Way to Language" Heidegger pointedly sets himself against the tradition, extending from the Greeks to Wilhelm von Humboldt, that perceives language in terms of the activity of human speech. For Heidegger, this account of language does not actually look at language *as* language; rather, it looks *to* language and *through* it in order to arrive at its real end – understanding the human who uses it. It does not seek "to speak about speech *qua* speech." As such, it is too anthropocentric and metaphysical. Buber, who utilizes Humboldt's distinction between language as firm system (*ergon*) and language as a living human phenomenon of speech (*energiea*) in his own account, and who refers favorably to Humboldt in his lecture, is heir to this legacy of language as the product of subjectivity. It is thus not surprising to find that in "A Dialogue on Language," the figure representing Heidegger notes to his Japanese interlocutor: "the much discussed I/Thou experience, too, belongs within the metaphysical sphere of subjectivity."[166]

---

[162] Heidegger, *On the Way to Language*, 129.   [163] Ibid., 112.
[164] Ibid.,124. Translation amended.
[165] Heidegger, *Hebel – Friend of the House*, 99/GA 13, 148.
[166] Heidegger, *On the Way to Language*, 35–36.

While Heidegger stresses monologue and implicitly criticizes Buber's notion of language as ontic dialogue or relation, it should not be concluded from this that Heidegger perceives language as non-relational. To the contrary. Through his account of language his fundamentally relational ontology comes to light. Time and again in his essay he deliberately employs the terms – in this context recognizably Buberian – *Dialog* and *Gespräch*, only to reconceptualize and transvalue their meaning. Already in *Sein und Zeit* he introduces the function of "understanding" as the disclosure of entities unto their possibilities by projecting them on a world. In this disclosive modality, understanding involves projecting an entity into a web of meaningful interconnected possibilities that hang together. Understanding is a referential structure: For example, I am a basketball player by virtue of my relation to, and projected possibilities onto, other entities, activities, and possibilities, such as coaches, trainings, shoes, rules, fans, injuries, championships, and so forth. Heidegger continues to hold a version of relational ontology later as well when he argues that an entity only *is* by virtue of its gathered and stabilized relationships to other entities, contexts, activities. "Language is, as saying that forms the world's ways, the relation of all relations. It relates, maintains, proffers, holds, and keeps them."[167] The relationalism of Heidegger's account of language is conveyed in his close reading of Georg's poem "Das Wort," a reflection on the poet's transforming relation to language and being, to which Buber alludes, as we have seen above.[168] The "word" is not a signifier in common language but logos, that which relates and gathers being into stable meanings. When Heidegger explains that "The word *is* the clearing [*die Lichtung*] of being itself"[169] or that "The word makes [*bedingt*] the thing into a thing," he gestures toward the *conditioning* of language which allows beings to show up as what they are, the dynamic of a thing coming into itself, *be-dingt*. This understanding of "words" as ontological relations rather than representations is what Heidegger referred to when he states in "Letter on Humanism" that the question of God can only be approached seriously when we are "able to hear and understand all these words" – Holy, divinity, God – "carefully."

[167] Heidegger, *On the Way to Language*, 107.
[168] On Heidegger's relational ontology and Georg, see Wrathall, H*eidegger and Unconcealment*, 119–155; and see also Backman, "The Transitional Breakdown of the Word."
[169] GA 74, 72.

From Heidegger's perspective, the goal of the Buberian dialogical moment is both overambitious and counterproductive. The insoluble dialectic of presencing and absencing performed by originary language entails that Heidegger can make little sense of ultimate transparency as the goal of ordinary language as set by Buber. "The poetic work speaks out of an ambiguous ambiguousness," an ambiguity that is inexhaustible and insurmountable. It is, moreover, not a contingent feature, but the condition, and conditioning, of language. In "On the Way to Language" he confirms: "the language of our dialogue might constantly destroy the possibility of saying that of which we are speaking."[170] Thus, Heidegger interprets Hölderlin's "since we are dialogue"– "even when man's ability to speak is present and is put into practice, the essential event of language – conversation – does not necessarily occur," followed by the statement Buber criticized above.[171] This is intimately tied to "the essence of being," which for Heidegger "is such that, as a self-revealing, being reveals itself in a way such that a self-concealing, that means, a withdrawal – belongs to this revealing."[172] Though the concealing unconcealment of being, beings are disclosed by means of concealment of alternative ways of disclosure. Expecting to reach a final theoretical grasp overlooks the "concealed fullness" from which beings are disclosed as what they are. Recognizing the unspeakableness of the becoming-speakable of entities opens up the possibility of having an experience with language. Heidegger seemingly has Buber's idea of the spokenness of language in mind when he states:

Everything spoken stems in a variety of ways from the unspoken, whether this be something not yet spoken, or whether it be what must remain unspoken in the sense that it is beyond the reach of speaking. Thus, that which is spoken in various ways begins to appear as if it were cut off from speaking and the speakers, and did not belong to them, while in fact it alone offers to speaking and to the speakers whatever it is they attend to, no matter in what way they stay within what is spoken of the unspoken.[173]

The reconstruction of the concealed Heidegger–Buber debate over the essence of language presented here demonstrates once again the differing applications of their parallel concerns. Both reject representational models of language and caution against overlooking its essential "happening," and both find this "happening" to unfold not simply in a unitary manner but relationally, in the between. But what for Heidegger is derivative and

---

[170] Heidegger, *On the Way to Language*, 15.
[171] Heidegger, *Elucidations of Hölderlin's Poetry*, 57.
[172] *GA* 10, 121/Heidegger, *The Principle of Reason*, 25.   [173] Ibid., 120.

metaphysical, for Buber is concrete, and what for Buber is abstract and metaphysical, for Heidegger is non-metaphysical and most urgent.

Much distinguishes the anonymous and faceless ontological account of language presented by Heidegger from the personal and interpersonal account of language presented by Buber.[174] For the present discussion, when we take into consideration Heidegger's account of language, another aspect of the misattribution of magic emerges: The definitive correspondence between human language and being which allows magic to create the link between sign and signified, is far removed from Heidegger's position. The notion that being and language can be completely accessible, unconcealed, and present-at-hand in such a way that humans can control them is intelligible according to Buber's program, but completely foreign to Heidegger's manner of thinking. Buber crowns the poetic, but "incomparably still more" the "messagelike [*botschaftsartigen*] saying" – *Botschaft* being a term frequently employed by theologians at the time to denote the prophetic or divine Word – but Heidegger claims that "the word is a hint."[175] Turning Buber's structure on its head, Heidegger asserts in the essay "Language" that "Poetry proper is never merely a higher mode [*melos*] of everyday language. It is rather the reverse: everyday language is a forgotten and therefore used-up poem, from which there hardly resounds a call any longer.'"[176] In Buber's account, language belongs to the present moment and hence lacks hermeneutic mediation, while for Heidegger, language essences ecstatically, historically. The "moment of surprise" in language does not emerge from the not-yet-known response of one's interlocutor, but from language's "releasing into the open whatever might be said" wherein the partners in dialogue "confidently entrust themselves to the hidden drift."[177] The "otherness" Buber proclaims absent in Heidegger's account is in truth the more acute otherness of what is left concealed, rather than

---

[174] One might find an intermediating position in Paul Celan, the Romanian-Jewish-German poet who was deeply influenced by both men. Celan sides with Heidegger that language speaks to the poet and that the poem, ultimately, exists in solitude, but also with Buber that the self of the poet is profoundly present in the poem, and that a poem, while in solitude, is "on the way" toward an other, a despairing call or plea for dialogue. Celan, *Gesammelte Werke in fünf Bänden*, 186. On Celan's troubled relationship with Heidegger, see Lyon, *Paul Celan and Martin Heidegger*. An early version of Celan's famous poem "Todnauberg" began with the Hölderlinian citation "Seit ein Gespräch wir sind." See Gellhaus "Seit ein Gespräch wir sind . . . "; Lebovic, "Near the End."

[175] *On the Way to Language*, 27. For example, Karl Barth's *Die Botschaft von der freien Gnade Gottes* (1947).

[176] Ibid., 208.   [177] Ibid., 30.

the merely not-yet-spoken. In his meditations on Georg's poem "Das Wort," it is toward this understanding of the last stanza, "where word is lacking no thing may be," that Heidegger signals.

The examination of aspects of Buber's ontological scheme as an alternative to Heidegger illuminates the fact that the fullness of this philosophical encounter lies beyond the framing of dialogism versus monologism. In his thinking, Buber seeks to salvage the West's monolithic and monological manner of thought by pointing to the implicit multivalence and tension within reality. The numerous dualisms that mark his writings testify to this. But for all of Buber's talk of the "between," duality, dialogue, and relation, his scheme is oriented toward ultimate synthesis. This synthesis, of course, does not represent a Hegelian climax, the I–Thou encounter always founders back to the I–It, and Buber insists on an apophatic element in the human–divine meeting. Nevertheless, the openness to the multeity and flux of being that constitutes the dialogical disposition is undergirded by a transcendental wholeness that makes possible the attainment of full transparency, presence, and encounter – even if it is only momentary, fleeting, and rare. It acknowledges the dimension of It but strives to the Thou; emerges from the historical but points toward pure presence. Even poetry strives toward the "message-like" saying. In this respect, the duality and multiplicity that feature prominently in Buber's dialogical thinking presuppose a monotheistic unity of being, while the monologism of Heidegger, with its interaction between presencing and absencing and with the ec-statically temporal features of Dasein and language, reveal an unsynthesizable dialogism, a dialectic that cannot promise full transparency or arrival. Since there is no stepping out of the hermeneutical circle and being is always also concealed, Heidegger's scheme can make no sense of "ultimate unconcealment" as its goal. Heidegger confers an ontology of non-synthesis while Buber strives for wholeness and higher unity. Buber's debt to the metaphysical ontological tradition is testified in his non-ecstatic account of selfhood, climactic moment of presence, and unmediated account of language. In the final analysis, the conceptuality framing Buber's call to "dwell prophetically" remains within the ontological constrictions that Heidegger's poetic dwelling seeks to overcome.

CONCLUSION

According to Buber, the Heideggerian account of Dasein has dire existential, theological, moral, and political ramifications. Heidegger's existential analysis in *Sein und Zeit* as well as his urge to "dwell poetically" in his later writings reflect a monological existence confined to a hermetical imma-nence, lacking the possibility of a full and unmediated encounter with the plenitude of the other and God. While it is questionable whether Heidegger would identify himself in these polemical representations, Buber puts forth his dialogical worldview as the Jewish-biblical alternative to this monolo-gical outlook. Buber offers the prophet as the model of truthful and dialo-gical existence, driven by a religious, political, and ethical impulse and animated by trust and poetical openness toward the possibility of an encounter with a Thou at any given moment. This, Buber believes, is the message that can reinvigorate the precipitating decline of the modern world, a decline of which Heidegger's philosophy is both a symptom and a glaring manifestation. By examining his efforts to promote his dialogical attitude both before and after the war, as well as the related endeavor to counteract Heidegger's position, it can be suggested that Buber perceived himself as a modern-day prophet, performatively addressing the world from within a situation, combating the idolatry of false prophets and proclaiming the salvific message of prophetic dwelling. As we shall see in the following chapter, also Leo Strauss perceives Heidegger's philosophy to be the exemplar of the modern crisis. Yet for Strauss, it is not Heidegger's monologism that typifies the crisis that ought to be overcome, but his assault on "truth," and its ramifications for the possibility of political philosophy and authentic Judaism.

5

The *Destruktion* of Jerusalem: Leo Strauss on Heidegger

INTRODUCTION

Heidegger's pivotal impact on Leo Strauss's thought is widely acknowledged. As one commentator notes: "One could almost say that Heidegger is the unnamed presence to whom or against whom all of Strauss's writings are in large part directed."[1] This view is confirmed by Strauss himself, who proclaimed that "the only question of importance ... is the question whether Heidegger's teaching is true or not."[2] While much has been written on Strauss and Heidegger, here I wish to focus on the intersections of Strauss's understanding of Heidegger and Judaism. The chapter's argument is threefold: first, that Strauss's lifelong grappling with matters Jewish are importantly marked by the philosophical, theological, and political challenges reflected in Heidegger; second, that his engagement with Heidegger unfolds within the context of his reflections on the Jewish engagement with modernity, understood as a project indebted to the Christian horizon; and third, that while he sees Heidegger as representing the "danger" and high point of the modern crisis in both philosophy and religion, it is, paradoxically, Heidegger who offers the theoretical breakthrough that directs out of the crisis.

Strauss's initial personal and philosophical encounter with Heidegger took place when he was a young Jewish student, in the momentous Weimar years.[3] In 1921, Strauss submitted his dissertation on

---

[1] Smith, "'Destruktion' or Recovery?" 346. On Heidegger and Strauss, see the insightful work by Velkley, *Heidegger, Strauss and the Premises of Philosophy*; Mewes, "Leo Strauss and Martin Heidegger," 105–120; Ward, "Political Philosophy and History," 273–295.

[2] Strauss, "Existentialism," 305.

[3] On Strauss's early years, see Sheppard, *Leo Strauss and the Politics of Exile*; Janssens, *Between Athens and Jerusalem*; Tanguay, *Leo Strauss*.

Friedrich Heinrich Jacobi, written under the supervision of Ernst Cassirer. He would later remark that Cassirer "was a distinguished professor of philosophy but he was no philosopher."[4] We shall see, however, that by formulating his critique of Heidegger in terms of historicism and nihilism, Strauss essentially echoes his *Doktorvater*. By contrast, during the 1920s Strauss was completely taken by Heidegger. According to a recollection of one of Strauss's friends of youth, "Heidegger was the only living philosopher about whom Strauss regularly spoke."[5] As was the case with Hannah Arendt and Herbert Marcuse, it was particularly Heidegger's analysis of Aristotle that left an indelible mark on the young Strauss and in many respects put him on the track to his later philosophical innovations.[6] Strauss himself later attested that on one occasion he related to Rosenzweig that in comparison to Heidegger, the admired Max Weber looked "like an orphan child." Moving to Freiburg for a postdoctoral year, Strauss attended Heidegger's lectures, and although not part of the close circle of his students, he followed him back to Marburg. Strauss ultimately fled Germany and eventually settled in the United States, but throughout his entire intellectual life, he would repeatedly note the great impression Heidegger had had on him.[7] He claims to have ceased to take interest in Heidegger "for about two decades" after the latter's siding with the Nazi Party, but recent publication of previously unknown material, including various lectures and correspondences, shows that while taking a back seat, his occupation with Heidegger persisted throughout this period as well, and indeed continued until the very end of his life.

ATHENS, JERUSALEM, AND THE CRISIS OF MODERNITY

Strauss is known for asserting that two compelling yet distinct attempts to address the ultimate question of the life worth living have animated the West. The determinative question is this:

whether men can acquire knowledge of the good without which they cannot guide their life individually or collectively by the unaided effort of their natural powers, or whether they are dependent for that knowledge on Divine Revelation. No alternative is more fundamental than this: human guidance or divine guidance.[8]

---

[4] Strauss, "Kurt Riezler (1882–1955)," 246.   [5] Udoff, "On Leo Strauss," 26–27n63.
[6] See, for example, Chacón, "Reading Strauss from the Start."
[7] Strauss, "A Giving of Accounts," 461.   [8] Strauss, *Natural Right and History*, 74.

The one advocates obedience to divine law as the proper life path, while the other promotes the path of life based on human wisdom. Symbolically formulated through the binary of Athens and Jerusalem, these two competing alternatives promote incompatible accounts of human perfection, reason, morality, and law. They derive from divergent assumptions and are conceptually irreconcilable, but since at times they concur in implication, they can be practically coordinated. While there is ample evidence that Strauss perceived himself as a citizen of Athens, his anti-dogmatic understanding of the task of philosophy behooved him to second-guess the claims of Athens and take the claims of Jerusalem seriously. As he writes:

No one can be both a philosopher and a theologian, or, for that matter, some possibility which transcends the conflict between philosophy and theology, or pretends to be a synthesis of both. But every one of us can be and ought to be either one or the other, the philosopher open to the challenge of theology, or the theologian open to the challenge of philosophy.[9]

In Strauss's view, upholding and engaging with the dialectical tension between Athens and Jerusalem is the secret of the West's vitality. However, this is no longer the case in the modern world, due to its continuous repression of this conflict, resulting in an overall crisis.

This fundamental schematization of the forms of life of Athens and Jerusalem is comprehensively articulated in Strauss's mature works, but its seeds are present in his thinking from early on. From its very beginning, Strauss diagnoses in his first book, *Spinoza's Critique of Religion* (1930), modern thought has posited that the Enlightenment has successfully refuted revelation.[10] Athens has been announced victorious over Jerusalem. Strauss claims that the basis of the modern rejection of revelation is the Epicurean idea that the liberation from fear of the gods is the path to *eudaimonia*. For modern Epicureanism, it is modern reason and science that bestows this liberating knowledge. Yet Strauss's scholarly explorations into the works of Spinoza and other early founders of the modern enterprise failed to find a *refutation* of revelation. Utilizing a *factum brutum* conception of revelation as put forth by Barth and Rosenzweig, Strauss posits revelation to be miraculous and thus irrefutable.[11] The all-encompassing modern faith in reason and science as the standards of truth, he submits, is precisely that – faith, a *petitio*

---

[9] Strauss, "Progress or Return," 116.   [10] Strauss, *Die Religionskritik Spinozas*.
[11] Strauss, "A Giving of Accounts," 460. On Strauss's attraction to dialectical theology en route to his mature thought, see Moyn, "From Experience to Law"; Lazier, *God*

principii, an unproved decision, reflecting a *will* against revealed religion. Strauss announces that modern thought is problematically established on unsteady grounds, for in its center lay a failed confrontation with the question of revelation. The fundamental question of the life worth living, the cardinal concern of political philosophy, is no longer raised, even though the dispute between reason and revelation was never settled. This dispute is as open as it was in the past, and ever so pressing. For this reason, Strauss calls modern philosophy into question and seeks to reactivate the quarrel between reason and revealed religion in order to return to the fundamental questions. He calls for a return to the wisdom of ancient and medieval philosophy, where a confrontation with this question takes place, as well as to take seriously what for him is the supreme embodiment of revealed religion, the Hebrew Bible and premodern Jewish monotheism. Reconsidering Athens and Jerusalem, he believes, can serve as the remedy of modern thought, which reached the peak of its crisis with the moral, intellectual, and political bankruptcy of Martin Heidegger.

HEIDEGGER AND THE MODERN JEWISH CRISIS

While Strauss's thinking undergoes significant developments over the years, the philosophical issues that occupy his early interwar writings, such as the crisis of liberalism and rationalism, and questions regarding God, revelation, political authority, and law, remain consistent themes throughout his life.[12] The philosophical innovations he is most known for, such as his discovery of the art of "exoteric writing," the precarious political relation between philosophy and the city, and the question of natural law and natural right, all draw on, and further develop, sustained outlooks that were shaped between the wars. In this respect, Strauss's thought as a whole can be seen as stemming fundamentally from his wrestling with what he would later call "the theologico-political predicament" as a German Jew during the Weimar years.

Strauss also testifies that "I believe I can say, without any exaggeration that since a very, very early time the main theme of my reflections has been what is called the 'Jewish question.'"[13] Underlying the "Jewish question," in his analysis, is a particular conception of religion

---

    Interrupted, 93–110. See also Meyer, "Leo Strauss and Religious Rhetoric (1924–1938)."

[12] For instance, Strauss, *Persecution and the Art of Writing*.

[13] Strauss, "Why We Remain Jews," 312.

matching liberal democracy, wherein "the bond of society is universal human morality, whereas religion (positive religion) is a private affair."[14] This privatization forced modern Judaism to compromise its traditional heritage, for which the stringent compartmentalization between internal (faith) and external (law) is foreign, and accommodate itself to the new political and theological conceptuality of the age. Strauss's investigations into the early founders of modern thought, and above all Spinoza, are best understood in light of this background and conceptual drive. The Dutch philosopher did not only level a blistering critique of revealed religion and was not only an early and important advocate of the modern liberal state, he also understood the two as interlinked, treating them as a *theologico-political* issue.[15] Moreover, Spinoza's defense of the modern liberal state is the condition of possibility for Jewish emancipation, and political Zionism, representing the failure of the liberal promises to the Jews, is also associated with Spinoza's name. Spinoza therefore offers an entry into the basic premises of the intellectual project of modernity, and at the same time he sheds light on the possibilities and limitations of modern Judaism. There is no rift between Strauss's "philosophical" and "Jewish" writings: his lifelong occupation with political philosophy is grounded in and touches on how he understood the very fabric of the modern Jewish experience and its conceptual underpinnings.

In a similar token, the terms and premises of Strauss's continuous encounter with Heidegger are shaped in the interwar years. His early attraction to Heidegger (and Carl Schmitt) betrays his proclivity toward a general anti-liberalism that furnished his desire to combat the "lack of reality" (*Entwirklichtheit*) of exilic Jewish existence. The mark of Heidegger can be discerned already in the context of his early aversion to assimilationist liberalism and his attraction to Zionism, when he uses the Heideggerian notion of *Daseinsmöglichkeit* to describe the conundrum of Jewish existence in exile.[16] This occurs within the wider context of Strauss's critique of the contemporary Jewish situation and his conviction that syntheses and reconciliations with Christian or German post-Enlightenment values are detrimental to both Judaism and Jews. "Germany," he writes, hinting to Hegel, is "the land of 'reconciliations' [*Versöhnungen*] and sublations [*Aufhebungen*]," but "as Jews we are

[14] Strauss, "Preface to the English Translation," 3.
[15] Spinoza, *Theologico-Political Treatise*.
[16] Sheppard, *Leo Strauss and the Politics of Exile*, 44.

radical: we do not like compromises."[17] The aversion to syntheses will
soon manifest itself in the assumption that the synthesis between philosophy and revelation is not the result of a bold confrontation between
competing compelling worldviews but of the avoidance of such
a confrontation. Syntheses on these matters amount to a conciliatory
self-effacing and are an obstacle to truth. Reconciling Jewish tradition
with modern values always consists in the denial of core aspects of
Judaism. "One cannot simply absorb somewhat deeper German things,"
Strauss writes in an early essay, "without absorbing along with them,
among other things, a dose of specifically Christian spirit."[18] However,
modern Judaism has done just that by incorporating the Enlightenment's
presuppositions. Translating this assessment into a piercing critique of
present-day Jewish society, Strauss judges that cultural and religious
Zionism, and especially liberal Judaism, are all hybrid systems that
cannot satisfyingly solve the tensions between Judaism and modernity.
They all offer modern secular solutions to a problem concerning revelation. His initial involvement with political Zionism also eventually
recedes for similar reasons.[19] The synthetic character of modern
Judaism attests to the victory of the modern Enlightenment and its
alleged refutation of revelation.

CHRISTIANITY, SECULARISM, AND HISTORICISM

One completely misunderstands Strauss's critique of modern Judaism if
one overlooks its intimate connection to his assessment of Heidegger as
a historicist, and his reflections on Christianity and secularization.[20]

Strauss does not mention Heidegger much in his early publications, but
his correspondences reveal the extent to which his thinking is impacted by,

---

[17] Strauss, "Biblical History and Science," in *Gesammelte Schriften*, vol. 2: 359. In English: *Leo Strauss: The Early Writings (1921–1932)*, 33.

[18] Ibid., 69.

[19] Although he continues to appreciate political Zionism. Muller, "Leo Strauss."

[20] My approach to Strauss is indebted to Batnitzky's rebuttal of Meier's claim that Strauss perceived the position of revelation as a refutable straw man serving the sole purpose of emboldening philosophy, and thus also as holding no fundamental difference between Jewish, Christian, and Islamic revelation. In fact, as Batnitzky shows, Strauss draws a distinction between the Jewish and Islamic conception of revelation as law and Christian revelation as doctrinal knowledge, and important corollaries derive from this distinction. See Batnitzky, "Leo Strauss's Disenchantment with Secular Society"; Batnitzky, *Leo Strauss and Emmanuel Levinas*, 117–139, and 238n39; Batnitzky, "Leo Strauss and the 'Theologico-Political Predicament,'" 41–62; Merrill, "Leo Strauss's Indictment of Christian Philosophy"; Pelluchon, "Strauss and Christianity."

and entangled with, Heidegger's. Strauss's correspondence with Gerhard Krüger from the early 1930s in particular sheds light on the manner in which he develops and consolidates his critical approach toward his former teacher.[21] Shortly after the publication of his book on Spinoza, which was written during his time as a research fellow in Jewish philosophy at the Academy for the Science of Judaism in Berlin, Strauss writes to Krüger on July 1, 1930 that the will against revealed religion that he identified among the early advocates of modern atheism – Machiavelli, Bruno, and Spinoza – "attains its most extreme representation in Nietzsche and reaches its completion in – *Being and Time*." What demonstrates the completion of the modern atheistic tradition in Heidegger's early masterpiece is the notion of "the call of consciousness." "I mean," he continues, "in the interpretation of the *call* of conscience, and in the answer given there to the question; *who* is calling? Only from Heidegger's Dasein-interpretation can an appropriate *atheistic* interpretation of the Bible be possible."[22] Two important points can be gleaned from this letter: First, Heidegger's philosophy is inserted into an analysis of modern critique of religion and ascribed a salient stage in its development. The analysis of Dasein in *Sein und Zeit* participates, indeed peaks a modern anti-religious tradition. This means that the condition of possibility of Heidegger's philosophy is the Enlightenment world that originated in Spinoza. Second, Strauss considers Heidegger an atheist. Both points are provocative. By terming his philosophy atheistic, Strauss denies the self-attested neutrality of Heidegger's philosophy; his existential framework is not uncommitted, for it advances a *positive* claim with respect to matters theological: atheism, indeed, *adequate* atheism. And by linking Heidegger to Spinoza's innovations and claiming his thought is the completion of this breakthrough, Heidegger's pretense of constituting a break from modern philosophy is discredited. Rather than overcoming it, Heidegger represents the "highest self-consciousness" of modern philosophy.

But there remains some unclarity with regards to Heidegger's status in Strauss's narrative. Insofar as only in Heidegger has an adequately atheistic account become available, then it follows that his predecessors' anti-religious philosophies were inadequately atheistic; revealed religion has not been fully overcome. If Heidegger is said to complete

---

[21] For a different interpretation of this correspondence, see Pangle, "The Light Shed on the Crucial Development of Strauss's Thought," 57–68.
[22] Letter to Krüger, July 1, 1930, *Gesammelte Schriften* 3: 380–381.

this tradition, then this must mean that he has overcome its insufficient atheism and successfully liberated himself from all remaining ties to its theistic past. Yet complication emerges when we consider the moment Strauss crowns as the "extreme representation" of the modern tradition of atheism: Heidegger's notion of the "call of consciousness," which Strauss interprets as a moment in which the idea of divine revelation from transcendence is replaced with the idea that Dasein is the caller of the immanent "call" from itself to itself, thereby presenting a godless depiction of human existence. It is, in other words, a moment in which a notion of discernible religious origin is stripped of its theistic content and presented anew as secular. Thus Strauss's emphasis: "*who* is calling?" – not God, but Dasein. Indeed, he later explicitly refers to Heidegger's "call" as an "atheistic interpretation of revelation" where "guilt, conscience, action, lose their meaning."[23] Can Heidegger's philosophy be said to constitute an "adequate atheistic interpretation," which unlike his predecessors is completely bereft of theistic determinations, when the notion chosen to prove its utter secularity is precisely one in which the remnants of its theological past are apparent and admitted? Can the Christian horizon of anti-religious modern philosophy be said to be overcome with a notion in which a mark of its Christian horizon is in plain sight? The continuation of the letter offers some clarification:

Religion will only have been overcome when it can be adequately interpreted atheistically. Thus: The Enlightenment's victory, i.e. the victory of the "scientific worldview" – by which I *only* mean the loss of the possibility of believing in miracles – is defensible only on the basis of a certain *attitude*, not on the basis of this worldview itself.

Religion, it appears, has *not yet* received an adequate atheistic interpretation, and the Enlightenment's victory cannot be defended by philosophical argumentation. Heidegger's atheism is thus the most radical manifestation of modern philosophy, but it is a manifestation of its still-inadequate atheism nonetheless.

---

[23] In a letter to Eric Voegelin, dated June 4, 1951, in Emberley and Cooper, eds., *Faith and Political Philosophy*, 88–89. Strauss's repeated evocation of the Heideggerian motif of "the call" sheds important light on his attitude toward Christianity and his conceptualization of historicism, experientialism, and secularism. On this, see Herskowitz, "The Call." For an alternative analysis, see Meier, "Death as God." Following Meier are McIlwain, "'The East within Us': Leo Strauss's Reinterpretation of Heidegger," and Vega, "'God Is Death': The Oblivion of Esotericism and Stimmungen in Leo Strauss's Heidegger."

It is important to see that Strauss's concern with Heidegger's atheism is not merely an intellectual exercise, but rather driven by his existential conundrum as a Jew in a modern world. As he reveals in this letter, his Spinoza book was an attempt to clarify his own disbelief and to *distinguish* it from Heidegger's atheism. Strauss could not believe in God, but he felt he must justify himself "before the forum of the Jewish tradition ... simply because I hold it to be unacceptable that I abandon out of recklessness and convenience a matter for which my ancestors took upon themselves everything conceivable."[24] He thus set out to "gain clarity about the various reasons for atheism," and his exploration into Spinoza's critique of religion constitutes this effort. But his conclusion is that Spinoza's critique misses the mark and consequently modern atheism, typified by Heidegger, as well as modern philosophy's sense of superiority, is based on shaky ground. It is celebrating a victory over a straw man. Strauss's search can be said to be after an adequate atheism, unlike its modern version. At the same time, he is not only after Athens, but also after Jerusalem, a revealed religion worthy of the confrontation with Athens.

Shortly after the completion of his book on Spinoza, Strauss comes to recognize that what is standing in the way of recouping the dispute between Athens and Jerusalem is the historical consciousness that emerged in the nineteenth century.[25] Historicism, for him, brought about the present crisis, and combating it is the most pressing intellectual challenge of the age. The challenge of repealing one's historicist commitments is portrayed by the image of leaving the "second cave," the cave below the Platonic cave. Only by leaving the cave of historicism can the task of philosophy, "the first cave," be approached, and only in so doing can the possibility of addressing the fundamental question, the question of the life worth living as raised in ancient Greece by Socrates, emerge again.

It is sometimes overlooked that Strauss locates the roots of this philosophical crisis in a *religious* source. What ultimately caused the departure from the Greek manner of thinking, he insists, is "Christian knowledge." On November 17, 1932, he writes to Krüger:

---

[24] Strauss, *Gesammelte Schriften* 3: 414.
[25] Strauss claimed this reorientation in his thought found its initial expression in his review of Carl Schmitt's *The Concept of the Political* (1932), although there are sufficient grounds to locate the beginning of this shift at the completion of his Spinoza book in 1928. See the collection of essays *Reorientation* (2014). On Strauss and Schmitt, see: Meier, *Carl Schmitt and Leo Strauss: The Hidden Dialogue*, and a critique of Meier's reading in Howse, *Leo Strauss: Man of Peace*, 25–50.

From its inception until Heidegger (*including* the latter), modern philosophy understood itself to be progress and progressive (with some justification, you will say, insofar as it had knowledge to impart that the Greeks did not possess: Christian knowledge. *Thus* the unradicality of modern philosophy: it thinks it can presume that the fundamental questions have already been answered, and can therefore "progress."[26]

He repeats this judgment almost a month and a half later, on December 27, when he writes: "The problem of the 'second cave' is the problem of historicism. The 'substantive and historical core' of historicism is . . . 'Christ's factual dominion over post-classical humanity.'"[27] The knowledge that Christianity introduced is the historical character of truth, that the human situation is determined not by universal and unchangeable principles, as per the Greeks, but in and by history. With this, Strauss is following Dilthey's conceptualization of the contribution of historical consciousness by early Christianity that we noted in Chapter 1. This "knowledge," Strauss relates, is the ground of modern historicism. For the focus on historicity ultimately led to the view that ahistorical eternity is an essentially empty category. Historicism, in Strauss's rendition, is the belief that human thought and existence are historically conditioned, contextualized, and relative to certain periods and places. It denies "nature," timeless principles and permanent characteristics, and accepts that right and justice are not objective or determined by nature but are mere convention and determined by arbitrary decision. Historicism, therefore, leads to relativism and nihilism.[28] It also baselessly presupposes progress insofar as it privileges the present perspective for judging the past. Driven by an unfounded sense of superiority, modern historicist thinking mistakenly assumes that the fundamental questions have already been answered, and therefore it can "progress." Importantly, Strauss claims that the modern historicist tendencies are epitomized in the centrality of Dasein's historicity and finitude in *Sein und Zeit* and in its method of *Destruktion*. "If historical

---

[26] Strauss, *Gesammelte Schriften* 3: 406. In English: Shell, ed., *The Strauss–Krüger Correspondence*, 40. Strauss does not close the parenthesis he opened in "with some justification."

[27] Ibid., 52–53.

[28] Velkley claims that Strauss obscures a significant common ground with Heidegger by portraying their dispute as centering on relativism. Velkley, *Heidegger, Strauss and the Premises of Philosophy*, 4. The charge of relativism is a common attack on the historicist outlook from the perspective of neo-Kantianism and Husserl, although it is important to remember that not one of the historicists considered himself a relativist. Beiser, "Historicism," 167.

consciousness isn't a carriage that one can stop whenever one pleases," he writes to Krüger on November 16, 1931, "then one arrives at a historical destruction of historical consciousness."[29] This position is soon termed "radical historicism," a code word for Heidegger's thought. In contrast to this, according to Strauss, proper philosophizing consists of raising the fundamental question in search for timeless truths, the validity of which transcend any given historical epoch. Historicism hampers this effort and forces upon philosophy an additional hindrance to its already difficult endeavor. "It seems to me," Strauss remarks in a draft to the December 27, 1932 letter to Krüger, "that modern philosophy, taken to its *conclusion*, leads to the point where Socrates begins." Alluding to Heidegger's role as the epitome of modern thought, he concludes, "modern philosophy proves to be a daunting 'destruction of tradition,' but not 'progress.'"[30]

According to Strauss, the overall denial of eternity and nature in Heidegger's work results in a moral depravity that is manifested politically in the latter's Nazism. While Strauss refuses to reduce Heidegger's philosophy to his political misdeeds – it would be "the most stupid thing I could do," he writes later, because Heidegger's political commitment "afford[s] too small a basis for the proper understanding of his thought" – at the same time he also identifies an "intimate connection" between Heidegger's thought and his embrace of Hitler.[31] "It was the contempt for these permanencies," Strauss writes,

which permitted the most radical historicist in 1933 to submit to, or rather to welcome, as a dispensation of fate, the verdict of the least wise and least moderate part of his nation, while it was in its least wise and least moderate mood, and at the same time to speak of wisdom and moderation.[32]

Likewise, he links the lack of enduring values and timeless principles to Heidegger's religious shortcomings. On September 5, 1933, after receiving from Löwith copies of Heidegger's *Rektoratsrede* and Karl Barth's "Theological Existence Today," where the theologian called to oppose the political powers of the time, Strauss replies:

[29] *The Strauss-Krüger Correspondence*, 29–30.   [30] Ibid., 48.
[31] Strauss, "Existentialism," 307.
[32] Strauss, "What Is Political Philosophy?" 26–27. It is not entirely clear what Strauss is referring to, but it may be to Heidegger's notion of *Verhaltenheit*, often translated as "reservedness" or "restraint." See Dahlstrom, *The Heidegger Dictionary*, 182–184. See also Strauss, *On Tyranny*, 212; Strauss, "Philosophy as Rigorous Science and Political Philosophy," 30; Strauss, "A Giving of Accounts," 461.

I like Barth very much, much better than H. It will be a long time before atheism is "competitive" with Christianity. Compare only B's open personal confession [*Bekenntnis*] to revelation with H's confession [*Bekenntnis*] to atheism behind the back of Nietzsche, and Barth's Christian critique of what is happening to H's uncritical submission [*kritikloser Unterwerfung*]. So I repeat my initial judgment of H.[33]

In contrast to Barth, whose critique of Nazism is theologically grounded, Strauss interprets Heidegger's notorious rectorial address and his "uncritical submission" to Hitler as rooted in his nihilistic atheism. Heidegger's atheistic amoralism cannot compete with religion in terms of the ethical posture it promotes.[34]

In the letter from December 27, Strauss picks up on some of the issues that were discussed previously in his correspondence with Krüger and asks what the current options are for someone, like himself, "who does *not* believe" and therefore would not be interested in subjecting himself to this Christian "dominion"? What is the right way of life completely unsupported by revelation? Two options present themselves: the first, represented by Heidegger's atheistic philosophy, and the second, the return to the question of natural law as raised by Greek philosophy.

The most proximate consequence – Heidegger's, among others – is: Christianity has brought to light facts about human life that were not known or not known sufficiently to classical philosophy; at least it understood these facts more *deeply* than the ancients; therefore the understanding of historicity first made possible by Christianity is a *deeper*, in this sense a *more radical* understanding of human beings ... Fundamentally: the philosophy still possible, and first made possible, after the decay of Christianity preserves the "truth" of Christianity ... I stated that the most proximate consequence of modern unbelief is the assumption: post-Christian philosophy represents a *progress* over against classical philosophy even if Christianity is not "*true.*"[35]

Strauss directly addresses the issue of secularization here: "Against this consequence," he continues, "there arises the suspicion that it always just leads to 'secularizations' that is, to positions that one cannot enter

---

[33] Strauss, *Gesammelte Schriften*, 3: 636.
[34] Elsewhere, Strauss expresses a common point, made by Buber and Levinas as well, about the link between Heidegger's philosophy and his politics: Heidegger's fixation with the loftiness of the ontological led him to indifference with respect to the concreteness of the ontic. To Alexandre Kojève he writes: "we both apparently turned away from Being to Tyranny because we have seen that those who lacked the courage to face the issue of Tyranny ... were forced to evade the issue of Being as well, precisely because they did nothing but talk of Being." Strauss, *On Tyranny*, 213.
[35] *The Strauss–Krüger Correspondence*, 52–53.

into without Christianity and in which one cannot remain *with* it." The modern anti-religious philosophical impulse in which Heidegger participates is made possible by, and indeed preserves, the legacy of the Christian tradition. Insofar as this is the case, and the Heideggerian option and modern philosophy as a whole is rejected for its covert but nevertheless persisting adherence to the speculative horizon introduced by Christianity, then "one has to ask oneself: Is there not a simply a-Christian philosophy? Is ancient philosophy – be it Platonic or Aristotelian – not *the* philosophy? ... Do we really know more about the roots of life, about the questionability of life, than the Greeks?"[36] This means, in effect, that according to Strauss, there is actually only *one* option to entertain within the sphere of philosophy: Greek philosophy. The option of modern philosophy, culminating in Heidegger, does not in truth qualify as purely philosophical because it is still beholden to the Christian legacy it believes itself to have left behind. As secularized, modern philosophy obscures the incommensurability between revealed religion and philosophy and thus hampers Strauss's attempt to renew the confrontation between these two traditions. That Strauss considers the deficiency of modern philosophy to be the continued presence of its Christian roots is confirmed by a draft of the letter (dated December 12) eventually sent on December 27, 1932, in which he claims that the continuity of biblical (Christian) faith and modern philosophy – *including* modern atheism – is indisputable:

It is true of modern philosophy that without biblical faith one could not and cannot enter into it, and especially not into its "atheism," and with faith one cannot remain in it. It fundamentally lives by grace of a factum that corrodes it. "Modern philosophy" is thus only possible as long as faith in the Bible has not been shaken in its foundations.[37]

It may be surprising to see that Strauss adheres to this understanding of secularization, which stresses the continuity between the premodern and the modern world.[38] After all, few thinkers emphasize the *discontinuity* between the premodern and the modern as he does. However, one can find plenty of textual evidence of Strauss's usage of this conception in his critical approach to modern philosophy. Moreover, he continues to adhere to the idea that modern philosophy is indebted to

---

[36] Ibid.   [37] Ibid., 47.
[38] On rare occasions Strauss expresses reservations on the idea of secularization. See Strauss, the long footnote on Max Weber in *Natural Right and History*, 61 n20, and "The Three Waves of Modernity," 82–83.

Christianity also after further developments in his thinking. In the 1948 lecture "Reason and Revelation" he claims that "a case can be made for the view that all specifically modern ideas are merely secularized versions of Biblical ideas."[39] In *On Tyranny*, also from 1948, he explains the present-day "universal and *homogeneous* State" as deriving from "philosophy (being the *negation* of religious Christianity)" which "is in turn derivative from St. Paul" but adds that it has only been able to achieve actual political import "once modern philosophy succeeded in *secularizing* it (= rationalizing it, transforming it into coherent discourse)."[40] In a letter to Löwith from August 15, 1946, he writes: "On the *querelle des anciens et des modernes*: I do not deny, but assert, that modern philosophy has much that is essential in common with Christian medieval philosophy, but that means that the attack of the moderns is directed decisively, against *ancient* philosophy."[41] And in 1952 he puts it openly: "modern philosophy emerged by way of transformation of, if in opposition to, Latin or Christian scholasticism."[42] The alleged disparity between Strauss's stress on the discontinuity of the premodern and the modern and his claim regarding their continuity can be explained by recognizing that the continuity relates to the enduring bearings of a specific tradition, namely, Christianity, and the discontinuity relates to the absence of another specific tradition, namely, the Judeo-Islamic medieval tradition. According to Strauss, historical Christianity sits comfortably neither in Athens nor in Jerusalem, because it commits the fallacy of attempting to encompass both. The reason for this is its understanding of revelation in terms of epistemological content and doctrinal knowledge which gives itself to the Scholastic effort of fusing philosophy and theology. The modern conception of reason is rooted in this Christian attempt to blend and reconcile philosophy and revelation.[43] The mutual trespassing of revelation and philosophy into the domain of the other made possible modernity's dogmatic assumption that reason can and has refuted revelation. The implied ramification, that reason is sufficient, able to provide answers to all questions, and that it can offer an exhaustive account of "the whole," is an impractical expectation that ultimately prompted the pervasive distrust in reason that followed suit, and

---

[39] Strauss, "Reason and Revelation," 143.   [40] Strauss, *On Tyranny*, 173.
[41] Strauss, *Gesammelte Schriften*, 3: 661.
[42] Strauss, "Preface to Isaac Husik, *Philosophical Essays*," 252.
[43] Strauss attributes this view to Aquinas. See Strauss, *Natural Right and History*, 163–164.

culminated in the nihilism of Nietzsche and Heidegger. The road to the modern secular society, according to Strauss, runs through Christian tradition.

Thus, not only is modernity's self-perceived superiority rooted in an imagined victory in a battle it is actually dodging, its Christian heritage makes it secularized rather than secular. It is based on the foundation of a particular religious legacy that obstructs the possibility of recovering the quarrel between Athens and Jerusalem. The ramification is that the intellectual project of the modern mind, from its founders in Machiavelli, Hobbes, and Spinoza, to its completion in Heidegger's historicism, aims to negate Christianity while at the same time it preserves its truth. The crises-laden post-Christian modern world is thus in an important sense post-*Christian*. We shall soon see that Strauss believes that the theoretical underpinnings of medieval Jewish and Islamic traditions are different from those of Christianity and therefore present themselves as optimal resources for thinking beyond the modern paradigm.

Modern philosophy is plagued by secularization, historicism, and nihilism, and Heidegger – even more than Nietzsche – represents the pinnacle of this dire state of affairs. His atheism and historicism ultimately deny the possibility of moving from opinion to knowledge, that is, the possibility of philosophy correctly understood, as well as the validity of revealed religion. In short, Heidegger obscures the possibility of attending to the pressing questions of political philosophy, namely, the question of human excellence and *the* good society. The peak of modernity and its most profound thinker, Heidegger also typifies the modern crisis. The hope for modern philosophy, then, resides in the ability to overcome Heidegger.

MODERN JUDAISM: FROM HEIDEGGER TO MAIMONIDES

Strauss perceives all the modern Jewish options to be victim of the modern historicist condition. In an unpublished essay from 1930, "The Religious Situation of the Present," he suggests that the one great contemporary thinker who can provide a portal into understanding "the religious situation of the present as *Jews*" is Heidegger, because the present religious situation is engulfed in the crisis represented by his thought. "If we want to know the present," he writes, "... then we must be free of the present."[44]

---

[44] Strauss, "Religiöse Lage der Gegenwart," *Gesammelte Schriften* 2: 377–391. In English, Strauss, "The Religious Situation of the Present," 225–235.

Once the historicist commitments and prejudices are rescinded, a search
for truth that transcends the present historical epoch becomes possible.
Strauss thus calls on his fellow non-believing Jews to leave "the cave" and
return to "the old, eternal, question, *the* primordial question [*die
Urfrage*]," namely, "what is the *right* life? How *should* I live? What
matters? What is needful?"[45]

That Strauss's imploration to "leave the cave" is directed at his contemporary Jewish world is made clear in his book *Philosophy and Law:
Contributions to the Understanding of Maimonides and His Predecessors*
(1935).[46] In the introduction to this work he organizes his critique of the
various strands of modern Judaism that he has been developing over the
last few years in order to, ultimately, develop a response to modern
atheism and historicism from the "sources of Judaism." "The present
situation ... is determined by the Enlightenment," Strauss claims, and
while the Enlightenment seems to have been long since overcome, modern
Judaism has in fact incorporated and thus perpetuated its
presuppositions.[47] The severe impact of what Strauss calls "radical
Enlightenment," of the likes of Spinoza, who posits the incompatibility
of revelation and reason and the decisive superiority of the latter over the
former, undermines the foundation of Jewish tradition. The same is true
with respect to "moderate Enlightenment," of the likes of Mendelssohn,
who evinces a method of "internalization" (*Verinnerlichung*) of religious
tenets and their "harmonization" (*Vereinbarungen*) with the
Enlightenment's terms. This features especially in the Jewish thinking of
Hermann Cohen, who, as Strauss testifies, was the revered "master" in the
Jewish environment in which he grew up. Even the new thinking of
Rosenzweig's "return" to Judaism cannot accept the traditional sense of
miracles and the afterlife. The synthetic character of the various strands
of modern Judaism, Strauss affirms, attests to the victory of the modern
Enlightenment and its alleged refutation of revelation.

While not mentioned by name, Heidegger is not absent from the book.
In the introduction, Strauss contends that the Enlightenment's critique of
religion originally targeted its delusionary character, its diversion "from
the real 'this-worldliness' to an imaginary 'other-wordliness.'" But this
critique has been eclipsed by "its last and purest expression" which
perceives the consoling quality of religion to be reprehensible. According
to this view, religion is an escape mechanism from the terror of existence

---

[45] Ibid., 380–382, 285.
[46] Strauss, *Philosophie und Gesetz*: in English, *Philosophy and Law*.   [47] Ibid., 22.

and the fearful truth of man's abandonment. And yet, according to Strauss, this "new kind of fortitude" which "accepts the eloquent depictions of the misery of man without God as a proof of the goodness of its case" is rooted in the virtue of "probity" (*Redlichkeit*), which is "a descendent of the tradition grounded in the Bible ... a way of thinking which became possible only through the Bible."[48] This means that even this version of radical modern atheism should be rejected as well: "it itself is the latest, most radical, most unassailable harmonization of these opposing positions" of Enlightenment and orthodoxy.[49] The adherers of this radical version of atheism remain nameless, but in the draft of a letter to Krüger from December 1932, Strauss takes Nietzsche as the example illustrating that modern atheistic philosophy betrays the secularized presence of its Christian roots. Despite his vitriolic attacks on Christianity, "[t]here is also a Christian heritage in Nietzsche," Strauss informs. "Nietzsche never broke away from certain Christian 'tendencies of thought,'" he argues, "because he ... did not proceed to an *unbelieving* critique of this ideal. Nietzsche went back *behind* philosophy." Nietzsche holds a "trans-Christian ideal" that "preserved nothing of Christianity," but his guide toward that ideal is a "(secularized-) Christian attitude of 'probity' [*Redlichkeit*] ... which as such is only necessary and possible as long as there still is a Christianity to be combated."[50] We saw above that Strauss finds Nietzsche's radical modern atheism to reach its completion in Heidegger's *Sein und Zeit*, and in a later essay, to be discussed below, Strauss openly lists Nietzsche and Heidegger as adherents of the biblical virtue of "probity." Even in his radical atheism, Heidegger proves to be entangled in the very religious conceptuality he seeks to overcome. His critique of modernity is not radical enough and his secularism is not secular enough.

The crux of *Philosophy and Law* is a chapter-long attack on Julius Guttmann's 1933 classic work *Die Philosophie des Judentums*.[51] Specifically, Strauss accuses Guttmann of betraying modern biases in his analysis of medieval Jewish philosophy: underlying his interpretation of medieval thought in terms of "philosophy of religion," understood through the framework of "culture," is the belief in the superiority of

---

[48] Ibid., 37.   [49] Ibid., 37–38.   [50] *The Strauss-Krüger Correspondence*, 47.

[51] Guttmann responded to Strauss in a posthumously published piece, "Philosophie der Religion oder Philosophie des Gesetz?" 146–173. The Strauss–Guttmann debate is beginning to garner a significant amount of secondary literature. See Adorisio, "Philosophy of Religion or Political Philosophy?"; Schweid, "Religion and Philosophy"; Wurgaft, "Culture and Law in Weimar Jewish Medievalism."

the modern perspective over the medieval. Guttmann's inability to understand the past on its own terms results in a misrepresentation of the entirety of medieval philosophy, according to Strauss. The fact that Guttmann believes that revelation and philosophy can be harmonized "substantively" means that "if the content of the Bible is to be perfectly preserved in the element of philosophy, the traditional conception of its form, that is, the belief that it is revealed, must be surrendered. The Bible must no longer be understood as revealed, but as the product of the religious consciousness."[52] Guttmann's post-Kantian and post-Schleiermacherian perspective leads to the peculiar claim that modern philosophy enables Judaism to "preserve intellectually the content of its tradition" better than medieval philosophy, albeit with the surrender of the belief of revelation. Strauss argues that Guttmann's program is conditioned by the shift from the ancient and medieval focus on metaphysics and the cosmos to the modern focus on epistemology and subjectivity. This shift has left a crucial mark on religious conceptions, because the absolute actuality and reality of God is no longer self-evident, but taken to be dependent on human consciousness. "The difficulty becomes no less, but even greater," Strauss adds, "as soon as 'consciousness' is replaced by 'existence,' by 'man.'"[53] This conception of religion renders the absolute actuality of God "fundamentally incomprehensible" and therefore stands in unsolvable tension with traditional belief.

Strauss admits that besides one dismissive and indirect remark, Guttmann does not address *Existenzphilosophie* in his work. Yet notwithstanding his idealistic predilections and rejection of the new philosophical perspective as "irrationalistic," Guttmann shares more with existential philosophy than he perhaps recognizes. Both operate within the horizon established after the "fundamental cosmological distinction eternal/corruptible" had become obsolete and within the subjectivist model of religion tailored to human measures. To illustrate his point, Strauss takes as a representative of *Existenzphilosophie* Barth's fellow dialectical theologian Friedrich Gogarten's doctrine of creation, whereby "creation has meaning only as the creation of man."[54] The passages cited by Strauss are as follows: "the works of God, in which God's being-for-us and, correspondingly, our being-from-God come to sight ... this being from [is] the primary being of man, and therefore the being proper to man." Noticeably, Gogarten's account is marked by Heidegger and reads like

---

[52] Strauss, *Philosophy and Law*, 45.   [53] Ibid., 48.
[54] Ibid., 49. The quotes are from Gogarten, *Wider die Ächtung der Autorität*, 41f.

a theological corrective to the Dasein analytic in *Sein und Zeit*. Strauss, like many, identifies in *Existenzphilosophie* the particular mark of the Christian emphasis on the individual's interiority that frames religion into a subjectivistic model. From the perspective of religious existential philosophy, as Strauss interprets it, creation means the creation of man. Idealism – Strauss has Cohen in mind – wherein "creation" is rendered as the illumination of human reason, is only slightly better, as its Kantianism leads it to take notice of the "causal being" of nature. But this is still only the "memory" of the doctrine of creation, and existential philosophy is superior to idealism in that it "grasp[s] more securely . . . the 'existential' sense of the Bible."[55] This confirms, for Strauss, that both are impoverished by modern limitations. In their religious renditions, both follow Schleiermacher's breakthrough and thus confer "the betrayal of the Biblical heritage for the sake of an alien 'piety.'"[56] Neither, moreover, can do justice to the traditional belief in creation or to the reality of revelation and the obligation to obey it. Idealism and *Existenzphilosophie*, while seemingly different, represent only "a progression," but qualitatively they are similar. Their modern lapse is deep, and destructive – "such at least would have to be the verdict of one who acknowledges the Jewish tradition as the judge of modern thought."[57] The primary reason Strauss couples Guttmann and *Existenzphilosophie* is to disclose the modern biases of Guttmann's interpretation of medieval Jewish philosophy and more generally of the modern theoretical approach toward the question of revelation and philosophy and the obscuration of political philosophy. But for our purpose here, this juxtaposition informs us how deeply inadequate Strauss considered the entire effort, which Heidegger is associated with, to ground religious and philosophical truths in anthropocentric ideas of consciousness, experience, and existence.

The critical tenor against Guttmann continues the social-religious critique of present-day Jewish life that was set forth in the introduction. For the attack on scientific idealism and *Existenzphilosophie* targets the intellectualized and experiential versions of post-Enlightenment Judaism. Strauss's overarching aim, in contrast, is to propose to leave the horizon of modern Enlightenment and "apply for aid to the medieval Enlightenment – the Enlightenment of Moses Maimonides."[58] The

---

[55] Strauss, *Philosophy and Law*, 50.   [56] Ibid., 54.   [57] Ibid., 55.
[58] On Strauss and Maimonides, see Green, *Jew and Philosopher*; Green, *Leo Strauss and the Rediscovery of Maimonides*; Green, *Leo Strauss on Maimonides*; Zank, "Arousing Suspicion Against a Prejudice."

inevitable step must be a shift from modern to premodern modes of
thinking; to transition from Heidegger to Maimonides. Within the modern philosophical horizon, it is this return that is paradoxically the true
"new thinking."

What the Maimonidean Enlightenment has to offer to the modern
person, according to *Philosophy and Law*, is an account of revelation
understood neither as matter of belief nor as knowledge – which, Strauss
claims, is found in Christianity and made modern atheism possible – but
rather understood as revealed law:

> mediaeval (Islamic and Jewish) philosophy differs specifically from both ancient
> and modern philosophy in that, understanding itself as both bound and authorized
> by revelation, it sees as its first and most pressing concern the foundation of
> philosophy as a legal foundation of philosophy. With this statement we have
> acquired a first indication of how the medieval philosophers understand religion:
> they understand it not as a "field of validity," nor as a "turn to consciousness,"
> least of all as a "field of culture," but as *law*.[59]

In Strauss's rendition, the Maimonidean account of revelation as law
focuses on the intermediary figure of the prophet and his political function. In his "Farabian-Platonic" interpretation of Maimonides' prophetology, the prophet, who unlike the philosopher is naturally perfected in
wisdom *and* imagination, has access to truths beyond the scope of human
cognition (such as creation), and transmits truths that are essential to the
existence and stability of the community to the unqualified multitude
through imaginative renditions. The prophet communicates esoteric
knowledge exoterically for the sake of political stability and human
perfection. Unlike the modern epistemological versions of prophecy, this
Maimonidean account of revelation as law secures the separate domains
of reason and revelation and hence their nature and integrity. The notion
of the prophet as lawgiver highlights the premodern rationalism whereby
reason is indispensable but also insufficient and acknowledges the pre-
philosophical, public, and distinctly political function of revelation.

The theoretical framework developed in *Philosophy and Law* is critical
of the interwar German intellectual world while also reflecting its contours. Channeling the critique of the "younger generation" of Jewish
intellectuals, Strauss rejects Guttmann's Kantian-inflected Judaism,
according to which "the religion of the Bible has its specific character in
the ethical personalism of its consciousness of God."[60] The charge that

---

[59] Strauss, *Philosophy and Law*, 59–60.
[60] See Guttmann, *Religion und Wissenschaft*, 63–67.

"scientific knowledge of Judaism is purchased at the price of belief in the authority of revelation" is a theologically inflected expression of the contestation against the neo-Kantian emphasis on "science" common at the time. Most importantly, the call to return to the non-atheistic, "moderate" Maimonidean Enlightenment is a call to transcend the modern, faith-based construction of theism–atheism as well as the prevailing rational–irrational binary that figured prominently during the period between the wars. Indeed, Strauss's celebration of Maimonides exhibits an aspiration to overcome the framework he claims was imposed by Christianity and to endorse a conceptuality that addresses the philosophical and existential issues essential to the nature of the human being in a way that Christianity and modern thought – and modern Judaism, beholden to their assumptions – cannot. "The Islamic and Jewish philosophes of the Middle Ages are 'more primitive' than the modern philosophers," he writes, "because they are guided not, like them, by the derived idea of natural right, but by the *primary, ancient* idea of *law* as a unified, total regimen of human life; in other words, because they are pupils of Plato and not pupils of Christians."[61]

Through his rebuttal of Guttmann, Strauss conveys his rejection of the quasi-universalistic liberal conception of religion that vouches for neutrality with regards to Judaism and Christianity only insofar as the former is modeled according to the latter, and particularly, insofar as revelation is defined epistemologically or experientially rather than as ceremonial law. Strauss wishes to revive the *nomos* tradition of Jewish and Islamic medieval philosophy, which, he believes, finds its foremost articulation in the thought of Maimonides. This tradition, with its restrained form of rationalism, politicized centrality of revealed law, and disinclination toward sublations and syntheses, is offered as a way to overcome the synthetic configuration of modern Judaism marked by the Christian horizon and Heideggerian historicism and relativism.

THE DESTRUKTION OF ATHENS, THE DESTRUKTION OF JERUSALEM

Philosophy and Law portrays the "danger" in the position attributed to Heidegger, but it also indicates its potential "saving power." In the introduction, Strauss speaks of idealism as fulfilling itself with "the discovery of the radical 'historicity' [*radikalen Geschichtlichkeit*] of man and

---

[61] Strauss, *Philosophy and Law*, 73.

his world" – a likely hint to Heidegger – "as the definitive overcoming of the idea of an eternal nature, an eternal truth."[62] This discovery leads to a relativization of the modern scientific worldview, now perceived as "one historically conditioned form of 'world construction' among others." Strauss does not agree with this relativization, but as a historical observation, he identifies in it a precious opportunity to revive philosophical thought. For calling into question the Enlightenment's victory "makes possible the rehabilitation of the 'natural world view' on which the Bible depends."[63] Once "the old concept of truth" no longer rules the modern mind, "the traditional view that the right life is a life according to nature," which has become "meaningless under modern premise," can be reconsidered.[64]

It is significant that Strauss repeatedly claims that his own move to recover the wisdom of the past is enabled and motivated by the constructive dismantling of Heidegger's "destruction." "Under the guidance of Heidegger," he writes, "people came to see that Aristotle and Plato had *not* been understood ... If Plato and Aristotle are not understood and consequently not refuted, return to Plato and Aristotle is an open possibility."[65] He credits his friend Jacob Klein to be "the first to understand the possibility which Heidegger had opened without intending it: the possibility of a genuine return to classical philosophy, to the philosophy of Aristotle and Plato, a return with open eyes and in full clarity about the infinite difficulties which it entails."[66] Strauss's adaptation of the Heideggerian "destruction," however, is also a correction. For he believes that Heidegger presupposes that he understands past thinkers better than they understood themselves, which means his "return" to the past is overwhelmed by modern historicist assumptions and hence not a return at all.

In truth, Heidegger's view on the matter evolved over the years. In the 1927–1928 winter lectures on Kant's First Critique he contends that "to understand Kant properly means to understand him better than he understood himself,"[67] and in the same year he repeats: "we not only wish to

---

[62] Ibid., 33.

[63] Ibid. In *Natural Right and History* he writes: "we ought therefore to welcome historicism as an ally in our fight against dogmatism" (p. 22).

[64] Strauss, *Philosophy and Law*, 34.

[65] Strauss, "The Living Issues," 134–135. Cf. Strauss, "A Giving of Accounts," 462; Strauss, *Gesammelte Schriften*, 3: xix.

[66] Strauss, "An Unspoken Prologue," 450.

[67] Heidegger, *Phenomenological Interpretation of Kant's* Critique of Pure Reason, 2ff.

but must understand the Greeks better than they understood themselves."[68] Later on, he complicates this pretension. "A proper commentary," he observes in his reflections in "Nietzsche's Word: God Is Dead," "never understands the text better than its author understood it, though it certainly understands it differently. Only this differing in understanding must be such that it encounters the same thing which the explicated is mediating."[69] And in his "A Dialogue on Language" he grants: "our thinking today is charged with the task to think what the Greeks have thought in an even more Greek manner." To this his Japanese interlocutor replies: "and so to understand the Greeks better than they have understood themselves," to which the speaker representing Heidegger answers: "no, that is not it; for all great thinking always understands itself best of all, that is to say, *itself* within the limits set for it," and so what is needed is "to pursue more originally what the Greeks have thought, to see it in the source of its reality. To see it so in its own way Greek, and yet in respect of what it sees is no longer, is never again, Greek."[70]

In appropriating and correcting the Heideggerian "Destruktion," Strauss seeks to understand past thinkers as they understood themselves. While in Strauss's judgment Heidegger fails to do so successfully himself, he nevertheless opened the door to recovering neglected past possibilities, a task Strauss sets out to undertake.

Heidegger's mark on Strauss here is clear: He adopts the framing of the modern predicament as an original forgetting of a specific *question*, to which the suitable response is "Destruktion" and retrieval. He also highlights Christianity's role in this forgetting and the preparatory nature of the task of selectively reappropriated tradition. Yet this does not mean that Strauss believed a naïve "return" to the past is simple or even fully attainable. Strauss's anti-historicism is not anti-historical; indeed, it is historical through and through. He envisions a careful, tentative recovery of enduring insights from the history of philosophy, the very recovery of which holds, he believes, saving power for the modern predicament.[71] Not only is he aware of the fundamental difficulty of this endeavor, he also walks a delicate line, for he tries to

---

[68] GA 24, 157/Heidegger, *The Basic Problems of Phenomenology*, 111.
[69] GA 5, 213–214/Heidegger, *Off the Beaten Track*, 160.
[70] GA 12, 134/Heidegger, *On the Way to Language*, 39.
[71] It follows that a simple opposition between "Destruktion" and "recovery," as framed by Smith, misconstrues the differences between the two thinkers: they are, in truth, occupied with both, albeit differently.

overcome historicism by following in the path of the worst of historicists. Yet he is ready to admit: "There is no inquiry into the history of
philosophy that is not at the same time a philosophical inquiry."[72] The
return to premodern philosophy as a post-Heideggerian mindset
betrays how Strauss follows Heidegger's footsteps in order to rehabilitate an intellectual trajectory in which "nature" rather than "history" is
central, that is, one which does not result in Heidegger. Strauss appropriates Heidegger's trope in order to turn it against him. Seemingly,
what Strauss writes in a different context applies for his own strategy
vis-à-vis Heidegger: "that is always so: in order to defeat an enemy, you
have to take a leaf from his book."[73] In this way, Heidegger's historicism exposes the modern crisis in all its acuteness *and* points to the
history of thought as its possible remedy.

A crucial implication of the fact that, according to Strauss, the project
of modernity must be reconsidered and the past is a repository of
operative ideas for the contemporary world is that the possibility of
recovering a Judaism emancipated from Christian determinations is
revealed. The Straussian "destruction" thus also seeks to overcome the
unsolvable tensions between Judaism and modernity and open the door
for reassessing the options facing modern Judaism. As he writes in 1932,
"the possibility emerged that European reservations vis-à-vis the Jewish
tradition were no longer possible and necessary: the whole [*das inte-
grale*] of Judaism appeared to become possible again."[74] The task of
surmounting the great obstacle standing before both philosophy and
authentic Judaism is therefore the task of overcoming Heidegger. This,
then, is the paradoxical effect of Heidegger's philosophy: it typifies the
crisis to which it also offers a direction for solution. By exposing the
bankruptcy of modern philosophy and Jewish thought, it also opens the
door to rehabilitate past positions long neglected or considered refuted.
Heidegger's philosophy thus can be likened to the darkest room in
the second cave, but it is also in this room that an ascending passageway
to the natural cave can be found.

Like Heidegger, Strauss follows the Grecocentric German tradition
and finds ancient Greece and the tradition it espoused as the possible
location from which germane insights can be retrieved. In this regard, he
is comparable to Hans Jonas, about whom Strauss writes to Klein on
February 14, 1934 that he too seeks "to return beyond Heidegger in the

---

[72] Strauss, *Philosophy and Law*, 41.   [73] Strauss, "Why We Remain Jews," 316.
[74] Strauss, "Die geistige Lage der Gegenwart," *Gesammelte Schriften* 2: 444.

same direction as we do, although not so clearly."[75] Strauss's project can also be compared to that of Hannah Arendt, who similarly returns to the Greeks and the Romans and who likewise claims that Heidegger's historicism and fixation with being reflects his neglect of the "classical and persistent problems of political philosophy" and the urgent questions of "what is politics? Who is man as a political being? What is freedom?"[76] Unlike Heidegger, however, whose "return" to Athens excludes the tradition of "Jerusalem," Strauss believes it should inaugurate anew the dispute between the two traditions of thought. Evidently, while stringent, his conception of "tradition" is considerably richer, more expansive, and more inclusive than Heidegger's. For not only is the Jewish tradition taken seriously from a philosophical perspective, but so is the Islamic tradition. Heidegger, for his part, does not seem to even consider the medieval Islamic tradition to be worthy of dismissal.

It is clear, then, that it is Heidegger and the challenge his philosophy poses that inspires Strauss to turn to medieval philosophy and rehabilitate Maimonides, who is then set against Heidegger. In fact, the wingspan of "the Great Eagle" is intended to be even wider, for he is pitted both against Spinoza, whose life and critique of revealed religion inaugurated the contradictions that define liberalism and modern Judaism and whose assertion of the sufficiency of human reason dominates modern thought, and against Heidegger, whose dubious thought and political affiliation exposes the impasse of modern thought and the predicament of modern Judaism in its utmost extreme. And insofar as Spinoza and Heidegger mark the prologue and epilogue of the modern crisis, the Maimonidean program emerges not only as the savior of modern Judaism, but as the savior of the Western philosophical tradition as a whole.

HISTORICISM, HISTORICITY, AND NIHILISM

Because scholars of Strauss tend to accept his reading of Heidegger and reproduce it in their works, and scholars of Heidegger do not usually read Strauss, it is worthwhile, before we continue, to pause and try to

---

[75] Strauss, *Gesammelte Schriften* 3: 494. On Strauss and Jonas and their responses to Heidegger, see Vogel, "Overcoming Heidegger's Nihilism," 131–150; Wiese, "Revolt Against Escapism," 151–177.

[76] Arendt, "Concern with Politics in Recent European Philosophical Thought," 432. On Arendt and Strauss, see Beiner, "Hannah Arendt and Leo Strauss"; Keedus, *The Crisis of German Historicism*; Wurgaft, *Thinking in Public: Strauss, Levinas, Arendt*; Zuckert and Zuckert, *Strauss and the Problem of Political Philosophy*, 254–288.

assess his interpretation of Heidegger. It is evident that his philosophy
serves as the ultimate foil for Strauss's constructive program, but it is
worth asking whether his critique is entirely justified. First, Strauss mis-
reads the godless framing of *Sein und Zeit* to indicate that Heidegger
presupposes that philosophy can and has refuted revelation. As we have
seen in Chapter 1, Heidegger designates each to a different domain, with
the implication being that such a refutation is pointless and impossible.
Strauss's own separationist position regarding the relations between
philosophy and revelation is actually reminiscent of Heidegger's, though
it is dissimilar in at least one crucial way: For Strauss, revelation cannot
be refuted by philosophy, but it can offer itself as a moral challenge,
contesting it with a competing way of life. For Heidegger, revelation
presents no such challenge. The affinity to Heidegger's actual view,
however, allows us to see that Strauss's position concerning the impossibility of refuting revelation itself reflects the theologically rooted strand
advocating for the separation of theology and philosophy which, as has
been noted, was dominant in Germany at the time of his philosophical
maturation. His projection of an ancient tradition that upholds a radical
distinction between philosophy and theology reflects the theological and
philosophical currents of his own time. His early attraction to
Rosenzweig's and dialectical theology's irrefutable account of revelation
demonstrates this well. Even his ensuing attempt to bracket Christianity
out of the rivalry between Athens and Jerusalem and the effort to pose
a Jewish-Islamic account of revelation as law while consciously chiding
the Rosenzweig–Barth position is nevertheless conducted within
a framework laid out by these concealed theological assumptions.

  Another point in Strauss's analysis of Heidegger that deserves attention is
the very attribution of radical historicism. In *Natural Right and History*
Strauss outlines the development of the historicist outlook, differentiating
between the first stage, when the historical school took to history for truth,
but claimed that universal principles can be gleaned from historical reality,
and the second stage, when these universal principles were depreciated in
favor of local and particular principles – "a particular temporal state of
a particular local society."[77] Strauss argues that these versions of historicism
are ultimately self-refuting, as their thesis can be construed as transhistorical.
The third stage, radical historicism, was prepared by Nietzsche and executed
by Heidegger, who, as Strauss writes to Alexandre Kojève on June 26, 1950,
is "the only radical historicist."[78] According to this view, "All knowledge,

[77] Strauss, *Natural Right and History*, 15.   [78] Strauss, *On Tyranny*, 251.

however, limited and 'scientific' presupposes a frame of reference ... [or] horizon ... within which understanding and knowing take place." This horizon is given or imposed by fate and "cannot be validated by reasoning, since it is the basis of all reasoning."[79] Radical historicism denies the possibility of reaching the transhistorical meta-principle of historicism, because it denies "the possibility of a theoretical or objective analysis." In this respect, radical historicism completely excludes the possibility of natural right, because unlike historicism, it repudiates the possibility of arriving at actual, universalized, enduring knowledge. From the perspective of radical historicism, "reality" itself should be blamed for the historicists' self-contradiction. All thought is historical, and "only to thought that is itself committed or 'historical' does the true meaning of the 'historicity' of all genuine thought disclose itself." It is, moreover, anti-religious by definition, as it denies the hallowing "by sacred powers" of the historical "meaningless process," and it is conceptually wedded to subjectivism, as the subjective standard of the individual's free choice is the only standard that remains.[80]

In some respects, this is a fair description of Heidegger's position. It does, however, covertly conflate historicism with historicity, resulting in an interpretation of Heidegger that demands to be nuanced. Historicism denotes that knowledge and truth is conditioned by historical context, while historicity means that human existence takes shape in a hermeneutical process within the factical-historical experience of one's situation. These often overlap, but they are not identical. That this is the case can be evinced from the program of *Sein und Zeit* itself, in which Heidegger outlines the ontological preconditions of the possibilities of Dasein's historical existence as such. He remarks, for example, that his analysis of average everydayness is after "not just any accidental structures, but essential ones which, in every kind of being that factical Dasein may possess, persist as determinative for the character of its being."[81] Dasein's temporality and historicity are precisely such persisting and fixed structures. The tension within *Sein und Zeit* between the search for enduring essences and the particularities of the historically manifest can be portrayed as the tension between two of his sources of influence, Husserl and Dilthey. This tension has been pointed out and debated by early and recent readers.[82] In contradistinction to Strauss, for example,

---

[79] Strauss, *Natural Right and History*, 26–27.   [80] Ibid., 18.   [81] *SZ*, 16–17/*BT*, 38.
[82] See, for example, from 1929, Misch, "Lebensphilosophie und Phänomenologie" and from 1931 Plessner, "Macht und menschliche Natur." More recently, see Guignon, "The Twofold Task."

Jürgen Habermas determines that "with his steady focus on the invariant structures of Dasein, Heidegger from the start cuts off the road from historicity to real history."[83] Likewise, Adorno, in his 1931 essay "The Actuality of Philosophy," makes the point that Heidegger is hardly a historicist because by ontologizing time, temporality itself emerges as a-temporal.[84] This tension is also present in Heidegger's later thought, where his reflections on the history of the happening of being disclose that being essences differently in different epochs. Even "time" was presumably understood differently before the first inception where the Greeks understood its temporality, and the anticipated new inception will similarly bring about a new ordering of how things show up to us. At the same time, the structures of logos and language, as well as that of *Ereignis*, appear to transcend specific historical epochs. It seems correct, therefore, to say that Heidegger is a radical historicist in arguing that ontic orderings are historically conditioned and that this conditioning changes in accordance with being's mysterious sending, but there is evidently no escaping general and lasting principles or structures that govern these shifting historical orderings, however formally. It must be stressed, however, that these are never a-temporal or a-historical. Strauss is correct when he writes to Löwith on December 13, 1960 about later Heidegger: "It is, I believe, essential to Heidegger that there is nothing eternal in the sense of the *nunc stans*, or sempiternal: the finiteness of being or of the world, temporally and also spatially is, as far as I understand, still essential to Heidegger."[85] Even when Heidegger considers beyng to be "everlasting" and "imperishable," as he does in his lecture course on Heraclitus from 1944,[86] or when he stresses the "everlasting" in his interpretations of Heraclitus's Fragment 30,[87] these characterizations should not be understood metaphysically. For he also says that "originary temporality [is] the 'temporalizing' of the eternal!"[88] and that eternity is "the deepest oscillation [*Durchschwingung*] of time."[89] "Eternity," thus, denotes a temporal quality of the givingness of being, a richness of the inceptive moment of ecstatic time, not anything beyond history or an unending chronological endurance.

The equation of historicism with historicity or the assumption that the one necessarily implies the other leads to a further misrepresentation of Heidegger's position. From the perspective of historicism, the gap

[83] Habermas, "Work and Weltanschauung," 140–172.
[84] Adorno, "The Actuality of Philosophy."   [85] Strauss, *Gesammelte Schriften* 3: 684.
[86] GA 55, 345.   [87] GA 15, 280.   [88] GA 73, 15.   [89] GA 95, 120.

between the past and the present is irreparable; history can shed no light on our current situation and thus recovering it is futile. From the position of historicity, however, the past can potentially hold valuable insights for the present when understood ecstatically. Indeed, the conviction that the debris of traditional philosophy is worthy of engagement is precisely what drives Heidegger's desire to retrieve an authentic way to the past through "Destruktion." Strauss is thus correct in emphasizing the non-absolute, thrown situatedness and circular hermeneutics of human understanding in his critique of Heidegger. Yet "Husserlian" determinations are still present, not in the form of a search for an a-temporal essence or *Hypokeimenon*, but as enduring structures of possible meaning-assembling nexuses or formal indications. What is most crucial for Heidegger is the question *how* the transcending of the transhistorical takes place, and how this endurance is conceived. Is its account of history present to hand and nihilistic, or is it grounded in Dasein's ecstatic finitude and appropriative of being's unconcealment? Being "free of the present," as Strauss urges, is foreign to Heidegger's perspective.

Strauss's interpretation also conceals the related point that Heidegger categorically rejects the category of progress. Not unlike in Strauss, the narrative animating *Sein und Zeit* is not of progress, but a *Verfallsgeschichte* with the hope for retrieval. The same is true of his later thought: The implication of the idea that the forgetting of being is not the philosophers' doing but the result of being's own mysterious self-concealment is that the present epoch is not privileged but actually in a particularly deprived state with regards to what is most urgent to thinking. Moreover, Heidegger is relentlessly devoted to one concern, and has no intention of "moving on," nor does he think such an advancement is really possible. "My essential intention," he declares in *The Metaphysical Foundations of Logic*, "is to first pose the problem and work it out in such a way that the essentials of the entire Western tradition will be concentrated in the simplicity of a basic problem."[90] A narrative of progression, from Heidegger's perspective, is technological in its teleology and logic of accumulation, and it is subjectivist in its belief that humans are the agents responsible for the perceived advancement. It presupposes an understanding of history as *Vorgang*, a process or series of events in which the present is in a more advanced point in time than the past, which can therefore be jettisoned. As noted before, Heidegger considers this conception of history to be present at hand, derivative, and an obstacle

---

[90] Heidegger, *The Metaphysical Foundations of Logic*, 132.

to a genuine reformation of the question of being. History for him is primarily *Geschichte*, a fateful happening latched to Dasein's ecstatic temporalizing and bound to inceptive moments that initiate new ways of ordering beings and new domains of truth.

It can be seen, thus, that the two men are aligned in their rejection of modern historicism, although their anti-historicist sentiments play out differently. For Strauss, the peril of historicism and its resulting nihilism is to be countered by the pursuit after permanencies and "nature," irrespective of historical situation.[91] For Heidegger, the problem lies not in the fear of a contextualized truth that leads to nihilism, but in the philosophical assumptions that make this kind of logic possible in the first place. For him, "relativism and scepticism spring from a partially justified opposition to an absurd absolutism and dogmatism of the concept of truth."[92] By claiming that truth is irreparably affixed to the temporality of human existence and to the disclosure of being, Heidegger seeks to dispose of the category of a-historical perpetuity as an operative concept against which the problem of nihilism and relativism, as understood by Strauss, can emerge at all. From his perspective, Strauss and the historicists differ in their expressed position but share an underlying nihilist logic: the projection of a-historicality is itself an attestation of nihilism. Strauss is a nihilist for Heidegger, and Heidegger is a nihilist for Strauss.

There is little doubt that from Heidegger's perspective, Strauss's return to Plato and Socrates is futile, for it is precisely these figures who are responsible for the forgetting of being in the first place. Strauss is equipped with the Platonic conception of truth as enduring correctness of assertion and therefore perpetuates rather than confounds the problem. Strauss's ontic concern with political philosophy thus inherently fall short of the urgent ontological challenges, and in principle is unable to offer a compelling alternative to his own program. But Strauss is no doubt aware of this, and his return to Plato, among other things, can be read as an intentional move to undercut Heidegger's ontological fixation as well as his interpretation of Plato as an ontologist who reinterpreted being in terms of the "most unhidden" and the illuminating *Idea*. For Strauss, "the beginning of philosophy is not the beginning," nor is the legitimacy of philosophy the correct starting point or a guaranteed presupposition. Heidegger's *Seinsfrage*, he posits, ignores the fact that philosophy is always conducted within a city, within a social and political context in

---

[91] Strauss, *Natural Right and History*, 30–33.
[92] GA 24, 316/Heidegger, *The Basic Problems of Phenomenology*, 221–222.

which the very possibility of philosophizing has stakes, indeed, is under threat. Not only does Heidegger insufficiently account for the actual political stakes of the poets and thinkers he glorifies, Strauss implicitly argues, but politics and revelation can fundamentally call philosophy into question in a manner unrecognized by Heidegger. Thus, rather than affirming the priority of the *Seinsfrage*, Strauss defiantly writes in 1949: "The question Plato *or* existentialism is today the ontological question."[93]

HEIDEGGER IN LATER STRAUSS'S CRITIQUE OF MODERN JUDAISM

While the buds of Strauss's later developments are easily identifiable in *Philosophy and Law*, it is nevertheless a transitionary work, and one that does not reach an unequivocal conclusion. How do we square the sub-jugation of divine law by practical philosophy and the claim that it imparts truth not given by philosophy? Does revealed law limit or expand the autonomy of philosophy? Who is superior – the philosopher or the prophet? This inconclusiveness is reflected in how this work was under-stood by some of its early readers: Scholem interpreted Strauss as promot-ing atheism, Löwith thought he was endorsing orthodoxy, and Klein claimed that "everything remains open."[94]

Soon after the publication of this work, following his interpretation of medieval Islamic philosophers, Strauss deepens and alters his political interpretation of Maimonides' prophetology. Announced to be a citizen of Athens rather than Jerusalem, Maimonides is now depicted, most famously in the essay "The Literary Character of the Guide for the Perplexed," as seeking to covertly vindicate *philosophy* within the ten-sion-filled relation between the philosopher and the multitude. The Maimonidean law-giving prophet is portrayed as a disguised Platonic philosopher-king whose main purpose is to establish a just polis, which requires the mysterious notion of divine law for its foundation, and at the same time to enable the possibility of philosophy by navigating between the mutual threats that the philosopher and the city pose each other. It is in this context that Strauss, following Lessing, develops his idea of "exoteric writing," most famously propounded in the essay "Persecution and the Art of Writing," as a path to mask subversive philosophical ideas from the masses. With this idea, Strauss attempts to lay bare, but also to balance

[93] Letter to Eric Voegelin from December 17, 1949, *Faith and Political Philosophy*, 63.
[94] Strauss, *Gesammelte Schriften*, 2: xxvii–xxviii.

without syntheses, the tensions between revelation and philosophy, praxis and theory, the philosopher and the city.

The modified portrayal of the "Great Eagle" notwithstanding, it is important to recognize that Maimonides stands in the center of his later thought as well, and for our purpose, three crucial points remain unchanged.[95] The first: Maimonides' functional role as a non-modern alternative to modern thought is retained. By submitting to the conception of reason that allows for the non-intelligibility of "the whole," Maimonides circumvents the modern philosophical shortcomings and as such serves as a beacon toward which modern thought should proceed. The second: by exposing Maimonides' acknowledgment of the political and legislative impositions on philosophy, Strauss continues to underscore the centrality of law. This, as he repeatedly insists, requires a return to Plato and a siding with the Jewish (and Islamic) notion of revelation, over against Christianity. The third: the critical assessment of modern Judaism that underpins the call to return to Maimonides endures. This can be seen by looking to Strauss's famous "Preface to the English Translation" of his book on Spinoza. Here, in the reflections on his intellectual development as "a young Jew born and raised in Germany who found himself in the grip of the theologico-political predicament," not only are his previous critical judgments of modern Judaism reiterated, but also Heidegger plays a central role in this critique.

In this preface, Strauss echoes his critical assessments of modern Judaism: liberalism as well as political, cultural, and religious Zionism are tempting yet ultimately unsatisfactory stances for the modern Jew. He then turns to Rosenzweig's option of "return" to Judaism, a path based on the experience of God. Here Strauss sets Heidegger and Rosenzweig, who he reads as a historicist, against each other. The purpose of this confrontation is to debunk "experience" as an adequate category for philosophy or revealed religion. He begins by suggesting that there are significant differences between the two thinkers, for example, their stance on revelation. But as his analysis unravels, it becomes clear that this difference is eclipsed by more crucial similarities. To show this, Buber's experience-based theology is introduced as a stand-in for Rosenzweig and contrasted with Heidegger's atheistic new thinking. Strauss recounts the Buber–Heidegger debate over the prophets' desire for comfort and "certainty of salvation" that was discussed in the previous chapter – clearly siding with

---

[95] A penetrating analysis of Maimonides' centrality for Strauss is Bernstein, *Leo Strauss on the Borders of Judaism, Philosophy, and History.*

Heidegger – but only as a way to raise the question of how humans can attain certainty about divine revelation. The prism of "experience," he argues, is impractical for such certainty. For if revelation is thought of through human categories, even as "absolute experience," it still remains not "absolute"; there is no objective standard by which its content can be confirmed. "Experience" is subjectivist, private, and unverifiable, and as such, it is interpreted according to the predetermined assumptions of the experiencer.

> Every assertion about the absolute experience which says more than that what is experienced is the Presence or the Call, is not the experiencer, is not flesh and blood, is the wholly other, is death or nothingness, is an "image" or interpretation; that any one interpretation is the simply true interpretation is not known but "merely believed."[96]

The reduction of divine revelation to the immanence of human experience results in inconclusiveness, because how one interprets the experience is predetermined by one's assumptions. That Buber renders the absolute experience as an experience of a Thou reflects more on Buber than on the nature of revelation itself. Strauss takes Heidegger's notion of the "call of consciousness" as an example for one possible way in which an absolute experience can be rendered, but one that emerges, like Buber's, from a set of inadequate assumptions about revelation and the human role in its giving. As noted, the Heideggerian "call" is a notion Strauss repeatedly returns to in order to demonstrate the flaws of modern anthropocentric thinking. It is, for him, an example of a secularized category improperly focusing on subjectivist human experience and existence, manifesting Heidegger's debt to Christian tradition and subsequently the impoverishment of his philosophical categories.

Strauss accentuates Heidegger's debt to Christianity in the "Preface" by making plain the latter's commitment to the biblically rooted principle of "probity." As before, Strauss's departure point is Nietzsche's principle that "the denial of the Biblical God demands the denial of Biblical morality however secularized."[97] He repeats his view from the 1930s that Nietzsche himself has failed to overcome the mark of Christianity in his

---

[96] Strauss, "Preface to the English Translation," 11. Strauss's opposition to "experience" is in some respects comparable to Scholem's. See Magid, "Gershom Scholem's Ambivalence." It is worth pointing out the extremely scarce mentions of Heidegger in Scholem's vast *oeuvre*. Curiously, Heidegger's name is completely absent from the recently published Arendt–Scholem correspondence.

[97] Ibid., 12.

own thought, as evident by his preservation of biblical morality through his operative principle of intellectual probity. "What is true of Nietzsche is no less true of the author of *Sein und Zeit*," Strauss proclaims.

> Heidegger wishes to expel from philosophy the last relics of Christian theology, like the notions of "eternal truths" and "the idealized absolute subject." But the understanding of man as the rational animal is, as he emphasizes, primarily the Biblical understanding of man as created in the image of God. Accordingly, he interprets human life in light of "being towards death," "anguish," "conscience," and "guilt"; in this most important respect he is much more Christian than Nietzsche.[98]

Strauss grounds his claim in the references to *Sein und Zeit* in the footnotes to the preface, where he signals to Heidegger's inconclusive relationship with Christian traditions. He references §9, where "the anthropology of Christianity" is said to obstruct an appropriate investigation into Dasein's being; §44, where Heidegger declares the idea of "eternal truths" and human "ideality" as "residues of Christian theology within philosophical problematics which have not as yet been radically extruded"; §40, where Heidegger remarks on the ontic Christian dealings with anxiety by Augustine, Luther, and Kierkegaard; and §49, where Heidegger mentions the concept of death in "the anthropology worked out in Christian theology" from Paul to Calvin. Through these references, Strauss gestures to the Christian horizon of Heidegger's existential analysis (though in some of these references Heidegger is *critical* of Christian tradition), and by implication, of the new thinking of Rosenzweig and Buber as well. "The fundamental awareness characteristic of the new thinking," be it by Heidegger, Rosenzweig, or Buber, "is a secularized version of the biblical faith as interpreted by Christian theology ... The efforts of the new thinking to escape from the evidence of the Biblical understanding of man, i.e., from Biblical morality, have failed."[99] All three thinkers depend on the Christian theoretical framework which makes the recourse to experience possible. Their differences merely derive from dissimilar points of view: Rosenzweig and Buber experience "the call" with reference to the revelatory Jewish God, while in Heidegger's "atheist" framework the call is disclosed as nothingness.[100] But insofar as their formulizations of revelation refer to an experience and are tailored to human measures, they are fundamentally all operating within a shared horizon. The

---

[98] Ibid., 12–13.   [99] Ibid.

[100] Strauss also refers to "the call" as "the Wholly Other" and "death" in a letter to Seth Benardete from January 1965. Quoted in Meier, "Death as God," 45–51.

"Jewish" thought of Rosenzweig and Buber does not differ *in essence* from Heidegger's Christianly inflected atheistic scheme. The confrontation with Heidegger, therefore, reveals that the thought of Rosenzweig and Buber is all too modern, all too Christian.[101] Rosenzweig does not call for a return to traditional Judaism, but to a Judaism conditioned by the Enlightenment and its Christian residues.

Thus, even if Strauss concludes the "Preface" by declaring that his reading of Spinoza has changed since his youthful days, his belated portrayal of the Weimar scene reconfirms his early conviction that Heidegger's historicist, existentialist, and secularized Christian thinking discloses the deficiency of modern Jewish thinking.

STRAUSS AND LATER HEIDEGGER

As Strauss's thought develops, he continues to respond to Heidegger, overtly or covertly, in many of his writings, including, most critically, in *Natural Right and History* (1953). To be sure, he continues to conceive *Sein und Zeit* as a most important and challenging work, but he takes note of Heidegger's later developments as well. From different statements and references, it can be concluded that Strauss was fairly up to date on Heidegger's ongoing publications. For example, in a footnote to his article "Philosophy as Rigorous Science," Strauss refers to five different later works by Heidegger – *Was Heisst Denken?*, *Der Satz von Grund*, *Einführung in die Metaphysik*, *Wegmarken*, and *Gelassenheit*.[102] It is significant that Strauss submits to the view that Heidegger's thought underwent a robust *Kehre*. With reference to Heidegger's recent publications, Strauss intimates in a letter to Löwith from 1951 that the transition from *Existenz* to *Sein* marks a "remarkable maturity."[103] After reading the Nietzsche lectures, he proclaims: "I myself feel now more strongly than ever the attraction exercised by Heidegger."[104] Two years earlier, in 1949, he admits that "much has become clear to me which I actually no longer knew – above all, Heidegger, whose *deinotes* [ἰδεινότες] really far surpass everything done in our time" – though he still regards Heidegger's

---

[101] For a different reading of the relation between Rosenzweig and Heidegger in the preface, see Green, "Editor's Introduction: Leo Strauss as a Modern Jewish Thinker."

[102] Velkley identifies two stages in Strauss's reaction to later Heidegger, corresponding to the publications of *Holzwege* in 1950 and *Nietzsche* in 1961. Velkley, *Heidegger, Strauss and the Premises of Philosophy*, 54–61.

[103] Strauss, *Gesammelte Schriften* 3: 67, cf. 3: 674.   [104] Ibid., 684–685.

solution "absurd."[105] The departure from the focus on Dasein's historicity confirms that Heidegger, "insofar as he is true to himself, in no way
makes concessions to faith [*Glauben*]."[106] The deviation from
Existenzphilosophie and its focus on subjectivist interiority represents
for Strauss a crucial step in the direction of de-Christianizing
Heidegger's thought. However, insofar as modern philosophy is as
a whole an outgrowth of Christianity, Heidegger's later thought does
not succeed in transcending its purview. Indeed, while Löwith claims in
their correspondence that also in his later writings "Heidegger's effort is
a religious one," Strauss maintains that it is "religious" only to the extent
that it is modern. Heidegger's *Kehre*, Strauss suggests, can be formulated
as a movement from Kierkegaard to Nietzsche: both are beholden to the
Christian horizon, yet the movement itself, he writes to Löwith, "strongly
speaks to me," as it displays "where Heidegger wants to go."[107]

Heidegger's later thought presents Strauss with a puzzle that he does
not entirely manage to work out. The notion of the *Seinsgeschichte* – the
radical idea that being is unconcealed differently in different historical
epochs – can serve as an example to demonstrate this puzzle. Does this
constitute a deepening of the grip of relativistic historicism, and by implication, of Christianity? Or is it a stepping beyond Christianity, insofar as
it betrays a diminished focus on the existential status of the individual
subject? Moreover, as noted above, Heidegger's later works betray
the tension between historical manifestations and underlying enduring
structures, as does *Sein und Zeit*, though more covertly. This puzzle is
aptly expressed by Löwith, who in a letter to Strauss dated February 21,
1950 interprets Heidegger's development in Hegelian terms: "'Being' is
certainly a super-Hegelian 'absolute' and at the same time it absorbs the
historicity of *Dasein* and renders it metaphysical. It is an 'overcoming' of
historicism (in the usual sense) and at the same time the most radical
historicism (in the Straussian sense)."[108]

Strauss's response to the puzzle of Heidegger's later thinking is inconclusive. On the one hand, he finds in Heidegger's later thinking a reduced
mark of Christianity and hence a more compelling form of philosophizing.
In a letter from 1971 to Löwith he comments that "for some time it has
struck me that to my knowledge there is not a single place in Heidegger's
writing where the name of Jesus appears, not once 'Christus' (unless it is in
a Hölderlin interpretation that I do not know). That is indeed very
noteworthy."[109] This is an odd observation, because Strauss himself

[105] Ibid., 598–599.   [106] Ibid., 675.   [107] Ibid., 673.   [108] Ibid.   [109] Ibid., 697.

cites from Heidegger's *Was heißt Denken?* where one finds a discussion of Christ, Hercules, and Dionysus in Hölderlin's poetry.[110] Nevertheless, this statement reflects Strauss's view that Heidegger's later thought has distanced itself from the Christian determinations that plagued his early writings. On the other hand, one can also find remarks by Strauss that point to secularized biblical and Christian notions featuring in Heidegger's later work. In the sixteenth session of a 1966 winter lecture course on Montesquieu at the University of Chicago, he associates Heidegger with Christianity, stating in a near-quote from Löwith's essay on Heidegger and Rosenzweig: "In our age someone has taken the passage from the New Testament, 'The truth will make us free' and has said, 'Freedom will make you true.' This is only another formulation of the same thing. This was Heidegger, by the way."[111] Similarly, in the lecture "The Problem of Socrates," delivered on April 17, 1970, on the Annapolis campus of St. John's College, Strauss discusses the insufficiency of Heidegger's claim that *Sein* is "*the* ground of all beings, and especially of man," because the question remains as to "what is responsible for the emergence of man and of Sein, or of what brings them out of nothing."[112] Heidegger's answer, that it is nothing from which being emerges, reminds Strauss of "the Biblical doctrine of creation [out of nothing]," yet he hastens to note that "Heidegger has no place for the Creator-God." He adds that "the mystery which Heidegger claims to have discovered is meant to be deeper, and less based on questionable presuppositions, than the mysteries of God."[113] Strauss's equivocal attitude toward Heidegger's later works thus springs from the assessment that it exhibits an estrangement from existentialism and as such reflects an attempt – not always successful – at gesturing beyond the grips of Christianity, but at the same time it remains incongruous with the idea of nature, and hence with political philosophy and its moral objectives.

EAST AND WEST

Among the ideas Heidegger develops in his later work, Strauss is intrigued by the claim that the East possesses important insights for the revival of

---

[110] As pointed out in Velkley, *Heidegger, Strauss and the Premises of Philosophy*, 59.

[111] Transcript available at: http://leostrausstranscripts.uchicago.edu/navigate/7/19/? byte=818732.

[112] Leo Strauss, "The Problem of Socrates," 338. The brackets are in the original.

[113] Ibid., 338 n82.

Western thinking.[114] Heidegger's fascination with Eastern thinking – or a certain construction of it – can be traced to his early years, but it intensifies in the 1950s, when he speaks of the "inevitable dialogue with the East Asian world."[115] It is not difficult to understand why the notion that the East could potentially provide an alternative solution to the West's crisis, alongside and perhaps in place of Athens and Jerusalem, would draw Strauss's attention. To be sure, he contends that Heidegger's formulation of the "dialogue and everything that it entails" between East and West discourages "political action of any kind" and is thus flawed, but he does endorse the idea of an East–West dialogue, albeit on his own terms.[116] In the lecture "The Problem of Socrates" Strauss notes that for Heidegger the solution to the fragmentation of our thinking "cannot lie in a return to the supra-temporal or eternal but only in something historical: in a meeting of the most different ways of understanding life and the world, a meeting of East and West." In order to prepare for this fateful meeting, "our first task would be the one in which we are already engaged – the task of understanding the Great *Western* Books."[117] In this telling statement, Strauss situates his own project of reviving political philosophy as complying with this Heideggerian imperative.

Earlier, however, in a lecture titled "Existentialism" from February 8, 1956, Strauss draws the Heideggerian trope of East–West dialogue into the orbit of modern Judaism. This lecture, delivered at the Hillel Foundation of the University of Chicago, the Jewish campus organization, likely to a crowd of considerable Jewish representation, can be read as a reevaluation of the relations between Heidegger's philosophy and the modern Jewish person. It should be noted that the lecture was first published, posthumously, with two crucial deviations from the original transcript: the title was emended to "An Introduction to Heideggerian Existentialism," and more importantly, the opening sentence, which runs as follows, was omitted: "This series of lectures – a reminder of the perplexities of modern man – should help the Jewish students in particular towards facing the perplexities of the modern Jew with somewhat greater clarity."[118] This initially omitted opening remark reveals that Strauss

---

[114] Strauss, "Philosophy as Rigorous Science," 33.
[115] *GA* 8, 136/Heidegger, *The Question Concerning Technology*, 158. Much has been written on the topic. See for instance: Parkes, *Heidegger and Asian Thought*; Ma, *Heidegger on East–West Dialogue*, esp. 113–116.
[116] Ibid., 33–34.   [117] Strauss, "The Problem of Socrates," 330.
[118] Strauss, "Existentialism," 303. See Pangle's introduction to *The Rebirth of Classical Political Rationalism*, xxix.

perceives the lecture series to be particularly relevant to Jewish students struggling with issues pertaining to their identity. His analysis of Heidegger, in other words, addresses the existential perplexities of the modern Jew. But how so?

This lecture offers a challenge to anyone seeking to understand Heidegger through it, because its exposition of his philosophy is overwhelmed by Strauss's own concerns, resulting in a deeply "Straussian" Heidegger. Indeed, this lecture demonstrates Strauss's deep dependence on Heidegger's thought, so much so that at times it is difficult to ascertain exactly whose view is being outlined. Rather than offering an "introduction to Heideggerian existentialism," as its amended title suggests, this lecture sheds light primarily on how Strauss comes to interpret the developments in Heidegger's thought. Characteristically, he begins with accolades to Heidegger and with personal recollections from his student years. Heidegger's philosophy is a "revolution"; he is "the only great thinker in our time," and with respect to philosophical dominance and stature, he is to be compared to Hegel.[119] At the same time, Heidegger is presented as the most pressing political, philosophical, and theological challenge. After a long buildup, Strauss attends to Heidegger's earlier philosophy and poses the difference between, on the one side, the ontology of Plato and Aristotle, wherein "to be in the highest sense means to be always," and on the other side, Heidegger's ontology, wherein "to be in the highest sense means to exist, that is to say, to be in the manner in which man is: to be in the highest sense is constituted by mortality."[120] This path of thought proved to be problematic for Heidegger, Strauss explains, eventually leading him "to break with existentialism." Strauss lists a number of difficulties that induced Heidegger to take a different route, the first being the prevalent Protestant anthropological undertones in the Dasein analysis, which were inconsistent with Heidegger's professed philosophical goals. Strauss writes:

Heidegger demanded from philosophy that it should liberate itself completely from traditional or inherited notions which were mere survivals of former ways of thinking. He mentioned especially concepts that were of Christian theological origin. Yet his understanding of existence was obviously of Christian origin (conscience, guilt, being unto death, anguish).[121]

---

[119] Strauss, "Existentialism," 304.
[120] Ibid. Some passages of this lecture are taken verbatim from sections dealing with "radical historicism" in *Natural Right and History*, confirming that Strauss is indeed referring to Heidegger, whose name is not mentioned in the book.
[121] Ibid., 313.

What motivated Heidegger to carry out a "turn" in his thought, among other things, is *Sein und Zeit*'s inadequate debt to Christian anthropology. His later thinking, accordingly, purges itself from this debt.

Strauss's depiction of Heidegger's later thinking becomes particularly interesting when he discusses Heidegger's fear of planetary technological domination, stating that the only hope that remains is for a world society that is "genuinely united by a world religion." Since Heidegger says no such thing, Strauss's statement appears to be a very loose interpretation of the notion of the advent of a new god, cast by his own worries over the question of technology and world politics in the time of the Cold War.[122] To combat this threat of technology, Strauss commentates, Heidegger believes that the tradition that brought about the present situation must be counteracted by exploring its limitations. Pithily, Heidegger's line of reasoning, according to Strauss, is recounted: "technology is the fruit of rationalism and rationalism is the fruit of Greek philosophy." This is a misinterpretation, for when Heidegger speaks of technology he means a mode of disclosure; it cannot be the fruit of rationalism – if anything, it is the other way around. The Greek understanding of being as presence, Strauss continues, presupposes the intelligibility of the whole, which renders it at the disposal of "human mastery."[123] Therefore, in order to bypass this conceptual heritage, the dogmatic assumption at the heart of rationalism – or better, metaphysics – that "to be means primarily to be present," must be disposed of. And over against the ontology of presence, an alternative understanding of being is offered, namely, "that to be means to be elusive or to be a mystery." This ontological understanding is attributed to "the east," and thus Strauss concludes that for Heidegger, salvaging the West from the threat of technology requires a philosophical encounter between the innermost roots of both worlds.

It is at this point that the importance of the initially omitted introductory statement regarding the significance of the lecture series for Jewish identity comes to light. For in Strauss's restatement of Heidegger, the way the West is to prepare for the meeting with the East is by examining its own roots and seeking a resembling, non-Greek conception of being as mystery *within itself*. According to Strauss, such an ontology can be found in the Bible. "Within the west," he determines, "the limitations of rationalism were always seen by the biblical tradition." Consulting with the Bible is particularly appropriate, for "biblical thought is one form of Eastern thought ... the Bible is the east within us, within western

---

[122] On this see Howse, *Leo Strauss: Man of Peace.*   [123] Strauss, "Existentialism," 317.

man."[124] To caution against misunderstandings, Strauss clarifies that he does not mean "taking the Bible as absolute" or as a set of beliefs or commandments. "Not the Bible as Bible," he assures, "but the Bible as eastern can help us in overcoming Greek rationalism." Clearly, Strauss reworks Heidegger's call to overcome Western metaphysics by engaging with the East as an appeal to take seriously a philosophical stance that resembles the one found in the biblical tradition. Not the pre-Socratics, who in Heidegger's scheme possess a non-metaphysical conception of being in the Western tradition, but rather the Bible can offset the ontology of presence. Strauss, in other words, likens Heidegger's conception of being to the mysterious "Eastern" biblical God. This, it is important to add, is not an identification, for it is said that Heidegger's understanding of being is "as impersonal as the Platonic ideas and as elusive as the biblical God."[125] The conclusion of Strauss's analysis, in any event, is this: the hope of the West lies in the contribution of a philosophically construed biblical-Heideggerian understanding of being. It is this ontological conception that can counter the Greek dogmatism of reason and the accelerating technological domination it espouses.

It should be clear that the claim that the biblical position is "the east within us" as well as the belief that it presents the possible avenue for rebooting the West's perverse conception of being are Strauss's views, not Heidegger's. Indeed, also in *Natural Right and History* Strauss suggests that classical rationalism's reconstruction of "the essential character of "the natural world" should be "supplemented by consideration of the most elementary premises of the Bible," and he speaks of the Bible as "the East within us, Western men" a few months before his lecture at the Hillel House.[126] On the other hand, Heidegger takes the Hebrew Bible to possess no competing ontology to Greek metaphysics whatsoever, and

---

[124] Ibid.

[125] Ibid., 318. On the mysterious and incomprehensible nature of the biblical God, see also Strauss, "On the Interpretation of Genesis," 359–376. Strauss's association of Judaism with the unrepresentable is in line with a prominent tradition in German philosophy and also brings to mind Jean-François Lyotard's *Heidegger and "the jews"* (1997), where "the jews" are formulated as the reminder of the futility of the West's desire for complete representation, presencing, and control. In this sense – and perhaps in this sense only – Strauss and Lyotard are in agreement. Shlomo Zemach, the translator of Heidegger's "Origin of the Work of Art" into Hebrew, explains Heidegger's idea of *aletheia*, often rendered as *das Unverborgene*, through the idea of the biblical self-concealing God as expressed in the verse in Isaiah 45:15: "You are a God who hides Himself [*El mistater*]." See Herskowitz, "Heidegger in Hebrew," 120.

[126] Strauss, *Natural Right and History*, 80; Strauss, "Letter to the Editor," 23.

moreover, he situates Judaism and the "Old Testament" alongside the Christian tradition as offering conceptions of the Creator God and *ens creatum* participating in the grip of technological disclosure of being as produced. It should not go unnoticed, moreover, that Strauss's invocation of the Bible in this lecture *excludes* Christianity, as his earlier portrayal of the overcoming of the Christian layers in Heidegger's existentialism makes clear. As we have by now come to learn, Strauss's overarching impulse is to break the ties between Judaism and Christianity and secure the dignity of the former as a self-standing tradition over against the latter. In a passing remark he avers: "'the Judaeo-Christian tradition'? This means to blur and to conceal grave differences."[127] A younger Strauss is even harsher: "There is no reconciliation between Judaism and Christianity; Judaism is the anti-Christian principle pure and simple."[128] It can be suggested, thus, that from the perspective of this essay, the so-called "turn" in Heidegger's thinking can be tentatively schematized as a move from a philosophy nested in the Christian tradition to one reflecting philosophical formulations approximating Jewish teachings. And apparently it is in this respect that the perplexed Jew can find remedy in the direction proposed by Heidegger, whose productive conceptual framework reflects the philosophical significance of the insights found in the Jewish tradition for the contemporary predicament.

This conclusion, however, makes Strauss's lecture a perplexing piece. Not only does it present a curious interpretation of Heidegger, it is also unclear how it should be reconciled with the aforementioned interpretation of the initiation of the East–West dialogue as pertaining to Strauss's liberal-arts Great Books project. But more importantly, Strauss speaks approvingly of the wane of evocations of secularized Christian categories in Heidegger, while at the same time he introduces a biblical category in a secularized register as holding the key to rethinking the foundations of philosophical rationalism. Is Strauss not committing the exact flaw he repeatedly rebukes in modern Jewish thought?[129] In his lecture "Why We Remain Jews" Strauss makes a related remark, immediately after he calls

---

[127] Strauss, "Existentialism," 307.   [128] Strauss, "Paul de Lagarde," 94.

[129] For different interpretations of this lecture, see Altman. *The German Stranger*, 190–191, n43. While Altman recognizes that the lecture offers "a *distorted* vision of the Bible," McIlwain seems to take the secularization of the Bible in it as unproblematic. See McIlwain, "The East within Us." I do not share Altman's view that Strauss was and remained a closet National Socialist his entire mature life. The Zuckerts disassociate Strauss from the opinions expressed in this lecture. See their *Strauss and the Problem of Political Philosophy*, 261–264.

Judaism a "heroic delusion" for holding tight to the conviction that "the one thing needful is righteousness or charity," which in Judaism "are one and the same thing." He then clarifies, more generously, that by "delusion" he means "dream":

No nobler dream was ever dreamt. It is surely nobler to be a victim of the most noble dream than to profit from a sordid reality and to wallow in it. Dream is akin to aspiration. And aspiration is a kind of divination of an enigmatic vision. And an enigmatic vision in the emphatic sense is the perception of the ultimate mystery, of the truth of the ultimate mystery. The truth of the ultimate mystery – the truth that there is an ultimate mystery, that being is radically mysterious – cannot be denied even by the unbelieving Jew of our age.[130]

The loftiness of this passage notwithstanding, it too, like his lecture on Heidegger, betrays a version of Judaism that is secularized and formulized according to terms set out by philosophy and indeed presented *as* a philosophical stance. Strauss appears to be offering a synthesis between philosophy and faith that has "internalized" modern atheism and disavowed the truth of the Bible. Does this not consist of surrendering the traditional belief in God and revelation, and is it not thus incommensurable with his most fundamental assumptions?

Through his creative interpretation of Heidegger, Strauss reveals himself as a modern Jewish thinker on another account, namely, in participating in the tradition common among modern German-Jewish thinkers who identify modern existence as crisis-laden and believe Judaism can contribute to its overcoming. Strauss understands the crisis not, as is sometimes the case, in the lack of fulfillment of modern precepts, but rather in these very precepts themselves. Judaism, in his view, is not the epitome of modern sensibilities but rather counteracts them. In this respect he is unlike Cohen and perhaps more akin to Buber. Similarly, in his analysis of the biblical as Eastern, Strauss invokes a view that emerged toward the *fin de siècle* and gained popularity in the first decades of the twentieth century, according to which Judaism and the biblical world are not in essence Western, but rooted in the Orient. Many of those who held this view were driven by an antisemitic motivation to efface the place of Judaism from the story of the West. But for others – once again, like Buber – it served the opposite goal. Fueled with an increasing sense of the West's decadence and by a fascination with non-Western cultures, they portrayed Judaism as exotic, irrational, and authentic, and thus as

---

[130] Strauss, "Why We Remain Jews," 328.

possessing the key to the revitalization of the modern European spirit, plagued by urbanization, rationalization, and alienation.[131] Strauss calls upon this constructed model, with its strong Romantic resonances, but in his interpretation of Heidegger's notion of being as biblical-oriental, the Jewish-biblical worldview represents not irrationalism, but a rationalism aware of its limitations. In this respect Strauss's "utopianism" is markedly "anti-utopian" in that he posits the limitations of human abilities and rejects the premises that "every problem can be solved."[132] It constitutes a moderate, nondogmatic form of rationalism that, as he claims, generates a moderate, nontotalitarian form of politics. By promoting this mode of thinking, however, Strauss is once again revealed to be situated precisely within the modern Jewish tradition he so dedicatedly toiled to overcome.

CONCLUSION

In his thought, Strauss's efforts to strengthen Jerusalem serve the purpose of reactivating the quarrel between philosophy and revelation in all its severity. In his understanding, while one is either from Athens or from Jerusalem, one must remain open to the option of the competing doctrine. Revelation is the only worthy rival to philosophy and as such must be taken seriously. Strauss's occupation with political philosophy is thoroughly marked by his youthful Weimarian concerns about the shortcomings of liberalism's promise of modern emancipation, the question of the modern critique of religion, and the desire to secure the integrity of modern Judaism vis-à-vis its tradition. As we have seen, Heidegger hovers over Strauss's diagnosis of the modern crisis in philosophy, as well as the possibility of its recovery. The Freiburg philosopher represents the height of modern nihilism, and overcoming his philosophy and the tradition that made it possible is therefore of paramount importance. At the same time, it is also he who directs Strauss toward the possibility of reconsidering the neglected strife between Athens and Jerusalem as a way out of the modern impasse. And in a similar manner to other thinkers we have already discussed, Strauss too understands Heidegger's philosophy of existence to be a secularized inheritor of the Christian tradition which, he believes,

---

[131] Mendes-Flohr, "Fin de Siècle Orientalism"; Marchand, "Eastern Wisdom in an Era of Western Despair," 341–360; Marchand, *German Orientalism in the Age of Empire*. The "orientalist" background of Strauss's view here is often overlooked. For example, Zuckert, "Leo Strauss: Jewish, Yes, but Heideggerian?" 95.

[132] Strauss, "Why We Remain Jews," 317.

is part of the problem. In this respect, his lifelong encounter with Heidegger springs from, and is best understood as, part of the interwar effort of Jewish self-assertion in the face of Christianity and modern secularism. Heidegger also plays a crucial role in Strauss's explorations into modern Judaism, reflecting its flaws and inauthenticity as well as offering a way to reconstruct a respectable Judaism. Indeed, his critique of Heidegger and his analysis of Judaism are closely knitted. In this manner, Strauss too identifies an opposition between Heidegger and Judaism and poses a construction of the latter as a possible alternative to the former. In the next chapter, we examine how Abraham Joshua Heschel frames a similar opposition between what he takes to be Heidegger's pagan phenomenology and his own existential-biblical thought.

6

God, Being, Pathos: Abraham Joshua Heschel's Theological Rejoinder to Heidegger

INTRODUCTION

In May 1963, Abraham Joshua Heschel delivered the Raymond Fred West Memorial Lectures at Stanford University. The three lectures – "In the Likeness and Unlikeness of God," "In Search of Meaning," and "Existence and Exaltation" – were later compiled in the book *Who Is Man?*, published in 1965. In this condensed and mature expression of many steadfast positions, Heschel challenges modern secularism through presenting his phenomenological "theology of man" in an implicit and explicit confrontation with Heidegger's existential ontology. In Heschel's formulation, Heidegger's philosophy "seeks to relate the human being to a transcendence called being as such" while his own thought, "realizing that human being is more than just being, that human being is living being, seeks to relate man to divine living, to a transcendence called the living God."[1] The aim of this chapter is to organize Heschel's otherwise unsystematic critique of Heidegger as a unified theological argument and critically assess it.[2]

EARLY ENCOUNTERS WITH PHENOMENOLOGY

Heschel studied philosophy in Berlin at the end of the 1920s and beginning of the 1930s, in the very years of Heidegger's rise to philosophical

---

[1] Heschel, *Who Is Man?*, 69.
[2] Heschel's rejoinder to Heidegger has been discussed in Perlman, *The Eclipse of Humanity*. However, further consideration seems to be required, as Perlman's analysis lacks almost any critical distance from Heschel, barely addresses Heschel's references to Heidegger outside of *Who Is Man?*, and reduces Heidegger's philosophy to his politics. Moreover, some of Heschel's misrepresentations of Heidegger's philosophy are reiterated in Perlman's book. An earlier version of this chapter was published as Herskowitz, "God, Being, Pathos."

stardom. From the very beginning, Heschel found phenomenology to be a constructive method of philosophical inquiry. As attested in his doctoral dissertation, *Das prophetische Bewusstsein*, which he was then writing, Husserl's phenomenology provided him with a methodology to overcome the historicistic standards and aims of *Religionswissenschaft* and investigate the "actual singularity" (*eigentümlichen Besonderheit*) of the biblical prophetic consciousness – or as he describes it in the introduction to its 1962 expanded English edition, "the decisive categories or the structural forms of prophetic thinking."[3] By means of Husserlian phenomenology, Heschel treated biblical prophecy as an actual phenomenon not to be reduced to psychological states or historical background.[4]

But Heschel never actually adheres to the worldview that sustains Husserl's notion of "transcendental ego." Like many of his generational peers, he too rejects a detached a-historical rationalism in favor of an engaged, experiential, and situational perspective. From early on, Heschel attends to the *Erlebnis* and *Ereignis* of human existence as explored by the "new thinking," and thus is allied with some of the philosophical presuppositions that led Heidegger to rebel against Husserl.[5] In 1936, Heschel befriended Henry Corbin, the French expert on Islamic studies who was among the first to translate Heidegger into French.[6] Their conversations and correspondence dealt with, among other things, Heidegger's thought and Corbin's progress with the translations.[7] Heschel is said to have "admired" Cassirer at the time, although it should be recalled that Cassirer had by then taken serious strides toward anthropological phenomenology, and it is unlikely that this admiration pertained to the vision of Judaism that Cassirer shared with Hermann Cohen, a vision Heschel considered an artificial Hellenization of Judaism.[8] Heschel's early work on the prophets constitutes an inaugural attempt, which will continue to occupy him throughout his entire life, to develop a "biblical" thought that challenges the "German-Greek way of thinking" within which his professors and members of the intellectual milieu that surrounded him, were

---

[3] Heschel, *Die Prophetie*, xvi; Heschel, *The Prophets*, xi. On Heschel and phenomenology, see Novak, "Heschel's Phenomenology of Revelation"; Kavka, "The Meaning of This Hour."

[4] Erlewine, *Judaism and the West*, 105–128.

[5] The marks of Dilthey and Scheler in his published dissertation confirm this, as well as Heschel's early attraction to Buber.

[6] On their relationship, see Fenton, "Henry Corbin and Abraham Heschel."

[7] Kaplan and Dresner, *Abraham Joshua Heschel*, 235, 258.   [8] Ibid., 99.

entangled. It is in his early years in Berlin that he realizes: "there is much that philosophy could learn from Jewish life."[9]

After Heschel fled from Nazi Germany to America, occasional references to Heideggerian ideas and vocabulary are discernible in his works. *Who Is Man?* is his most comprehensive treatment of Heidegger and could be rightfully seen as the culmination of an ongoing albeit sporadic engagement with the German thinker. The relative scarcity of references to Heidegger before *Who Is Man?* largely reflects the intellectual environment in America at that time. In the 1940s and most of the 1950s, only a few works by Heidegger were available in English – *Sein und Zeit* not among them (a failed attempt by Hannah Arendt and Paul Tillich to set in motion the project of translating Heidegger's early masterpiece into English took place in 1954).[10] Heschel's *Who Is Man?* both reflects and should be read as an attempt to counter the theological surge of interest in Heidegger's philosophy that took place in the United States at the end of the 1950s and through the 1960s. Some notable indications of the "Heidegger surge" include a conference at Drew University in April 1964, dedicated to the theological potential in Heidegger's thought, which drew public attention through a *New York Times* article reporting the controversial keynote address by Hans Jonas, "Heidegger and Theology"; the publication of a book entitled *The Later Heidegger and Theology* (1963), collecting various perspectives on the theological import of Heidegger's later philosophy; and the extensive popularity of Paul Tillich's existentialist theology, overtly influenced by Heidegger. As we shall see, some of the misrepresentations of Heidegger's thought typical of the time are apparent in Heschel's reading.

That *Who Is Man?* reflects this theological fascination can be confirmed by a comparison of Heschel's published dissertation, entitled *Die Prophetie* (1936) with its expanded English version *The Prophets* (1962). After the section "Die ontologische Voraussetzung" in the original edition, the English edition has an added section entitled "The

---

[9] Heschel, *Man's Quest for God*, 95.
[10] On the reception of Heidegger in America, see Woessner, *Heidegger in America*. Woessner does not mention Heschel. In *Who Is Man?* Heschel quotes a translated passage from *Sein und Zeit* as it is found in Langan, *The Meaning of Heidegger*, which he evidently consulted. It is noteworthy that Heschel does not translate this passage on his own from the original German or use the English version of the now-canonical Macquarrie and Robinson translation which had been published in 1962. This suggests Heschel's later encounter with Heidegger's thought is mainly secondhand and not in-depth. Heschel seems to be unfamiliar with William Richardson's work *Heidegger: Through Phenomenology to Thought* (1963) as well.

Ontocentric Predicament," parts of which appear verbatim in *Who Is Man?* as a polemic against Heidegger. In this added section, a pagan experience, characterized as "experiencing being," is contrasted to the prophetic experience in which "experiencing concern" is the center of existence.[11] This, indeed, offers a condensed encapsulation of the issue from Heschel's point of view. His engagement with Heidegger consists of a confrontation between the biblical perspective of the prophets and what he defines as Heidegger's paganism.

HESCHEL'S RELIGIOUS EXISTENTIALISM

It is easy to confirm from Heschel's writings that his existential perspective concurs with many of Heidegger's philosophical assumptions. For example, he effectively sides with Heidegger's notion of phenomenology when he exercises a phenomenological "exegesis of human existence" in-the-world, "an attempt to describe some modes of being human."[12] Moreover, he is after the meaning of being, which he believes can be known only through temporal life. Indeed, temporality and historicity figure largely in his thought. In a chapter from *Man Is Not Alone*, entitled "The Temporality of Existence," he writes: "it is obvious that the relation of existence to time is more intimate and unique than its relation to space ... temporality, therefore, is an essential feature of existence."[13] The celebration of time is also extended in Heschel's work *The Sabbath: Its Meaning for Modern Man* (1951). Like Heidegger, Heschel's existential positioning also prioritizes possibility over actuality – "the outstanding mark of man," he announces, "is the superiority of the possibilities of his being over the actuality of his being."[14] Heschel, however, maintains that this overall outlook derives from, and is reflected in, the Hebrew Bible. For this reason, he rejects the prospects of an adequate phenomenology of human existence by means of Heidegger's a-theistic methodology. Springing from the conviction that God is essential to the very constitution of the human being, Heschel perceives Heidegger's Dasein analytic to be misguided from the very outset. There is simply no sense in which the godless explication of Dasein's existence and the lack of any reference to Dasein's being-from or -toward God can refer to the actual human's

[11] Heschel, *Die Prophetie*, 153–160; Heschel, *The Prophets*, 260–267.
[12] Heschel, *Who Is Man?*, 31.   [13] Heschel, *Man Is Not Alone*, 200.
[14] Heschel, *Who Is Man?*, 40.

being. In practice, Heidegger's a-theism is atheism. Heschel writes so in reference to Heidegger in a handwritten note kept in his private papers: "The issue is not being itself, for being itself is the invention of meta-physicians. Being in the world as expressing man's existence confines man and limits the problem. The true issue is *being with God.*"[15]

In his theology, Heschel attempts to counter the demythologized modern perspective and reestablish the account in which the good is an actual, objective constituent of the nature of things due to their origin in a benevolent God. "After the Lord had created the universe," Heschel muses, "He took a look at His creation. What was the word that conveyed His expression? If an artist were to find a word describing how the universe looked to God at the dawn of its existence, the word would be sublime or beautiful. But the word that the Bible has is *good.*"[16] Being is good because God created it; it has an implicit nor-mative value that is derived from its status as creation. Without this understanding, we cannot espouse normativity at all. "We may explore things without God," he states, but "we cannot decide about values without him."[17] A supernatural God and consequently a supernatural good are the condition of possibility of human existence.

Importantly, only the biblical God can be the source of good and therefore inhabit the path toward human fulfillment. As pathetic, that is, compassionate, caring, and animated by what Heschel terms "tran-sitive concern," the biblical God engages with the world, makes demands on humanity, and is in need of human partnership for redemp-tion. Heschel's fundamental premises is this: any framework that denies the essential link between humans and an ineffable but at the same time personal, compassionate, and demanding God, viz., the biblical God of pathos, is ultimately nihilistic and tied to paganism. In his understand-ing, Heidegger's philosophy falls squarely into this category. Like Buber and others, Heschel approaches Heidegger from an ontic vantage point and in effect provides an ontic reading of Heidegger. It is similarly apparent that Heidegger's lack of theological commitments is con-tested. Heidegger, in Heschel's anti-Bultmannian view, advocates a religious perspective in contrast to which the Hebrew biblical tradi-tion stands.

---

[15] Heschel Papers: Prophets: En Shnei Nevi'im be-Signon Ehad, circa 1950s–1960s, box 154, folder 5.
[16] Heschel, *God in Search of Man*, 372.   [17] Ibid., 377.

BEING AND LIVING

The fundamental assumption with which Heschel approaches Heidegger is that "the problem of being can never be treated in isolation but only in relation to God."[18] As such, the account of authenticity outlined in *Sein und Zeit* is severely distorted. Heidegger describes Dasein's existence as groundless, and authenticity consists of taking ownership of one's existence in the face of one's death. According to Heschel, however, the "existential paradox" of human life resides in the fact that "the self is in need of a meaning which it cannot furnish itself."[19] *Ens finitum* is unable to provide the sufficient stability and substance for a meaningful, fulfilled life. The implicit privation of human existence denies it the possibility of self-redemption. By ignoring the existential ground that God is, Heidegger substantiates a dangerous circularity by which the groundless Dasein, granted quasi-divine attributes, grounds its own being. With this, Heschel voices a prevailing critique of Heidegger. We encountered it already in our discussion of his early Christian readers, but also Hannah Arendt, in her expositional essay "What Is Existential Philosophy?," restates the argument that Dasein bears the attributes of a secularized God and reaches similar conclusions. With regards to Heidegger's notion of authenticity, she writes:

This ideal of the Self follows as a consequence of Heidegger's making of man what God was in earlier ontology. A being of the highest order is conceivable only as single and unique and knowing no equals. What Heidegger consequently designates as the "fall" includes all those modes of human existence in which man is not God but lives together with his own kind in the world.[20]

Likewise, Jacob Taubes proposes to translate Dasein into *homo absconditus*, while acknowledging and rejecting the analogy to *deus absconditus* and the suggestion that it is a mere secularization of the original theological notion. As to the question whether "man is his own source?," Taubes responds: "to this question Heidegger fails to give an answer."[21] This kind of circularity, Heschel asserts, is a pagan ideal, whereby "man becomes his own idol."[22] A trace of Heschel's befuddlement by the self-circuiting features of Dasein's being can be found in

---

[18] Heschel, *God in Search of Man*, 412. [19] Heschel, *Who Is Man?*, 56.
[20] Arendt, "What Is Existential Philosophy?" 180.
[21] Taubes, "The Development of the Ontological Question," 662.
[22] Heschel, *Who Is Man?*, 36.

another handwritten note in his personal papers, where he quotes from *Sein und Zeit*, "Dasein is *essentially guilty*," and then adds:

This means [Dasein] is not guilty some of the time, but all of the time. In everything man does, he is guilty, because he always has been guilty. This is a "primordial being guilty," which lies in the fact that, though Dasein is "thrown" and "fallen" being, it is somehow responsible for its thrownness and fallenness.[23]

Furthermore, the fact that human beings are created by God implies an inherent normative stamp on their existence. Values and normativity can be sustained only with recourse to God, and since such recourse is non-existent in *Sein und Zeit*, all that remains is neutral being, or being neutral. Decisions are made, actions are played out, but not in the name of a higher vocation or value: Dasein simply is. Heschel thus distinguishes between two accounts of existence: "living" and "being." In a likely allusion to Heidegger, he states "the term 'human being' is apt to suggest that the human is but a mode of being in general, with the emphasis placed on being." In contrast to this view, he asserts that "man's most important problem is not being but living";[24] that is, not leading an ethically void existence but engaging in the constant challenge of a life directed toward the good. Heidegger's ontological existential of "being-in-the-world," interpreted here as "being-neutral-in-the-world," is converted in *Who Is Man?* to the ontic and ethically charged category of "living-in-the-world," or "being-challenged-in-the-world."[25]

With this judgment, Heschel offers a variant of the critique of the immorality of Heidegger's system. Of course, in Heidegger's descriptive and transcendental project of delineating the a priori ontological precon-ditions of Dasein's existence in the world, few, if any, actual normative imperatives should to be found. *That* existential possibilities constitute Dasein's being is of dramatically greater interest to Heidegger than their *actual* ontic manifestations. Any encouragement or discouragement with respect to taking on one ontic possibility over another inherently under-mines the declared descriptive aim. This does not mean Heidegger's philosophical scheme is not normative in a more general sense. What Heidegger attempts to do, however, is to expose and remove the presumed objective ground of the value systems so often taken for granted. Heidegger articulates what Dasein *could* be, but according to Heschel's ontic perspective, a genuine portrayal of human being must include both

---

[23] Heschel Papers: box 243, folder 5.   [24] Heschel, *Who Is Man?*, 68.
[25] Ibid., 95, 105.

what one could *and* should be. "The central problem," Heschel affirms, "is not: 'What is it "to be"?' but rather: 'How to be and not to be'?"[26] It may be helpful to clarify Heschel's assessment by considering another common critique of Heidegger's descriptive methodology. Leveled most famously by Jean-Paul Sartre, this critique calls attention to the inevitable prescriptive character of Heidegger's distinction between authentic and inauthentic being. It simply cannot be the case, so this charge goes, that this distinction can be made without an implicit prescriptive impetus toward authenticity. Whatever its merits and shortcomings, this critique allows us to see that according to Heschel, Heidegger's fault lay not in his failure to live up to the descriptive aims of his existential ontology, but in what is missing in his basic assumptions that brings rise to a misguided desire to adhere to solely descriptive aims in the first place.

Critique of Heidegger's lack of constructive moral obligation permeates *Who Is Man?* For instance, Heschel agrees with Heidegger that a key element of human existence is the fundamental distress of existential alienation and misplacement. Yet unlike Heidegger's authentic Dasein that opens itself up for *Angst*, in Heschel's account, the sense of homelessness translates into an embedded existential urge toward a relation with what is beyond. More specifically, existential anguish is generated less "by the mystery of being, by the absence of being, or by the fear of non-being," as he reads Heidegger to be asserting, but by the prospect of "meaningless being."[27] Anxiety does not spring from Dasein's general uncanniness or portending nothingness but from the troubling awareness of an unfulfilled ethical demand. Heschel's insinuated castigation of Heidegger's notion of "boredom" draws on a similar view. In the lecture "What Is Metaphysics?" Heidegger states that the existential mood of boredom can serve as a portal into the truth of being, a gateway to awareness of the nothingness lurching behind being. For his part, Heidegger does not judge boredom positively or negatively, but rather seeks to uncover ontological insights through its attunement toward being.

We are occupied with beings even when we do not occupy ourselves with them explicitly; even then we are related to beings, indeed even in boredom. Boredom not in the sense of when we say: this book is boring, but rather in the attunement: I'm bored. Here there is a fusion of things, of beings as a whole, which in a certain way sink away in the attunement of boredom.[28]

---

[26] Ibid., 47.   [27] Ibid., 52.   [28] Heidegger, "What Is Metaphysics?," 738.

In Heschel's opinion, this reflects the absence of a compassionate God who instills vocation and meaning in human existence. "Boredom is a sickness of the self-consciousness," he writes, "the result of one's inability to sense the vital vocation" in life.[29] Our very existence is marked by vocation because "to be" implies the normative demand "to live." A related point can be detected in Heschel's intimation of the notion of "mineness" (*Jemeinigkeit*) in *Sein und Zeit*. Heidegger holds that Dasein understands its being as is in each case concretely "mine." In an earlier work Heschel polemicizes against this position: "the essence of what I am," he writes, "is not mine. *I am what is not mine.*"[30] Heidegger comprehends man from within this fundamental self-referencing, yet in truth, Heschel maintains, we belong to God, whose demands make ethical conduct the linchpin of authentic existence.

Demonstrating that he holds no meaningful distinction between Heidegger's earlier and later writings, Heschel ties the lack of normativity in *Sein und Zeit*'s version of authenticity, and the sheer being it promotes, to Heidegger's imperative to "let being be." Like Arendt, who in *Life of the Mind* judges Heidegger as someone who renounces the will and action, Heschel too understands this as a call for passivity, an expression of "despair" and mistrust in humanity. This grim view arises from a perverse account of human being, he maintains, for "it is self-deception to assume that man can ever be an innocent spectator. To be human is to be involved."[31] In one of the two explicit mentions of Heidegger in *Who Is Man?*, Heschel emphasizes that

> Man is not only being, he is also living, and if he were simply to "surrender to being," as Heidegger calls upon us to do, he would abdicate his power to decide and reduce his living to being. To be is both passive and intransitive. In living, man relates himself actively to the world.[32]

Heschel's charge notwithstanding, the accusation that Heidegger holds a position advocating passivity is somewhat misleading. While Heidegger does seem to retreat from a focus on praxis already in the mid-1930s, he makes clear in "The Question Concerning Technology" and other essays that "to let being be" means not the absence of action but a certain receptive and attentive comportment toward being, one that does not aggressively seek to exploit or transform it. Heidegger renounces "will" primarily insofar as it is the will to power; the act of thinking, which lets

---

[29] Ibid., 104.   [30] Heschel, *Between God and Man*, 62.   [31] Heschel, *Who Is Man?*, 68.
[32] Ibid., 94–95.

being be, "is neither theoretical nor practical. It takes place before that differentiation."[33] To speak of "passivity" in opposition to "activity" as Heschel does is implicitly to participate in the discourse of effectivity and productivity that Heidegger seeks to circumvent. In other words, one who lets being be is indeed involved and is certainly not (at least necessarily) an "innocent spectator."

OBJECTIFICATION AND NAZISM

A major corollary of Heidegger's advancement of "being" over "living," according to Heschel, is his inability to appropriately differentiate between human and thing. For without the fundamental ethical imperative in human being, Heidegger's system cannot account for the intrinsic quality and value of man. Heschel connects this fault to the way in which Heidegger carries out his phenomenology. "There are two ways of facing and inspecting human being," he observes: "from within or from without."[34] The former is when "I face my own being, here and now." The latter is when "I encounter my fellow man's being-there" – evoking the term Da-sein in English. It is important for Heschel to make a clear distinction between the two. While it is "possible and legitimate to ponder being in general or the being of all beings" as Heidegger does, it is nevertheless "futile and impossible to ponder human being in general, the being of human species." Since the irreplaceably unique relation one has with oneself is missing in the reflection of other human beings, then "there is only one way of comprehending man's being-there, and that is by way of inspecting my own being."[35] In taking the "from without" perspective, Heidegger overlooks the elements of human existence that are attained by means of our self-relation. Any methodology that ignores this crucial feature is guilty of applying the method for investigating objects onto human beings and will therefore inevitably yield an objectivized and distorted portrayal of human existence. The title '*Who Is Man?*' deliberately conveys this point: *who* applies to humans alone. In Heidegger's depiction, however, Dasein is objectivized: it is a *what*, not a *who*.

This is confirmed, in Heschel's view, by the portrayal of inauthentic Dasein as an impersonal, generalized, dispensable, and plainly ordinary being. Against Heidegger's somewhat patronizing depiction of average everyday Dasein, Heschel argues that "my own being, placed as it is in the midst of many beings, is not simply being here, being around, being part of

[33] *GA* 9, 362/Heidegger, *Pathmarks*, 263.   [34] Ibid., 34.   [35] Ibid.

the environment. It is at the very center of my consciousness that I am distinct."[36] It should be noted that the phrasing "being here, being around, being part of" is an unmistakable nod to the plethora of terms used to describe Dasein's various ontological conditions in *Sein und Zeit*. But more importantly, what is implied here is that since the internal experience of other human beings is inaccessible to Heidegger, his only resort is to blunt generalizations that obscure uniqueness: "Generalization ... fails in trying to understand man."[37] Had he taken the "from within" perspective, Heschel continues, he would have known that "it is through the awareness that I am not only an everybody that I evolve as a self, as somebody, as a person, as something that cannot be repeated, something for which there is no duplicate, no substitute." Admittedly, "in the eyes of the world ... I am an average man, but to my heart I am not an average person. To my heart I am of great moment."[38] According to Heschel, Heidegger's derogatory descriptions of everyday Dasein reflect a fundamental disdain toward human beings that is fastened to an even more fundamental disdain toward being: "it is as a result of extreme abuse and desecration of being that man brings upon himself the punishment of disgust with being." Echoing the assessment of Hans Jonas, who found parallels between Heidegger's existential philosophy and ancient Gnosticism as well as Buber's confirmation of the Gnostic charge of the notion of *Das Man*, Heschel judges that Heidegger suffers from a "disgust of being, a sense of being trapped in the world."[39] For Heschel it is clear that "in the actual lives of actual men, life even when felt to be a burden is cherished deeply, valued supremely, accepted in its reality."[40]

Heidegger, however, holds a clear distinction between the being of things – either ready to hand (*zuhanden*) or present at hand (*vorhanden*) – and the being of Dasein. For him, Dasein is an entity like no other in its fundamental feature of disclosiveness of other beings and in that it lacks a fixed and determined essence: "if existence is definitive for Dasein's Being and if its essence is constituted in part by potentiality-for-Being, then, as long as Dasein exists it must in each case, as such potentiality, *not yet be* something."[41] Unlike objects that are constituted by their facticity alone, Dasein is an open-ended being and as such its essence is determined by the unfolding of its life – hence the central role of death, the ultimate projection of this formative unfolding. The *how* of Dasein constitutes its

---

[36] Ibid., 34–35.   [37] Ibid., 37.   [38] Ibid., 35.   [39] Ibid., 35–36.   [40] Ibid., 35.
[41] *SZ*, 233/*BT*, 276.

being. Heidegger explicitly asserts that "the person is not a Thing, not a substance, not an object."[42] Heidegger in fact contrasts Dasein to all other entities that are constituted by their essence in language similar to that used by Heschel:

The being that we are ourselves, the Dasein, cannot at all be interrogated by the question *What* is this? We gain access to this being only if we ask: *Who* is it? Dasein is not constituted by whatness but – if we may coin the expression – by *whoness*. The answer does not give a thing but an I, you, we.[43]

Similarly, Heschel's "within–without" critique seems to rest on the subject–object distinction so forcefully rejected by Heidegger and which he himself repudiates. That Dasein is primordially always already outside itself, in-the-world, and with-others, that is, always already attesting to and constituted by the existence of others, illustrates the inappropriateness of the rigid inside–outside axis upon which Heschel bases his criticism. Tellingly, not only does Heschel attribute to Heidegger a stance he fervently rejects, he also argues that this Heideggerian "subject," as a "what" and not a "who," is not even worthy of the term. Moreover, given that Heidegger seeks a phenomenological and transcendental investigation of human existence and being, there is no escaping general and uniform preconditions. Indeed, that Heschel ventures to provide an apt description of modalities of human existence solely by means of self-inspection is incoherent if it is not grounded in the covert assumption that one's personal self-relational experiences can be generalized and applied to those of others.

The fault of generalizing human beings and treating them as "average" is linked to Heidegger's notorious political affiliation. In Heschel's view, brutality – "the opposite of humanity" – is tied to "the tendency to treat a person as a generality, to regard a person as an average man."[44] The accusation of Heidegger's philosophical objectification and contempt for human beings is also associated with Heidegger's Nazism. After quoting a passage written in pre-Nazi Germany describing the industrial resourcefulness of the human physique, Heschel suggests that "perhaps there was a connection between this statement and what the Nazis actually did in the extermination camps: make soap of human flesh."[45] The direct result of "moral annihilation" is "physical extermination."[46] Heidegger's

---

[42] *SZ*, 48/*BT*, 73.   [43] Heidegger, *The Basic Problems of Phenomenology*, 120.
[44] Ibid., 47.   [45] Ibid., 24.
[46] It cannot go without mentioning that Heschel's mother and sister were both murdered by the Nazis. Maurice Friedman, a long-time friend of Heschel, shares a short anecdote: "Heschel confided in me that an American professor told him that while he was visiting

immanence goes hand in hand with the pagan monstrosity of the Nazis: "existence without transcendence is a way of living where things become idols and idols become monsters."[47] Inasmuch as the world and humanity are perceived from within an immanent and self-contained framework that denies a transcendent and relational God, there is nothing to prevent the reduction of human beings to objects readily exploited, abused, or exterminated in accordance with benefit or the whimsicality of will. Heschel thus reiterates the view we have encountered earlier, connecting Heidegger's Nazism to his immanentism.

In Heschel's understanding, the tragic unfolding of the twentieth century is the direct result of the paganism of modern secularism. And as Heidegger embodies this mode of thinking, the confrontation with his thought typifies the confrontation with the deficient spiritual underpinning of the age. Like the prophets, his biblical heroes of the past, and equipped with their message, Heschel feels obligated to confront and repudiate the modern manifestation of paganism he saw Heidegger's ontology to be.[48] Ultimately, this is a constructive task, one which does not only repudiate but also offers an alternative. And the alternative Heschel seeks to recover as a response to the present-day resurgence of paganism – manifested in the political sphere by Nazism and in the sphere of thought by Heidegger – is the biblical tradition. As he announces: "Biblical religion is in a sense rebellion against the tyranny of things, a revolt against confinement in the world. Man is given the choice of being lost in the world or of being a partner in mastering and redeeming the world."[49]

It is not incidental that Heschel contrasts Heidegger with "biblical religion." No doubt, first and foremost, he has Judaism in mind, but he includes Christianity under this category as well. Surely after the

Heidegger, the latter expressed regret that so many Jewish professors were able to emigrate to America. This can have only one meaning since the fate of German Jewish professors who stayed in Germany was extermination!" Friedman, "Buber, Heschel and Heidegger," 133. While it is doubtful whether "this can have only one meaning," this anecdote, assuming its credibility, conveys something of Heschel's personal opinion of the German thinker. And yet also Harold Stern's counterpoint is worth noting: "as a Jew, a brand plucked from the fire, [Heschel] had the right to relate negatively to Martin Heidegger whose Nazis sympathies were well-attested … Yet in *Who Is Man?* Heschel shows a distinct respect for the author of *Being and Time*." Stern, "A. J. Heschel, Irenic Polemicist," 176–177.

[47] Heschel, *Who Is Man?*, 86.
[48] Magid, "The Role of the Secular in the Theology of Abraham Joshua Heschel's Theology," 151.
[49] Heschel, *Who Is Man?*, 83.

Holocaust, he holds that Judaism and Christianity share a fate in the war against paganism. In his famous address "No Religion is an Island" he proclaims:

Nazism in its very root was a rebellion against the Bible, against the God of Abraham. Realizing that it was Christianity that implanted attachment to the God of Abraham and involvement with the Hebrew Bible in the hearts of Western man, Nazism resolved that it must both exterminate the Jews and eliminate Christianity, and bring about instead a revival of Teutonic paganism.[50]

This shared fate generates a shared task: Both Judaism and Christianity must "recognize our vocation to preserve and to teach the legacy of Hebrew scripture, accept our aid in fighting Marcionite trends as an act of love."[51] Significantly, Heschel situates Heidegger on the side of Athens, and both Judaism and Christianity on the side of Jerusalem – only insofar, that is, as Christianity, "a wayward, rebellious" child of Judaism, preaches the Jewish message.

LIVING-TOWARD-DEATH

Generally, for Heschel, the preoccupation with death is the mark of paganism: "to the pagan eye the mystery of life is *Ruh*,' death, oblivion."[52] This preoccupation can appear as an intense anxiety over death or as an excessive concern over the afterlife. The centrality of Dasein's being-toward-death in Heidegger's account of authenticity demonstrates this pagan disposition. The idea of living anxiously in light of a portended death is interpreted by Heschel as an expression of an unrealistic fantasy: "[I]s not the exaggerated anxiety about death due to presumption: the unspoken claim to go on living without dying?"[53] In "Death as Homecoming" (1969), an expressive essay discussing death and peppered with critical references to Heidegger, Heschel also maintains that "anxiety about death is really an anxiety about the ultimate confrontation that follows death. In other words, it is an anxiety about the

---

[50] Heschel, "No Religion Is an Island," 236.
[51] Ibid., 242. The published version mistakenly reads "anti-Marcionite." See Erlewine, *Judaism and the West*, 216n149.
[52] Quoted in Kaplan and Dresner, *Prophetic Witness*, 159.
[53] Heschel, *Who Is Man?*, 36. This misrepresentation of Heidegger could perhaps be traced to Langan's aforementioned book, where it is stated that "the Dasein's ultimate possibility is death, i.e., the radical impossibility that a finite being should continue to exist forever" (p. 36).

afterlife rather than dying itself."[54] Directing his reproach against Heidegger, the Jewish thinker states that "it is a distortion to characterize the life of man as moving toward death ... Death is the end of the road, but not its meaning, not a refutation of living. That every moment of life is a step toward death is a mechanical view."[55] To consider death as the final and ultimate end of human existence is to adhere to a secular-paganist view. "Death then is not simply man's coming to an end. It is also entering a beginning."[56] Not the beginning of nothingness, but rather, inasmuch as human being is grounded in the divine, "the beginning of exaltation, an ultimate celebration, a reunion of the divine image with the divine source of being."[57] As opposed to ancient forms of paganism, Heschel confirms, "the Hebrew Bible calls for a concern for the problem of living rather than the problem of dying."[58]

The normative task instilled into human existence, Heschel claims, is signaled in one's relation to finitude. "The thought of death is a necessary component for human existence," he writes, for "it enables us to be open to ultimate demands regardless of personal needs."[59] Or, as he remarks in an unpublished handwritten note, "The fear of death is an apprehension of the debt we may have failed to pay. Death is a balance. Existence is not thrown 'being-toward-its-end.'"[60] Thus, "the real issue," Heschel contends, "is whether my existence here and now is exclusively being-in-the-world or whether it is also being-in-God's-knowledge, whether being in the world is not also living in the presence of God."[61] In opposition to Heidegger's perspective, when approached through the Jewish perspective, whereby life is a "gift" granted by God, "then death ceases to be a radical, absolute negation of what life stands for. For life and death are aspects of a greater mystery, the mystery of being."[62]

Heschel is clearly correct in pointing to the importance of death in Heidegger's scheme. Yet in *Sein und Zeit*, resolute anticipatory anxiety in the face of death does not spring from the fear of the event of death or from the desire for eternal life. Nor, moreover, is it in any way an "absolute negation of what life stands for." Heschel attributes to Heidegger the view that death is an event that occurs in some moment and that renders every moment a mechanical "step toward" it. This,

---

[54] Heschel, "Death as Homecoming," 366–378.   [55] Ibid., 375.   [56] Ibid., 367.
[57] Ibid., 371.   [58] Ibid., 369.   [59] Ibid., 376.
[60] Heschel Papers: Box 239 folder 4: Death, undated.
[61] Heschel, "Death as Homecoming," 372.
[62] Ibid., 366. On Heidegger's account of death and Jewish traditions, see Wolfson, "Not Yet Now: Speaking of the End and the End of Speaking."

however, is precisely the inauthentic account of death characterizing *das Man*, according to which the reaction to death is that of awaiting, not anticipation. In Heidegger's account, death is the ultimate closure of the futural projection of Dasein's *ex-tasis*, the marking of Dasein's historicity. Being-toward-death is an ontological character of Dasein's being-in-the-world, what designates its being-ahead-of-itself (*sich-vorweg-sein*). "The ending meant by death is not the being-at-an-end of Dasein," which is the position Heschel attributes to Heidegger, "but the being-towards-the-end of this being."[63] Heschel's perception of Heidegger's notion of death does not take into account the discussion on "possibility" and the structure of "care" in *Sein und Zeit*, without which the philosophical and existential force of "death," as well as the difference between Dasein and a Cartesian "subject," cannot be properly comprehended. Inasmuch as one's own death is not, to quote Wittgenstein, "an event in life," and is thus always "the possibility of the pure and simple impossibility of Dasein,"[64] then "death is a way to be, which Dasein takes over as soon as it is";[65] or as one commentator put it, "being-towards-death is essentially a matter of being-towards-life."[66]

BEING AND PATHOS

As stated, Heschel characterizes Heidegger's scheme as one that "seeks to relate the human being to a transcendence called being as such," while his own biblical thought "seeks to relate man to divine living, to a transcendence called the living God."[67] Following a dominant understanding of the time, expressed also in Jonas's "Heidegger and Theology" address, Heschel takes Heidegger's notion of being to be a proxy for God. This may explain the motivation behind the confrontation with Heidegger's ontology in the first place. In *God in Search of Man* Heschel announces that one of the tasks of philosophy of religion is "to refute the claim of philosophy when it presumes to become a substitute for religion."[68] A central problem with positing being as the ultimate, in Heschel's view, is its lack of pathos – its lack of care and compassion toward humanity: "Man is in need of meaning, but if ultimate meaning is

---

[63] *SZ*, 245/*BT*, 289.   [64] *SZ*, 250/*BT*, 294.   [65] *SZ*, 245/*BT*, 289.
[66] Mulhall, *The Routledge Guide to Heidegger's Being and Time*, 123. For a simultaneously traditional and innovative application of the Heideggerian notion of being-toward-death in a Jewish context, see Herskowitz and Shalev, "Being-Toward-Eternity."
[67] Heschel, *Who Is Man?*, 69.   [68] Heschel, *God in Search of Man*, 11–12.

not in need of man, and he cannot relate himself to it, then ultimate meaning is meaningless to him."[69] This argument is identical to Heschel's recurring reproach of the "philosopher's god," his paradigmatic specimen of a lifeless religious concept and the embodiment of the intrusion of Athens into the shrine of Jerusalem. "There is only one way to define Jewish religion," he insists, "it is the *awareness of God's interest in man*, the awareness of a *covenant*, of a responsibility that lies on Him as well as on us."[70] Heidegger's notion of being, on the other hand, is portrayed as a dead metaphysical entity: distant, detached, and aloof. As such, it is necessarily incapable of furnishing significant religious and existential meaning. In a comparable manner to Buber (and Levinas, as we shall see), Heschel opposes the anonymity of Heidegger's being and instead posits the personal and pathetic God of the Hebrew Bible.

Heschel contends, moreover, that positing being as the ultimate espouses nihilism. In continuation to his earlier argument against the lack of normative value in Heidegger's account, he declares against Heidegger's ontological fixation and the apathetic nature of being: "the ultimate problem is not being, but the concern for being. What precedes being is not nothingness, but rather concern for beings; logos as well as *pathos*."[71] Heschel is alluding again to "What is Metaphysics?" where Heidegger speaks of the dependency and commingledness of being with Nothing. The ramifications of conferring ultimacy on that which is entangled with nothingness, Heschel claims, are dire: "If the ultimate is sheer being, the human living has nothing to relate himself to as living. He can only relate himself to nothing."[72] In contrast to the nihilism of an ontology entwined with nothingness, Heschel's theology of pathos is focused on God's transitive concern. "There is a care that hovers over beings," he writes. "Being is surpassed by concern for being. Being would cease to be were it not for God's care for Being."[73] Overall, Heschel laments, Heidegger suffers from "the ontocentric predicament," that is, the prioritization of ontology over anthropology, by which Heschel means not an anthropocentric worldview but rather the one that focuses on a God whose pathos toward humans grants value and meaning to their lives.

Here the discrepancy between Heidegger's nonhumanist ontology and Heschel's humanist existentialism is thrown into sharp relief. For the German philosopher's ontological project endeavors to delineate the existential structures of Dasein's being in order to better come to grips with

---

[69] Heschel, *Who Is Man?*, 73.   [70] Heschel, *Man Is Not Alone*, 241.
[71] Heschel, *Who Is Man?*, 92.   [72] Ibid., 69.   [73] Ibid., 92.

the *Seinsfrage*. The question "Who is man?" does not stand alone, but must be addressed as part of the question of being. Heschel attributes Heidegger's ontological quest to a Greek mode of thinking which is marked by abstractions and confined to the realm of thought. The Greeks ask "what is being?" while the biblical mind thinks concretely and ethically and asks "what is required of me?"[74] For the biblical man, "Being is not *all*." Heschel claims that Heidegger's ontocentric predicament grants that Dasein's value depends on and corresponds to the manner in which it contributes to the inquiry into being – which means it is derivative, diminished, and ultimately hinged on nothingness. Insofar as being is said to be inherently valueless, the integrity and meaning of human beings cannot be derived from it. As he states, "[human] existence does not receive its meaning from the realm of being."[75] Heidegger's tie between Dasein and *Sein* circumvents the constitutive place of God in human existence and once again bespeaks pagan tendencies.

As noted, Heschel's treatment of Heidegger's notion of being reveals a misunderstanding at the heart of his critique. The ontology ascribed to Heidegger is precisely the one he dedicated extended philosophical efforts in order to overcome, or at least "get over." In Heschel's presentation, being is an "ultimate," something Dasein is in need of, an "object" that Dasein strives for but that cannot grant affection in return. However, the rendition of being as a substantive ignores Heidegger's fundamental point regarding the ontological difference between being and beings and the related point that being (*Sein*) is always and only manifested in beings (*Seiendes*). This point is best explained by Derrida in his early response to Levinas: "Being, since it is *nothing* outside the existent ... could in no way *precede* the existent, whether in time, or in dignity, etc. ... being is but the *being of* the existent, and does not exist outside it as a foreign power, or as a hostile or neutral impersonal element."[76] Heidegger is regarded by Heschel as a traditional ontologist, adhering to "the metaphysics of presence" against which he contests. Heidegger sometimes employs the ancient and defamiliarizing form of *Seyn* instead of *Sein* in order to disassociate it from precisely Heschel's misconception. Being is not a Platonic form or Aristotle's unmoved mover, but rather contingent, finite, historical, and always elusive. It does not act nor is it acted upon; it is disclosure as such.

It is also important to remind that the identification of being and God is explicitly denied by Heidegger, who proclaims, as mentioned in

---

[74] Ibid., 107.   [75] Ibid., 67.   [76] Derrida, "Violence and Metaphysics," 136.

Chapter 1, that "God and being are not identical, and I would never attempt to think the essence of God via being." Heidegger's own assault on the Aristotelian god and what he terms "ontotheology" makes clear why Heschel's rendering of the notion of being as an unmoved mover is so misguided. While appropriately a philosophical critique, Heidegger is well aware that his critique of the *causa sui* God can amount to a theological critique as well, indeed, one mirroring Heschel's own protest against the philosopher's god.[77] Relatedly, Heschel's implication that in Heidegger's scheme Dasein's value is diminished because it is derived from being is based on the errant assumption that being is a thing from which value can be derived. Heidegger considers the connection between being and value to be the hallmark of Western metaphysics, from Plato to Nietzsche, its last victim. It should be added that Heschel's understanding of Nothing in Heidegger as an absence or negation of something stands in direct opposition to Heidegger's statement that "the nothing [*das Nichts*] is more original than the 'not' and negation."[78] Such a rendering misses the sense of Nothing as the force, so to speak, that draws being out to the openness of its disclosure, or, as Heidegger explains in his 1943 postscript to "What Is Metaphysics," as a word for being itself.

BEING AS CREATION

Seemingly nowhere is the variance between Heschel's religious existentialism and Heidegger's a-theistic methodology better attested than in their diverging responses to Leibniz's question, "Why is there something rather than nothing?" Both thinkers situate the fundamental wonder from the very fact of being in the center of their thought. According to Heidegger, attending to the mystery of being is the zenith of thinking and the limit of phenomenology. In Heschel's view, being generates radical amazement and invites questioning, and although evasive, it steers the inquirer toward a further investigation after its origin. Against the Heideggerian position, Heschel stresses that "the mind dares to go beyond being in asking about the source of being ... a Being that calls a reality into being is endowed with the kind of being that transcends mysteriously all conceivable being." Heschel would have probably agreed with Eric Voegelin's point that, in Leibniz's thought, the aforementioned question is coupled with an additional vital question – "why

---

[77] Held, *Abraham Joshua Heschel*, 50.   [78] *Pathmarks*, 97.

is something as it is, and not different?" – a question which, Voegelin observes, Heidegger neglects to address.[79] Voegelin's point is not a complaint about a disloyal reading of Leibniz; rather, it is directed at Heidegger's hidden theological presuppositions that hold him back from inquiring further beyond the being of beings. Heschel would agree: accepting that "the Supreme Being is total mystery" and subsequently rejecting that "there is meaning beyond the mystery" is a manifestation of "pagan heritage."[80] The mystery of being cannot be the final point of investigation, for both being and nothing are "transcended." It is for this reason that Heschel contends that Heidegger's immanentism suffers from a logical fallacy – "the acceptance of the ultimacy of being is a *petitio principii*; it mistakes the problem for the solution."[81] The intrigue of the question of being points beyond itself, to the condition of being, to the question of the *coming into being* of being: "Being points to the question of how being is possible," Heschel remarks. "The act of bringing being into being, creation, stands higher in the ladder of problems than being."[82] In a clear reference to Heidegger, he asserts: "Being is a mystery, being is concealment, but there is meaning beyond the mystery."[83] Being is not the ultimate, as Heidegger allegedly holds, but rather the result of the concern of God, the creator and Lord of Being.

As Heschel points out, understanding being as creation has ethical ramifications: "Philosophically the primacy of creation over being means that the 'ought' precedes the 'is'."[84] This view resembles the general thrust of Levinas's critique of Heidegger, as we shall see. For Heschel, the immanentist worldview lacks this inherent ethical imperative toward being. As such, it generates an increasing posture of exploitation, manipulation, and objectification toward the world. Heschel bemoans that "our age is one in which usefulness is thought to be the chief merit of nature . . . Man has . . . become primarily a tool-making animal, and the world is now a gigantic tool box for the satisfaction of his needs."[85] There are clearly some resemblances between Heschel's concern and Heidegger's thoughts about the modern enframing and the essence of technology.[86] For both, the technological disposition of manipulation betrays a woeful disassociation with the holiness of being that ought to be surmounted. Of course, Heschel would reject such a comparison. From his perspective, care for

---

[79] Voegelin, "On Debate and Existence," 43–44.
[80] Heschel, *Who Is Man?*, 77; Heschel, *God in Search of Man*, 126.
[81] Heschel, *Who Is Man?*, 70.   [82] Ibid., 71.   [83] Ibid., 77.   [84] Ibid., 97.
[85] Heschel, *God in Search of Man*, 98.   [86] Held, *Abraham Joshua Heschel*, 46–52.

the world stems from its status as creation. The pagan worldview championed by Heidegger cannot promote an attentive and delicate comportment toward the world since it cannot distill real value into the world. His pagan "disavowal of transcendence" turns nature into "a utensil, an object to be used. The world ceases to be that which is and becomes that which is available."[87] Heidegger seeks to prepare for a receptivity to the imminent radiance, transcendence, and mystery of the overflowing richness of being – that is, the *opposite* of manipulation. For Heschel, this is paganism; transcendence must arrive from without and be manifested and implemented within. Thus, while ostensibly holding comparative outlooks, from Heschel's perspective, Heidegger's stance is the problem, not the solution.

The view of being as creation allows Heschel to offer a theological corrective to Heidegger's notion of thrownness. With thrownness Heidegger points to the basic ontological feature that much in our life is not determined or controlled by us, that our very being is always conditioned by the world outside ourselves, that Dasein is born into its finite facticity. Heschel, like other theologians at the time, understands this notion as a description of arbitrary existence bereft of any overarching intention or plan, the abandonment of man by God. He therefore exclaims: "[God] has not thrown us out into the world and abandoned us."[88] Heschel quotes – without reference – (Thomas Langan's translation of) *Sein und Zeit* §53, where it is stated that through the idea of death Dasein "discovers himself confronted by Nothingness, the possible impossibility of his existence." He then paraphrases Heidegger's depiction of Dasein as an extended existence from its thrown birth to its extinction in death by alluding to Genesis 3:19: "Man may see himself between 'thrownness' at one end and death at the other and so maintain: Out of Nothingness I came and into Nothingness I shall return."[89] In the second explicit reference to Heidegger in the book, Heschel declares, "Heidegger's rhetorical question, 'Has the Dasein, as such, ever freely decided and will it ever be able to decide as to whether to come into existence or not?' has been answered long ago: 'It is against your will that you are born, it is against your will that you live, and it is against your

---

[87] Heschel, *Who Is Man?*, 83.   [88] Heschel, *Man Is Not Alone*, 269.

[89] Heschel, *Who Is Man?*, 69–70. This too may be traced back to Langan's book, where the discussion of this issue is formulated in a way that for a biblically inclined reader such as Heschel, these verses from Genesis would likely come to mind. Langan writes: "'Throwness' at one end and death at the other – these are the signs that Dasein draws its reality from Nothing and is destined to return it to the same indefinite night" (p. 36).

will that you are bound to give account ... .'"[90] The quote from Mishna *Avot* 4:22 ostensibly reiterates the idea that Dasein is thrown into a world with little control over the most momentous events of life. But inasmuch as being is creation, the implied idea of a caring creator indicates concern and intention behind one's thrownness. Offering his alternative, Heschel trumpets,

I have not brought my being into being. Nor was I thrown into being. My being is obeying the saying "Let there be!" ...
   Against the conception of the world as something just here, the Bible insists that the world is creation. Over all being stand the words: Let there be! And there was, and there is. To be is to obey the commandment of creation.[91]

Once again, the biblical notion of creation is culled as a counter-ontological concept to Heidegger's ontology. We've seen, however, that from his perspective this notion is inherently technological and incompatible with the radical questioning required of philosophy. Moreover, for him Dasein's role as the "open" in which beings are disclosed means that the question regarding the "beginning" of being must involve Dasein's role in its unconcealment. It is for this reason he is after the origin of the understandings of being but has little interest in the question of the origin of being as raised by theology. As he contends,

History begins only when beings themselves are expressly drawn up into their unconcealemnt and conserved in it, only when this conservation is conceived on the basis of questioning regarding being as such. The primordial disclosure of beings as a whole, the question concerning beings as such, and the beginning of Western history are the same.[92]

CONCLUSION

Heschel seeks to expose the religious and ethical deficiencies in Heidegger's work and to challenge it by placing his biblical theology as a contesting alternative, one that is not only more divinely attuned but also essential to human flourishing and promoting the good. The main problem with the German philosopher's ontology, in his view, is that it brackets the living God of the Bible outside its purview. As such, it is unable to be receptive to the holiness and value existing in the world and in every human being, and also unable to account for the spiritual and moral obligation this demands. Heidegger's philosophy is thus not neutral but

[90] Heschel, *Who Is Man?*, 97.   [91] Ibid.   [92] Heidegger, *Pathmarks*, 145.

straightforwardly pagan; it is the reemergence of the paganism of biblical times, against which the prophets pronounce their ever-reverberating message. In the next chapter, we turn to Emmanuel Levinas, who similarly likened Heideggerian ontology to paganism, and developed in its wake a radical ethics focused on the other.

7

Uprooting Paganism: Emmanuel Levinas Faces Heidegger

INTRODUCTION

Emmanuel Levinas is arguably the most famous Jewish student of Martin Heidegger (alongside, perhaps, Hannah Arendt). Levinas's philosophical effort could be summarized, somewhat succinctly, as the attempt to put to the fore the idea of "ethics as first philosophy." Levinas seeks to dethrone what he takes to be philosophy's prioritization of ontology and establish that undergirding ontology is infinite and asymmetrical responsibility for the other person. Often the ethical encounter is portrayed as a relation to the other's (*Autrui*) face, an "infinite," overabundant excess conditioning the finite; a relation beyond the horizon of being, through which the trace of the divine Other shines through. The revelation of the face does not manifest itself as, nor is it mediated through, concepts or representations, but rather as the demand and command of ethics. Intersubjectivity is not contingent on the self, but precedes and conditions it. I am obligated to the other person before comprehension. The insight of "ethics as first philosophy" is expressed with typical hyperbole: my responsibility to the other includes a responsibility for the other's responsibility, even for my oppressor and prosecutor; I am demanded to substitute for the other, to death. Throughout the course of Western thought, Levinas claims, Otherness has always been reduced to sameness, the unfamiliar quickly devoured by thematization and rendered familiar. Hence alterity – of the other person, of God – is consistently denied. Levinas's task then is to phenomenologically depict the ethical moment which exceeds phenomenality and argue for its originary status with regards to ontology.

According to Levinas's own testimony, his philosophical project is a "translation" of the "Hebrew" message of the primacy of the ethical into "Greek." Figuratively, he expresses this idea with the statement that "the Septuagint is incomplete."[1] His work presents itself as an attempt to convey Jewish wisdom in the language of philosophy, with the aim of reanimating the West by excising from it the unethical impulses dominating its traditional ontology. These unethical impulses, Levinas claims, reach their full and alarming expression in Heidegger. For him, Heidegger's exclusion of ethics from ontology, his admiration of the Greeks, and his anti-Jewish sentiments are all dimensions of a single configuration of thought in contrast to which Judaism and its ethical core stand. While the seemingly innocent metaphor of "translation" is misleading, for reasons that will be fleshed out below, in this chapter I argue that in his early essays, from the mid-1930s through the 1940s, Levinas mimics Heidegger's methodology and develops a secularized phenomenology of Jewish existence as an alternative to what he considers Heidegger's paganism. This Jewish phenomenological alternative to paganism is the foundation of his later opposition between "ethics" and "ontology" and remains reverberating in it. What emerges is that Levinas presents a philosophical alternative to Heidegger in which his account of Judaism is inscribed. At the same time, however, his account is also profoundly marked by Heidegger's own philosophical achievements, thereby problematizing any simplistic framings of confrontation between the Jewish and German philosophers.[2]

While Levinas lived most of his mature life in France, wrote in its language, and is hailed as one of its most renowned thinkers, the case for dealing with him in the context of the present study is not difficult to make. Not only did Levinas serve as a major conduit of German thought to France, alongside luminaries like Jean Wahl and Sartre, but as we shall soon see, the time he spent in Germany in the early stages of his philosophical development was formative and thoroughly determined the trajectory of his thinking.[3] An early advocate of phenomenology, Levinas was deeply impressed by the German interwar intellectual sensitivities and vocabulary, and its anxieties over issues of ontology, theology, radical otherness and intersubjectivity, and drew significantly on it. In this

---

[1] Levinas, "The Pact," 75.
[2] Manning's observation that "Levinas quite clearly situates himself beside Heidegger and it is *there* that he grows uncomfortable" has telling consequences on the formation of Levinas's thoughts on Judaism, a point often marginalized. Manning, *Interpreting Otherwise than Heidegger*, 17.
[3] Three excellent studies on Heidegger's French reception are Kleinberg, *Generation Existential*; Janicaud, *Heidegger in France*; Pettigrew and Raffoul, *French Interpretations of Heidegger*.

respect, while he was Lithuanian by birth and French by adoption, the inception of Levinas's philosophy as well as its core concerns and insights are marked by the powerful innovations of the interwar German discourse.[4] Similarly, his response to Heidegger, as we shall see, corresponds with typical features of the German-Jewish encounter with the philosopher from Freiburg.

LEVINAS AND HEIDEGGER: EARLY ENCOUNTERS

The difficulty in coming to terms with Levinas's critique of and rejoinder to Heidegger rests in part in the fact that it is based on a profound debt to Heidegger, one which often finds Levinas closer to his teacher than he is willing to admit.[5] To appreciate this intricate relation, it is best to begin at the beginning. From the very outset, Levinas was captivated by the phenomenological method. As a student, he spent two semesters in 1928–1929 in Freiburg, where he attended lectures by Heidegger and Husserl. While he recognized the latter's greatness, Levinas was quickly impressed by the philosophical rebellion Heidegger wrought against his mentor in *Sein und Zeit*. Already in his dissertation on Husserl's phenomenology, the analytical method with which Levinas approaches Husserl is Heideggerian.[6] Approving of Heidegger's rebuke of Husserl's notions of pure consciousness, intentionality, and transcendental ego for suffering from an overdose of theoretical intellectualism and abstraction, Levinas rhetorically inquires: "Is our main attitude toward reality that of theoretical contemplation? Is not the world presented in its very being as a centre of action, as a field of activity or of care – to speak the language of Martin Heidegger?"[7] Husserl continues to be an important philosophical resource for Levinas, but the recognition of Heidegger's eminence is never repealed.

Indeed, Levinas's appreciation of Heidegger's work begins in his early student years and persists throughout his entire life. In fact, it is rare to witness one philosopher speak of the work of another philosopher with such adoration. No superlatives are held back: *Sein und Zeit* is praised as

---

[4] Moyn, *Origins of the Other*.

[5] Cf. for example Zarader, *The Unthought Debt*, 138–149. Critchley terms this Levinas's "somewhat Oedipal conflict with Heidegger." Critchley, "Leaving the Climate of Heidegger's Thinking," 45. And see below.

[6] Published later as Levinas, *The Theory of Intuition in Husserl's Phenomenology*.

[7] Ibid., 119.

a "miracle,"[8] "a peak of phenomenology," "brilliant,"[9] "one of the finest books in the history of philosophy,"[10] "the great event of our century,"[11] and a personal "shock."[12] Levinas consistently speaks of his "admiration" of Heidegger,[13] "the greatest philosopher of the century, perhaps one of the very great philosophers of the millennium,"[14] and a "genius."[15] It is thus of little surprise that we find this appreciation expressed in Levinas's first piece on Heidegger, "Martin Heidegger and Ontology" (1932), which aimed at introducing Heidegger's philosophical novelties to the French intelligentsia and expresses little if any reservations toward Heidegger's ontological project.

While his initial veneration is severely marred by Heidegger's decision to follow Hitler, Levinas continually, if painfully, expresses his admiration also after 1933.[16] That he perceived Heidegger's political views to be directly related to the latter's philosophy manifested for him an acute philosophical flaw at its very heart. His early essays strive to address the broader import of this flaw and begin to sketch out an alternative from *within* the philosophical horizons outlined by Heidegger. Levinas's *oeuvre* as a whole is markedly governed by Heidegger's itinerary, concerns, terminology, and method; the Levinasian problematic is only intelligible from within the groundwork staked out by Heidegger. His discomfort, critique, and effort to pose an alternative to it presupposes a profound acceptance of some of its fundamental features. Later, in a programmatic response to his interviewer's question as to whether it is correct to say that he "went through Heidegger, beyond Heidegger, by means of Heidegger," Levinas admits: "always with pain and suffering. But I cannot deny it. Mont Blanc is Mont Blanc."[17]

THE EARLIEST LEVINAS: BEING-PAGAN, BEING-JEWISH

The beginning of Levinas's effort to formulate a rejoinder to Heidegger coincides with a personal rekindling of interest in Judaism. While never completely abandoning it, the occupation with the tradition of his youth dwindled throughout his student years, only to forcefully reemerge in the

[8] Levinas, *Is It Righteous to Be?*, 140.   [9] Levinas, *Ethics and Infinity*, 116.
[10] Ibid., 37.   [11] Ibid., 42.
[12] Kearney, *Dialogues with Contemporary Continental Thinkers*, 51.
[13] Levinas, *Ethics and Infinity*, 38   [14] Ibid., 116.   [15] Levinas, "Being Jewish," 209.
[16] Indeed, the majority of the cited adulations are expressed after 1933, and even after the Holocaust.
[17] Levinas, *Is It Righteous to Be?*, 154.

1930s. This biographical point is significant because in this initial stage of his intellectual maturation, Levinas cultivates a philosophical conceptualization of Judaism in response to Heidegger. His recovery of Judaism can be explained by the historical circumstances of the rise of Hitler and the imperative forced upon Jews to take hold of their Jewish facticity. It can perhaps also be explained by the fact that Levinas understands Heidegger's ontological project itself to be theologically charged. "In 1928–29, as I read him for the first time," he recalls, "it sounded, resounded, *theological* as well. You know, 'guilt.' It looked as if it were a secularization of theology. Do you know the saying from Max Scheler, 'it is a mixture of genius and Sunday school preaching'?, that was the echo."[18] Like so many of Heidegger's early readers, Levinas too identified in *Sein und Zeit* a constitutive Christian mark. Interestingly, he makes a similar argument with respect to Heidegger's later thought. As he points out in a 1975 lecture course on "Death and Time": "There are many Christian virtues in the 'pre-Socratic' being (generosity, modesty, humility, etc.), and Heidegger's teaching would have it that these structures or these virtues have a root in being itself." In a lecture series, "God and Onto-theo-logy," from the same year, this judgment is repeated: "the 'being' of the pre-Socratics would be close to a biblical, and singularly Christian, conception."[19] It appears that for him, as for others, the Christian categories stripped of their theistic content and ontologically formulized are not a-theological, as Heidegger confers, but a secularized immanentism which he would later term "paganism," a 'code word' for the general worldview Levinas took Heidegger to be advancing.[20]

In a handful of essays throughout the 1930s and 1940s, Levinas formulates phenomenologically two ways of inhabiting the world: the first, a sense of rootedness in an impenetrable totality of the self and of being; the second, a sense of uprootedness and estrangement in a totality punctured by exteriority. The former is dubbed a pagan being-in-the-world and associated with the radically hermetical immanent world of Heidegger.

---

[18] Ibid., 141.   [19] Levinas, *God, Death, and Time*, 30–31, 136.
[20] On Levinas's early critique of Heidegger's paganism see Moyn, "Judaism against Paganism." For a different reading of the development of Levinas's thought vis-à-vis Heidegger, see Fagenblat, "Levinas and Heidegger," 103–134. Fagenblat claims that Moyn's reading (and by implication also my own) is a "retrojection" of Levinas's critique from the 1950s back to the 1930s. As I argue throughout this chapter, Levinas's later critique of Heidegger, as well as his philosophical scheme more generally, develops out of his earlier writings and indeed draws out what was in many cases already implicit to it, in substance if not in exact terminology.

The latter is proposed as an alternative existential modality of being-in-the world, "being-Jewish." In Levinas's understanding, these alternatives bear political, ontological, ethical, and religious ramifications, all of which are developed throughout his intellectual corpus. Perhaps the cardinal assumption driving Levinas's writings is that "mere" or "pure" being is the site of evil, power, and idolatry. Moral justification, peace, and true religiosity are accessible only in being touched by transcendence, by otherness. As he writes in *On Escape* (1935), "every civilization that accepts being – the tragic despair it contains and the crimes it justifies – merits the name 'barbarian.'"[21] This assumption is latent in many of the writings of the young Levinas, fleshed out more explicitly in his discussion of *il y a* in the 1947 *Existence and Existents*, and lies at the very heart of the ethical philosophy he develops in numerous later texts.

In one of his earliest essays, "Reflections on the Philosophy of Hitlerism" (1934), Levinas begins to draw out the conceptual ties between political totalitarianism and a totalizing ontology that he will immediately term paganism. The political phenomena of Hitler, he claims in this piece, is rooted in a set of ideas that have been made possible by long-standing yet impoverished liberal understandings of time, freedom, the will, and the body. The philosophy of Hitlerism is established on the dissolution of these understandings, but in such a way that their negation results in the acceptance of the inescapable bondage to the body, the temporality of "fatedness," and the immanent order. "Man's essence no longer lies in freedom, but in a kind of bondage. To be truly oneself . . . means becoming aware of the ineluctable origin chain that is unique to our bodies, and above all accepting this chaining." A society governed by the ideals of this framework, Levinas posits, gives itself to racism and the will for power. This society "does not see that the true ideal requires effort and instead enjoys those aspects of the ideal that make life easier. It is to a society in such a condition that the Germanic ideal of man seems to promise sincerity and authenticity." And it is this philosophy of immanentism that is in the heart of the aggressive desire for universal expansion that now threatens the Judeo-Christian legacy of Western humanism. Heidegger's name is absent from this essay, but the conceptual link between Heideggerian ontology and "the philosophy of Hitlerism" is easily established, and indeed in a later edition Levinas openly confirms that the essay was written to address the dangers he identified in the conception of being that was advanced by Heidegger, namely, being completely concerned

---

[21] Levinas, *On Escape, De l'évasion*, 73.

with itself, wherein the possibility of its breaching from without is denied.[22]

It is hardly surprising that Levinas approaches the political and philosophical challenges of Hitlerism from his perspective as a Jew. For him, Hitlerism confronts Judaism with the greatest trial it has ever faced, while also provoking it to reassert its essence and proclaim its message to the nations.[23] An early expression of what Levinas understands by this is found in a 1935 text entitled "The Contemporary Relevance of Maimonides."[24] This short article is an exposition of how the "Great Eagle" bears on "current concerns," above all, on the "paganism" that has reemerged in Europe. Levinas claims that Maimonides can serve as a guide for the perplexed of the day, though in the present situation the perplexed are not those who are caught between the apparent contradictory truths of scripture and science, but those who are tempted by the philosophical appeals of this reemerging "arrogant barbarism." Since the philosophical and political perversion of Hitlerism is bound to a certain comportment toward being, Maimonides' contribution to the current predicament can be teased out ontologically from the way he deals with the plunder of "creation." This vital notion was considered philosophically obsolete from the then-reigning Aristotelian commitment to the eternity of the world and divine perfection. But in the discussion of the topic in a series of chapters in book II of *The Guide*, Maimonides argues that applying the laws by which the world is governed, as outlined by Aristotle, to the event of creation, is erroneous. As Levinas explains, there is an "abyss separating creation from manufacturing," and it is the conceptual distinction between "notions borrowed from the world" and "that which is beyond the world" undergirding this abyss that holds the key to Maimonides' contemporary relevance.[25] For, as Levinas states, "the clarity of this distinction between the thought that thinks the world and the thought that surpasses it comprises the definitive victory of Judaism over paganism." Levinas's definition of "paganism" is important

---

[22] Levinas, "Reflections on the Philosophy of Hitlerism"; Hammerschlag, *The Figural Jew*, 124–125.

[23] Levinas, "L'actualité religieuse de l'Alliance," 4.

[24] Levinas, "The Contemporary Relevance of Maimonides." On Levinas and Maimonides, see Fagenblat, *Covenant of Creatures*, 67–96 and 111–139; Wurgaft, "How to Read Maimonides after Heidegger: The Case of Strauss and Levinas"; Levinas's approach toward Maimonides is addressed from a different angle in Kavka, "Screening the Canon: Levinas and Medieval Jewish Philosophy."

[25] Ibid., 92.

in this context, for it denotes an expansive and existential state of being-in
-the-world rather than a proposition regarding the numbers of existing
divine entities: Paganism is "a radical incapacity to break out of the world.
It does not amount to denying spirits and gods but in situating them within
the world."[26] The refusal to accept a world-picture of imprisonment in
being and the ability to acknowledge an "otherwise" that surpasses it is
the meaning of "creation," and Judaism's contribution and "*raison
d'être.*"

Levinas's appropriation of Maimonides in this short essay is profoundly modern. The argument in the *Guide* against the "eternal world
position" is that it commits the methodological fallacy of inferring potentiality from actuality, that is, deducing from what is actual – the state of
the world – to what must have been potential – the question of whether the
world is created or eternal. While Maimonides accepts the correctness of
the Aristotelean framework for the laws of nature in the sublunar sphere,
he insists that we cannot deduce from the aftermath that the same laws
apply to the origin, and therefore cannot *rule out* the possibility of creation. Levinas takes this Maimonidean argument and draws it into
a contemporary context. Rescinding the Aristotelian logic regarding actuality and potentiality, he centers, in a modern register, on the implications
of Maimonides' stance in terms of its bearings on matters of transcendence and immanence, in order to target the radical immanence of
Heidegger's worldview. Moreover, in the discussion about the origin of
the world in *The Guide* Maimonides discusses three options: creation *ex
nihilo*, which he describes, not without ambiguity, as "the opinion of
everyone who believes in the Torah of Moses," Plato's creation out of
eternal matter, and the Aristotelian view of eternal world. Without entering into the question of whether these are fair representations of these
philosophers' position on the subject, Maimonides famously does not take
unequivocal sides with any position or argue anything decisively, but
rather demonstrates that creation is philosophically *possible* (and morally
and theologically preferable). Levinas, however, takes Maimonides' crea-
tionism as a given and, drawing on the point that there can be no revelation without the created status of the world, advocates the view regarding
the breaching effects of divine transcendence to counter Heidegger's godless and immanent world.

An analogy thus surfaces between Aristotelian and Heideggerian
paganism on the one side, and the Maimonidean and Levinasian Jewish

---

[26] Ibid., 94.

challenges to this paganism, on the other side. The former positions accept being as an impenetrable and incontestable totality, while the latter positions confirm the immanent world *as well as* a radical externality that disturbs and disputes its purported totality. This analogy reveals a fundamental point about Levinas's relation to Heidegger. Just as Maimonides' contesting position does not deny the truth of the Aristotelian worldview, so too Levinas's position does not refute the ontological view. Rather, he claims that there is an otherness conditioning the dominant worldview that subverts its totality. Insofar as Levinas's effort to overcome the pagan confinement to being is analogous to his attempt to supersede Heideggerian philosophy, in both cases the task involves a dialectic that includes displacing and conserving its basic elements.

Since Levinas's main concern in his early writings is ontological phenomenology, countering Heidegger's conception of being with the notion of "creation" is not a speculative theological rejoinder, but a formulation of a distinctive way of experiencing being. The pagan's refusal of transcendence generates a mode of being-in-the-world of confidence and a sense of sufficiency with being that brings about a fundamental experience of stability and rootedness. "The Jew," in contrast, "does not have the fundamental basis in the world that the pagan has," Levinas affirms. "Within a milieu of complete confidence in things, he is eaten away by a mute unease."[27] Being-in-creation, that is, the existence in being the totality of which is called into question by beyond, generates an ingrained element of insecurity and alienation. The Jew is truly *unheimlich*. The phenomenological opposition between being-pagan and the Jewish being-in-creation will be expressed in Levinas's later works in the claim that the experience governing the encounter with the Other is not that of givenness from within, as per Heidegger, but of fundamental separation, of holiness. In other words, it will be reformulated as the distinction between ontology and what he calls "ethics."[28]

An essay from 1937, "The Meaning of Religious Practice," manifests this very structure.[29] The essay's subject matter seems far removed from anything Heideggerian, and characteristically Heidegger's name is not evoked. Yet closer examination suggests that the German philosopher is

---

[27] Levinas, "The Contemporary Relevance of Maimonides," 94.
[28] Cf. Hammerschlag, *Figural Jew*, 141.
[29] Atterton, Calarco, and Hansel, "The Meaning of Religious Practice by Emmanuel Levinas," 285–289.

indeed in the background, and similar features of the confrontation between Judaism and paganism are evident here as well. In this essay Jewish ritual and practice is described as a "pause" from, or "interruption" of, the familiar order of being. Jews do not "feel themselves immediately at home" in a world in which entities "are familiar, everyday, and profane." To the contrary, "nothing is entirely familiar, entirely profane" to them.[30] Interrupting the simple familiarity of the world with its strange misplacedness, Jewish ritual sheds a new light on the world, making the very existence of anything "infinitely surprising." In Levinas's presentation, Jewish ritual takes on existential and ontological significance through the estranged attunement to being it produces. Levinas claims that the Jew "experiences wonder at every instant at the fact – so simple and yet so extraordinary – that the world is there."[31] This wonder, he continues, is equated to the belief in creation, "the basis of Judaism." While Levinas will leave behind some of the views expressed in this early essay, the seeds of the later bond between the priority of obligation and the category of creation are present here. Particularly important, if somewhat striking, is the portrayal of Judaism as outside the natural order of the world. In Levinas's account, its commandments are so utterly misplaced and alien that it destabilizes the totality of what is and prompts an effect of ontological significance. Judaism, which for Levinas means primarily rabbinic Judaism with its emphasis on commandments, laws, and obligations, is presented here as the "other" of ontology, refashioning it by means of interruption. The basic phenomenological structure governing Levinas's early writings reemerges here: the distinction between a non-Jewish, pagan mode of existence in which one is comfortably rooted in being, and a Jewish mode of existence in which one's sense of rootedness is interrupted and revamped from without. "Judaism," Levinas announces in 1939, "is nothing, in the final synthesis, but anti-paganism. It is anti-paganism *par excellence*."[32]

In this early stage, the task of overcoming Heidegger is complicated by the fact that Levinas implicitly accepts the priority of the *Seinsfrage*, and hence must also accept the riveted character of being. He therefore centers on Heidegger's notion of *Geworfenheit* and refashions it in order to construct a Jewish experience of being-in-creation that shares a departure point but ultimately differs from being-pagan. This begins already in the 1935 essay "On Escape," where Levinas delineates what he considers to be the fundamental experience of human existence: the sense

---

[30] Ibid., 288.   [31] Ibid.   [32] Quoted in Moyn, "Judaism against Paganism," 46.

of being nauseatingly trapped in being, the urge to escape its suffocating effect, and the inability to do so.

Temporal existence takes on the inexpressible flavour of the absolute. The elementary truth that *there is being* ... is revealed at a depth that measures its brutality and its seriousness. The pleasant game of life ceases to be just a game. It is not that the sufferings with which life threatens us render it displeasing: rather it is because the ground of suffering consists of the impossibility of interrupting it, and of an acute feeling of being held fast [*rivé*].[33]

The rivetedness to being is a pressing experience, one which smothers the freedom and activity governing the possibility-actualizing Dasein and evinces pure passivity. It has been noted that this portrayal of human existence reflects the historical experience of a Jew in Europe with the rise of Nazism, entrapped and unable to escape the fateful facticity of her Jewishness.[34] This judgment seems to be correct, for in a short text from the same year Levinas describes the specific existential features of the Jew in a world plagued by Hitlerism with similar terms: "the pathetic fate of a Jew becomes a fatality. One can no longer flee it. The Jew is ineluctably fixed to his Judaism."[35] Indeed, Levinas later states:

During these years before the war I wrote philosophical texts which had no specific Jewish thematic to them but which probably stemmed from that which the Judaic classifies or suggests as the human. One of these texts, *De l'évasion*, was republished a short while ago ... In the original text, written in 1935, one can distinguish the anxieties of the war to come. And the whole fatigue of being, the condition of that period.[36]

Additionally, the existential feature of entrapment in being is conceptualized by Levinas as a sense of persecution, which is precisely the trope with which he will soon describe the Jewish experience in his private notebooks from his captivity in a German camp for French prisoners of war. "In persecution I rediscover the original sense of J[udasim], its initial emotion," he writes. "This is not just any persecution," but rather – offering an early and undeveloped version of the notion of radical persecution central to *Otherwise than Being* – "an

---

[33] Levinas, *On Escape*, 52. Levinas consistently describes the existential feature of rivetedness in being with variations of *être rivé* and *irrémisibilité*. Schonfeld, "Jewish Philosophy as Existential Hermeneutics," 381 (Hebrew).
[34] Rolland, "Getting Out of Being by a New Path," 29–32.
[35] Levinas, "L'actualité," 4. Quoted in Moyn, *Origins of the Other*, 190.
[36] Levinas, *Is It Righteous to Be?*, 39.

absolute persecution, which pursues the being everywhere so as to enclose it in the bare fact of its existence."[37]

This phenomenological description has a political dimension, for just as Heidegger's pagan phenomenology suggests a totalitarian political program of violence, the divergent phenomenology of Jewish existence translates into a scheme of nonviolence. As Levinas writes in his 1939 eulogy for Pope Pius XI, the Jewish (and Christian) experience of estrangement from the natural world constitutes a "resistance to the cult of power and earthly greatness" of paganism.[38] The conceptualization of Judaism as a nonviolent force opposing the dominance and power of an ontology of totality prefigures the prophetic messianism of peace enveloped in *Totality and Infinity* and the fraternity of prophetic witnessing in *Otherwise than Being*, signaling to the clear political impulse in Levinas's philosophy.

While the sealed being within which humans are imprisoned is the self-enclosed pagan world brought to bear by Heidegger, there is a fundamental difference between pagan *Geworfenheit* and Jewish rivetedness. Especially in the 1940s, in the midst of the Holocaust, Levinas finds the Jewish modality of being to be personified in the biblical figures of Job and the suffering servant from chapter 53 of Isaiah, who take ownership over their painful facticity, pure passivity, and submission, and turn these into elected purposefulness. In a passage from his wartime notebooks, he writes:

[I]t is here also (chapter 53 of Isaiah) – in the despondency which no one would know how to comprehend – that the divine presence is revealed. The situation of pure submission where there is an election in the sense of the love of a person who brushes against you (caress). Or rather revelation of an order different from the natural order – real despite all the failures of the natural order. An intoxication of this useless suffering, of this *pure passivity* by which one becomes like the son of God.

He then continues:

This is very important: the pure "submission" is not a sensation of the arbitrariness of the world. It can be thus when the eyes are turned toward the world. But submission here becomes: filiality.[39]

---

[37] Quoted in Fagenblat, "The Passion of Israel," 307.

[38] Levinas, "A propos de la mort du pape Pie XI," 3. Quoted in Hammerschlag, *Figural Jew*, 135. Hammerschlag's work is particularly important for its clarification of the political context and resonances of Levinas's thought.

[39] Fagenblat, "The Passion of Israel," 307. Fagenblat notes that "it is through theology that Levinas understands the very meaning of passivity," over against Hammerschlag's emphasis on the "fact, not form" of Jewish existence.

Levinas introduces here, in the context of "the original sense of
J[udaism]," the idea of filiality and fecundity that will figure in *Totality
and Infinity* as paradigmatic of the eschatological time of being-toward-
beyond-death and "having time for the other." The emblematic character
of these biblical characters, who are also invoked in the 1957 essay "A
Religion For Adults" and the 1963 essay "The Trace of the Other," and
whose resonances are palpable in the discussion of vicarious suffering in
Otherwise than Being, is reasserted in a 1945 essay, "The Jewish
Experience of the Prisoner," where Levinas announces: "what is
Judaism if not an experience, since Isaiah, since Job, of the possibility of
this reversal – prior to hope, from the depth of despair – of pain to
happiness; the discovery of signs of election in pain itself."⁴⁰ This idea is
similarly disclosed in an important essay two years later, where being-
Jewish is said to bear "the odd resonance of Isaiah chapter 53 and the
book of Job," which for Levinas amounts to achieving the "unexpected
transformation of misfortune into praise."⁴¹

In this 1947 essay, appropriately named "Being Jewish," Levinas
openly elaborates on what was thus far only implied, namely, that he is
developing a hermeneutic of Jewish facticity as an ontological category.
A few years earlier, in his wartime notebook number 7, he already indicates this by noting – "to begin from *Dasein* or begin from J' [*Juif*]. J' as
a category." In "Being Jewish" Levinas primarily responds to the existentialist notions articulated by "the great talent of Sartre" in "Anti-Semite
and Jew" (1944), and by "the genius of Heidegger." His ontological
alternative of being-Jewish centers on countering the categories of "facticity," "thrownness," and "resoluteness" with phenomenologically determined notions of "creation," "election," and '"commandment." Unlike
the existentialists' stress on the present or futural orientation, Levinas
presents an alternative temporality whereby being-created, having an
origin, opens a dimension of past – "the infinite time behind us" – into
the present. The Jew is not simply thrown, she is riveted to her being, but
this rivetedness is experienced positively, as finding herself *already* chosen
and commanded into being. "The imperative of the creation that is
continued in the imperative of the commandment and of the law inaugu-
rates a total passivity," he writes. "To do the will of God is in this sense the
condition of facticity." Unlike Heschel, who too argues that "to be"
fulfills the divine command of creation, and unlike Heidegger's account

⁴⁰ Quoted in Schonfeld, "Jewish Philosophy as Existential Hermeneutics," 390.
⁴¹ Levinas, "Being Jewish," 208. Translation amended.

of authenticity whereby Dasein owns up to its thrownness and conceives it as Fate and Destiny, for Levinas being-Jewish, as created, chosen, and commanded, is utterly passive. In this respect, Jewish rivetedness antecedes and intensifies Dasein's *Geworfenheit*, but at the same time, it bears a positivity that is inaccessible in a hermetically immanent Heideggerian world.

The dimension of origin and beyond in "a world that is without origin and simply present" Levinas terms "religion," which he considers to be the Jewish contribution to the illumination of human existence: "The Jew is the very entrance of the religious event into the world; better yet, he is the impossibility of a world without religion."[42] This allows Levinas to declare that Jewish existence is "the fulfilment of the human condition." The airtight immanence of Dasein's existential structure and its temporal constitution rules out the perspective that gives access to this begotten positivity. These phenomenologically construed notions emerge as a competing Jewish account of existence to the one extended by Sartre and by Heidegger, and they will assume an emphatic ethical charge in Levinas's later works, where they are transformed into the an-archical passivity and the immemorial past of the being-for-the-other and by-the-other. Indeed, the model of election presented in "Being-Jewish" is formulized and universalized in the important section "Substitution" in *Otherwise than Being*. Phrased almost verbatim though flipped in application, it exhibits the structure of the subject as already commanded to ethical responsibility by the other person.[43]

A SECULARIZED JUDAISM

As we can see, in his early writings Levinas set out to forge an alternative to the Heideggerian being-in-the-world by formalizing the experience of being-Jewish into a modality of existence, thereby challenging the claim for exclusivity of Heidegger's analysis of Dasein. The ontological category of being-Jewish, he believes, is not only a more apt phenomenology of human existence, but it also avoids the interconnected philosophical, theological, political, and ethical pitfalls of which Heidegger's framework is guilty.

From the way in which Levinas structures his thought vis-à-vis Heidegger, an apparent binary emerges between pagan existence and

---

[42] Ibid., 209.
[43] Levinas, *Otherwise than Being*, 99–121. This has been pointed out by Hammerschlag, *Figural Jew*, 142.

Jewish existence, Dasein and J.' Testifying to the impact of the dualistic structures of the German interwar theological discourse, these binaries permeate Levinas's thought and concur with the "logic of interruption" that finds its initial expression in his youthful writings and becomes dominant in his mature works. Clearly the either/or rhetoric inserts an urgency into the discussion and plays into Levinas's attempt to distinguish himself as decisively as possible from his teacher. This rhetoric, however, does not do justice to the internal logic of Levinas's arguments. The main trouble is not, as Dominique Janicaud charges, *that* Levinas smuggles theological categories and structures into his phenomenology, but rather *which* ones he smuggles in and *whether* they serve his purposes well. Already in his early essays and certainly in his mature works, Levinas's overriding aim is not simply to reject the concept of totality, but to object to its presumptuous claim for exclusivity and hence to reconceive it in light of, or in relation to, otherness. Levinas must presuppose the ontology of totality, as described above all by Heidegger, for it to be fissured by alterity. In this respect, Levinas's Jewish alternative subverts Heidegger's totalitarian framework but at all times still stands in relation to it and indeed depends on it.

The dichotomous façade is further problematized by the Heideggerian approach Levinas takes in order to set it up. This is best seen if we consider Hermann Cohen, who developed a text-based philosophical structure "from the sources of Judaism." A cautious comparison between Levinas and Cohen is surely appropriate, due to their shared emphasis on ethics, their prophetically inspired conception of Jewish-universal messianism, and their adherence to reason, among other points. Yet Levinas does not follow Cohen's path – nor even Husserl's, for that matter – but rather Heidegger's, and carves out a basic mode of existence which he associates with a distinctive Jewish being-in-the-world.[44] Stated otherwise, Levinas opposes Heidegger's philosophy of radical immanence *by means* of Heideggerian phenomenology. Apparently, Levinas prefigures Habermas's better-known postwar suggestion to proceed *"mit Heidegger gegen Heideggers Denken,"* rendered in a Jewish key.[45] Predictably, the dialectical tension between *mit* and *gegen* results in a countering Jewish account that struggles to leave the orbit of Heidegger's thought.

[44] See Schonfeld, "Jewish Philosophy as Existential Hermeneutics."
[45] Habermas, "Zur Veröffentlichung von Vorlesungen aus dem Jahre 1935," 67–75.

Levinas's tangled effort to articulate a hermeneutic of Jewish facticity as an alternative to Heidegger's existential analysis of Dasein is also driven by a desire to elaborate on what Rosenzweig called *Judensein*.[46] Generally, it can be suggested that Hegel to Rosenzweig is what Heidegger is to Levinas. Levinas adopts Rosenzweig's view that the essence of Judaism is disclosed in Jewish existence. In a later essay, he asserts that for Rosenzweig, "Judaism is no longer just a teaching whose theses can be true or false; Jewish existence . . . itself is an essential event of being; Jewish existence is a category of being."[47] As noted in Chapter 2, in his own work Levinas affirms Rosenzweig's view and pits it against Heidegger's existential analysis. However, it is crucial to notice that Rosenzweig's particularistic notion of being-Jewish is reemployed by Levinas as an ontological and universal category. Levinas's move requires some clarification, as Jewish existence seems to be by definition particularistic and hence in tension with the universal and all-encompassing ontological category of which Levinas speaks. Karl Jaspers, in a different context, points to this tension in a response to a copy of a written lecture by the young Hannah Arendt on the "Jewish existence" of Rahel Varnhagen, the writer and famed Berlin salon hostess who experienced her Jewishness as an obstacle to her cultural and literary hopes. Arendt was making use of the perspective of *Existenzphilosophie* which Jaspers, Arendt's *Doktorvater*, knew well, but he could make little sense of the idea of "Jewishness" as a distinct ontological category of existence. "You objectify 'Jewish existence' existentially – and in so doing perhaps cut existential thinking off at its roots," he wrote her on March 30, 1930. "The concept of being-thrown-back-on-oneself can no longer be taken altogether seriously if it is *grounded* in terms of the fate of the Jews instead of being rooted in itself." Arendt responded by denying that being-Jewish constitutes a distinct ontological status, though she insists that it does have a particular facticity that gives rise to certain possibilities of existence.[48] Unlike Arendt, for whom being Jewish is an ontic category, and unlike Rosenzweig, for whom the ontological meaning of being Jewish is grounded in the membership in the Jewish *Blutsgemeinschaft*, for Levinas it is a peculiar mode of being that gives

---

[46] The Rosenzweig–Levinas link has been widely explored and debated. Among many, see Gibbs, *Correlations in Rosenzweig and Levinas*; Cohen, *Elevations, passim*; Handelman, *Fragments of Redemption*, 177–345; Kavka, *Jewish Messianism and the History of Philosophy*, 129–192.

[47] Levinas, "Between Two Worlds (The Way of Franz Rosenzweig)," 183.

[48] Kohler and Saner, eds., *Hanna Arendt, Karl Jaspers: Correspondence*, 10–12.

itself to the generality of universal existence and is clarified and illuminated through an ontologized set of traditional content and connotations, such as the notions of persecution, election, commandment, and creation.

This leads us to the important issue of secularization. Levinas constantly uses terminology from Jewish tradition to convey his thought, while often denying it has any theological import.[49] He openly and repeatedly professes that by "Jewish" he does not mean a specific nation, tradition, or confessional faith. "Jewish election," for example, is not interpreted traditionally but is rather "the very mystery of personhood."[50] The inescapable Jewish condition reflects the human condition, and the Jewish fate is the human fate. "Jew," in other words, is a universal category. "The recourse of Hitlerian anti-Semitics to racial myth," he relates, "reminded the Jew of the irremissibility of his being. Not to be able to flee one's condition – for me this was like vertigo. Granted, this is a human situation, and in this the human soul is perhaps naturally Jewish."[51] Levinas thus develops an alternative universal phenomenology from the particular existential experience of being-Jewish, whereby the employed Jewish categories are stripped of their particularistic traditional content and formulized into a phenomenological structure. Once formulized, they are perceived as the factical or existential ground capturing an elemental truth about human existence and being. By defusing their initial particularistic and theological charge, Levinas constructs an all-inclusive Jewish corrective to paganism. This of course bears resemblance to the common interpretation of Heidegger's Dasein analytic and indeed presents itself as a deliberate response to it. By means of Heideggerian phenomenology, Levinas discovers, analyzes, and disperses the truth about the human condition that is disclosed in his understanding of being-Jewish.[52]

---

[49] Levinas's statements on the matter are inconsistent, varying from insistence on the absolute separation between faith and his thought to more frequent descriptions of proximity and even reconciliation. Levinas presents contradicting claims relating to his designation as a Jewish thinker as well. As he grew older and as his standing in the French philosophical world was secured, he was increasingly willing to admit to the Jewish sources and objectives of his thinking. For a discussion of the religious charge and potentiality in Levinas's thought that does not emphasize its Jewish layers, see Kosky, *Levinas and the Philosophy of Religion.*

[50] Levinas, "Being Jewish," 209–210.   [51] Ibid., 208.

[52] Fagenblat suggests reading Levinas's philosophy as a secularization of what he calls the "Jewish covenant of faith," yet he mainly takes the "Judaic" to be ideas expressed in Jewish traditional texts. In following studies this view is modified, and the secularization enacted by Levinas is likened to Heidegger's idea of "formal indication" of the factical life. Fagenblat, *A Covenant of Creatures*, xxv, 140–170; see also Fagenblat's "Levinas,

Seemingly, here is another moment in which Levinas follows his teacher's principles: he approves that even if fundamental revelations regarding human existence may be imparted in a religious context, a phenomenological investigation into these revelations necessitates a formal indication that gains access to originary manifestations of modalities of being through the directive of theistic categories disposed of their original content. On this account, phenomenology is a nontheological, or at least a-theological, endeavor. Levinas's repeated insistence on the theological neutrality of what we called "being-in-creation" and the religiously infused terminology of his later philosophy seems to cohere with Heidegger's a-theistic methodology. But here too the secularization enacted by Levinas would not only neutralize, but also preserve existential features of the repressed theological background, and his formulized notions of existential facticity would continue to harbor the imprint of Jewish categories and historical experiences – as Levinas himself eventually comes to admit. Alluding to the German philosopher, Levinas later writes in *Humanism of the Other*: "Biblical verses do not function here as proof but as testimony of a tradition and an experience. Don't they have as much right as Hölderlin and Trakl to be cited?"[53]

There is, however, a crucial difference between the ways in which Heidegger and Levinas activate phenomenology a-theistically. For while Heidegger's attitude toward phenomenology is at times tottered, as he senses that as a methodology it is still too metaphysical, he is reluctant to do away with it and never, in final analysis, does he stop being occupied with the givenness of being and its disclosure to thought. In his 1963 "My Way to Phenomenology," he even proposes that the label "phenomenology," understood correctly as the possibility of thinking, is actually one and the same as "the *Sache* of thinking" and therefore could all but disappear as a label.[54] Levinas, on the other hand, resolves to tread beyond phenomenality and representation and think the resonances or traces of transcendence in phenomenality, which he calls "the religious."

Judaism, Heidegger," 51–63. I think Fagenblat is absolutely right, but wish to develop his point further – or perhaps flesh out what he may be implying – and state not only that there is an analogy with Heidegger's formal indication, but that Levinas is deliberately following what he understands Heidegger to be doing methodologically in order to formulate an alternative to his program.
[53] Levinas, *The Humanism of the Other*, 66.
[54] Von Herrmann, "Way and Method: Hermeneutic Phenomenology in Thinking the History of Being."

His grammar of secularization opens a sphere of religiosity that affords a God "not contaminated by being" and thus is part of an effort to situate his thought outside the boundaries of ontology and what he calls "theology," or onto-theological determinations.[55] This dynamic is present in his conception of "atheism" and is intensified in *Otherwise than Being* and later essays where he veers toward – or beyond – negative theology.[56] "Theological language," he maintains, "destroys the religious situation of transcendence."[57] Heidegger would no doubt agree with this; for him, too, philosophy gestures toward the religious, into an opening to a purer modality of religiosity. But for Levinas Heidegger's grounding of meaning in being amounts to partaking in the very onto-theological scheme Heidegger himself finds faulty, and against it Levinas posits a philosophy conditioned by the ethical demand of otherness formulated as a secularized account of Judaism. And *as* ethics, it springs from the fixation with the Other, which also charts how God is given without capitulating to onto-theological pitfalls. For both Heidegger and Levinas, "secular" philosophy is propaedeutic to a deeper and more genuine de-secularization, but for Heidegger this never leaves the boundaries of philosophy, which is in principle distinct from religion, while for Levinas there is, ultimately, a unison of the holiness in philosophy and the God of religion. That the sublation of the ontological ultimately arrives at the religious, that the divine is approached through the height of the face, that the ethical life obsessed by the other is perceived as holy, and that as we shall see, this is all equated to Judaism – these points expose that for Levinas, the ethical life is the religious life and vice versa; ethics for him, to use Derrida's words, is the "religiosity of the religious."[58]

LOST IN TRANSLATION

I have thus far suggested that after Heidegger endorsed Hitler, Levinas comes to understand the latent theological biases in *Sein und Zeit* as germane to his teacher's philosophical and political failures. In response,

---

[55] Levinas, *Otherwise than Being*, xlii.
[56] On Levinas's negative theology, particularly with reference to Plotinus see, among many, Wolosky, "Two Types of Negative Theology."
[57] Ibid., 197.
[58] Levinas, *Is It Righteous to Be?*, 49. Levinas told Derrida: "You know, one often speaks of ethics to describe what I do, but what really interests me in the end is not ethics, not ethics alone, but the holy, the holiness of the holy." Derrida, *Adieu to Emmanuel Levinas*, 4.

he turns to his own tradition and experience to develop a Jewish corrective
to Heidegger's paganism. The best way to understand what he is doing
methodologically is to perceive him as deploying Heidegger's formal
indication and secularization. Levinas believes that the formal structures
of Judaism, understood phenomenologically and hence, following
Heidegger's footsteps, ontologized, universalized, and secularized, can
serve as an appropriate philosophical rejoinder to the plight of the West
embodied in Heidegger.

What comes into focus here is that the language of translation used by
Levinas to describe his work is misleading.[59] Among the ambiguities and
difficulties attached to this metaphor is the fact that it presupposes
a solidified, stable, and unchanging account of Judaism, and overlooks
many of its historical manifestations. It also gives the impression that his
philosophy is exclusively channeling Jewish wisdom while other sources
of influence, such as Protestant theology, Russian literature, and indeed
Heidegger's philosophy, are disregarded. The metaphor of translation
presupposes two distinct registers of thought, wherein there is some content in one – in this case Judaism – that is unavailable in the other – in this
case, philosophy – and which will remain unavailable until the act of
translation. Yet in our case, if the translation is to succeed, it is only
because the content being translated can fully give itself to philosophy.
This means that it *is* available to philosophy, thereby making the endow-
ing role of Judaism, and the act of translation, redundant. On the other
hand, if there is some untranslatable core content in Judaism, then the
translation becomes futile, for what is most important is nontransferable.
The language of translation ostensibly entails that Levinas identifies nothing ethical in philosophy and nothing philosophical in Judaism. Yet
neither is correct: Descartes's idea of the infinity of God as thought by
the *res cogitans* wherein "the I from the first *thinks more that it thinks*"
and Plato's notion of the "Good beyond Being" are taken up by Levinas

---

[59] For different views on this matter, see for example, Gibbs, "Jewish Dimensions of Radical
Ethics," 13–23; Gibbs, *Correlations in Rosenzweig and Levinas*, 155–175; Batnitzky,
"On Reaffirming a Distinction between Athens and Jerusalem"; Batnitzky, *The Politics of
Revelation*, 3–24 and *passim*. In his *Levinas's Jewish Thought* Ephraim Meir accepts the
metaphor of translation at face value – "Levinas was a master of translation" (ibid.,
262) – without attending to the problems it generates. A reading of Levinas with the
background of two millennia of "Jewish philosophy" is offered by Trigano, "Levinas and
the Project of Jewish Philosophy." Trigano shows that some notions of Levinas's idiosyncratic terminology are in fact translations from Hebrew; see also Chalier, "The
Philosophy of Emmanuel Levinas and the Hebraic Tradition," 3–12; Wright, *The
Twilight of Jewish Philosophy*; Putnam, "Levinas and Judaism," 33–62.

and interpreted ethically as "prophetic moments" situated within the philosophical tradition. Likewise, his Jewish writings demonstrate time and again the philosophical layer of Judaism. It can be seen that Levinas's rhetoric obscures the underlying logic that neither Greece nor Jerusalem represent pure forms, nor are they mutually exclusive. Greece possesses an internal ethical sensitivity and Judaism is not foreign to philosophical conceptuality.[60]

Our examination of Levinas's early writings allows us to nuance one of the prevailing assumptions of the critical research of Levinas, namely, that the main thrust of his thought is a response to the Holocaust.[61] Guiding this view is the sense that the construction of a philosophy of absolute ethical commitment reflects a noble response to the ultimate betrayal of being manifested in the Holocaust. In the wake of such unprecedented evil, so this common view goes, Levinas concludes that goodness cannot reside in being but instead must erupt from without.[62] There is also a "Jewish" inflection at play: The ethical philosophy of Levinas, the Jew, is a response to the Nazi murder of the Jewish people (including some of Levinas's family members). There is no denying the momentous impact of the Holocaust on Levinas and his thought, nor that it became the "resonance chamber" of his philosophical corpus, nor still that his postwar writings are fixated on the ethical. Yet we have seen that the development of some of the core structures and central features of his later thought predate the trauma of the Holocaust and are concocted in his pre-Holocaust phenomenological framing of being-Jewish in opposition to being-pagan. It is true that the markedly ethical tenor of Levinas's thought is not yet fleshed out to the same depth, extent, and radicalism as it is in his post-Holocaust writings. One might suggest that this is because in his early stage Levinas is still wedded to the general Heideggerian presumption that one's fundamental relation to being is ontological, and thus his Jewish alternative denotes a different *manner* of exercising this relation. But Levinas never completely abandons this perspective: he resolves to advance beyond being because he *accepts* both the prominence and the

---

[60] Fagenbalt, *Covenant of Creatures*, 1–20, makes a compelling argument to this effect.

[61] On this see Moyn, *Origins of the Other*, 195–196.

[62] Bernstein writes that "the primary thrust of Levinas's thought is to be understood as his response to the horror of evil that has erupted in the twentieth century," and particularly Auschwitz "casts its shadow over everything [Levinas] has ever written." Bernstein, "Evil and the Temptation of Theodicy," 253. See also Shaw, "Is Levinas's Philosophy a Response to the Holocaust?"; Eaglestone, *The Holocaust and the Postmodern*, 249–278.

final impotence of the Heideggerian *Seinsfrage*. In the preface to his 1947 *From Existence to Existents*, he states: "if at the beginning our reflections are in large measure inspired by the philosophy of Martin Heidegger ... they are also governed by a profound need to leave the climate of that philosophy, and by the conviction that we cannot leave it for a philosophy that would be pre-Heideggerian."[63] Yet even if the commanding quality of the face and the thematic of substitution are yet to emerge, an ethical impulse is nevertheless already present in the link between Hitlerism and Heideggerianism and in the conceptualization of sheer being as harboring an evil expunged only by the acute effect of transcendence.

There is, no doubt, a danger of overstating the argument and presenting a simplistic picture of a single, linear trajectory in Levinas's thought while ignoring important shifts and developments, which certainly exist.[64] Nor should it be argued that every idea of Levinas's mature works originates in his earlier writings. His thought certainly evolves, and the postwar French intellectual scene, and particularly his personal relationship with Derrida, among others, had a fateful impact on him. Yet the significant continuity of Levinas's pre- and postwar writings and the manner in which central building blocks of his mature philosophy find their nascent articulation in his early writings should not be underestimated. Thus, insofar as Levinas's philosophy *as a whole* is to be conceived as a response to anything, it seems justified to locate the earlier moment of Heidegger's enrolment in the Nazi party on May 3, 1933 as the event that woke Levinas from his "Heideggerian slumber" and urged him to set out on the philosophical path that ultimately laid the foundation for his post-Holocaust reflections. This also means that the ethical imperative figuring so prominently in Levinas's thought is first and foremost the result of the way in which he conceptualizes the ramifications of a radically immanent worldview and the breaching effect of radical otherness.

AGAINST PAGANISM: ETHICS

Throughout the 1950s and onwards, Levinas develops a robust philosophical account underscoring the primacy of the ethical, culminating in the doubled peak of *Totality and Infinity* (1961) and *Otherwise than Being or Beyond Essence* (1974). Heidegger remains a central foil and adversary of

---

[63] Levinas, *Existence and Existents*, 19.
[64] An overview of developments in a few central themes is Bergo, "Ontology, Transcendence, and Immanence in Emmanuel Levinas."

Levinas's postwar writings, now more directly than before.[65] The previous strategy of posing an alternative ontological outlook now gives way to a questioning of the ultimacy of the ontological. Initially in "Is Ontology Fundamental?" (1951) as well as "Philosophy and the Idea of Infinity" (1957), Levinas articulates his sustained accusation that "Heideggerian ontology subordinates the relation with the other to the relation with the Neuter, Being." In effect, it participates in the violent reduction of otherness to sameness and the denial of transcendence typical of traditional ontology. This, Levinas insists, is especially true with regards to "being-with-the-other-person – *Miteinandersein*," which is a relation with a being and thus within the compass of ontology.[66] Despite his originality, then, Heidegger is not a break from the history of Western philosophy but rather its prime representative. With the solidification of Levinas's ethical fixation, the transcendence to which Heidegger's pagan ontology is said to be impenetrable is first and foremost the transcendence of the other person. This means that the familiar claim that in Levinas the 'face' dons the trait of God as radical otherness is true but incomplete, for as we have seen, in his early writings, the monotheistic God, Judaism, and the Jew are all depicted as radical exteriority interrupting the familiar order.

Like in the prewar essays, the conceptual ties between ontology, violence, paganism, and rootedness are emphatic in Levinas's postwar rejoinder to Heidegger. "Ontology as first philosophy is a philosophy of power," he declares, for the eradication of the Other through its subordination to being in general "leads inevitably to another power, to imperialist domination, to tyranny."[67] With recognizable vocabulary, Levinas claims that the origin of this tyranny lies "in the pagan 'moods,' in the enrootedness in the earth." The centrality of being in Heidegger both undergirds and is manifested in the "pagan existing" advocated by National Socialism. Yet the consequence of the pagan impulse of "this earth-maternity" is more wide-ranging, as it "determines the whole Western civilization of property, exploitation, political tyranny, and war."[68] Ultimately, the ideational project that occupies Levinas in his mature philosophical works is to reverse the priorities of "the well-known theses of Heideggerian philosophy" and

[65] Cf. for example, Taminiaux, "The Presence of *Being and Time* in *Totality and Infinity*," 3–22.
[66] Levinas, "Is Ontology Fundamental?" 1–11; Levinas, "Philosophy and the Idea of Infinity," 47–59.
[67] Levinas, *Totality and Infinity*, 46–47.   [68] Ibid., 52, 53.

establish the precedence of beings over being, metaphysics over ontology, justice and obligation over freedom and thought. These reversals are enacted by setting the Other as primal to the Same, a task described as overturning the philosophical priorities set by the Greeks and "following a tradition at least as ancient" – the biblical prophetic tradition. This tradition, which is "not necessarily religious" but rather "philosophical," respects Otherness and "does not read right in might."[69] Levinas thus delineates a philosophical program that challenges Western ontology through what he calls the revelation of the face and the absolute submission to the needs of the other. The encounter with the other person exceeds the confines of ontology and hence repels its inherent dynamic of power and violence.

For Levinas in *Totality and Infinity*, we comport our life with a desire for mastery over our surroundings. This provides enjoyment, which precedes the practical instrumentality of Dasein and manifests our concrete freedom. But the revelation of the other in its nudity, defencelessness, and defiance of conceptualization disrupts the self's freedom and spontaneity and resists its passion for mastery. To the desire for control and assimilation the face expresses a command: "thou shall not kill." The intrinsic ethical quality of the "nonallergic" ethical encounter with the other is rooted in its plea to respect its alterity, resist the urge of effacement, and respond to its plight. In place of the Heideggerian Dasein, of which, according to Levinas, *mit-Sein* is encompassed in the "mineness" of its own project and thus lodged in egology, he posits an account of human being whose responsibility toward the suffering of the other person constitutes the very structure of subjectivity. In *Otherwise than Being*, Levinas radicalizes this perspective once more, now calling for an absolute responsibility to the Other *prior* to the emergence of any such subjectivity.

THE VIOLENCE OF HISTORY AND PROPHETIC MESSIANISM

Examining Levinas's conception of history is particularly conducive for illuminating the way in which Heideggerianism is contrasted to his philosophy and account of Judaism. In *Totality and Infinity* Levinas challenges Heidegger's paganist ontological totalitarianism and the militancy of the philosophical ontology rooted in Greece with a philosophy of "originary peace" drawn from the prophetic tradition – "prophetic eschatology." As he establishes, the non-intuitional relation with the Other

---

[69] Levinas, "Philosophy and the Idea of Infinity," 53.

produces a life oriented by eschatology. This loaded term is understood not as a scheme of the "last things," but as a sense of direction and obligation for history through "institut[ing] a relation with being *beyond the totality* or beyond history." History is totality; it is where justice is passed over and the pain of the conquered is ignored. Ubiquitous oppression is superficially appeased by contextualization or abjectly explained away by theodicies. As is made clear in the "Preface" and "Conclusions" to this work, this historical account is exemplified above all by Hegel and Heidegger, for whom history is said to be a homogeneous plane that allows for nothing outside it and subjugates any given moment to the crowning purpose of the course of history. It can only account for time as synchrony and is stitched to the tyranny of the State. Levinas seeks to destabilize this conception of history, and in so doing, he even wishes to undercut the distinction at play in Heidegger between the "objective" constructivism of narratives in *Historie* and the enactment of being in *Geschichte* – neither spring from the relation with the other.[70] For Levinas, "when man truly approaches the Other he is uprooted from history."[71] In his anti-teleological, eschatological model, the interruption of the infinite institutes "judgment" and "restores to each instance its full signification in that very instant."[72] Thus the eschatological interruption dismantles totality and the logic of war and beckons a peace more originary than an extended ceasefire.

Levinas is no doubt correct that Heidegger's concerns intersect with Hegel's philosophy in significant moments. Heidegger believes that his philosophical project necessitates a "historical confrontation" with Hegel, who represents the high point of the metaphysical tradition he seeks to overcome.[73] There are clear points of comparison between the two, especially in their histories of philosophy and being and in their insistence on the immanence of their unfolding. Yet Heidegger says that "Christian and rationalist thought converge in Hegel," and he rejects the concept of history at play in Hegel.[74] It may be more accurate to say that Heidegger's depiction of the history of philosophy is an "inversion of Hegelianism," whereby history does not progress toward absolute knowledge but advances into the oblivion of the truth of being.[75] In fact, Heidegger's core objection to the Hegelian system is that it does not take

---

[70] On this see Nelson, "Heidegger, Levinas, and the Other of History."
[71] Levinas, *Totality and Infinity*, 52.   [72] Ibid., 23.
[73] GA 36/37, 13–14/Heidegger, *Being and Truth*, 10.   [74] GA 36–37, 151.
[75] This observation is made by Haar, *The Song of the Earth*, 72.

negativity and nothingness "seriously," but rather methodologically sub-limates them in its dialectical advancement toward the fulfillment of absolute *Geist*.[76] This, indeed, sails close to Levinas's own critique of Heidegger, indicating that animating the German philosopher's thought is a strong impulse *against* subjugating alterity. Moreover, Heidegger's hermeneutical approach to Dasein's historicity and the negation and nothingness at the heart of what he calls the a-byss of the clearing, or *Aletheia*, signals toward multiplicity, incompleteness, and non-absolutism, and is thus inconsistent with the confidence, privileging of unity, and triumphalism attributed to Hegel by Levinas.

It should be recalled that we encountered the resistance to Heidegger's philosophy of history as an extension of the resistance to Hegel already in our analysis of Buber. Both Levinas and Buber find ties between Hegel's and Heidegger's totalized conception of history and their com-mitment to totalitarian leaders and states, and both confront this con-ception of history with a vision of prophetic history. Levinas parallels Buber in a related issue: he too rejects the portrayal of history as the march of the triumphant and embraces a contrasting view of history as the chronicle of the oppressed and conquered. Also discernible is an anti-assimilationist impulse at play: Both oppose Hegel's dialectical frame-work whereby Judaism is superseded by Christianity, and correspond-ingly grant Judaism a vital role on the world stage. Among other things, they differ in that Buber's vision locates the prophetic within the political arena and hence seeks to sanctify history, while Levinas's offers an ethics prior to any state or political situation and his prophetic messianism is, at least prima facie, beyond the political and the historical. Buber's account of prophetic history is also grounded in actual exegesis of the biblical prophets' books – however idiosyncratic – while Levinas's view of prophetic messianism is instructed by a loosely substantiated affilia-tion of nonviolence and ethical obligations with what he takes to be the core message of the prophets.[77]

Before continuing, it may be worth questioning the nonviolence of the interruptive prophetic eschatology of peace in Levinas's account. For it is undeniable that there is an inherent violence in the unexpected, vertical rupture of the Other. From a political-theological perspective, this inter-ruption features an authoritative, despotic modality projecting force

[76] GA 68, 45–49.
[77] On Buber and Levinas, see the collection of essays *Levinas and Buber: Dialogue and Difference*.

rather than peace. The aggressive model of *Totality and Infinity* is repeated and intensified in *Otherwise than Being* where, for example, in the notion of interrupted temporality in the discussion of "proximity," Levinas considers the neighbor to be "a disturbance of the memorable time. One can call that apocalyptically the break-up of time."[78] Perhaps inadvertently fleshing out the internal logic of his position and radicalizing it, his terminology in this work is openly violent. He describes the subject as engrossed by a nonreciprocal "obsession" with the other, as being "disturbed" by and "hostage" of the other, against its will – "condemned without being able to speak, persecuted." Levinas also asserts that the self is "traumatized" by the proximity to the other and the infinite "debt" to it. Anarchy, suffering, psychosis, and hatred are some of the more alarming terms employed to describe the total ownership of the other over the displaced self. Levinas claims that these experiences, pointing to the radical passivity of the subject, make compassion possible and without them there would be no ethics. Yet he does not sufficiently justify why the complete subordination of one's self to the other or the radical demand for substitution is not inversed violence against the self. In the tripartite division of duties to God, the other, and ourselves familiar from eighteenth-century moral philosophy, Levinas unites the former two and seems to ignore the latter. Derrida's Levinasian-inspired notion of hospitality, defined as "to let oneself be overtaken, to not even *let* oneself be overtaken, to be surprised, in a fashion almost violent, to be raped, stolen," testifies to the violence of the interruption of the other, the violence of the other's binding command in Levinas's scheme.[79] Does Levinas not substitute one violent picture for another? This point was raised by Paul Ricoeur, who states that "there is no such thing as a one-way ethics, to think myself uniquely as the other's hostage without any form of reciprocity is to underestimate the other's importance." Levinas's response, that "holiness excludes all interest," implies a justification for violence in the name of holiness and only makes matters worse.[80] Perhaps this should be expected, since Levinas's ethical picture is rooted in the hermeneutic of facticity of Jewish existence pressed by the violence of persecution and victimization, which he claims affords access to constitutive features of being as such.

---

[78] Levinas, *Otherwise than Being*, 89.
[79] Derrida, "Hospitality," 361. This is a point made by Haar, "The Obsession of the Other." See also Weber, "The Notion of Persecution."
[80] De Saint Cheron, *Conversations with Emmanuel Levinas*, 22.

Levinas accuses Heidegger of formulating an ontology of violence, but in so doing he in fact taps into an already-present critical impulse within Heidegger's philosophy itself, which gradually deepens and becomes more expressed. According to Heidegger's own admittance, the accent on Dasein's self-assertion and potency in his early works can be seen as reflecting some form of dominion over being. Still in *Introduction to Metaphysics* (1935) he insists on the necessity of human "violence" with respect to being. But immediately after (probably in light of the political situation in Germany at the time) he reconfigures this relation, and in the remainder of his writings and lectures from the 1930s, including *Contributions* (1936–1938), *Besinnung* (1938–1939), *Elucidations*, and the *Nietzsche* lectures, and virtually all subsequent writings, the under-standing of power as control and violence is taken to be a crucial feature of metaphysics. Being is powerful, Heidegger writes in *Elucidations*, but not in the sense of control: "The essence of power is determined from the all-presence of nature, which Hölderlin calls 'powerful, divinely beautiful.' Nature is powerful because she is god-like in beauty."[81] Being is a struggle, a confrontation, he explains, but his recourse to the notion of *Polemos* in Heraclitus should not be understood as any form of combat or violence, but in the sense of "'making-it-stand-out' [*hervorstellen*] in open view. That is the essence *of battle* as it is philosophically thought."[82] Indeed, the relation between Dasein and *Sein* is a resolute *machtlos* co-respondence and co-belonging, and his opposition to *Machenschaft* is precisely rooted in its forceful manipulation of being and its opposition to the nonviolent freedom that lets being be. "Restraint [*Die Verhaltenheit*] is the ground of care," Heidegger writes.[83] At least in terms of *philosophical* credentials, therefore, Heidegger's amended frame-work can be seen as presenting an economy of lesser violence than the one Levinas sets forth.

ETHICS, JUDAISM, AND DEMYTHOLOGIZATION

Some of Levinas's early readers were quick to pick up on the Judaic accent of his philosophy. Gabriel Marcel, for example, asks Levinas: "Why do you always say 'the Other' when you know that the term exists in the

---

[81] Heidegger, *Elucidations of Hölderlin's Poetry*, 76.
[82] Heidegger, "The Rectorate 1933/1934," 19. On the importance of *Polemos* and its role in Heidegger's politics, see Fried, *Heidegger's Polemos*.
[83] GA 65, 35/Heidegger, *Contributions to Philosophy*, 29.

biblical tradition as 'the neighbour'?"[84] Jean-François Lyotard describes Levinas's philosophy as the thought of the Old Testament God and echoes its contrast to Heidegger's paganism. "Heidegger's god is merely pagan-Christian, the god of bread, wine, earth and blood," Lyotard writes. "He is not the god of the unreadable book, which only demands respect and does not tolerate that one liberates oneself from respect and disrespect."[85] Most famously, Derrida in his "Violence and Metaphysics" discloses that in contrast to Levinas's claim that his ethics condition theology, his version of ethics is in fact informed by a deeply theological, indeed Jewish, sensitivity. "Independent of its 'theological context' (an expression that Levinas would most likely reject)," Derrida asks, "does not this entire discourse collapse?"[86] Indeed, both Levinas's major philosophical works as well as countless essays are dotted with terminology associated with the Hebrew Bible and the Jewish tradition, such as revelation, monotheism, creation, election, face, holiness, prophecy, epiphany, glory, judgment, and trace. The face's plea is expressed as a biblical commandment, and the other in need is rendered a widow, orphan, stranger, or neighbor. Levinas commonly equates the philosophical program he is offering to the journey of Abraham, who is awakened by an external call and leaves the rootedness of his fatherland for the non-belonging of the unknown. The Abrahamic linear trajectory, constantly proceeding into the unfamiliar, is contrasted to the circular motion of Ulysses, who embodies the Greek ontology of final arrival, whereby the Same returns unchanged to the nativity of its immanence.[87] No wonder it is with the Abrahamic response that Levinas chooses to express the ethical responsiveness – *me voici*, here I am, *hineni*.

At this point, the writing of Levinas's philosophical works coincided with a significant output of writings on Jewish matters by him in which parallel teachings are expressed. Most noteworthy among these are his Talmudic readings, originating in an annual colloquium of French-Jewish intellectuals that was launched in 1957, and his 1963 collection of essays on Judaism entitled *Difficult Freedom*.[88] In his Jewish writings, Levinas describes the Jewish orthopraxy as preeminently focused on the responsibility for the other and bearing precisely the ethical core exhibited in his

---

[84] Malka, *Emmanuel Levinas*, 268.   [85] Lyotard, *Heidegger and "the jews,"* 22–23.

[86] Derrida, "Violence and Metaphysics," 103.

[87] Levinas, "The Trace of the Other," 346; Levinas, *Totality and Infinity*, 102; Levinas, "Meaning and Sense," 75–107.

[88] Levinas, *Nine Talmudic Readings*.

philosophical works. Equally important, many of the features associated with being-Jewish in Levinas's early writings reappear as the components of ethical existence. He later admits that "it is a Jewish ordeal [*épreuve*] which is translated [*in Otherwise than Being*]," only to then make two further illustrative clarifications: that he makes no attempt to assert a dogmatic truth and that "Judaism is an essential modality of all that is human."[89]

One way in which the construction of an alternative can be perceived is the manner in which Levinas conceptualizes holiness and atheism. In conversation with Part I of Rosenzweig's *The Star*, Levinas describes the initial mode of selfhood in its absorption in the solitude of its interiority as "atheism," and its emergence is described as the death of "mythical" gods. Separation, that is, atheism – which for Levinas comes *before* the question of the affirmation or denial of God is even raised – is the precondition of the revelation of the infinitude of the face and of sociality. In an instructive passage, Levinas claims that "the separated being must run the risk of the paganism which evinces its separation and in which this separation is accomplished, until the moment that the death of these gods will lead it back to atheism and to the true transcendence."[90] Atheism is thus placed at the heart of the religious journey toward the self's ethical agency, since religion also demands the rejection of idolatry. "Faith purged of myth, the monotheistic faith, itself implies metaphysical atheism."[91] For the sanctity of the Other to be revealed, the world must be disenchanted and vacated of gods. Elsewhere Levinas notes that traditional philosophy "is atheism, or rather unreligion," and it is above all Heidegger who reveals how philosophy's "anti-religious essence become a religion in reverse." This is because in Heidegger's thought "atheism is a paganism, the pre-Socratic texts are anti-Scriptures."[92] It is clear, however, that while rejected, Heidegger's paganism inhabits a role in Levinas's overall scheme, for evacuating its gods serves as *praeparatio* to the emergence of the holiness of transcendence. In the essay "A Religion for Adults," the role and essence of Judaism is described precisely as enacting "a desacralization of the Sacred."[93] Corresponding to his statement about "true transcendence" quoted above, here it is proclaimed that "Judaism teaches us a *real* transcendence." And as before, the distinction between paganism and

---

[89] Levinas, *Is It Righteous to Be?*, 97.   [90] Levinas, *Totality and Infinity*, 142.
[91] Ibid., 77.   [92] Levinas, "Philosophy and the Idea of Infinity," 49.
[93] Levinas, "A Religion for Adults," 11–23; Cf. Levinas, "Desacralization and Disenchantment," 141.

Jewish monotheism does not revolve around the question of the number of existing deities – "Monotheism is not an arithmetics of the Divine," Levinas quips – but rather marks the difference between a mystified and demystified world.[94] The radical expulsion of the divine from the world runs the risk of the denial of God, yet it is a risk that must be taken. "To ignore the true God is in fact only half an evil," he writes. "Atheism is better than the piety bestowed on mythical gods."[95] He similarly contends that "only through [atheism] can man be raised to the spiritual notion of the Transcendent. It is a great glory for the Creator to have set up a being capable of seeking Him or hearing Him from afar, having experienced separation and atheism." This, indeed, is "the paradox of creation."[96]

For Levinas there is an inherent link between the sacralized world of Heideggerian paganism, and mystical, numinous experiences, as both accept an immediate encounter with the holy. His aversion to mysticism is the other side of the coin of his rejection of systematized theology: both boast a direct access to God by ignoring separation and compromising transcendence, and both do not pass through the encounter with the other person. He expresses his concerns with the Christian notion of incarnation in similar terms: "the direct encounter with God, *this* is a Christian concept."[97] In his discussion of language in *Totality and Infinity*, Levinas is careful to note that the "holiness" of the Other "is without any odour of the 'numinous.'"[98] And as he makes clear through the epigraph of part 1 of *Difficult Freedom*, this is the Jewish attitude toward the holy. The epigraph, a citation of Rashi's commentary on Leviticus 10:2, "Let them not enter the sanctuary drunk," links the death of Aaron's sons by the strange fire to their drunkenness, which Levinas takes to

---

[94] Levinas, "Monotheism and Language," 178.
[95] Levinas, "A Religion for Adults," 16.   [96] Levinas, *Totality and Infinity*, 103.
[97] Levinas, "Ideology and Idealism," 247. While this seems to be a polemical oversimplification of the notion of "incarnation," Levinas commends Jesus as an exemplar of what he calls "substitution." In so doing Levinas is one with a long line of modern Jewish thinkers who endorse Jesus as a Jewish exemplar of ethics. Levinas does claim however that we are each called upon to be messiahs; our responsibility is ours alone, and no one, not even Jesus, can substitute our absolute obligation toward the other. See Levinas, "A Man-God?" Christian engagements with Levinas abound. For example, Webb, "The Rhetoric of Ethics as Excess"; Morrison, "Emmanuel Levinas and Christian Theology"; Zimmerman, *Levinas and Theology*; Ward, *Barth, Derrida*, esp. 147–170. Purcell, *Levinas and Theology*. Purcell basically ignores any Jewish coloration of Levinas's philosophy, while Ward claims that notwithstanding the Jewish layers of his thought, Levinas can be read Christologically as well. See also *The Exorbitant: Emmanuel Levinas Between Jews and Christians*.
[98] Levinas, *Totality and Infinity*, 195

symbolize the idolatrous enthusiasm of numinal religiosity. It is no coincidence that Levinas claims Heidegger's philosophy illustrates "in what intoxication the lucid sobriety of philosophers is steeped."[99] While Levinas's rejection of the numinal form of spirituality is often rightly attributed to the Lithuanian rabbinic *Mitnagdik* tradition within which he was raised, and which is eminently critical of Hasidism's ecstaticism, it would be a mistake to overlook its anti-Heideggerian connotations. Thus, with clear Kantian reverberations, Levinas poses an opposition between Heidegger's juvenile, mystical, ecstatic, and nonethical mode of being, and the Jewish, rational, ethical, atheistic monotheism, "a religion for adults."

We have seen that at first, Levinas rebukes Heidegger's framework for its radical immanence. The world of Dasein, he contends, is impenetrable to and hence void of *real* transcendence. The denial of transcendence leads to the situating of the gods *within* a sacralized world, and thus Heidegger's being becomes permeated with, rather than emptied of, the sacred. From Levinas's perspective, the godless world he advances in the name of Judaism differs decisively from the godless world of Heideggerian paganism. The crucial difference is that Heidegger's hermetically immanent world amounts to a denial of transcendence, while Judaism acknowledges and hence safeguards the transcendence of God by accepting the immanent world as bearing only a trace of the divine. But what safeguards this "infinite qualitative difference" between the world and God from turning into a radical dualism or collapsing into a framework of radical immanence? There is apparently a fateful but thin line separating paganism and religion, violence and ethics, totalitarianism and messianism, the absolutization of totality and the vindication of totality by infinity. In "Violence and Metaphysics" Derrida observes that "God alone keeps Levinas's world from being a world of pure and worst violence."[100] However, Levinas's response to Derrida's critique of the unsustainability of the purity of the sameness–otherness divide in *Totality and Infinity* is to double down on the radicalism of the distance between the two in his later writings. Especially in *Otherwise than Being*, as God is pushed further and further into the darkness and becomes "not simply the 'first other,' or the 'other *par excellence*,' or the 'absolutely other,' but other than the other, other otherwise," it is questionable whether this thin line can still uphold the weight of these distinctions.[101]

---

[99] Levinas, "Philosophy and the Idea of Infinity," 53.
[100] Derrida, "Violence and Metaphysics," 107.   [101] Levinas, *Otherwise than Being*, 69.

JUDAISM, TECHNOLOGY, AND THE GODS

With respect to Heidegger's philosophy, Levinas often emphasizes his near exclusive attention to *Sein und Zeit* and general disregard of Heidegger's later thought. This early work "is much more significant and profound than any of Heidegger's later works," Levinas states; and "as for the later Heidegger," he admits, "I am much less familiar with him."[102] However, notwithstanding his long-standing wrestling with the 1927 masterpiece, Levinas's dismissive remarks about later Heidegger deserve our skepticism. There are simply too many references to too many of Heidegger's later works to argue otherwise, and Levinas's writings testify to his close reading of these later writings. For example, a few years after the publication of the lecture "The Question Concerning Technology" in Heidegger's 1954 *Vorträge und Aufsätze*, Levinas draws on it in the wider context of his Jewish polemic against Heidegger. His 1961 essay "Heidegger, Gagarin, and Us," prompted by the impression of Russian Astronaut Yuri Gagarin's successful journey into outer space, is a reflection on the philosophico-religious significance of this event, within the explicit context of Heidegger's critique of technology. The Cold War "space race" between the United States and the Soviet Union in general and Gagarin's flight in particular elicited both enthusiasm and apprehension and generated much debates over the promises and perils of the human triumph over nature by means of modern technology that it immediately came to symbolize. Arendt, for example, like others who contemplated the effect of this historical moment on what it means to be human, begins her 1958 work *The Human Condition* with a sober reflection on the launch of the Sputnik on October 4, 1957, an event she considers "second in importance to no other."[103] Levinas, as his essay makes clear, is among the enthusiasts. For him the potential danger in "technological things" is far exceeded by its "great hopes." Gagarin's flight represents a strategic blow to "the eternal seductiveness of paganism," that is, rootedness and transcendence in the world. Levinas draws on a variety of familiar Heideggerian images from a multitude of later essays to describe the pagan framework of transcendence in the mundane that is purportedly shattered by this flight:

[T]o follow a path that winds its way through fields, to feel the unity created by the bridge, the bridge that links two river banks and by the architecture of building, the presence of a tree, the chiaroscuro, of the forests, the mystery of things, of a jug,

---

[102] Kearney, *Dialogues*, 51.   [103] Arendt, *The Human Condition*, 1.

or worn-out shoes of a peasant girl, the gleam from a carafe of wine sitting on a white tablecloth.[104]

Levinas rightly identifies that Heidegger's critique of technology participates in his effort to retrieve a sense of immanent sacredness and mystery to the world. "Technology," he declares in response, "wrenches us out of the Heideggerian world and the superstitions surrounding Place."[105] Thus technology is paired with Judaism as two anti-pagan, anti-Heideggerian forces spearheading the crusade against the pagan gods and the re-mystification of the world. Both are modeled as fundamentally iconoclastic: unlike Christianity, "Judaism has not sublimated idols – on the contrary, it has demanded that they be destroyed. Like technology, it has demystified the universe."[106] Interestingly, Levinas here comes close to Cassirer, who speaks of the rise of technology as the *Götterdämmerung* of myth and who attributes the role of combating and overcoming mythical paganism to Judaism. Echoing his definition of Judaism as anti-paganism par excellence almost two decades earlier, Levinas now proclaims that "*The Sacred filtering into the world* – Judaism is perhaps no more than the negation of all that."[107] In this respect, one might say that for Levinas, Gagarin is Jewish. The sense of estrangement associated from early on with being-Jewish, in contrast to the Heideggerian *der Ort*, reappears here as well – "Judaism has always been free with regard to place." The "politics of space" at play here should not be missed, for as beyond place, as non-place, Judaism is utopian, messianic, while Heideggerian pagan rootedness is totalitarian.

In his essay Levinas accuses Heidegger of holding a "reactionary" view, but Heidegger was not a Luddite. In fact, aware of this common misinterpretation, he specifically emphasizes that "I am not against technology" and that "it would be foolish to attack technology blindly. It would be shortsighted to condemn it as the work of the devil."[108] Nor is he against technological advancement – he calls this "false romanticism."[109] One may be skeptical about whether Heidegger's account is entirely free of romanticism – some passages describing the pre-technological Greek world betray more than a smack of sentimental nostalgia – but his main imperative in this context remains to unmask the metaphysical approach toward being underpinning technology, which "drives out every other possibility of revealing."[110] As such, the technological disclosure of truth

[104] Levinas, "Heidegger, Gagarin, and Us," 232.   [105] Ibid., 233.   [106] Ibid., 234.
[107] Ibid., 232. Italics in the original.   [108] Heidegger, *Discourse on Thinking*, 53.
[109] GA 94, 356–357/Heidegger, *Ponderings II–VI*, 260.
[110] Heidegger, *The Question Concerning Technology*, 27.

constitutes a detachment, an uprooting of beings from the excess of their being, and deepens the forgetfulness of being. Even as he opposes the technological outlook once perceived as the exclusive horizon of disclosure and mode of truth, as is the case in the present age of *das Gestell*, Heidegger does not sweepingly condemn technology, for he also recognizes in it a saving power.

It should not go unnoticed, however, that Levinas's critique of Heidegger's stance on technological actually rests on a fundamental agreement. Levinas mirrors Heidegger's view that technology is a configuration of truth, that *Technik* no longer denotes a certain aspect of human activity but rather a historical condition defining the modern era, and that technology is a demystifying force antithetical to "dwelling." He also concurs with Heidegger regarding the solidarity of technology and Judaism as well as the coupling of Judaism, technology, and uprootedness. While he would replace Heidegger's ontological emphasis with a humanistic intonation, Levinas apparently complies with the proclamation in the *Black Notebooks*, that *Weltjudentum* is "the sort of human singularity [*Menschentümlichkeit*] which, being utterly unattached [*schlechthin ungebunden*], can undertake the uprooting of all beings from being as world-historical 'mission.'"[111]

Clearly, the crux of their difference lies in the appraisal of technology and of the Jews as the technological people. Indeed, while Levinas takes the contrast between what he understands as Heidegger's enrooted Nazi paganism and the Jewish ethos of ethically loaded uprootedness as reflecting the radical opposition between his own philosophical project and Heidegger's, it can be seen that he maintains the Heideggerian and volkish discourse, with its focus on the notion of rootedness, while inverting its valuation. In this respect, too, the mark of the early decades of the twentieth-century German intellectual climate are evident in his thinking. But it is here that Levinas's identification of the mission of Judaism with the project of modernity, its technological progress, and the disenchantment of the world, is curious. Seemingly carried away by his anti-Heideggerian polemic or by the enthusiasm from the historical flight, Levinas accepts a dichotomy between technology and monotheistic iconoclasm on the one hand, and anti-technological Ludditism and paganism on the other. Not only does he minimize the perils that an overly enthusiastic technological frenzy holds in store for both humans and the world,

---

[111] *GA* 96, 243. For an alternative view, see Maloney "Dreaming Otherwise than Icarus," 41.

he also grants it religious justification and dangerously conflates technological and ethical progress. Unlike Hans Jonas, who calls for "biblical
restraints" on technology, in this article Levinas embraces technology as
an instantiation of the biblical worldview.[112] This is puzzling, for at the
heart of modern technological progress is precisely the calculative, instru-
mentalizing approach that would seem to be guilty of the reductive and
unchecked desire of the Same for prediction, assimilation, and control
against which Levinas wages battle. And insofar as the scale and brutality
of the horrors of the twentieth century are inconceivable without modern
technology (an argument made by many, including Zygmunt Bauman,
Theodor Adorno, and Hannah Arendt), Levinas effectively downplays the
link between Nazism and technology – a link that ultimately led
a dismayed Heidegger *away* from the party.

For Heidegger, modern technology is a stage in the history of being
whereby the metaphysical force of the will to power has outdone itself and
wills nothing but blind will itself. On the other hand, for Levinas, all
human endeavors, including ontology, epistemology, history, and culture,
are in themselves manifestations of the pagan will to power – all, that is,
except for ethics, Judaism, and apparently, also modern technology.
Consequently, the coupling of the Jewish mission with the progress of
modernity inadvertently concedes to some Hegelian presuppositions
regarding history that Levinas overtly rejects. The religious quality
instilled into technological advancement grants it an overarching purpo-
seful and almost teleological character. This is at odds with his understanding of an interruptive eschatological temporality and his attack on
"vulgar" spatializing temporality. To be sure, unlike Hegelianism,
Levinas intends to depict this historical development as a progression
toward or motivated by alterity. Yet in the way in which it is presented,
it approximates the establishment of a *Heilsgeschichte* and can function as
what he calls "theodicy."

The difficulty that leads Levinas to signal in two opposing directions is
this: his account of ontology and eschatology indicates that the meaning
of history cannot be given within the historical order; hence the face, and
Judaism, are interruptions. Indeed, in both his early and later writings he
presents an ahistorical Judaism constituting of one central message or
impulse, bereft of developments, shifting historical contexts, internal or
external debates and influences, or any other manifestation of a live
tradition enacted historically. It is, in his words, "a rupture of the natural

---

[112] Jonas, "Contemporary Problems in Ethics from a Jewish Perspective," 177.

and historical."[113] Its absolute unconditionality is so decontextualized, self-contained, and ossified, that it invites the deconstructive readings to which Derrida submitted it. On the other hand, for Judaism to have actual effect, it must relate to the historical order. But once Judaism is defined extra-historically, attaching it to a historical development as Levinas does in the "Gagarin" essay makes it susceptible to the very shortcomings of history he wishes to avoid. Is Judaism the motor of eschatology or its result? Does it interrupt history or operate within it? Levinas seems to affirm both "prophetic" and Hegelian stances while presenting them as mutually exclusive.[114]

This is the difficulty that the attempt to set a radically dichotomous distinction between ethics on the one side and ontology, politics, and history on the other will inevitably run into. This difficulty is crystalized toward the end of *Otherwise than Being*, where the notions of "justice" and "the third" are developed to attend to a certain insufficiency in *Totality and Infinity* and account for the more general social and political realm, as well as for other others, outside the dyad of the face-to-face encounter, whose demand on the subject is equally infinite and pressing. How is the transition from an-archial and nonviolent ethics to totalizing and violent politics achievable? Levinas claims that the third interrupts the responsibility emerging from the face-to-face encounter, which "is troubled and becomes a problem when the third party enters."[115] But he also describes the ethical as interrupting the ontological and the political. Is the third readily given or an interruption? Is it beyond the face or in some way present in the other's face? The same contradictory impulses are displayed here too: on the one hand, the political concretizes ethics which would otherwise be an abstraction, and on the other hand, there is a refusal to compromise the purity and radicalism of the face-to-face encounter with the other.[116] Ethics and politics, like Judaism and history – and therefore, *also Judaism and Heidegger* – must be concurrent while distinct, neither entirely dependent nor entirely independent.

---

[113] Levinas, "Demanding Judaism," 4. Here he writes explicitly that "Judaism has not changed much through the millennia and the planetary space of its 'dispersion.'"

[114] Here we should note another ambiguity in Levinas, mentioned by many, regarding the interpretation of the ethical relation, which could be understood transcendentally, as the condition of possibility of being and meaning as such, or as an actual encounter that interrupts antecedent being and intelligibility.

[115] Levinas, *Otherwise than Being*, 157. The notion of "the third" is introduced briefly toward the end of *Totality and Infinity*, but is not developed.

[116] Bernasconi, "The Third Party." For an attempt to formulate a coherent account of Levinas's reflections on ethics and politics, see Morgan, *Levinas's Ethical Politics*.

Levinas's approach toward technology in "Gagarin, Heidegger, and Us" appears therefore overblown. Surely one can appreciate the objection to the status of "the earth as a coal mining district, the soil as a mineral deposit"[117] without being charged a pagan or a reactionary. Eventually, Levinas appears to have come close to doing just that. A decade later he retracts his enthusiasm from Gagarin's flight, and in the essay "Ideology and Idealism" (1972) he responds to Gagarin's alleged declaration that he did not find God in outer space:

> The new condition of existence in the weightlessness of a space "without sites" is still experienced, by the first man to be launched into space, as a *here*, as the *same* without a veritable alterity. The marvels of technology do not open the *beyond* where Science, their mother, was born! No outside at all in all these movements! What an immanence! What a bad infinite![118]

A year earlier, in the essay "Antihumanism and Education," Levinas considers the sciences in which man "is reduced purely and simply to the fields in which the operations of numbers unfold" to be inhumane. To stay clear of coming too close to Heidegger on this point, he immediately differentiates himself from the "ambitious philosophical enterprise in aid of thought and against pure calculation," which is guilty of "subordinating the human to the anonymous gains of Being and, despite its 'Letters on Humanism,' bringing understanding to Hitlerism itself."[119] Also in his "Secularization and Hunger" (1976), Levinas asserts that "no one is mad enough to fail to recognize the contradictions and the miscalculations of technology and its new, murderous dangers and bondage, and the mythologies which it threatens, and the pollution which results from it." But he also goes on to stress that the condemnation of technology forgets its implicit ethical promise, for in the present world, "without the development of technology, [humanity] could not be fed."[120]

Evidently, Levinas revisits his previous enthusiasm and posits that technology is not one with ethical advancement, but rather valuable only insofar as it promotes ethical justice and reduces mythicization, that is, only insofar as it reveals the world as a space opened by ethically charged human interaction.[121] "The sciences of man and Heidegger," he

---

[117] *GA* 7, 15.   [118] Levinas, "Ideology and Idealism," 8.
[119] Levinas, "Antihumanism and Education," 281.
[120] Levinas, "Secularization and Hunger," 9.
[121] Levinas acknowledges that according to some, "my article on Gagarin and Heidegger went too far." He does however insist that "there are texts in Heidegger on the place of man in Central Europe. Europe and the German West are central to him. There is a whole geopolitics in Heidegger." Levinas, "Philosophy, Justice, and Love," 118.

states, "end either in the triumph of mathematical intelligibility, repressing the subject, the person, his uniqueness and election, into ideology, or else in the enrootedness of man in being."[122] For Levinas, then, the essence of technology *ought* to be the ethical promise of feeding the hungry. We might recall, in this context, his complaint that Heidegger's Dasein is never hungry.[123] Whether it is directed toward being or toward the other person determines for Levinas whether technology gives itself to the anti-humanism of Heideggerian pagan enrootedness or rehabilitates a Jewish humanism and ethics.

Levinas's stance with respect to technology rests on the distinction between a nomadic ethics and the Heideggerian anti-ethics of rooted dwelling, a distinction for which he finds confirmation in the link between Heidegger's notion of *Bodenständigkeit* and his volkish support of Hitler. Indeed, in texts that Levinas did not know, Heidegger himself contrasts the aspired German enrooted existence with the prolonged unrootedness and "worldlessness of Jewry," which is grounded in "the tenacious facility in calculating, manipulating, and interfering."[124] Yet as Heidegger's personal affiliation with the party dwindled in the mid-1930s and in the years that followed, he construed a more sophisticated account of the homely *as well as* exilic quality of modern existence. Levinas is surely correct in pointing to the enduring importance of rootedness in a "place" for Heidegger. Over against the technological world, Heidegger implores us to dwell in a world structured by the unified "wrestling" of the fourfold of earth, sky, mortals, and divinities; nurturing and being nurtured by our localized essence, place, and customs.[125] But this *Heimat* is not merely the soil of one's land, but a special approach or attunement to the question of being, a sense of nearness that allows the holiness and mystery of being to be present. There is, he acknowledges, a simultaneity of at-homeness and homelessness, of exile and homecoming, of rootedness and displacement in the *Heimat*, and hence it is at once *unheimlich* and a *Geheimnis*. This point is stressed in the 1940s in his lectures on Hölderlin's "Andenken" and particularly "Der Ister," where an analysis of the first choral ode from Sophocles' *Antigone* offers an in-depth investigation into the meaning of being-at-home. There he muses on the Greek word *deinon*, which he translates as *das Unheimliche*, and announces that "the saying 'the human being is the uncanniest' provides the authentic *Greek* definition

[122] Levinas, *The Humanism of the Other*, 61.   [123] Levinas, *Totality and Infinity*, 134.
[124] GA 95, 97/Heidegger, *Ponderings VII–IX*, 76.
[125] On this see Wrathall, *Heidegger and Unconcealment*, 195–211.

of humanity [*Mensch*]."[126] He similarly writes that "Antigone herself is
the poem of coming-to-be-at-home in not-being-at-home [*des
Heimischwerdens im Unheimischsein*]." In "Letter on Humanism," to
which Levinas occasionally refers, Heidegger proposes alleviating the
homelessness of the modern person by dwelling not in the *Boden*, but in
language, the house of being. Also in the 1960 lecture "*Sprache und
Heimat*," *Sprache* is said to be best understood *as Heimat*.[127] Indeed,
already in *Sein und Zeit* Heidegger grants that "the 'not-at-home' must be
conceived as the more primordial phenomenon."[128] But not only does
Heidegger not simplistically advocate for vulgar enrootedness in German
soil à la Hermann Göring; it is also the case that Levinas himself concedes
some legitimacy to being-at-home in one's self and in being, for example,
when he speaks of the "interiority of the Home" and describes the hospitality toward the Other: "I welcome the Other who presents in my home
by opening my home to him." Once more Derrida's notion of "hospitality" can help shed light on Levinas, for, as he points out, "I cannot offer
you hospitality without saying: 'this is mine, I am at home.'"[129]

<h2 style="text-align:center">DISRUPTING DICHOTOMIES</h2>

At this point, it is worthwhile to situate Levinas's response to Heidegger
within the broader context of other Jewish engagements with the German
philosopher. In light of the previous chapters of this study, it becomes
apparent that with regards to some central themes, Levinass' response is
hardly untypical. In insinuating that Heidegger's existential analysis of
Dasein does not aptly portray Jewish existence; in linking this inaccuracy
to a theological deficiency; in identifying it as "paganism," a term possessing obvious negative connotations; in focusing on the theme of immanence and transcendence as the heart of this theological flaw; in
conjoining the political, philosophical, and theological to make sense of
Heidegger's Nazi sympathies; in posing an opposing, alternative Jewish
account to contrast with that of Heidegger; in charging the Jewish alternative with an ethical import said to be lacking in Heidegger's account; in
suggesting that this Jewish alternative is instructive and pertinent to non-

---

[126] Heidegger, *Introduction to Metaphysics*, 161. Cf. Wolfson, *The Duplicity of
Philosophy's Shadow*, 33–86; Withy, *Heidegger on Being Uncanny*.
[127] GA 13, 180.   [128] SZ, 189/BT, 234.
[129] This theme is discussed by Eubanks and Gauthier, "The Politics of Homeless Spirit";
Tijmes, "Home and Homelessness: Heidegger and Levinas on Dwelling."

Jews as well; in identifying Heidegger not as a break from philosophical tradition but as its emblematic culmination; and in perceiving his Jewish rejoinder to be not only the antithesis to Heideggerianism but a remedy to the overall spiritual sickness it represents – in all these features, Levinas concurs with a central line of contemporary Jewish reactions to Heidegger. One might say that Levinas's novelty in comparison with other Jewish intellectuals is the extent to which he is profoundly *in debt* to Heidegger. He seeks to outstrip Heidegger's innovations without altogether dismissing their cogency; his rejoinder offers an alternative from within, as it were. His emphasis on the absolute obligation to the other person accounts for and presupposes Heidegger's ontology, and his vision of Judaism is correspondingly developed *through* his engagement with Heidegger. Indeed, he reads the one in light of the other. The result is a Heideggerian-inspired and -based exposition of being-Jewish-in-the-world, further developed and expanded as his ethics. Thus, more than any other thinker discussed in this study, it stands true that without Heidegger, Levinas would not be.

The crux of Levinas's critique of Heidegger's ontology is that it repudiates otherness. On this account, the category of being in Heidegger is identical to the traditional metaphysical category of "essence" and hence promotes "constant presence" and is allergic to difference. This understanding, however, has elicited much opposition.[130] Levinas's conflation of Heidegger's being with "the Same" is ill-conceived. Heidegger repeatedly insists that "being," in the sense in which he uses the term, has been forgotten throughout the history of Western thought and is distinguished from the metaphysical "essence." Being it is not *a* being and thus cannot be the mediating ontological concept Levinas says it is. Heidegger's understanding of being, the ontological difference, and his attempt to think its originary openness lead him to claim that the otherness to which this difference testifies is "neither an ontic nor an ontological relation."[131] In fact, Levinas's Other is in some important respects rather similar to Heidegger's being, which too is at once the farthest and oddly near, present but inaccessible. Levinas's vigilance against metaphysical remnants, ontotheology, and the nullification of difference is in truth an internal impulse within Heidegger's thought, present already in *Sein und Zeit* and intensified thereafter. Heidegger's ardent call for releasement

[130] This has been argued by Derrida and repeated ever since. On a specific focus on the question of the holy, see Sikka, "Questioning the Sacred."
[131] Heidegger, *Discourse on Thinking*, 77.

[*Gelassenheit*], to let being be, is a call to curb our disposition of forcing the unfamiliar into familiar forms and to cultivate a modest and respectful approach to alterity.[132] It is not without reason that Philippe Lacoue-Labarthe admits that "I have a lot of trouble not seeing in Heidegger's 'Being,' if it is still Being and if it is Heidegger's Being, the same thing as (if not the very possibility of) Levinas's 'otherwise than Being.'"[133] Jacques Rolland similarly contends that "the concepts of *Otherwise than Being* function according to a scheme formally identical to what governs Being in Heidegger's sense of the term."[134] For both Levinas and Heidegger, difference demands non-indifference, though in Levinas (as in Buber and Heschel) there is a crucial personalized accent to otherness absent in the anonymity of Heidegger's being.

Perhaps surprisingly, we can find support for the claim that Heidegger's ontology strongly signals toward what Levinas calls ethics from Levinas himself. In a number of late occasions, the Jewish-French philosopher comes close to admitting precisely that. In "Diachrony and Representation" (1982), he comments on Heidegger's 1946 "The Anaximander Fragment" in *Holzwege*, where the latter renounces metaphysical ontology of presence and reads his modification of being as *Anwesen*, in which a radical and irreducible absence and otherness is acknowledged, into the pre-Socratic's fragment. Recognizing what surely qualifies as an ethical moment in Heidegger, Levinas exclaims:

A putting into question of that "positivity" of the *esse* in its presence, signifying – brusquely – encroachment and usurpation! Did not Heidegger, despite all he wants to teach about the priority of the "thought of being" – here run up against the original significance of ethics?[135]

Also Levinas's somewhat unexpected defense of Heidegger against Buber's charge of monological solipsism exposes a rather decisive identification of his own ethical perspective with a Heideggerian category.

---

[132] This has been suggested, for example, in Nancy, "Heidegger's Originary Ethics," 65–86, and Raffoul, "Heidegger and the Origins of Responsibility," 87–98. Dastur sketches out Levinas's misreading of Heidegger on this point in her "Levinas and Heidegger: Ethics or Ontology?" 175–206. Cohen accepts that Heidegger's fundamental ontology is indeed an ethics, but that it is still a different, and inferior, account of ethics to Levinas's. Cohen, *Ethics, Exegesis and Philosophy*, 120–142.
[133] Lacoue-Labarthe, *Typography*, 23.
[134] Quoted in Zarader, *The Unthought Debt*, 146. Echoing this judgment, Zarader contends that "Levinas 'forgets' all that which in Being, in Heidegger's sense, might be liable to approximate it to the Other ... yet this forgetting is a decision" (p. 145).
[135] Levinas, "Diachrony and Representation," 108–109.

"Buber rises in violent opposition to the Heideggerian notion of *Fürsorge* which, to the German philosopher, would be access to Others," Levinas writes,

it is certainly not from Heidegger that one should take lessons on the love of man or social justice. But *Fürsorge* as response to an essential destitution accedes to the alterity of the Other. It takes into account that dimension of height and misery through which the very epiphany of others takes place.[136]

Here Levinas differentiates between Heidegger's philosophy and his personal actions. The philosophy bears witness to the ethical relation, but the philosopher has little credit in these matters. Levinas carries on and accuses Buber of abstraction and unethical monologicalism – that is, exactly what Buber finds faulty in Heidegger: "One may wonder whether clothing the naked and feeding the hungry do not bring us closer to the neighbour than the rarefied atmosphere in which Buber's Meeting sometimes takes place." For Buber's dialogue to occur as an ethical encounter, it must base itself on the structure related by Heidegger. "Is dialogue possible without *Fürsorge*?," Levinas wonders.[137] On another occasion, Levinas forthrightly equates his conception of responsibility with Heidegger's *Sorge*. "The central idea of my argument," he explains in an interview, "is that the other's alterity is my responsibility for him, which is heavy and evasive. The sign of being human is caring for the other – *die Sorge*, as Heidegger says."[138]

Interestingly, these examples refer to both Heidegger's earlier and later writings, indicating that apparently Heidegger has *always* approximated the ethical sensitivity of which Levinas speaks. This observation is important for anyone who seeks to arrive at an honest judgment of Levinas's attitude toward his former teacher, and it is crucial for the interest of the present chapter, because Levinas's belated acknowledgment of the ethical impulse animating Heidegger's stance invites the need to revisit the trenchant adversarial framing of ethical Judaism over against Heideggerian paganism.

Unsurprisingly, Levinas does not engage in such a revision. On one occasion, however, he is somewhat ambivalent about his indictment of Heideggerian ontology as paganism. In one of the many interviews he

[136] Levinas, "Martin Buber and Contemporary Judaism," 18. Cf. the chapter "Buber and Levinas – and Heidegger" in Cohen's *Levinasian Meditations*, 80–93. Cohen offers an analysis of this philosophical triangle from a decidedly Levinasian perspective.
[137] Ibid. [138] De Saint Cheron, *Conversations with Emmanuel Levinas*, 36.

gave later in his life, he is asked: "do you think that Heidegger would make a kind of sacralization of the world, and that his thought represents a culmination of paganism?" The answer to this question would presumably be a simple affirmation, as Levinas has been arguing precisely this for decades.[139] Yet his response is far from being straightforward: "Whatever the case may be, he has a very great sense for everything that is part of the landscape; not the artistic landscape, but the place in which man is enrooted. It is absolutely not a philosophy of the émigré!"[140] Levinas evokes Heidegger's proclivity toward rootedness but avoids reaffirming his steadfast identification of Heideggerianism and paganism. Does this mean he finally acknowledges the discrepancies between Heidegger and "Levinas's Heidegger"?[141] Or that the clean-cut contrast posed between his teacher's thought and his own is overstated? Is he prepared to problematize the plain association between Heidegger and paganism? It is unlikely. Too much is at stake – philosophically and personally.[142] There are, however, moments when a mild admittance to the inadequacy of the contrastive disposition between Heidegger and Levinas's construction of Judaism can be found. With respect to the Heideggerian idea of being manifesting itself in a silent language, for example, Levinas remarks that "in this way, without realizing it, Heidegger would have Judaized the Greeks."[143] Marlène Zarader attempts to explain Levinas's oversight of this overall proximity:

Levinas is led to mark a distance, even to exaggerate it deliberately, not in order to caricature Heidegger's thought, but on the contrary to disclose that which is most proper to it. And what is most proper to it is the absence of the only Other that might give meaning to the concept of alterity. In this sense, Heidegger's work stands farthest from the Levinasian endeavor, as also from the heritage to which the latter claims to be faithful.[144]

---

[139] The contrast between the universal uprooting of Judaism and the nationalistic rooting of paganism is utilized in Levinas's 1951 scold of Simone Weil, "Simone Weil Against the Bible," 136–138.

[140] Levinas, "Philosophy, Justice, and Love," 117.

[141] "Levinas's Heidegger" is David Boothroyd's formulation, signifying "a representative of Heidegger that functions internally within Levinas's own thesis." See his "Responding to Levinas," 17.

[142] Cf. Levinas's reading of the Babylonian Talmud, Tractate *Yoma*, 85a–85b in the context of the theme of "forgiveness," where he proclaims movingly: "One can forgive many Germans, but there are some Germans it is difficult to forgive. It is difficult to forgive Heidegger." Levinas, *Nine Talmudic Readings*, 25.

[143] Levinas, *God, Death, and Time*, 151. Cf. Wolfson, *Giving Beyond the Gift*, 123–135.

[144] Zarader, *The Unthought Debt*, 146.

Zarader opines that the reason Levinas deliberately effaces their similarities is his former teacher's godless framework, which neutralizes the
concept of alterity. This core absence makes the many semblances
between the two, important as they may seem, "absolutely
negligible."[145] Yet this does not explain why Levinas does not simply
state this rather than recurrently and polemically deride a strawman for
years while expressing what otherwise appears to be at the very least
comparable views. Zarader's explanation also insufficiently attends to
the aforementioned moments in which Levinas does finally seem to
admit to affinities with Heidegger. The difference between the two
thinkers, moreover, is not whether or not God is an Other, but rather
regards the apparatus through which God can be approached. Another
matter is that Zarader's point rests on the implicit depiction of Athens
as ontotheology and Judaism as its "other." According to this logic,
which Zarader shares with Levinas, although he is less willing to
acknowledge it, Heidegger is much closer to the "Hebraic," which
serves as the "unthought" of his philosophy. To accept this judgment,
however, one must hold a very specific (and static) understanding of
what "Hebraic" means, and be prepared to make some coarse generalizations with respect to Christianity. It is easy to see that mapping the
philosophies of Levinas and Heidegger onto "Jerusalem" and
"Athens," respectively, is misguided. Not only because both Levinas's
philosophical works *and* his Jewish writings are "Greek" in that they
are presented in a philosophical medium as a discourse of *logos*, but
because Heidegger's philosophy simply does not concur with Levinas's
description of what constitutes Athens.[146] The philosopher who titled
his collected works *Wege: Nicht Werke* and who claims that "questioning is the piety of thought" is no Ulysses. But this does not mean he
necessarily is Abraham either. It only means that, with respect to
Levinas, Judaism and philosophy are not, as it is popular to say, each
other's other. Once again, Levinas's dualistic disjunction between his
ethical thought and Judaism on the one hand, and Heidegger's philosophy on the other hand, covers up the intricate ways in which
Levinas's account is marked by Heidegger, both positively and
negatively.

---

[145] Ibid., 145.
[146] Eisenstadt argues that Levinas's Jewish writings "emerge as more Greek, or
Greekjewish, than the philosophical works." See Eisenstadt, "Levinas Versus
Levinas," 148.

CODA

In Levinas's scheme, no internal development within the ego or within the world generates the revelation of the other person. The calling into question of totality comes from without, as rupture and interruption. Any predisposed presence of the Other in the Same is by definition ruled out. Yet for the interruption to *interrupt*, that is, to have an effect, there must be – to borrow language from theology – a *Kontaktpunkt* that makes possible an interaction-in-difference between the two divided spheres. Such a point of contact is rejected by Levinas, leading to Derrida's claim that with this rejection Levinas announces a "dream" of "pure thought of pure difference."[147] But at the same time, this point of contact is also assumed in his understanding of "religion" and ethics as a non-violating approach toward transcendence. Indeed, alongside the logic of interruption operating in Levinas there is another model of logic wherein not mutual exclusivism but dialectic of priorities and relations is at play. His proposed reversal of traditional ontological priorities must not lead to the formation of a new totalizing ontology wherein the Other adopts the oppressing role of the Same. Levinas does not reject ontology per se, but rather only the totalizing and deifying propensity of its self-perception as first philosophy. Binary expositions are deceptive. Ontology, the Same, philosophy, are not invalidated, only churned up by an ethical shift. It is for this reason that describing his contention with Heidegger as a dispute over the question of primacy between ontology and ethics as "first philosophy" is problematic. For according to Levinas's logic – and, in truth, also Heidegger's – the very conception of first philosophy can all too easily operate as a violent site of metaphysical fundamentalism.[148] The counter-ontology that he calls "metaphysics" consists of both Athens and Jerusalem, totality and infinity, being and otherwise than being, ethics and justice, the Saying and the Said, philosophy and skepticism.[149] When asked, "is transcendence inseparable from immanence?," Levinas replies: "absolutely."[150] Thus, even if Heidegger is misinterpreted by Levinas as a paragon of totality, it is still not disjunction but dialectical sublation that defines their philosophical relations. J' and Dasein are not mutually exclusive.

[147] Derrida, "Violence and Metaphysics," 151.
[148] On this see Murphey, "Critique, Power, and Ontological Violence," 15–30.
[149] Handelman, *Fragments*, 324.
[150] De Saint Cheron, *Conversations with Emmanuel Levinas*, 33.

It is ultimately also the logic of dialectics that serves Levinas's aim of opening Greek thought to the philosophical contributions of the Jewish monotheistic perspective as he understands it. Judaism's universal vocation hinges on the possibility of the interaction of its otherness with the world. Without it, the statements about the human soul being naturally Jewish, or that a Jew is not a particularity but a modality of being, are empty. Levinas states that in his philosophy, Hebrew is the content and Greek the form; Greek needs Hebrew for it to be meaningful and Hebrew needs Greece to expose its universalism.[151] Ultimately, then, Levinas proposes an *Aufhebung*, a sublation and modification of totality in relation to infinity, of being in relation to its beyond, which, in order to sustain this fragile relation and not proceed to a higher synthesis of a new Same, must deconstruct itself and collapse, over and over again.[152] Derrida is therefore correct that Levinas is, and must be, "Jewgreek. Greekjew."

---

[151] Kearney, *Dialogues*, 57; Levinas, "The Translation of Scripture," 147.
[152] On this see Critchley, *The Ethics of Deconstruction*.

CONCLUSION

Which God Will Save Us? Heidegger and Judaism

Only a great thinker can help us in our plight. But here is the great trouble: the only great thinker in our time is Heidegger.[1]

A man who undertakes to philosophize in the twentieth century cannot *not* have gone through Heidegger's philosophy, even to escape it.[2]

Man kann verjuden ...

HEIDEGGER AND JUDAISM: AUSEINANDERSETZUNG

From many, the publication of the *Black Notebooks* introduced Judaism into the orbit of Heidegger's thought. The sorry insertion of *Judentum* and the *Judenfrage* into the apparatus of Heidegger's deliberations on the *Seinsfrage* in these notebooks has led to much reflection on whether and how to situate Judaism in the task of thinking. However, thinking about Judaism vis-à-vis Heidegger is in fact a long-standing endeavor. Throughout the twentieth century, leading Jewish thinkers have transgressed Heidegger's objection to confessional readings of his philosophy and engaged with it as a provocation and challenge to Judaism.

When one sets out to study the reception of a certain philosopher, one can certainly chose to ignore historical backgrounds and political contexts and focus solely on the contours of the theoretical positions and stakes. Such a study could be written on Heidegger's Jewish receptions as well, but much – too much – would be lost. Heidegger's much-quoted statement about Aristotle, that he "was born, worked, and died," simply cannot be

---

[1] Strauss, "An Introduction to Heideggerian Existentialism," 28.
[2] Levinas, *Ethics and Infinity*, 42.

said of the German philosopher: biography, history, and politics are part and parcel of this intellectual encounter.

There is a sense in which the Jewish reception of Heidegger can be recited as the story of reactions to the two major crises of the twentieth century: the breakdown of the faith in progress and reason around the First World War, and the catastrophe of the Second World War and the Holocaust. From this perspective, the encounter with Heidegger is placed in the context of two major intersections of twentieth-century European and Jewish history – and appropriately so, for he is personally and philosophically tied to both. He was a prominent representative of the new mode of thinking challenging the old worldview in the era between the wars, and he was personally involved with National Socialism and refused to publicly come to terms with his error after the war, branding his name to this calamity. In terms of Heidegger's *Rezeptionsgeschichte*, however, it is misleading to think of these two crises as distinct from each other. For it is eminently clear that the later crisis continued, drew on, and intensified the earlier one, and the conceptual terms of the postwar responses to this thought were set up in, and determined by, the fraught intellectual climate of the interwar period and the pressing prewar experiences of Jews in Germany. It seems fair to say that the determining event, if such is at all identifiable, certifying a constitutive "before" and "after" in terms of the Jewish receptions of Heidegger would be his enlistment to the Nazi party in 1933. For many students and readers, it was this scandalous moment that either verified their disapproval of his philosophy or led them to rethink their initial attraction to it. The horrors of the Holocaust confirmed and profoundly aggravated this already present consternation – aggravated further by his postwar silence and inability to publicly come to terms with his political misadventure – and the denunciations were voiced with increased prevalence, volume, and tenacity.

And yet, merely seeing this episode as mirroring Jewish reactions to the advent and outcome of Nazism misses out on its broader and more substantial import. To be sure, the notoriety of Heidegger's biography framed the terms of the engagement with his thought as almost inevitably negative, but it is worthy of note that in the Jewish reception we have examined, his philosophy is never completely contracted to his politics, nor does his Nazism lead to the simple ostracization of his philosophy. While the view that his politics derive from his philosophy is common-place – and indeed, as we now know, sanctioned by the philosopher himself – time and again Heidegger is recognized as a thinker of historical rank whose philosophy must be addressed and wrestled with in a serious manner. The critique he leveled against the foundations of the thought-structure of "old" thinking demanded a rebuttal, but to those who shared his hostility to the rationalism of neo-Kantianism, Heidegger presented a serious challenge as well. His philosophy reflected either a stark mani-festation of the "crisis of reason" or a perverse way of responding to it and conducting postliberal "new" thinking. Blamed for either insufficiently breaking free of the depraved philosophical traditions of the past or for overenthusiastically dismantling the entire fundamentals of Western civi-lization, Heidegger's philosophy came to represent post-metaphysical thought "gone bad," a speculative scheme deepening rather than solving the present predicament. From the perspective of the Jewish adherents of "old" and "new" thinking alike, Heidegger embodied the overarching spiritual, cultural, and political crises of the day, and these crises are rooted, most fundamentally, in the theological deficiencies embedded or reflected in his philosophy. Denying his self-professed neutrality, Heidegger's philosophy was read as both deriving from and promoting repudiated religious positions. He was associated with Christianity in general, as well as Protestantism, secularism, atheism, paganism, and Gnosticism – all of which are disavowed from Jewish standpoints. Indeed, the absolutization of immanence, depiction of a godless world, secularized Christian theological categories, or invocation of the "gods" featured in his thought are seen as inextricably connected to his political blunder.

Certainly in terms of the religious stance he is associated with, it is justified to speak of receptions of Heidegger's philosophy by his Jewish readers. Speaking in the plural is also warranted in terms of the geographies in which these interpretations were developed. As we have seen, the com-mencing moment and location of the story chronicled in this book is interwar Germany, but it unravels as a story of diffusion and displacement, generating what can be termed a "Heidegger diaspora" in the United States, France, pre-state Palestine and later Israel, Canada, even in postwar Germany, and elsewhere, where his reception continued. Indeed, even as the figures discussed in this study left Germany for various other locations and hence for other political, cultural, and intellectual environments, their ideas remained marked by the crisis of German-Jewish relations that Weimar witnessed and the speculative terms and premises developed in this historical context. Their emigration out of Germany to other countries and settings explains, in part, the nuances of their thought and the variety of their postwar responses to Heidegger – even if the roots of these responses are often already present in their prewar reflections. The implication of this is not only that Heidegger remained forcibly present in the minds of Jewish thinkers also after the war, when they continued to grapple with *Sein und Zeit* while also making sure to remain informed of his later writings as these were published. It is also that from the perspective of Jewish thought coming out of Europe, since this period was enormously fertile for new conceptualizations of Judaism and Jewish identity, the twentieth century indeed was "Weimar Century" – and consequently, given the philosopher's centrality in its intellectual world, it can also be termed "Heidegger Century."[3]

But while the plurality of Heidegger's Jewish receptions is undeniable, we should not lose sight of the overarching contrarian model that governs the varying manifestations of the Heidegger–Judaism moment. This is the case, firstly, with regards to Heidegger's conceptualization of his own thought vis-à-vis Judaism, where for him Judaism is a dominant force in the technological and nihilistic oblivion of being, and his own philosophy discloses *poiesis* as its noninstrumental antithetical alternative. But a similar confrontational mentality hovers over the Jewish receptions of his thought, too. In the minds of leading Jewish thinkers of the previous century Judaism does not only stand in opposition to Heidegger's thought and the deficient religious categories associated with it, but it also serves as its spiritual and moral antidote. Judaism, or better, *Judentum*, is posited as *the* alternative to Heidegger and the comprehensive crisis his philosophy represents. Indeed, Heidegger is repeatedly portrayed as the "negative" to the constructive task of the thinkers we have discussed. He represents irrationalism in a world in need of rational order; a godless worldview in a world in need of God; the monological existence in a world in need of dialogue; the totalitarianism of the Same in a world in need of respect for otherness; historicism and relativism in a world in need of enduring truth; world-denial in a world in need of world-affirmation; or the paganism of a disinterested deity in a world in need of divine care. The Heidegger-Judaism opposition is played out differently in each case; and, indeed, in each case a different Heidegger is confronted with a different Judaism. Yet one thing remains fixed amid the many Heideggers and Judaisms: that the relation between them is that of opposition.

---

[3] "Weimar Century" is, of course, the title of a work by Greenberg, *The Weimar Century*, in which he argues that the origins of Germany's postwar political and cultural transformation into a democracy, as well as the ideological foundation of the Cold War, are to be found in the work of Weimarian theorists who emigrated to the United States.

It is important to emphasize that the Jewish critiques of Heidegger are motivated, first and foremost, by philosophical and theological reasoning, targeting what is recognized as theoretical deficiencies in his thought. These include, as noted, claims against the "pseudo-concreteness" of his philosophy and against the ethical and political deficiencies that arise from his privileging of the ontological at the expense of the ontic, as well as flaws in his analysis of human existence, such as insufficient attention to Dasein's embodied nature or a skewed account of the human–divine relationship. At the same time, it is noteworthy that the responses to Heidegger's philosophical flaws are claimed to be channeling insights from Jewish tradition and heritage. There is, it appears, a convergence of philosophically motivated critiques and an apologetic effort, whereby the polemical engagement with Heidegger, while grounded conceptually, also offers an opportunity, albeit a painful one, to self-assert and advocate for the legitimacy of Judaism in the modern world. Indeed, in the contrarian model that is put forth, this petition for legitimacy is presented in a very specific way: Judaism is constructed as the redemptive and Heidegger, correspondingly, as apocalyptic. Judaism's social, political, and ideational message is formulated in accordance with society's values and presented as holding the salvific key to the ills of modernity, which are said to be epitomized in Heidegger's philosophy. By portraying Judaism as messianic in this way, what is petitioned is the "Judaization" of the modern (European) world. Accordingly, the more "Jewish" the world becomes, the better off it will be. Indeed, it is not Heidegger's god, but *Judentum* that will save us.

Perceiving a philosopher in such a way is no doubt unusual, but this form of petition for legitimacy is not unique to the encounter with Heidegger. It is rather a common, if also paradoxical, feature of modern German-Jewish thought more broadly, which Derrida calls the "paradox of exemplarity." "No cultural identity presents itself as the opaque body of an untranslatable idiom," he writes in the context of his reflections on "Europe," "but always, on the contrary, as the irreplaceable inscription of the universal in the singular, the unique testimony to the human essence and to what is proper to man."[4] According to this discourse, Jewish particularity is crystallized as a chief *universal* sensitivity or principle summoning endorsement by non-Jews. Through this inclusive exclusivity, not only does Jewishness becomes a general modality of being human, but Jewish particularity is upheld *by* reconceiving itself as a specific form of

---

[4] Derrida, *The Other Heading*, 73.

universality. Paul Celan expresses precisely this impulse when he writes that "One can become a Jew ... one can Judaize [*Man kann verjuden*]."⁵ Derrida points to the internal incongruity of this "exemplarity" model's attempt to vouch for particularity by appealing to universal categories, though he finds in its very incongruity a redemptive, ethical dimension, wherein sealed and stabilized identities are destabilized and breached by that which is not them. This is articulated in a characteristically paradoxical manner in his powerful explication of Celan: "Jewish is not Jewish ... The Jew is also the other, myself and the other; I am Jewish in saying: the Jew is the other who has no essence, who has nothing of his own or whose own essence is not to have one."⁶ But the price of this model of self-difference, paradoxical as it is and redemptive as it may be, is that Jewishness remains hanging in abstraction. At the same time, the effort to construct an alternative to Heidegger by priming existentialism with Jewish traditions – each reading and misreading allowing for the further development of a form of exemplarity or the emergence of a new one – leads to an expansion of the category of "religion" beyond private belief to bear a range of social and political ramifications.

While no doubt self-laudatory, this reductive and redemptive hermeneutics of exemplarity reflects the historically shaky position of Judaism and Jews vis-à-vis modern European culture and tradition. Reconstrued as a philosophical category, the Jew, Judaism, or Jewishness embody the "other," the pariah, looking in from the outside and offering a critical reflection of, as well as an alternative to, the center. But this very status as "other" is only made possible by its preceding belonging; the Jew is "the inside outsider," a "participating outsider" whose speaking from "without" is only possible by its already being "within." When applied to the theme of this study, this means that the grappling with Heidegger we have detailed is deeply misconceived if considered as solely an internally Jewish intellectual activity. The look "inward" is at the same time a look "outward." It challenges the hegemony from its peripheral position but, paradoxically, at the same time also reinforces the hegemonic order by disturbing it according to the vocabulary and boundaries of its own discourse. The result is the complication of any definite distinction

---

⁵ Celan, *The Meridian*, 131. I am indebted here to the beautiful analysis in Liska, *German-Jewish Thought and Its Afterlife*, 125–134. On the impulse of exemplarity in Cohen and Rosenzweig, see Erlewine, *Judaism and the West*, 14–33, and Hollander, *Exemplarity and Chosenness*.
⁶ Derrida, "Shibboleth: For Paul Celan," 35.

between center and periphery, and for the present context, also the complication of the presentation of the encounter with Heidegger as a clash
between two diametrically opposing programs.

It is important to see, at any rate, that the aforementioned discursive
procedure of exemplarity constitutes the mirror image of Heidegger's own
fear of the Judaization of the German spirit. According to Heidegger's
narrative, the salvation of Germany, and hence the world, will occur only
once the epoch of Jewish machination has passed. This confirms Derrida's
fascination with the "double exemplarism" encapsulated in the title of
Hermann Cohen's *Deutschtum und Judentum*: "in what sense and how
have the Jewish and German 'peoples' – or those who have called
themselves thus – been able to declare themselves exemplary of this
'exemplarity'? in what sense and how, since the *Aufklärung* ... has ...
the Jewish-German pair, been doubly exemplary of this exemplarity?"[7]
What forcefully emerges here is the presumed privileged status of the
German and the Jewish dominating the conceptual architecture of the
Heidegger–Judaism moment, as well as its outstanding allosemitism.
From both anti-Semitic and philosemitic perspectives, the Jews are conceived as prioritized others, for good or for ill.

We have repeatedly encountered the leitmotiv of Athens and Jerusalem.
As noted, while ostensibly denoting a duality, this convenient structure
often entails the trinary of Judaism, Christianity, and paganism in the
context of the Christian-Jewish polemic over *Verus Israel*. Since the
Jewish encounter with Heidegger takes place as part of the Jewish
exchange with Christianity and in the context of the advent of modern
secularism ("paganism"), there is little surprise that the trinal application
of the Athens and Jerusalem model is dominant. Indeed, one can trace the
different paradigms associated with Heidegger by the figures we have
discussed to their conception of the Jewish-Christian coupling and its
relation to paganism. Often, the reason some read *Sein und Zeit* as
a secularized Christianity while others read it as a pagan treatise is linked
to whether they uphold a general conception of a shared Judeo-Christian
legacy to which paganism constitutes a common threat, or whether they
interpret Judaism as standing over against Christianity, which possesses
the seeds of its own secularized undoing due to it pagan roots. Notably,
also Heidegger makes use of the Athens–Jerusalem paradigm when he
objects to the monotheistic worldview he associates with Christianity and
Judaism, and identifies in ancient Greece a pregnant ontological moment.

[7] Derrida, "Interpretations at War: Kant, the Jew, the German."

Yet the shortcomings of this simplified binary are manifested in the various Jewish responses to Heidegger, where not only "Athens" and "Jerusalem" mean different things in each case, but the dichotomous separation between the two, so central to the argument, is often unsustainable, and the parallels, moments of agreement, and even overlaps between the two are admitted. Indeed, the instability of these signifiers is reflected in the fact that often what is constructed as "Jewish" is also, disturbingly, found in Heidegger.

This means that the seemingly stable dichotomizing model, shared by Heidegger and his Jewish readers alike, does not stand. As we have seen, these thinkers share with Heidegger significant philosophical assumptions and their thought was forged in a similar intellectual matrix. Despite their suspicion, even aversion, Heidegger himself was often a crucial source for their own reflections. Indeed, a key factor in the Jewish engagements with Heidegger is defining themselves as antithetical to him while at the same time ladling from common conceptual wells and even drawing directly from him. It becomes clear, therefore, that some of the symbolic binaries animating this encounter with Heidegger, such as the German/Jew and Athens/Jerusalem polarities, among others, are overly simplified and require a more nuanced treatment. This also means that the intellectual encounters we have been tracing cannot be isolated as a mere "Jewish moment." It is, most importantly, a German and indeed European episode. This can be demonstrated, among other examples, with the narratives of "historical forgetfulness" and "progress as return" that are employed by both Heidegger and many of the Jewish reactions to his thought. Following the outline of nineteenth-century German historicism, Heidegger structures the history of being according to the threefold model of origin, fall, and restoration. This structure allows him to speak of the intimacy of the Greek poetic openness to being and his envisioned Germany, *das Land der Dichter und Denker*. In a comparable manner, the tripartite historical structure features largely in the Jewish alternative. Here, it is not the conceptual revival of Athens and the pre-Socratics, but of Jerusalem and the biblical prophets. This is featured, as we have seen, in Cassirer, Strauss, Buber, Heschel, Levinas, and others. In this regard, it is telling that while the backdrop of this entire episode is the breakdown of the synthesizing model of liberal Judaism, the prominent and recurring featuring of the prophets to counter Heidegger, together with the almost uncontested assumption that the prophetic moment represents the normative heart of Judaism, attests to the lasting legacy of this model – as well as of the

Christian world through and against which it developed some of its definitive traits. Indeed, the critical and apologetic inflection of the encounter with Heidegger is highlighted when one considers that by positing the Hebrew prophets as possessing the kernel of the Jewish alternative to Heidegger, the nineteenth-century Jewish effort to reclaim the prophets from the hands of liberal Protestantism, who perceived them as the first stage in the Christian supersession of Judaism, is extended deep into the twentieth century.

The impulses of "defense" and "attack" animating these Jewish responses to Heidegger are further emphasized by another recurring theme in this encounter: that of secularization. Heidegger's roots in theology and his barely suppressed longing for the holy in a decidedly nontheological setting directs attention to the dialectic of continuity and break with regards to religious traditions marking his thought. As noted, Heidegger's problematic as a whole is driven by the attempt to rethink tradition by thinking *against* it, from *within* it, and *through* it. But how does one go against one's own tradition when one's hermeneutic circularity is recognized, that is, when one accepts that thought is always situated within a history, community, language, and heritage? This is a tension-fraught attempt, and Heidegger understood this better than most. Throughout the chapters of this study, I have argued that the Jewish encounter with Heidegger reflects a critical encounter with modernity and the theological structures informing it. As we have seen, there is an overarching skepticism of Heidegger's claim for neutrality and an emphasis on the religiously charged features of his philosophy. And if, as the thinkers examined in this study repeatedly argued, Heidegger embodies the gist of modern thought, then it follows that modernity is a religiously charged project. Yet modernity is in a state of crisis, they all sensed, and this crisis is rooted in a deficient religious grounding. Yet insofar as it is the presuppositions of certain philosophico-theological frameworks that made possible and facilitated the ills of modern life, then only an alternative philosophico-religious framework, one that is not susceptible to such pitfalls, can offer an apt antidote. As we have seen, the predominant conviction has been that the Jewish heritage offers the much-needed corrective to the spiritual crisis of the present. Thus, the Jewish responses to Heidegger reflect more than just a critical encounter with a challenging philosopher. They reflect an ongoing wrestling with the broken promises of emancipation and the perception that both modern secularism and Nazism are outcomes of the political-theological premises of the modern project, and of Western tradition more generally. What is proposed in response is an avenue for an alternative *kind* of modernity, a Jewish modernity. In this way, the Jewish receptions of Heidegger encompass the predicament of modern Jewish existence, with its hopes, disillusionment, tragedies, and attempts at reconstruction.

Bibliography

ARCHIVE MATERIAL

Abraham Joshua Heschel Papers, Duke University, North Carolina, USA.
Ernst Simon archive, in the Israel National Library in Jerusalem.
Shmuel Hugo Bergmann Archive, in the Israel National Library in Jerusalem.

WORKS BY HEIDEGGER IN GERMAN

Biemel, Walter, and Saner, Hans, eds. *Martin Heidegger/Karl Jaspers, Briefwechsel, 1920–1963.* Munich: Piper, 1990.
Heidegger, Gertrud, ed. *"Mein liebes Seelchen!" Briefe Martin Heideggers an seine Frau Elfride, 1915–1970.* Munich: Deutsche Verlags-Anstalt, 2005.
Heidegger, Martin. *Gesamtausgabe.* Frankfurt am Main: Klostermann, 1976–.
   GA 2, Sein und Zeit, edited by F. W. von Herrmann, 1977. Cited as *SZ.* References to this work will include pagination of both German and English editions.
   GA 3, Kant und das Problem der Metaphysik, edited by F. W. von Herrmann, 1991.
   GA 4, Erläuterung zu Hölderlins Dichtung, edited by F. W. von Herrmann, 1981.
   GA 5, Holzwege, edited by F. W. von Herrmann, 1977.
   GA 6.1, Nietzsche I, edited by B. Schillbach, 1996.
   GA 7, Vorträge und Aufsätze, edited by F. W. von Herrmann, 2000.
   GA 8, Was heisst Denken? edited by P. L. Coriando, 2002.
   GA 9, Wegmarken, edited by F. W. von Herrmann, 1976.
   GA 10, Der Satz vom Grund, edited by P. Jaeger, 1997.
   GA 11, Identität und Differenz, edited by F. W. von Herrmann, 2006.
   GA 12, Unterwegs zur Sprache, edited by F. W. von Herrmann, 1985.
   GA 13, Aus der Erfahrung des Denkens (1910–1976), edited by H. Heidegger, 1983.
   GA 14, Zur Sache des Denkens, edited by F. W. von Herrmann, 2007.

GA 15, *Seminare*, edited by C. Ochwadt, 1986.

GA 16, *Reden und andere Zeugnisse eines Lebensweges, 1910–1976*, edited by H. Heidegger, 2000.

GA 17, *Einführung in die phänomenologische Forschung (Winter semester 1923/24)*, edited by F. W. von Herrmann, 1994.

GA 20, *Prolegomena zur Geschichte des Zeitbegriffs (Summer semester 1925)*, edited by P. Jaeger, 1979.

GA 24, *Die Grundprobleme der Phänomenologie (Summer semester 1927)*, edited by F. W. von Herrmann, 1975.

GA 25, *Phänomenologische Interpretation von Kants* Kritik der reinen Vernuft *(Winter semester 1927/28)*, edited by I. Görland, 1995.

GA 32, *Hegels Phänomenologie des Geistes*, edited by I. Görland, 1980.

GA 34, *Vom Wesen der Wahrheit. Zu Platons Höhlengleichnis und Theätet (Winter semester 1931/32)*, edited by H. Mörchen, 1988 (2nd ed. 1997).

GA 36/37, *Sein und Wahrheit*, edited by H. Tietjen, 2001.

GA 38, *Logik als die Frage nach dem Wesen der Sprache*, edited by G. Seubold, 1998.

GA 40, *Einführung in die Metaphysik*, edited by P. Jaeger, 1983.

GA 41, *Die Frage nach dem Ding. Zu Kants Lehre von den transzendentalen Grundsätzen (Winter semester 1935/36)*, edited by P. Jaeger, 1984.

GA 47, *Nietzsches Lehre vom Willen zur Macht als Erkenntnis*, edited by Eberhard Hanser, 1989.

GA 50, *Nietzsches Metaphysik (announced for the Winter semester 1941/42)/ Einleitung in die Philosophie – Denken und Dichten (Winter semester 1944/ 45)*, edited by P. Jaeger, 1990.

GA 52, *Hölderlins Hymne "Andenken" (Winter semester 1941/42)*, edited by C. Ochwaldt, 1982.

GA 53, *Hölderlins Hymne "Der Ister" (Summer semester 1942)*, edited by W. Biemel, 1984.

GA 54, *Parmenides*, edited by M. S. Frings, 1982.

GA 55, *Heraklit. 1. Der Anfang des abendländischen Denkens/ 2. Logik. Heraklits Lehre vom Logos*, edited by M. S. Frings, 1979.

GA 58, *Grundprobleme der Phänomenologie (Winter semester 1919/20)*, edited by H. H. Gander,1992.

GA 60, *Phänomenologie des religiösen Lebens*, edited by C. Strube,1995.

GA 61, *Phänomenologische Interpretationen zu Aristoteles. Einführung in die Phänomenologische Forschung (Winter semester 1921/22)*, edited by W. Bröcker-Oltmanns, 1985.

GA 62, *Phänomenologische Interpretation ausgewählter Abhandlungen des Aristotles zur Ontologie und Logik*, edited by G. Neumann, 2005.

GA 63, *Ontologie. Hermeneutik der Faktizität (Summer semester 1923)*, edited by K. Bröcker-Oltmanns, 1988.

GA 64, *Der Begriff des Zeit*, edited by F. W. von Herrmann, 2004.

GA 65, *Beiträge zur Philosophie (Vom Ereignis)*, edited by F. W. von Herrmann, 1989.

GA 66, *Besinnung*, edited by F. W. von Herrmann, 2006.

GA 68, *Hegel*, edited by I. Schüssler, 1993.

GA 73, Zum Ereignis-Denken, edited by P. Trawny, 2013.
GA 74, Zum Wesen der Sprache und Zur Frage nach der Kunst, edited by T. Regehly, 2010.
GA 75, Zu Hölderlin/Griechenlandreisen, edited by C. Ochwadt, 2000.
GA 94, Überlegungen II–VI (Schwarze Hefte 1931–1938), edited by P. Trawny, 2014.
GA 95, Überlegungen VII–XI (Schwarze Hefte 1938–1939), edited by P. Trawny, 2014.
GA 96, Überlegungen XII–XV (Schwarze Hefte 1939–1941), edited by P. Trawny, 2014.
GA 97, Anmerkungen I–V (Schwarze Hefte 1942–1948), edited by P. Trawny, 2015.
Heidegger, Martin. "Das Problem der Sünde bei Luther," in *Sachgemässe Exegese: Die Protokolle aus Rudolf Bultmanns Neutestamentlichen Seminaren 1921–52,* edited by Bernd Jaspert. Marburg: N. G. Elwert, 1996a.
Heidegger, Martin and Kästner, Erhart. *Briefwechsel,* edited by Heinrich W. Petzet. Frankfurt am Main: Insel, 1986.
Storck, Joachim W., ed. *Martin Heidegger, Elisabeth Blochmann, Briefwechsel 1918–1969.* Marbach: Deutsche Schillergesellschaft, 1989.

WORKS BY HEIDEGGER IN ENGLISH

Biemel, Walter, and Saner, Hans, eds. *The Heidegger–Jaspers Correspondence (1920–1963),* translated by Gary E. Aylesworth. New York: Humanity Books, 2003.
Heidegger, Martin. *The Basic Problems of Phenomenology,* translated by Albert Hofstadter. Bloomington, IN: Indiana University Press, 1982. *GA 24.*
Basic Problems of Phenomenology: Winter Semester 1919/1920, translated by Scott M. Campbell. London: Bloomsbury, 2013a. *GA 58.*
Being and Time, translated by John Macquarrie and Edward Robinson. New York: Harper & Row, 2008. *GA 2;* cited as *BT.*
Being and Truth, translated by Gregory Fried and Richard Polt. Bloomington, IN: Indiana University Press, 2010b. *GA 36/37.*
The Concept of Time, English–German edition, translated by William McNeill. Oxford: Blackwell, 1992a. *GA 64.*
Contributions to Philosophy (of the Event), translated by Richard Rojcewicz and Daniela Vallega-Neu. Bloomington, IN: Indiana University, 2012. *GA 65.*
Discourse on Thinking: A Translation of Gelassenheit, translated by John M. Anderson and E. Hans Freund. New York: Harper & Row, 1969c.
Early Greek Thinking, translated by David Farrell Krell and Frank A. Capuzzi. San Francisco: Harper & Row, 1984a.
Elucidations of Hölderlin's Poetry, translated by Keith Hoeller. New York: Humanity Books, 2000a. *GA 4.*
The End of Philosophy, translated by Joan Stambaugh. New York: Harper & Row, 1973.

The Essence of Reason, translated by Terrence Malik. Evanston, IL: Northwestern University, 1969a.

"Hebel – Friend of the House," translated by Bruce V. Foltz and Michael Heim, *Contemporary German Philosophy* 3 (1983): 89–101.

Hegel's Phenomenology of Spirit, translated by Pravis Emad and Kenneth Maly. Bloomington, IN: Indiana University Press, 1980. *GA* 32.

History of the Concept of Time: Prolegomena, translated by Theodore Kisiel. Bloomington, IN: Indiana University Press, 1985a. *GA* 20.

Hölderlin's Hymn "Germania" and "The Rhine," translated by William McNeill and Julia Ireland. Bloomington, IN: Indiana University Press, 2014.

Hölderlin's Hymn "The Ister," translated by William McNeill and Julia Davis. Bloomington, IN: Indiana University Press, 1996b. *GA* 53.

Identity and Difference, translated by Joan Stambaugh. New York: Harper Row, 1969b. *GA* 11.

Introduction to Metaphysics, trans. George Fried and Richard Polt. New Haven, CT: Yale University Press, 2000b. *GA* 40.

Introduction to Phenomenological Research, translated by Daniel O. Dahlstrom. Bloomington, IN: Indiana University Press, 2005. *GA* 17.

Introduction to Philosophy – Thinking and Poetizing, translated by P. J. Braunstein. Bloomington, IN: Indiana University Press, 2011.

Kant and the Problem of Metaphysics, translated by Richard Taft. Bloomington, IN: Indiana University Press, 1990a. *GA* 3.

"Kant's Thesis about Being," translated by Ted Klein and William Pohl, *Southwestern Journal of Philosophy* 4(3) (1973): 7–33. *GA* 9.

Letters to His Wife, 1915–1970, edited by Gertrud Heidegger. Cambridge: Polity, 2008a.

Logic as the Question Concerning the Essence of Language, translated by Wanda Torres Gregory and Yvonne Unna. Albany, NY: State University of New York Press, 2009b.

The Metaphysical Foundations of Logic, translated by Michael Heim. Bloomington, IN: Indiana University Press, 1984b.

Mindfulness, translated by Parvis Emad and Thomas Kalary. London: Continuum, 2006. *GA* 66.

Nature, History, State, 1933–1934, translated and edited by Gregory Fried and Richard Polt. London: Bloomsbury, 2013b.

Nietzsche, vol. I, translated by David Farrell Krell. New York: Harper & Row Publishers, 1979.

Off the Beaten Track, translated by Julian Young and Kenneth Haynes. Cambridge, UK: Cambridge University Press, 2002. *GA* 5.

On Time and Being, translated by Joan Stambaugh. New York: Harper and Row, 1972. *GA* 14.

On the Way to Language, translated by Peter D. Hertz. New York: Harper & Row, 1971. *GA* 12.

"Only a God Can Save Us," *The Heidegger Reader*, edited by Günter Figal, translated by Jerome Veith. Bloomington and Indianapolis, IN: Indiana University Press, 2009a.

Ontology – The Hermeneutics of Facticity, translated by John van Buren. Bloomington: Indiana University Press, 1999a. *GA* 63.

Parmenides, translated by André Schuwer and Richard Rojcewicz. Bloomington and Indianapolis, IN: Indiana University Press, 1992b.

Pathmarks, edited by William McNeill. Cambridge, UK: Cambridge University Press, 1998. *GA* 9.

Phenomenological Interpretations of Aristotle: Initiation into Phenomenological Research, translated by Richard Rojcewicz. Bloomington, IN: Indiana University Press, 2001. *GA* 61.

Phenomenological Interpretation of Kant's Critique of Pure Reason, translated by Parvis Emad and Kenneth Maly. Bloomington and Indianapolis, IN: Indiana University Press, 1997. *GA* 25.

Phenomenology of Religious Life, translated by Matthias Fritsch and Anna Gosetti-Ferencei. Bloomington and Indianapolis, IN: Indiana University Press, 2004. *GA* 60.

The Piety of Thinking: Essays, edited and translated by James G. Hart and John C. Maraldo. Bloomington: Indiana University Press, 1976.

Plato's "Sophist," translated by Richard Rojcewicz and André Schuwer. Bloomington, IN: Indiana University Press, 1997b.

Poetry, Language, Thought, translated by Albert Hofstadtler. New York: Harper & Row. 1975.

Ponderings II–VI: Black Notebooks 1931–1938, translated by Richard Rojcewicz. Bloomington, IN: Indiana University Press, 2016. *GA* 94.

Ponderings VII–IX: Black Notebooks 1938–1939, translated by Richard Rojcewicz. Bloomington, IN: Indiana University Press, 2017a. *GA* 95.

Ponderings XII–XV: Black Notebooks 1939–1941, translated by Richard Rojcewicz. Bloomington, IN: Indiana University Press, 2017b. *GA* 96.

The Principle of Reason, translated by Reginald Lilly. Bloomington, IN: Indiana University Press, 2010a. *GA* 10.

The Question Concerning Technology and Other Essays, translated by William Lovitt. New York: Harper Torchbooks, 1977.

"The Rectorate 1933/1934: Facts and Thoughts," *Heidegger and National Socialism: Questions and Answers*, edited by Günther Neske and Emil Kettering, translated by Lisa Harries. New York: Paragon House, 1990b.

Schelling's Treatise on the Essence of Human Freedom, translated by Joan Stambaugh. Athens: Ohio University Press, 1985b.

"What Is Metaphysics? Original Version," edited by Dieter Thomä, translated by Ian Alexander Moore and Gregory Fried. *Philosophy Today* 62(3) (2018): 733–751.

"Wilhelm Dilthey's Research and the Struggle for a Historical Worldview," *New Yearbook for Phenomenology and Phenomenological Philosophy* 9 (2009a): 235–273.

BIBLIOGRAPHY

Adelmann, Dieter. *Einheit des Bewußtseins als Grundproblem der Philosophie Hermann Cohens*. Heidelberg: Inaugural-Dissertation, 1968.

Adorisio, Chiara. "Philosophy of Religion or Political Philosophy? The Debate Between Leo Strauss and Julius Guttmann," *European Journal of Jewish Studies* 1(1) (2007): 135–155.

Adorno, Theodor. "The Actuality of Philosophy," *Telos* 31(Spring 1977): 120–133.

The Jargon of Authenticity, translated by Knut Tarnowski and Fredric Will. London: Routledge, 2003.

Altman, William H. F. *The German Stranger: Leo Strauss and National Socialism*. Lanham: Lexington Books, 2001.

Altmann, Alexander. "Franz Rosenzweig's Legacy: Two Books by Ignaz Maybaum," *The Meaning of Jewish Existence, Theological Essays 1930–1939*, edited by Alfred L. Ivry. New Hampshire: Brandeis University Press, 1991, 100–104.

"Hermann Cohens Begriff der Korrelation," *Zwei Welten: Siegfried Moses zum Fünfundsiebzigsten Geburtstag*, edited by Hans Tramer. Tel Aviv: Verlag Bitaon, 1962, 377–399.

"Metaphysik und Religion," *Jeschurun: Monatsschrift für Lehre und Leben im Judentum*, 17(9–12) (1930): 321–347.

"Metaphysics and Religion," *The Meaning of Jewish Existence, Theological Essays 1930–1939*, edited by Alfred L. Ivry. New Hampshire: Brandeis University Press, 1991, 1–15.

"The God of Religion, the God of Metaphysics and Wittgenstein's 'Language-Games,'" *Zeitschrift für Religions- und Geistesgeschichte* 39(4) (1987): 304–305.

"Um das Erbe Franz Rosenzweigs: Zu Zwei Büchern von Ignaz Maybaum," *Jüdische Rundschau* (September 3, 1937): 6–8.

"Was ist Jüdische Theologie? Beiträge zur jüdischen Neuorientierung," *Der Israelit* 15, June 22 and July 6 (1933): 3.

"What Is Jewish Theology?" *The Meaning of Jewish Existence, Theological Essays 1930–1939*, edited by Alfred L. Ivry. New Hampshire: Brandeis University Press, 1991, 40–56.

Arendt, Hannah. "Concern with Politics in Recent European Philosophical Thought," *Essays on Understanding 1930–1954: Formation, Exile, and Totalitarianism*, edited by Jerome Kohn, translated by Robert Kimber and Rita Kimber. New York: Harcourt, Brace. New York: Schocken Books, 1994.

The Human Condition. Chicago, IL: University of Chicago Press, 1958.

"What Is Existential Philosophy?" *Essays on Understanding 1930–1954: Formation, Exile, and Totalitarianism*, edited by Jerome Kohn, translated by Robert Kimber and Rita Kimber. New York: Harcourt, Brace. New York: Schocken Books, 1994.

Armitage, Duane. "Heidegger's God: Against Caputo, Kearney, and Marion," *Philosophy and Theology* 26(2) (2014): 279–294.

Aschheim, Steven E. "'The Jew Within': The Myth of 'Judaization' in Germany," *Culture and Catastrophe: German and Jewish Confrontations with National Socialism and Other Crises*. London: Macmillan, 1996, 45–68.

Atkins, Zohar. *An Ethical and Theological Appropriation of Heidegger's Critique of Modernity: Unframing Existence*. New York: Palgrave Macmillan, 2018.

Atterton, Peter, Calarco, Matthew, and Friedman, Maurice, eds., *Levinas and Buber: Dialogue and Difference*. Pittsburgh, PA: Duquesne University Press, 2004.

Atterton, Peter, Calarco, Matthew, and Hansel, Joelle. "The Meaning of Religious Practice by Emmanuel Levinas: An Introduction and Translation," *Modern Judaism* 25(3) (Oct. 2005): 285–289.

Backman, Jussi. "The Transitional Breakdown of the Word: Heidegger and Stephan George's Encounter with Language," *Gatherings: The Heidegger Circle Annual* 1 (2001): 54–73.

Baeck, Leo. "Die Existenz des Juden," *Leo Baeck Werke, Band 6: Briefe, Reden Aufsätze*, edited by Michael A. Meyer. Gütersloh: Gütersloher Verlagshaus, 2003, 245–253.

Bambach, Charles R. *Heidegger, Dilthey, and the Crisis of Historicism*. Ithaca and London: Cornell University Press, 1995.

Heidegger's Roots: Nietzsche, National Socialism, and the Greeks. Ithaca: Cornell University Press, 2003.

Barash, Jeffrey A. "Ernst Cassirer's Theory of Myth: On the Ethico-Political Dimension of His Debate with Martin Heidegger," *The Legacy of Ernst Cassirer*, edited by Jeffrey Andrew Barash. Chicago, IL: University of Chicago Press, 2008, 114–132.

Baring, Edward. "Anxiety in Translation: Naming Existentialism before Sartre," *History of European Ideas* 41(4) (2015): 470–488.

Converts to the Real: Catholicism and the Making of Continental Philosophy. Boston: Harvard University Press, 2019.

Barrett, Lee C. "Karl Barth: The Dialectic of Attraction and Repulsion," *Kierkegaard's Influence on Theology*, vol. 10, tome I: *German Protestant Theology*, edited by Jon Stewart. Aldershot: Ashgate, 2012, 1–41.

Barth, Heinrich. "Ontologie und Idealismus," *Zwischen den Zeiten* 7 (1929): 511–512.

Barth, Karl. *Church Dogmatics* vol. III, 3, translated by G. W Bromiley and R. J. Ehrlich. Edinburgh: T&T Clark, 1961.

Letters 1961–1968, translated and edited by G. W. Bromiley. Edinburgh: T&T Clark, 1981.

Batnitzky, Leora. *Leo Strauss and Emmanuel Levinas: Philosophy and the Politics of Revelation*. New York: Cambridge University Press, 2006.

"Leo Strauss's Disenchantment with Secular Society," *New German Critique* 94 (2005): 106–126.

"Leo Strauss and the 'Theologico-Political Predicament,'" *The Cambridge Companion to Leo Strauss*, edited by Steven B. Smith. Cambridge: Cambridge University Press, 2009, 41–62.

"On Reaffirming a Distinction between Athens and Jerusalem," *Hebraic Political Studies* 2(2) (2007): 211–231.

Bauch, Bruno. "Leserbrief," *Der Panther. Deutsche Monatsschrift für Politik und Volkstum* 4(6) (1916): 148–154.

"Vom Begriff der Nation," *Kantstudien* (21) (1916): 139–162.

Beiner, Ronald. "Hannah Arendt and Leo Strauss: The Uncommenced Dialogue," *Political Theory* 18 (2) (1996): 238–254.

Beiser, Frederick. "Historicism," *The Oxford Handbook of Continental Philosophy*, edited by Brian Leiter and Michael Rosen. Oxford: Oxford University Press, 2007.

Benjamin, Walter. "Kierkegaard: The End of Philosophical Idealism," *Selected Writings*, vol. 2, *1927–1934*, translated by Rodney Livingstone and others, edited by Michael W. Jennings, Howard Eiland, and Gary Smith. Cambridge, MA: Harvard University Press, 1999, 703–705.

Bergmann, Samuel Hugo. *Hogay Ha'Dor*. Tel Aviv: Mitspa Publishing House, 1935.

Bergo, Bettina. "Ontology, Transcendence, and Immanence in Emmanuel Levinas," *Research in Phenomenology* 35(1) (2005): 141–180.

Berl, Heinrich. "Begegnung mit Jüdischer Zeitgenosse: Bergson, Husserl, Scheler, Buber, Gundolf, Mombert, Wasserman," *Menorah: jüdisches Familienblatt für Wissenschaft, Kunst und Literatur* 7–8 (July 1932): 317–335.

Bernasconi, Robert. "Poets as Prophets and as Painters: Heidegger's Turn to Language and the Hölderlinian Turn in Context," *Heidegger and Language*, edited by Jeffrey Powell. Bloomington, IN: Indiana University Press, 2013, 146–162.

"The Third Party: Levinas on the Intersection of the Ethical and the Political," *Journal of the British Society for Phenomenology* 30(1) (1999): 76–87.

Bernstein, Jeffrey A. *Leo Strauss on the Borders of Judaism, Philosophy, and History*. Albany, NY: State University of New York Press, 2015.

Bernstein, Richard. "Evil and the Temptation of Theodicy." *The Cambridge Companion to Levinas*, edited by Simon Critchley and Robert Bernasconi. Cambridge: Cambridge University Press, 2006, 252–267.

Bin Gorion, Emanuel. "Ernt Simons Bialik-Monographie Rezension," *Der Morgen: Monatsschrift der Juden in Deutschland* 4 (1936): 188–189.

Blumenberg, Hans. *The Legitimacy of the Modern Age*. Cambridge, MA: MIT Press, 1983.

Bongardt, Michael. "Must Religion Be Overcome? Myth, Religion and Liberation in the Thought of Ernst Cassirer," *Svensk Teologisk Kvartalskrift* 82 (2006): 5–15.

Boothroyd, David. "Responding to Levinas," *The Provocation of Levinas: Rethinking the Other*, edited by Robert Bernasconi and David Wood. London: Routledge, 1988.

Bourdieu, Pierre. *The Political Ontology of Martin Heidegger*, translated by Peter Collier. Stanford: Stanford University Press, 1991.

Brague, Rémi. "How to Be in the World: Gnosis, Religion and Philosophy," *Martin Buber: A Contemporary Perspective*, edited by Paul Mendes-Flohr. New York: Syracuse University Press, 2002, 133–147.

Brenner, Michael. "Gnosis and History: Polemics of German-Jewish Identity from Graetz to Scholem," *New German Critique* 77 (1999): 45–60.

The Renaissance of Jewish Culture in Weimar Germany. New Haven, CT: Yale University Press, 1996.

Brock, Werner. *An Introduction to Contemporary German Philosophy.* London: Cambridge University Press, 1935.

Brody, Samuel. *Buber's Theopolitics.* Bloomington, IN: Indiana University Press, 2018.

Brogan, Walter. *Heidegger and Aristotle: The Twofoldedness of Being.* Albany, NY: SUNY Press, 2005.

Brumlik, Micha. *Deutscher Geist und Judenhass: Das Verhältnis des philosophischen Idealismus zum Judentum.* Munich: Luchterhand, 2000.

Die Gnostiker. Der Traum von der Selbsterlösung des Menschen. Frankfurt am Main, 1992, 312–369.

Preussisch, konservative, Jüdisch: Hans-Joachim Schoeps' Leben und Werk. Vienna: Böhlau Verlag, 2000.

Brunner, Emil. "Theologie und Ontologie, oder: Die Theologie am Scheidewege," *Zeitschrift für Theologie und Kirche* 12 (1931): 111–122.

Buber, Martin. "Between Religion and Philosophy," *Davar* 3 (January 1954): 3 [Hebrew].

"Biblical Leadership," *On the Bible: Eighteen Studies by Martin Buber*, edited by Nahum N. Glatzer. New York: Schocken Books, 2000.

Briefwechsel aus sieben Jahrzehnten: Band III 1938–1965. Heidelberg: Lambert Schneider, 1975.

"The Burning Bush," *Biblical Humanism: Eighteen Studies by Martin Buber*, edited by Nahum N. Glatzer. London: Macdonald, 1968.

"Christ, Hasidism, Gnosis," *The Origin and Meaning of Hasidism*, edited and translated by Maurice Friedman. New York: Harper & Row, 1960, 241–254.

Daniel: Dialogues on Realization, translated by M. Friedman. New York: Holt, Rinehart and Winston, 1964.

"Der Glaube des Judentums," *Der Jude und sein Judentum.* Cologne: Joseph Melzer Verlag, 1963.

"Dialogue," *Between Man and Man*, translated by Ronald Gregor Smith. London: Kegan Paul, 1947.

"Die Verwirklichung des Menschen: Zur Anthropologie Martin Heideggers," *Philosophia* 3(1–4) (1938): 289–308.

"Distance and Relation," *The Knowledge of Man: Selected Essays*, translated by Maurice Friedman and Ronald Gregor Smith. Atlantic Highlands, NJ: Humanities Press, 1988.

Eclipse of God. New York: Harper & Row, 1965.

"Elements of the Interhuman," *The Knowledge of Man: Selected Essays*, translated by Maurice Friedman and Ronald Gregor Smith. Atlantic Highlands, NJ: Humanities Press, 1988.

"The Faith of Judaism," *Israel and the World: Essays in a Time of Crisis.* New York: Schocken Books, 1948.

I and Thou, translated by Ronald Gregor Smith. Edinburgh: T&T Clark, 1958.

"Man and His Image-Work," *The Knowledge of Man: Selected Essays*, translated by Maurice Friedman and Ronald Gregor Smith. Atlantic Highlands, NJ: Humanities Press, 1988.

Martin Buber: Briefwechsel aus sieben Jahrzehnten, 1918–1938, vol. 2. Heidelberg: Lambert Schneider, 1972–75.

Moses. Oxford: Easy & West Library, 1946.

"Myth in Judaism," *On Judaism*, edited by Nahum Glatzer. New York: Schocken Books, 1967.

"On the Situation of Philosophy," *A Believing Humanism: My Testament, 1902–1965*, translated by Maurice Friedman. New York: Simon and Schuster, 1967, 136–137.

"Prophecy, Apocalyptic, and the Historical Hour," *Pointing the Way: Collected Essays*, translated by Maurice Friedman. New York: Harper & Row, 1957, 192–207.

"The Question of the Single One," *Between Man and Man*, translated by Ronald Gregor Smith. London: Kegan Paul, 1947.

"Religion and Modern Thinking," *Eclipse of God*. New York: Harper & Row, 1965.

"Religion and Reality," *Eclipse of God*. New York: Harper & Row, 1965.

"Remarks on Goethe's Concept of Humanity," *Goethe and the Modern Age*, edited by Arnold Bergstraesser. Chicago, IL: Regnery, 1950, 227–233.

"Renewal of Judaism," *On Judaism*, edited by Nahum Glatzer. New York: Schocken Books, 1967.

"Replies to My Critics," *The Philosophy of Martin Buber*, edited by Paul Arthur Schilpp and Maurice Friedmann. Chicago, IL: Open Court, 1967.

"Seit ein Gespräch wir sind: Bemerkungen zu einem Vers Hölderlin," *Werkausgabe*, vol. 6, edited by Asher Bieman. Güterslohe: Gütersloher,2003, 83–85.

"Spinoza, Sabbatai Zevi, and Baalshem," *Hasidism*. New York: Philosophical Library, 1948.

"The Spirit of the Orient and Judaism," *On Judaism*, edited by Nahum Glatzer. New York: Schocken Books, 1967.

"Supplement: Reply to C. G. Jung," *Eclipse of God*. New York: Harper & Row, 1965.

"A Tentative Answer" in "Autobiographical Fragments," *The Philosophy of Martin Buber*, edited by Paul Arthur Schilpp and Maurice Friedmann. Chicago, IL: Open Court, 1967.

"The Two Foci of the Jewish Soul," *Israel and the World: Essays in a Time of Crisis*. New York: Schocken Books, 1948.

Two Types of Faith, translated by Norman P. Goldhawk. London: Routledge & Kegan Paul, 1951.

"The Validity and Limitation of the Political Principle," *Pointing the Way: Collected Essays*, translated by Maurice Friedman. New York: Harper & Row, 1957.

"What Is Common to All," *The Knowledge of Man: Selected Essays*, translated by Maurice Friedman and Ronald Gregor Smith. Atlantic Highlands, NJ: Humanities Press, 1988.

"What Is Man?" *Between Man and Man*, translated by Ronald Gregor Smith. London: Kegan Paul, 1947, 118–205.

"The Word that Is Spoken," *The Knowledge of Man: Selected Essays*, translated by Maurice Friedman and Ronald Gregor Smith. Atlantic Highlands, NJ: Humanities Press, 1988.

Bultmann, Rudolf. "Heidegger, Martin," *Die Religion in Geschichte und Gegenwart*, vol. 2. Tübingen: Mohr, 1928, 1687–1688.

"The Historicity of Faith," *Existence and Faith: Shorter Writings of Rudolf Bultmann*, edited by Schubert Ogden. New York: Meridian, 1960.

"New Testament and Mythology," *Kerygma and Myth: A Theological Debate*, edited by Hans Werner Bartsch, translated by Reginald H. Fuller. New York: Harper & Row, 1961.

Burns, Timothy W. "Strauss on the Religious and Intellectual Situation of the Present," *Reorientation: Leo Strauss in the 1930s*, edited by Martin D. Yaffe and Richard S. Ruderman. New York: Palgrave Macmillan, 2014.

Busch, Eberhard. *Barth – ein Porträt in Dialogen: Von Luther bis Benedikt XVI.* Zurich: Theologischer Verlag, 2015.

Cahana, Jonathan. "A Gnostic Critic of Modernity: Hans Jonas from Existentialism to Science," *Journal of the American Academy of Religion* 86(1) (2018): 158–180.

Cairns, Dorion. *Conversation with Husserl and Fink*. The Hague: Martinus Hijhoff, 1976.

Capobianco, Richard. *Heidegger's Way of Being*. Toronto: University of Toronto Press, 2014.

Caputo, John D. "Heidegger and Theology," *The Cambridge Companion to Heidegger*, edited by Charles B. Guignon. Cambridge: Cambridge University Press, 1993.

"People of God, People of Being; The Theological Presuppositions of Heidegger's Path of Thinking," *Appropriating Heidegger*, edited by James E. Faulconer and Mark A. Wrathall. Cambridge: Cambridge University Press, 2000, 85–100.

Radical Hermeneutics: Repetition, Deconstruction, and the Hermeneutic Project. Bloomington, IN: Indiana University Press, 1994.

Carman, Taylor. "Heidegger's Anti-Neo-Kantianism," *The Philosophical Forum* 41(1–2) (2010): 131–142.

Cassirer, Ernst. "Cohen's Philosophy of Religion," *Internationale Zeitschrift für Philosophie* 1 (1996): 101.

An Essay on Man: An Introduction to a Philosophy of Human Culture. New Haven, CT: Yale University Press, 1956.

"Judaism and the Modern Political Myths," *Contemporary Jewish Record* 7 (1944): 115–126.

"Kant und das Problem der Metaphysik: Bemerkungen zu Martin Heideggers Kantinterpretation," *Kantstudien* 36(1) (1931): 1–26.

Language and Myth, translated by Susanne K. Langer. New York: Harper, 1953.

"The Metaphysics of Symbolic Forms," *The Philosophy of Symbolic Forms*, vol. IV, edited by John Michael Krois and Donald Phillip Verene, translated by John Michael Krois. New Haven, CT: Yale University Press, 1994.

The Myth of the State. London: Oxford University Press, 1946.

"Mythical Thought," *The Philosophy of Symbolic Forms*, vol. II, translated by Ralph Manheim. New Haven, CT: Yale University Press, 1955.

"Zum Begriff der Nation. Eine Erwiderung auf den Aufsatz von Bruno Bauch," *Zu Politik und Philosophie. Mit Beilagen*, edited by John Michael Krois and Christian Möckel. Hamburg: Felix Meiner Verlag, 2008.

Cassirer, Toni. *Aus meinem Leben mit Ernst Cassirer*. New York: Published privately, 1948.

Celan, Paul. 1983. *Gesammelte Werke in fünf Bänden*, edited by Beda Allemann and Stefan Reichart, in conjunction with Rolf Bücher. Frankfurt am Main: Suhrkamp.

The Meridian: Final Version – Drafts – Materials. Stanford: Stanford University Press, 2011.

Chacón, Rodrigo. "Reading Strauss from the Start: On the Heideggerian Origins of 'Political Philosophy,'" *European Journal of Political Theory* 9 (3) (2010): 287–307.

Chalier, Catherine. "The Philosophy of Emmanuel Levinas and the Hebraic Tradition," *Ethics as First Philosophy: The Significance of Emmanuel Levinas for Philosophy, Literature and Religion*, edited by Adriaan T. Peperzak. New York, NY: Routledge, 1995, 3–12.

Cohen, Hermann. "Das soziale Ideal bei Platon und den Propheten," *Der Jude: Eine Monatsschrift* 10–11 (1923): 618–636.

"Deutschtum und Judentum I-II," *Hermann Cohens Jüdische Schriften*, vol. II. Berlin: C. A. Schwetschke, 1924, 237–301, 302–318.

Ethik des reinen Willens. Berlin: B. Cassirer, 1904.

Religion der Vernunft aus den Quellen des Judentums. Bruno Strauss: Leipzig, 1929.

Cohen, Richard A. *Elevations: The Height of the Good in Rosenzweig and Levinas*. Chicago, IL and London: University of Chicago Press, 1994.

Ethics, Exegesis and Philosophy: Interpretation After Levinas. Cambridge: Cambridge University Press, 2001.

Levinasian Meditations: Ethics, Philosophy, and Religion. Pittsburgh, PA: Duquesne University Press, 2010.

Cooke, Vincent M., S. J., "Kant's Godlike Self," *International Philosophical Quarterly* 28, 3(111) (1988): 313–323.

Coyne, Ryan. *Heidegger's Confessions: The Remains of Saint Augustine in Being and Time and Beyond*. Chicago, IL: Chicago University Press, 2015.

Cristaudo, Wayne. "Heidegger and Cassirer: Being, Knowing, and Politics," *Kant-Studien* 82 (1991): 469–483.

Critchley, Simon. *The Ethics of Deconstruction: Derrida and Levinas*. Oxford: Blackwell, 1992.

"Leaving the Climate of Heidegger's Thinking," *Levinas in Jerusalem: Phenomenology, Ethics, Politics, Aesthetics*, edited by Joëlle Hansel. Dordrecht: Springer, 2009, 45–55.

"Original Inauthenticity – on Heidegger's *Sein und Zeit*," *On Heidegger's Being and Time*, edited by Simon Critchley and Reiner Schürmann. London: Routledge, 2008, 145–147.

Crowe, Benjamin D. *Heidegger's Phenomenology of Religion: Realism and Cultural Criticism.* Bloomington, IN: Indiana University Press, 2007.

Heidegger's Religious Origins: Destruction and Authenticity. Bloomington, IN: Indiana University Press, 2006.

Dahlstrom, Daniel O. *The Heidegger Dictionary.* London: Bloomsbury, 2013.

"Heidegger's Method: Philosophical Concepts as Formal Indications," *Review of Metaphysics* 47(4) (1994): 775–795.

Dallmayr, Fred. "Heidegger on *Macht* and *Machenschaft.*" *Continental Philosophy Review* 34 (2001): 247–267.

Dastur, Françoise. "Levinas and Heidegger: Ethics or Ontology?" *Between Levinas and Heidegger,* edited by John E. Drabinski and Eric S. Nelson. New York, NY: SUNY Press, 2014, 175–206.

Davis, Bret W. *Heidegger and the Will: On the Way to Gelassenheit.* Evanston, IL: Northwestern University Press, 2007.

Delp, Alfred. "Sein als Existenz: Die Metaphysik von Heute," *Aufstieg zur Metaphysik heute und ehedem,* edited by Bernard Jansen. Freiburg: Herder, 1933, 441–484.

Tragische Existenz: Zur Philosophie Martin Heideggers. Freiburg: Herder, 1931.

De Saint Cheron, Michael de. *Conversations with Emmanuel Levinas, 1983–1994.* Pittsburgh, PA: Duquesne University Press, 2010.

Dennison, William D. *The Young Bultmann: Context for His Understanding of God, 1884–1925.* New York: Peter Lang, 2008.

Derrida, Jacques. *Adieu to Emmanuel Levinas,* translated by Pascale-Anne Brault and Michael Nass. Stanford, CA: Stanford University Press, 1994.

"Hospitality," *Acts of Religion,* edited by Gil Anidjar. New York: Routledge, 2002.

"Interpretations at War: Kant, the Jew, the German," *New Literary History* 22 (1) (1991): 39–95.

Of Spirit: Heidegger and the Question. Chicago, IL: University of Chicago, 1989.

The Other Heading: Reflections on Today's Europe, translated by Pascale-Anne Braut and Michael B. Naas. Bloomington, IN: Indiana University Press, 1992.

"Shibboleth: For Paul Celan," *Sovereignties in Question: The Poetics of Paul Celan,* edited by Thomas Dutoit and Outi Pasanen. New York: Fordham University Press, 2005.

"Violence and Metaphysics," *Writing and Difference,* translated by Alan Bass. London: Routledge, 1997.

Di Cesare, Donatella. *Heidegger, die Juden, die Shoah.* Frankfurt am Main: Klostermann, 2015.

Dilthey, Wilhelm. *Introduction to the Human Sciences,* translated by Ramon J. Betanzos. Detroit, MI: Wayne State University, 1988.

Disse, Jörg. "Philosophie der Angst: Kierkegaard und Heidegger im Vergleich," *Kierkegaardiana* 22 (2002): 64–88.

Dolgopolski, Sergey. "How Else Can One Think Earth? The Talmuds and Pre-Socratics." *Heidegger and Jewish Thought: Difficult Others,* edited by

Elad Lapidot and Micha Brumlik. London: Rowman and Littlefield, 2017, 221–44.

Eaglestone, Robert. *The Holocaust and the Postmodern*. New York: Oxford University Press, 2004, 249–278.

Eisenstadt, Oona. "Levinas Versus Levinas: Hebrew, Greek, and Linguistic Justice," *Philosophy & Rhetoric* 38(2) (2005): 145–158.

Emberley, Peter C. and Cooper, Barry, ed. and trans. *Faith and Political Philosophy: The Correspondence between Leo Strauss and Eric Voegelin: 1934–1964*. Pennsylvania, PA: Pennsylvania State University Press, 1993.

Erlewine, Robert A. *Judaism and the West*. Bloomington and Indianapolis, IN: Indiana University Press, 2016, 78–104.

Eubanks, Cecil L. and Gauthier, David J. "The Politics of Homeless Spirit: Heidegger and Levinas on Dwelling and Hospitality," *History of Political Thought* 32(1) (2001): 125–146.

Fackenheim, Emil L. *To Mend the World: Foundations of Post-Holocaust Jewish Thought*. Bloomington, IN: Indiana University Press, 1994.

Fagenblat, Michael. *Covenant of Creatures: Levinas's Philosophy of Judaism*. Stanford, CA: Stanford University Press, 2010.

  "'Heidegger' and the Jews," *Reading Heidegger's Black Notebooks: 1931–1941*, edited by Ingo Farin and Jeff Malpas. Cambridge, MA: MIT Press, 2016, 145–168.

  "Levinas and Heidegger: The Elemental Confrontation," *The Oxford Handbook of Levinas*, edited by Michael L. Morgan. Oxford: Oxford University Press, 2018, 103–134.

  "Levinas, Judaism, Heidegger," *Judaism in Contemporary Thought: Traces and Influences*, edited by Agata Bielik-Robson and Adam Lipszyc. London: Routledge, 2014, 51–63.

  "Of Dwelling Prophetically: On Heidegger and Jewish Political Theology," *Heidegger and Jewish Thought: Difficult Others*, edited by Elad Lapidot and Micha Brumlik. London: Rowman and Littlefield, 2017, 245–267.

  "The Passion of Israel, the True Israel according to Levinas, or Judaism as a Category of Being," *Sophia* 54 (2015): 297–320.

Farin, Ingo and Jeff Malpas, eds., *Reading Heidegger's Black Notebooks: 1931–1941*. Cambridge, MA: MIT Press, 2016.

Faye, Emmanuel. *Heidegger: The Introduction of Nazism to Philosophy in Light of the Unpublished Seminars of 1933–1935*, translated by Michael B. Smith. New Haven, CT: Yale University Press, 2009.

Fell, Joseph P. "Heidegger's Notion of Two Beginnings," *Review of Metaphysics* 25(2) (1971): 213–237.

Feller, Yaniv. "From Aher to Marcion: Martin Buber's Understanding of Gnosis," *Jewish Studies Quarterly* 20 (2013): 374–397.

Fenton, Paul. "Henry Corbin and Abraham Heschel," *Heschel: Philosophy, Theology, and Interreligious Dialogue*, edited by Stanislaw Krajewski and Adam Lipszyc. Wiesbaden: Harrassowitz, 2009, 102–111.

Feuchtwanger, Ludwig. "'Jüdischer Glaube in dieser Zeit': Der Versuch einer neuen jüdischen Glaubenslehre," *Bayerischen Israelitische Gemeindezeitung* 11 (June 1, 1932): 165–167.

"Review of Julius Kraft, *Von Husserl zu Heidegger: Kritik der phänomenologischen Philosophie*," *Bayerischen Israelitische Gemeindezeitung* 19 (Oct. 19, 1932): 298–299.

Fischer, Norbert and von Hermann, Friedrich-Wilhem, eds. *Heidegger und die christliche Tradition: Annäherungen an ein schwieriges Thema*. Hamburg: Felix Meiner, 2007.

Fischer-Barnicol, Hans A. "Spiegelungen-Vermittlungen," *Erinnerung an Martin Heidegger*, edited by Günther Naske. Pfullingen: Naske, 1977.

Flasch, Kurt. *Die geistige Mobilmachung. Die deutschen Intellektuellen und der Erste Weltkrieg*. Berlin: Alexander Fest Verlag, 2000.

Fleischacker, Samuel. "Heidegger's Affinities with Judaism," *Heidegger's Jewish Followers: Essays on Hannah Arendt, Leo Strauss, Hans Jonas and Emmanuel Levinas*, edited by Samuel Fleischacker. Pittsburgh, PA: Duquesne University Press, 2008, 1–27.

Fleteren, Frederick, van. *Martin Heidegger's Interpretations of Saint Augustine*. Lewiston: Edwin Mellen Press, 2005.

Freund, Else Rahel. *Die Existenzphilosophie Franz Rosenzweig: Ein Beitrag Zur Analyse Seines Werkes: "Der Stern Der Erlösung."* Leipzig: Felix Meiner Verlag, 1933.

Franz Rosenzweig's Philosophy of Existence: An Analysis of The Star of Redemption, translated by Stephen L. Weinstein and Robert Israel, edited by Paul Mendes-Flohr. The Hague/Boston/London: Martinus Nijhoff, 1979.

Haphilosophiya Hakiyumit shel Franz Rosenzweig: Lenitucho shel Kochav Hageula, translated by Jehoshua Amir. Tel Aviv: Schocken Publishing House, 1972 [Hebrew].

Freundenthal, Gideon. "The Hero of Enlightenment," *The Symbolic Construction of Reality: The Legacy of Ernst Cassirer*, edited by Jeffrey Andrew Barash. Chicago, IL: University of Chicago Press, 2008, 189–213.

Fried, Gregory. *Heidegger's Polemos: From Being to Politics*. New Haven, CT: Yale University Press, 2000.

"A Letter to Emmanuel Faye," *Philosophy Today* 55(3) (2011): 219–252.

Friedman, Maurice. "Buber, Heschel and Heidegger: Two Jewish Existentialists Confront a Great German Existentialist," *Journal of Humanistic Psychology* 51(1) (2011): 129–134.

Friedman, Michael. *A Parting of the Ways: Carnap, Cassirer and Heidegger*. Chicago, IL: Open Court, 2000.

Fritsche, Johannes. "Absence of Soil, Historicity, and Goethe in Heidegger's Being and Time: Sheehan on Faye," *Philosophy Today* 60 (2) (2016): 429–445.

Gadamer, Hans-Georg. "Existentialism and the Philosophy of Existence," *Heidegger's Ways*, trans. by John W. Stanely. New York: State University of New York Press, 1994, 1–14.

"The Marburg Theology," *Heidegger's Ways*, trans. by John W. Stanely. New York: State University of New York Press, 1994, 29–44.

Galli, Barbara Ellen. *Franz Rosenzweig and Judah Halevi: Translating, Translation and Translators.* Montreal and Kingston: McGill-Queen's University Press, 1995.

Gay, Peter. *Weimar Culture: The Outsider as Insider.* New York: Harper & Row, 1968.

Gellhaus, Axel. "'Seit ein Gespräch wir sind . . .' Paul Celan bei Martin Heidegger in Todnauberg," *Spuren* 60 (2002): 2–16.

Gibbs, Robert. *Correlations in Rosenzweig and Levinas.* Princeton, NJ: Princeton University Press, 1992.

"Jewish Dimensions of Radical Ethics," *Ethics as First Philosophy: The Significance of Emmanuel Levinas for Philosophy, Literature and Religion,* edited by Adriaan T. Peperzak. New York, NY: Routledge, 1995, 13–23.

Glatzer, Nahum N. *Franz Rosenzweig: His Life and Thought.* New York: Schocken Books, 1953.

Glatzer, Nahum N. and Strauss, Ludwig. *Sendung und Schicksal des Judentums. Aus nachbiblischen Quellen mitgeteilt.* Berlin: Schocken Verlag,1931.

Glatzer, Nahum N. and Mendes-Flohr, Paul, eds. *The Letters of Martin Buber: A Life of Dialogue,* translated by Richard Winston, Clara Winston, and Harry Zohn. New York: Schocken Books, 1991.

Gogarten, Friedrich. *Wider die Ächtung der Autorität.* Jena: Diederichs,1930.

Goldberg, Lea. "The German Intellectuals and Nazi Germany," *Al Ha'Mishmar* 5 (November 5, 1943), p. 5.

(Log). "Ha'Orchidea Mul Ha'Totach," *Davar* 27 (December, 9, 1935), p. 9.

Goldstein, Jeffrey. "Buber's Misunderstanding of Heidegger: Being and the Living God," *Philosophy Today* 22(2) (1978): 156–167.

Gordon, Haim. *The Heidegger-Buber Controversy: The Status of the I-Thou.* Westport, CT: Greenwood Press, 2001.

Gordon, Peter E. *Adorno and Existence.* Boston: Harvard University Press, 2016.

Continental Divide: Heidegger, Cassirer, Davos. Cambridge, MA: Harvard University Press, 2010.

Rosenzweig and Heidegger: Between Judaism and German Philosophy. Berkeley, CA: University of California Press, 2003.

Gordon, Peter E., and McCormick, John P., eds. *Weimar Thought: A Contested Legacy.* Princeton, NJ: Princeton University Press, 2013.

Greenberg, Udi. *The Weimar Century: German Émigrés and the Ideological Foundations of the Cold War.* Princeton, NJ: Princeton University Press, 2015.

Guignon, Charles. "The Twofold Task: Heidegger's Foundational Historicism in Being and Time," *Tulane Studies in Philosophy: The Thought of Martin Heidegger* 32(1984): 53–61.

Green, Kenneth Hart. "Editor's Introduction: Leo Strauss as a Modern Jewish Thinker," *Jewish Philosophy and the Crisis of Modernity.* Albany, NY: SUNY Press, 1997, 25–28.

Jew and Philosopher: The Return to Maimonides in the Jewish Thought of Leo Strauss. New York: State University of New York Press, 1993.

Leo Strauss on Maimonides: The Complete Writings. Chicago, IL and London: University of Chicago Press, 2013.

Leo Strauss and the Rediscovery of Maimonides. Chicago, IL and London: University of Chicago Press, 2013.

Guttmann, Julius. "Philosophie der Religion oder Philosophie des Gesetz?" *Proceedings of the Israel Academy of Sciences and Humanities* (1974): 146–173.

Philosophies of Judaism: A History of Jewish Philosophy from Biblical Times to Franz Rosenzweig, translated by David W. Silverman. New York: Schocken Books, 1964.

Religion und Wissenschaft im mittelalterlichen und im modernen Denken. Berlin: Philo-Verlag, 1922.

Haar, Michel. "Heidegger and the God of Hölderlin," translated by Reginald Lilly, *Research in Phenomenology* 19 (1) (1989): 89–100.

"The Obsession of the Other: Ethics as Traumatization," *Philosophy and Social Criticism* 23(6) (1997): 95–107.

The Song of the Earth: Heidegger and the Grounds of the History of Being. Bloomington, IN: Indiana University Press, 1993.

Habermas, Jürgen. "Work and Weltanschauung: The Heidegger Controversy from a German Perspective," *The New Conservatism: Cultural Criticism and the Historians' Debate,* translated by Shierry Weber Nicholsen. Cambridge, MA: MIT Press, 1989, 140–172.

"Zur Veröffentlichung von Vorlesungen aus dem Jahre 1935," *Philosophisch-politische Profile.* Frankfurt am Main: Suhrkamp Verlag, 1973, 67–75.

Hadad, Yemima. "Fruits of Forgetfulness: Politics and Nationalism in the Philosophies of Martin Buber and Martin Heidegger." *Heidegger and Jewish Thought: Difficult Others,* edited by Elad Lapidot and Micha Brumlik. London: Rowman and Littlefield, 2017, 201–220.

Hammerschlag, Sarah. *The Figural Jew: Politics and Identity in Postwar France.* Chicago, IL: Chicago University Press, 2010.

Handelman, Susan A. *Fragments of Redemption: Jewish Thought and Literary Theory in Benjamin, Scholem, and Levinas.* Bloomington and Indianapolis, IN: Indiana University Press, 1991.

Hart, Kevin and Signer, Michael Alan, eds. *The Exorbitant: Emmanuel Levinas Between Jews and Christians.* New York: Fordham University Press, 2010.

Heinemann, Fritz. *Neue Wege der Philosophie.* Leipzig: Quelle & Meyer, 1929.

Heinz, Marion and Kellerer, Sidonie, eds. *Martin Heideggers "Schwarze Hefte." Eine philosophische-politische Debatte.* Berlin: Suhrkamp, 2016.

Held, Shai. *Abraham Joshua Heschel: The Call of Transcendence.* Bloomington, IN: Indiana University Press, 2013.

Hemming, Laurence. *Heidegger's Atheism: The Refusal of a Theological Voice.* Notre Dame, IN: University of Notre Dame Press, 2002.

Herrigel, Hermann. "Denken dieser Zeit: Fakultäten und Nationen treffen sich in Davos," *Frankfurter Zeitung,* April 22, 1929. Abendblatt: Hochschuleblatt, "Für Hochschule und Jugend."

Herrmann, Friedrich-Wilhelm von. "Way and Method: Hermeneutic Phenomenology in Thinking the History of Being," translated by Parvis Emad, *Martin Heidegger: Critical Assessments,* edited by Christopher Macann, vol. 1. London: Routledge, 1992.

Herskowitz, Daniel, M. "Between Exclusion and Intersection: Heidegger's Philosophy and Jewish Volkism," *Leo Baeck Institute Year Book*. 2020 (in press).

"The Call: Leo Strauss on Heidegger, Secularization, and Revelation," *New German Critique* (in press).

"Everything Is Under Control: Buber's Critique of Heidegger's Magic," *International Journal for Philosophy of Religion* 86(2) (October 2019): 111–130.

"Franz Rosenzweig and Karl Barth: A Chapter in the Jewish Reception of Dialectical Theology," *The Journal of Religion* 97(1) (2017): 79–100.

"God, Being, Pathos: Abraham Joshua Heschel's Theological Rejoinder to Heidegger," *Journal of Jewish Thought and Philosophy* 26(1) (2018): 94–117.

"Heidegger as a Secularized Kierkegaard: Martin Buber and Hugo Bergmann Read Sein und Zeit," *Heidegger and Jewish Thought: Difficult Others*, edited by Elad Lapidot and Micha Brumlik. London: Rowman and Littlefield, 2017, 155–174.

"Heidegger in Hebrew: Translation, Politics, Reconciliation," *New German Critique* 135(3) (2018): 97–128.

"The Husserl–Heidegger Relationship in the Jewish Imagination," *Jewish Quarterly Review*, 110(3) (2020): 491–522.

"An Impossible Possibility? Jewish Barthianism in Interwar Germany," *Modern Theology* 33(3) 2017: 348–368.

"The Moment and the Future: Kierkegaard's Øieblikket and Soloveitchik's view of Repentance," *Association for Jewish Studies Review* 40(April 1, 2016): 87–99.

"Rabbi Joseph B. Soloveitchik's Endorsement and Critique of Volkish Thought," *Journal of Modern Jewish Studies* 14(3) (2015): 373–390.

Herskowitz, Daniel, M. and Shalev, Alon. "Being-Toward-Eternity: R. Hutner's Adaptation of a Heideggerian Notion," *Journal of Jewish Thought and Philosophy* 26 (2018): 254–277.

Hertzberg, Arthur. "A Reminiscence of Ernst Cassirer," *Leo Baeck Institute Year Book* 15 (1970): 245–246.

Heschel, Abraham J. *Between God and Man: An Interpretation of Judaism.* New York, NY: Free Press Paperbacks, 1959.

"Death as Homecoming," *Moral Grandeur and Spiritual Audacity: Essays*, edited by Susannah Heschel. New York: Farrar, Straus & Giroux, 1996, 366–378.

Die Prophetie. Krakow: Polish Academy of Sciences, 1936.

God in Search of Man: A Philosophy of Judaism. New York: Farrar, Straus and Giroux, 1955.

Man Is Not Alone: A Philosophy of Religion. New York: Farrar, Straus and Giroux, 1951.

Man's Quest for God: Studies in Prayer and Symbolism. New York: Charles Scribner's Sons, 1954.

Moral Grandeur and Spiritual Audacity: Essays, edited by Susannah Heschel. New York: Farrar, Straus & Giroux, 1996.

"No Religion Is an Island," *Moral Grandeur and Spiritual Audacity: Essays*, edited by Susannah Heschel. New York: Farrar, Straus & Giroux, 1996, 235–250.

The Prophets. New York, NY: Harper & Row, 1962.

Who Is Man? Stanford, CA: Stanford University Press, 1965.

Ho, Eugene Yue-Ching. "At 90, and Still Dynamic: Revisiting Sir Karl Popper and Attending His Birthday Party," *Intellectus*, 23 (1992): 1–5.

Hoeres, Peter. *Krieg der Philosophen: Die deutsche und die britische Philosophie im Ersten Weltkrieg*. Paderborn: Ferdinand Schöningh, 2004, 232–238.

Hollander. Dana. *Exemplarity and Chosenness: Rosenzweig and Derrida on the Nation of Philosophy*. Stanford, CA: Stanford University Press, 2008.

Homolka, Walter and Heidegger, Arnulf, eds. *Heidegger und der Antisemitismus. Positionen im Widerstreit*. Freiburg/Basel/Vienna: Herder, 2016.

Hook, Sidney. "A Personal Impression of Contemporary German Philosophy," *The Journal of Philosophy* 27(6) (1930): 141–160.

Howse, Robert. *Leo Strauss: Man of Peace*. New York, NY: Cambridge University Press, 2014.

Huntington, Patricia J. "Heidegger's Reading of Kierkegaard Revisited: From Ontological Abstraction to Ethical Concretion," *Kierkegaard in Post/Modernity*, edited by Martin J. Matuštík and Merold Westphal. Bloomington and Indianapolis, IN: Indiana University Press, 1995, 43–65.

Husserl, Edmund. *Ideas: General Introduction to Pure Phenomenology*, translated by W. R. Boyce Gibson. New York, NY: Humanities Press, 1976.

Jaegerschmidt, Adelgundis. "Conversations with Edmund Husserl, 1931–1938," *New Yearbook for Phenomenology and Phenomenological Philosophy* 1 (2001): 331–350.

Janicaud, Dominique. *Heidegger in France*, translated by François Raffoul and David Pettigrew. Bloomington, IN: Indiana University Press, 2015.

Phenomenology and the "Theological Turn": The French Debate. New York: Fordham University Press, 2000.

Janssens, David. *Between Athens and Jerusalem: Philosophy, Prophecy, and Politics in Leo Strauss's Early Thought*. New York: State University of New York, 2008.

Jaspers, Karl. *Notizen zu Martin Heidegger*. Munich: R. Piper & Co. Verlag, 1978.

Johnston, Murray. *Engagement and Dialogue: Pluralism in the Thought of Joseph B. Soloveitchik*. Master thesis, Department of Jewish Studies, McGill University, Montreal, 1999.

Jonas, Hans. *Augustin und das paulinische Freiheitsproblem*. Göttingen: Vandenhoeck & Ruprecht, 1930.

"The Concept of God after Auschwitz: A Jewish Voice," *Mortality and Morality: A Search for the Good after Auschwitz*, edited by Lawrence Vogel. Evanston, IL: Northwestern University Press, 1996.

"Contemporary Problems in Ethics from a Jewish Perspective," *Philosophical Essays: From Ancient Creed to Technological Man*. Upper Saddle River, NJ: Prentice-Hall, 1974.

Erinnerungen, edited by Christian Wiese. Frankfurt am Main: Insel, 2003.

Gnosis und spätantiker Geist. Teil I. Die mythologische Gnosis. Göttingen: Vandenhoeck und Rupprecht, 1934.

The Gnostic Religion: The Message of the Alien God and the Beginning of Christianity. Boston, MA: Beacon House, 1958.

"Gnosticism and Modern Nihilism," *Social Research* 19 (1952): 430–452.

"Heidegger and Theology," *Review of Metaphysics* 18(2) (1964): 207–233.

"Heidegger's Resoluteness and Resolve: An Interview," *Martin Heidegger and National Socialism*, edited by Günter Neske and Emil Kettering. New York, NY: Paragon House, 1990, 197–203.

"Jewish and Christian Elements in Philosophy: Their Share in the Emergence of the Modern Mind," *Philosophical Essays: From Ancient Creed to Technological Man.* Upper Saddle River, NJ: Prentice-Hall, 1974.

Philosophical Essays: From Ancient Creed to Technological Man. Upper Saddle River, NJ: Prentice-Hall, 1974.

Von der Mythologie zur mystischen Philosophie. Göttingen: Vandenhoeck & Ruprecht, 1954.

Kant, Immanuel. *Critique of Pure Reason*, translated by Norman Kemp Smith. New York: Palgrave Macmillan, 2003.

Kaplan, Edward K. and Dresner, Samuel H. *Abraham Joshua Heschel: Prophetic Witness.* New Haven, CT: Yale University Press, 1998.

Kaufmann, Fritz. "Cassirer, Neo-Kantianism, and Phenomenology," *The Philosophy of Ernst Cassirer*, edited by Paul Arthur Schilpp. Chicago, IL: Open Court Publishing, 1973, 799–854.

Kaufmann, Walter. "Buber's Religious Significance," *The Philosophy of Martin Buber*, edited by Paul Arthur Schilpp and Maurice Friedmann. Chicago, IL: Open Court, 1967.

Kavka, Martin. *Jewish Messianism and the History of Philosophy.* Cambridge: Cambridge University Press, 2004.

"The Meaning of This Hour: Prophecy, Phenomenology, and the Public Sphere in the Early Writings of Abraham Joshua Heschel," *Religion and Violence in a Secular World: Toward a New Political Theology*, edited by Clayton Crocket. Charlottesville, VA: University of Virginia Press, 2006, 108–136.

"Screening the Canon: Levinas and Medieval Jewish Philosophy," *New Directions in Jewish Philosophy*, edited by Aaron W. Hughes and Elliot R. Wolfson. Bloomington, IN: Indiana University Press, 2010, 19–51.

Kearney, Richard. *Dialogues with Contemporary Continental Thinkers: The Phenomenological Heritage.* Manchester: Manchester University Press, 1984.

Keedus, Liisi. *The Crisis of German Historicism: The Early Political Thought of Hannah Arendt and Leo Strauss.* Cambridge: Cambridge University Press, 2015.

Kenaan, Hagi, Rottem, Shmuel and Barnea, Dana. "Heidegger in Jerusalem: A Chapter in the Formation of a Local Philosophy," *Theory and Criticism* 40(Summer 2012): 35–66 [Hebrew].

Kerr, Fergus. *Immortal Longings: Versions of Transcending Humanity.* London: SPCK, 1997.

King, Karen L. "Translating History: Reframing Gnosticism in Postmodernity," *Tradition und Translation: Zum Problem der interkulturellen Übersetzbarkeit religiöser Phänomene.* Berlin: De Gruyter, 1994, 264–277.

Kisiel, Theodore. *The Genesis of Heidegger's Being and Time.* Oakland, CA: University of California Press, 1993.

Kisiel, Theodore and Sheehan, Thomas, eds. *Becoming Heidegger: On the Trail of His Early Occasional Writings, 1910–1927.* Evanston, IL: Northwestern University Press, 2007.

Kisiel, Theodore and Van Buren, John, eds. *Reading Heidegger from the Start: Essays in His Earliest Thought.* Albany, NY: State University of New York Press, 1994.

Kleinberg, Ethan. 2005. *Generation Existential: Heidegger's Philosophy in France, 1927–1961.* Ithaca: Cornell University Press.

Kohler, Lotte, and Saner, Hans, eds. *Hanna Arendt, Karl Jaspers: Correspondence,* translated by Robert and Rita Kimber. San Diego: Harvest Book, 1992.

Kosky, Jeffrey L. 2001. *Levinas and the Philosophy of Religion.* Bloomington, IN: Indiana University Press.

Kovacs, George. *The Question of God in Heidegger's Phenomenology.* Evanston, IL: Northwestern University Press, 1990.

Kraft, Werner. *Gespräche mit Martin Buber.* Munich: Kösel-Verlag, 1966.

Krois, John Michael. "Cassirer's Unpublished Critique of Heidegger," *Philosophy & Rhetoric* 16(3) (1983): 147–159.

"Why Did Cassirer and Heidegger Not Debate in Davos?" *Symbolic Forms and Cultural Studies,* edited by Cyrus Hamlin and John Michael Krois. New Haven, CT: Yale University Press, 2004, 244–262.

Kuhlmann, Gerhardt. "Zum theologischen Problem der Existenz. Fragen an Rudolf Bultmann," *Zeitschrift für Theologie und Kirche* 37 (1929): 28–57.

Lacoue-Labarthe, Philippe. *Typography: Mimesis, Philosophy, Politics,* translated by Christopher Fynsk. Stanford, CA: Stanford University Press, 1998.

Lafont, Cristina. *Heidegger, Language, and World Disclosure,* translated by Graham Harman. Cambridge: Cambridge University Press, 2000.

Langan, Thomas. *The Meaning of Heidegger: A Critical Study of an Existentialist Phenomenology.* New York: Columbia University Press, 1959.

Lapidot, Elad. "Das Fremde im Denken," *Heidegger und der Antisemitismus. Positionen im Widerstreit,* edited by Walter Homolka and Arnulf Heidegger. Freiburg/Basel/Vienna: Herder, 2016, 269–276.

"Geschichtsphilosophische Einleitung," *Kritische Gesamtausgabe der Werke von Hans Jonas,* vol. IV/1, Gnosis und spätantiker Geist, edited by E. Lapidot und R. Kampling. Freiburg/Berlin/Wien: Wissenschaftliche Buchgesellschaft, 2020.

"Heidegger's *Teshuva?*" *Heidegger Studies* 32 (2016): 33–52.

"People of Knowers: On Heideggerian and Jewish Epistemico-Politics," *Heidegger and Jewish Thought: Difficult Others,* edited by Elad Lapidot and Micha Brumlik, London: Rowman and Littlefield, 2017, 269–289.

Lazier, Benjamin. *God Interrupted: Heresy and the European Imagination Between the World Wars.* Princeton, NJ: Princeton University Press, 2012.

Lease, Gary. *"Odd Fellows" in the Politics of Religion: Modernism, National Socialism and German Judaism.* Berlin/New York: Mouton de Gruyter, 1995.

Lebovic, Nitzan. "The Jerusalem School: The Theopolitical Hour," *New German Critique* 35(3) (2008): 97–120.

"Near the End: Celan, between Scholem and Heidegger," *The German Quarterly* 83(4) (2010): 465–484.

Lehmann, Gerhard. *Die Deutsche Philosophie der Gegenwart.* Stuttgart: Alfred Kröner, 1943.

Lehmann, Karl Kardinal. 2007. "'Sagen, was Sache ist': der Blick auf die Wahrheit der Existenz. Heideggers Beziehung zu Luther," *Heidegger und die christliche Tradition: Annäherungen an ein schwieriges Thema*, edited by Norbert Fischer, and Friedrich-Wilhelm von Hermann. Hamburg: Felix Meiner, 2007, 149–166.

Levinas, Emmanuel. "Antihumanism and Education," *Difficult Freedom: Essays on Judaism*, translated by Seán Hand. London: The Athlone Press, 1990.

"A propos de la mort du pape Pie XI," *Paix et Droit* 19(March 1939): 3–4.

"Being Jewish," *Continental Philosophy Review* 40 (2007): 205–210.

"Between Two Worlds (The Way of Franz Rosenzweig)," *Difficult Freedom: Essays on Judaism*, translated by Seán Hand. London: The Athlone Press, 1990.

"The Contemporary Relevance of Maimonides" (1935), translated by Michael Fagenblat, *Journal of Jewish Thought and Philosophy* 16(1) (2008): 91–94.

"Demanding Judaism," *Beyond the Verse: Talmudic Readings and Lectures*, translated by Gary D. Mole. London: The Athlone Press, 1994.

"Desacralization and Disenchantment," *Nine Talmudic Readings*, translated by Annette Aronowicz. Bloomington, IN: Indiana University Press, 1990.

"Diachrony and Representation," *Time and the Other (and Additional Essays)*, translated by Richard A. Cohen. Pittsburgh, PA: Duquesne University Press, 1987.

Discovering Existence with Husserl, translated by Richard A. Cohen and Michael B. Smith. Evanston, IL: Northwestern University Press, 1998.

Ethics and Infinity: Conversations with Philippe Nemo, translated by Richard A. Cohen. Pittsburgh, PA: Duquesne University Press, 1985.

Existence and Existents, translated by Alphonso Lingis. London: Kluwer, 1978.

"God and Philosophy," *Of God Who Comes to Mind*, translated by Bettina Bergo. Stanford, CA: Stanford University Press, 1998, 55–78.

God, Death, and Time, translated by Bettina Bergo. Stanford, CA: Stanford University Press, 2000.

"Heidegger, Gagarin, and Us," *Difficult Freedom: Essays on Judaism*, translated by Seán Hand. London: The Athlone Press, 1990, 231–234.

The Humanism of the Other, translated by N. Poller. Urbana and Chicago, IL: University of Illinois, 2006.

"Ideology and Idealism," *Of God Who Comes to Mind*, translated by Bettina Bergo. Stanford, CA: Stanford University Press, 1998, 3–14.

Is It Righteous to Be? Interviews with Emmanuel Levinas, edited by Jill Robbins. Stanford, CA: Stanford University Press, 2001.

"Is Ontology Fundamental?" *Entre Nous: Thinking-of-the-Other*, translated by Michael B. Smith and Barbara Harshav. New York: Columbia University Press, 1991, 1–11.

"L'actualité religieuse de l'Alliance," *Paix et Droit* 15(8) (1935): 4.

"A Man-God?," *Entre Nous: Thinking-of-the-Other*, translated by Michael B. Smith and Barbara Harshav. New York: Columbia University Press, 1991, 53–60.

"Martin Buber and Contemporary Judaism," *Outside the Subject*, translated by Michael B. Smith. Stanford, CA: Stanford University Press, 1993, 4–19.

"Martin Heidegger and Ontology," translated by the committee of Public Safety, *Diacritics* 26(1) (1996): 11–32.

"Meaning and Sense," *Collected Philosophical Papers*, translated by Alphonso Lingis. Dordrecht: Martinus Nijhoff, 1987.

"Monotheism and Language," *Difficult Freedom: Essays on Judaism*, translated by Seán Hand. London: The Athlone Press, 1990, 178–180.

Nine Talmudic Readings, translated by Annette Aronowicz. Bloomington: Indiana University Press, 1990.

Oeuvres 1: Carnets de captivité et autres inédits, edited by R. Calin and C. Chalier. Paris: Bernard Grasset/IMEC, 2009.

On Escape, De l'évasion, translated by Bettina Bergo. Stanford, CA: Stanford University Press, 2003.

Otherwise than Being or Beyond Essence, translated by Alphonso Lingis. Dordrecht: Kluwer Academic Publishers, 1991.

"The Pact," *Beyond the Verse: Talmudic Readings and Lectures*, translated by Gary D. Mole. London: The Athlone Press, 1994, 68–87.

"Philosophy and the Idea of Infinity," *Collected Philosophical Papers*, translated by Alphonso Lingis. Dordrecht: Martinus Nijhoff, 1987, 47–59.

"Philosophy, Justice, and Love," *Entre Nous: Thinking-of-the-Other*, translated by Michael B. Smith and Barbara Harshav. New York: Columbia University Press, 1991, 88–104.

"Reflections on the Philosophy of Hitlerism," translated by Seán Hand, *Critical Inquiry* 17(1) (1990): 62–71.

"A Religion for Adults," *Difficult Freedom*. Baltimore, MD: Johns Hopkins University Press, 1997, 11–23.

"Secularization and Hunger," *Graduate Faculty Philosophy Journal*, 20–21 (2–1) (1998): 3–12.

"Simone Weil Against the Bible," *Difficult Freedom: Essays on Judaism*, translated by Seán Hand. London: The Athlone Press, 1990, 133–141.

The Theory of Intuition in Husserl's Phenomenology, translated by André Orianne. Evanston, IL: Northwestern University Press, 1973.

Totality and Infinity: An Essay on Exteriority, translated by Alphonso Lingis. Pittsburgh, PA: Duquesne University Press, 1969.

"The Trace of the Other," *Deconstruction in Context*, translated by Alphonso Lingis and edited by Mark Taylor. Chicago, IL: University of Chicago Press, 1986, 345–359.

"The Translation of Scripture," *In the Time of the Nations*, translated by Michael B. Smith. London: The Athlone Press, 1994, 46–52.

Lewkowitz, Albert. "Religion und Philosophie im jüdischen Denken der Gegenwart," *Monatsschrift für Geschichte und Wissenschaft des Judentums* 79 (1935): 1–11.

"Vom Sinn des Seins. Zur Existenzphilosophie Heideggers," *Monatsschrift für Geschichte und Wissenschaft des Judentums*, 80 (1936): 184–195.

Liebeschütz, Hans. *Von Georg Simmel zu Franz Rosenzweig: Studien zum Jüdischen Denken im deutschen Kulturbereich.* Tübingen: J. C. B. Mohr, Paul Siebeck, 1970.

Liska, Vivian. *German-Jewish Thought and Its Afterlife: A Tenuous Legacy.* Bloomington and Indianapolis, IN: Indiana University Press, 2017.

Löwith, Karl. *Das Individuum in der Rolle des Mitmenschen. Ein Beitrag zur anthropologischen Grundlegung der ethischen Probleme.* Munich: Drein Masken Verlag, 1982.

"Grundzüge der Entwicklung der Phänomenologie zur Philosophie und ihr Verhältnis zur protestantischen Theologie," *Theologische Rundschau* 2 (1930): 26–64, 333–361.

Martin Heidegger and European Nihilism, translated by Gary Steiner and edited by Richard Wolin. New York: Columbia University Press, 1995.

"M. Heidegger and F. Rosenzweig or Temporality and Eternity," *Philosophy and Phenomenological Research* 3(1) (Sept. 1942): 53–77.

Meaning in History: The Theological Implications of the Philosophy of History. Chicago, IL: University of Chicago Press, 1947.

"My Last Meeting with Heidegger in Rome, 1936," *The Heidegger Controversy: A Critical Reader,* edited by Richard Wolin. Cambridge, MA: MIT Press, 1993, 140–143.

My Life in Germany Before and After 1933: A Report, translated by Elizabeth King. Urbana and Chicago, IL: University of Illinois Press, 1994.

"Phänomenologische Ontologie und protestantische Theologie," *Zeitschrift für Theologie und Kirche* 28 (1930): 365–399.

Luz, Ehud. "Max Wiener as a Historian of Jewish Religion in the Emancipation Period," *Hebrew Union College Annual* 56 (1985): 29–46 [Hebrew].

Lynch, Dennis A. "Ernst Cassirer and Martin Heidegger: The Davos Debate," *Kant-Studien* 81 (1990): 360–370.

Lyon, James, K. *Paul Celan and Martin Heidegger: An Unresolved Conversation, 1951–1970.* Baltimore, MD: John Hopkins University Press, 2006.

Lyotard, Jean-François. *Heidegger and "the jews,"* translated by Andreas Michel and Mark Roberts. Minneapolis, MN/London: University of Minnesota Press, 1997.

Ma, Lin. *Heidegger on East–West Dialogue: Anticipating the Event.* New York and London: Routledge, 2008.

Mack, Michael. *German Idealism and the Jew: The Inner Antisemitism of German Philosophy and German Jewish Responses.* Chicago, IL: Chicago University Press, 2003.

Magid, Shaul. "Gershom Scholem's Ambivalence Toward Mystical Experience and his Critique of Martin Buber in Light of Hans Jonas and Martin Heidegger," *Journal of Jewish Thought and Philosophy* 4(2) (1995): 245–269.

"The Role of the Secular in the Theology of Abraham Joshua Heschel's Theology: (Re)Reading Heschel after 9/11," *Modern Judaism* 29(1)(Feb. 2009): 138–160.

Mali, Joseph. "Ernst Cassirer's Interpretation of Judaism and its Function in Modern Political Culture," *Juden in der deutschen Wissenschaft*, edited by Walter Grab. Tel Aviv: Otpaz, 1986, 187–215.

Malik, Habib C. *Receiving Søren Kierkegaard: The Early Impact and Transmission of His Thought*. Washington, DC: The Catholic University of America Press, 1997.

Malka, Salmon. *Emmanuel Levinas: His Life and Legacy*, translated by Michael Kigel and Sonja M. Embree. Pittsburgh, PA: Duquesne University Press, 1993.

Maloney, Philip J. "Dreaming Otherwise than Icarus: Heidegger, Levinas, and the Secularization of Transcendence," *Between Levinas and Heidegger*, edited by John E. Drabinski and Eric S. Nelson. New York, NY: SUNY Press, 2014, 31–50.

Manning, Robert John Sheffler. *Interpreting Otherwise than Heidegger: Emmanuel Levinas's Ethics as First Philosophy*. Pittsburgh, PA: Duquesne University Press, 1993.

Marchand, Suzanne L. "Eastern Wisdom in an Era of Western Despair: Orientalism in 1920s Central Europe," *Weimar Thought: A Contested Legacy*. Princeton, NJ: Princeton University Press, 2013, 341–360.

German Orientalism in the Age of Empire: Religion, Race and Scholarship. Cambridge: Cambridge University Press, 2000.

Marck, Siegfried. *Die Dialektik in der Philosophie der Gegenwart*. Tübingen: J.C. B. Mohr, 1929.

Marcuse, Herbert. "Heidegger's Politics: An Interview with Herbert Marcuse," *Marcuse: Critical Theory and the Promise of Utopia*, edited by Robert Pippin, Andrew Feenberg, and Charles P. Webel. South Hadley, MA: Bergin and Garvey, 1988, 165–175.

Marion, Jean-Luc. *God Without Being*, translated by Thomas A. Carlson. Chicago, IL: University of Chicago, 1991.

McCarthy, Vincent. "Martin Heidegger: Kierkegaard's Influence Hidden and in Full View," *Kierkegaard and Existentialism*, edited by Jon Stewart. Farnham: Ashgate, 2011, 95–125.

McGrath, S. J. *The Early Heidegger & Medieval Philosophy: Phenomenology for the Godforsaken*. Washington, DC: Catholic University of America Press, 2006.

"The Facticity of Being God-Forsaken: The Young Heidegger and Luther's Theology of the Cross," *American Catholic Philosophical Quarterly* 79(2) (2005): 273–290.

McGrath, S. J. and Wierciński, Andrzej, eds. *A Companion to Heidegger's "Phenomenology of Religious Life."* Amsterdam: Rodopi, 2010.

McIlwain, David. "'The East within Us': Leo Strauss's Reinterpretation of Heidegger," *Journal of Jewish Thought and Philosophy* 26 (2018): 233–253.

McNeill, William. "From Destruction to the History of Being," *Gatherings: The Heidegger Circle Annual* 2 (2012): 24–40.

The Glance of the Eye: Heidegger, Aristotle, and the Ends of Theory. Albany, NY: SUNY Press, 1999.

Meir, Ephraim. *Levinas's Jewish Thought: Between Jerusalem and Athens*. Jerusalem: Magnes Press, 2008.

Meier, Heinrich. *Carl Schmitt and Leo Strauss: The Hidden Dialogue*, translated by J. Harvey Lamox. Chicago, IL: Chicago University Press, 1995.

"Death as God: A Note on Martin Heidegger," *Leo Strauss and the Theologico-Political Problem*, translated by Marcus Brainard. New York: Cambridge University Press, 2006, 45–51.

Mendes-Flohr, Paul. "Buber and the Metaphysics of Contempt," *Divided Passions: Jewish Intellectuals and the Experience of Modernity*. Detroit, MI: Wayne University State Press, 1991, 207–236.

"Fin de Siècle Orientalism, the Ostjuden, and the Aesthetics of Jewish Self-Affirmation," *Divided Passions: Jewish Intellectuals and the Experience of Modernity*. Detroit, MI: Wayne University State Press, 1991, 77–132.

Martin Buber: A Life of Faith and Dissent. New Haven, CT: Yale University Press, 2019.

"Martin Buber and Martin Heidegger in Dialogue," *The Journal of Religion* 94 (January 2014): 2–25.

Merrill, Clark A. "Leo Strauss's Indictment of Christian Philosophy," *The Review of Politics* 62(1) (2000): 77–106.

Mewes, Horst. "Leo Strauss and Martin Heidegger: Greek Antiquity and the Meaning of Modernity," *Hannah Arendt and Leo Strauss: German Emigrés and American Political Thought after World War II*, edited by Peter Graf Kielmansegg, Horst Mewes, and Elisabeth Glaser-Schmidt. Cambridge: Cambridge University Press, 1995, 105–120.

Meyer, Thomas. *Ernst Cassirer*. Hamburg: Ellert & Richter, 2006.

"Ernst Cassirer, Judentum aus dem Geist der universalistischen Vernunft," *Aschkenas*, 10(2) (2000): 459–502.

"Leo Strauss and Religious Rhetoric (1924–1938)," *Daat: A Journal of Jewish Philosophy & Kabbalah* 88 (2019): 205–224.

Zwischen Philosophie und Gesetz: Jüdische Philosophie und Theologie Von 1933 bis 1938. Leiden: Brill, 2009.

Misch, Georg. "Lebensphilosophie und Phänomenologie. Eine Auseinandersetzung der Diltheyschen Richtung mit Heidegger und Husserl [1, 2]," *Philosophischer Anzeiger* 3(2) (1929): 267–368.

"Lebensphilosophie und Phänomenologie. Eine Auseinandersetzung der Diltheyschen Richtung mit Heidegger und Husserl [1, 2]," *Philosophischer Anzeiger* 3(3) (1929): 405–475.

Montgomery, Paul L. "Scholar Breaks with Heidegger," *New York Times*, April 11, 1964.

Moran, Dermot. *Edmund Husserl: The Founder of Phenomenology*. Oxford: Polity, 2005.

"What Does Heidegger Mean by the Transcendence of Dasein?" *International Journal of Philosophical Studies* 22(4) (2014): 491–514.

Morgan, Michael L. *Levinas's Ethical Politics*. Bloomington, IN: Indiana University Press, 2016.

Morrison, Glen J. "Emmanuel Levinas and Christian Theology," *Irish Theological Quarterly* 68 (2003): 3–24.

Moyn, Samuel. "Anxiety and Secularization: Søren Kierkegaard and the Twentieth-Century Invention of Existentialism," *Situating Existentialism: Key Texts in Context*, edited by Jonathan Judaken and Robert Bernasconi. New York: Columbia University Press, 2012, 279–304.

"From Experience to Law: Leo Strauss and the Weimar Crisis of the Philosophy of Religion," *History of European Ideas* 33(2) (2007): 174–194.

"Judaism against Paganism: Emmanuel Levinas's Response to Heidegger and Nazism in the 1930s," *History and Memory* 10(1) (1998): 25–58.

Origins of the Other: Emmanuel Levinas Between Revelation and Ethics. London: Cornell University Press, 2006, 113–163.

Moyn, Samuel and Yadin-Israel, Azzan. "The Creaturely Limits of Knowledge: Martin Heidegger's Theological Critique of Immanuel Kant," *The Weimar Moment: Liberalism, Political Theology, and Law*, edited by Leonard V. Kaplan and Rudy Koshar. Lanham, MD: Lexington Books, 2012, 123–144.

Mulhall, Stephen. *Philosophical Myths of the Fall.* Princeton, NJ: Princeton University Press, 2005.

The Routledge Guide to Heidegger's Being and Time. Oxford: Routledge, 2013.

Muller, Jerry. "Leo Strauss: The Political Philosopher as a Young Zionist," *Jewish Social Studies* 17(1) (2010): 88–115.

Murphey, Ann. "Critique, Power, And Ontological Violence: The Problem of 'First' Philosophy," *Between Levinas and Heidegger*, edited by John E. Drabinski and Eric S. Nelson. New York, NY: SUNY Press, 2014, 15–30.

Müller, Max. "Martin Heidegger: A Philosopher and Politics: A Conversation," *Martin Heidegger and National Socialism*, edited by Günter Neske and Emil Kettering. New York: Paragon House, 1990, 175–196.

Myers, David N. "Hermann Cohen and the Quest for Protestant Judaism," *Leo Baeck Institute Year Book* 46(1) (2001): 195–214.

Resisting History: Historicism and its Discontents in German-Jewish Thought. Princeton, NJ: Princeton University Press, 2003.

Nancy, Jean-Luc. "Heidegger's Originary Ethics," *Heidegger and Practical Philosophy*. Albany, NY: SUNY Press, 2002, 65–86.

The Banality of Heidegger. New York: Fordham University Press, 2017.

Nelson, Eric S. "Heidegger, Levinas, and the Other of History," *Between Levinas and Heidegger*, edited by John E. Drabinski and Eric S. Nelson. New York: SUNY Press, 2014, 51–72.

Nirenburg, David. "When Philosophy Mattered," *The New Republic*, February 3, 2011, 39–43.

Novak, David. "Buber's Critique of Heidegger," *Modern Judaism* 5(2) (May 1985): 125–140.

"Heschel's Phenomenology of Revelation," *Abraham Joshua Heschel: Philosophy, Theology, and Interreligious Dialogue*, edited by Stanislaw Krajewski and Adam Lipszyc. Wiesbaden: Harrassowitz, 2009, 36–46.

Nowotny, Joanna. *"Kierkegaard ist ein Jude!": Jüdische Kierkegaard-Lektüren in Literatur und Philosophie.* Wallstein Verlag: Göttingen, 2018.

O'Meara, Thomas F. "Heidegger and his Origins: Theological Perspectives," *Theological Studies* 47 (1986): 205–226.

Ott, Hugo. "Martin Heidegger's Catholic Origins," *American Catholic Philosophical Quarterly* 69(2) (1995): 137–156.

Ozar, Alex S. 2016. "The Emergence of Max Scheler: Understanding Rabbi Joseph Soloveitchik's Philosophical Anthropology," *Harvard Theological Review* 109(2): 178–206.

Pangle, Thomas L. 2014. "Introduction," *The Rebirth of Classical Political Rationalism: Essays and Lectures by Leo Strauss*, edited by Thomas L. Pangle. Chicago, IL: University of Chicago Press, 1989.

"The Light Shed on the Crucial Development of Strauss's Thought by his Correspondence with Gerhard Krüger," *Reorientation: Leo Strauss in the 1930s*, edited by Martin D. Yaffe and Richard S. Ruderman. New York: Palgrave Macmillan, 2014, 57–68.

Parkes, Graham, ed., *Heidegger and Asian Thought.* Honolulu: University of Hawaii Press, 1990.

Pelluchon, Corine. "Strauss and Christianity," *Interpretation: A Journal of Political Philosophy* 33(2) (Spring 2006): 185–203.

Perkins, Robert L. "Buber and Kierkegaard: A Philosophic Encounter," *Martin Buber: A Centenary Volume*, edited by Haim Gordon and Jochanan Bloch. New York, NY: Ktav, 1984, 275–303.

"The Politics of Existence. Buber and Kierkegaard," *Kierkegaard in Post/Modernity*, edited by Martin J. Matuštík and Merold Westphal. Bloomington and Indianapolis, IN: Indiana University Press, 1995, 167–181.

Perlman, Lawrence. *The Eclipse of Humanity: Heschel's Critique of Heidegger.* Berlin: De Gruyter, 2016.

Pettigrew, David, and Raffoul, François. *French Interpretations of Heidegger: An Exceptional Reception.* Albany, NY: SUNY Press, 2008.

Plessner, Helmuth. "Macht und menschliche Natur." *Gesammelte Schriften V.* Frankfurt am Main: Suhrkamp, 135–234.

Pöggeler, Otto. *Martin Heidegger's Path of Thinking*, translated by Daniel Magurshak and Sigmund Barber. Atlantic Highlands, NJ: Humanities Press, 1987.

The Paths of Heidegger's Life and Thought. Atlantic Highlands, NJ: Humanities Press, 1997.

Philosophie und hermeneutische Theologie: Heidegger, Bultmann und die Folgen. Munich: Fink, 2009.

Pollock, Benjamin. 2014. *Franz Rosenzweig's Conversions: World Denial and World Redemption.* Bloomington and Indianapolis, IN: Indiana University Press.

Polt, Richard. 2006. *The Emergency of Being: On Heidegger's Contributions to Philosophy.* Ithaca, NY and London: Cornell University Press.

2019. *Time and Trauma: Thinking Through Heidegger in the Thirties.* London and New York: Rowman and Littlefield.

Poma, Andrea. 1997. *The Critical Philosophy of Hermann Cohen*, translated by John Denton. Albany, NY: SUNY Press.

Possen, David D. "J. B. Soloveitchik: Between Neo-Kantianism and Kierkegaardian Existentialism," *Kierkegaard's Influence on Theology*, tome 3, *Catholic and Jewish Theology*, edited by Jon Stewart. Farnham, UK: Ashgate, 2012, 189–209.

Powell, Jeffrey. "The Way to Heidegger's 'Way to Language.'" *Heidegger and Language*, edited by Jeffrey Powell. Bloomington, IN: Indiana University Press, 2013, 180–200.

Przywara, Erich. *Augustinus. Gestalt als Gefüge*. Leipzig: Hegner, 1934.

Das Geheimnis Kierkegaards. Munich: Oldenbourg, 1929.

"Der Mensch des Adgrundes," *Stimmen der Zeit* 120 (1931): 252–266.

"Drei Richtungen der Phänomenologie," *Stimmen der Zeit* 115 (1928): 252–264.

"Gott in uns und über uns? (Immanenz und Transzendenz in heutigen Geistesleben)," *Stimmen der Zeit* 105 (1923): 343–362.

"Theologische Motive im Werk Martin Heideggers," *In und Gegen: Stellungnahmen zur Zeit*. Nuremberg: Glock und Lutz, 1955, 55–60.

"Wende zum Menschen," *Stimmen der Zeit* 199 (1930): 1–13.

Purcell, Michael. *Levinas and Theology*. Cambridge: Cambridge University Press, 2006.

Putnam, Hillary. "Levinas and Judaism," *The Cambridge Companion to Levinas*, edited by Simon Critchley and Robert Bernasconi. Cambridge: Cambridge University Press, 2006, 33–62.

Raffoul, François. "Heidegger and the Origins of Responsibility," *Heidegger and Practical Philosophy*. Albany, NY: SUNY Press, 2002, 87–98.

Rakeffet-Rothkoff, Aaron. *The Rav: The World of Rabbi Joseph B. Soloveitchik*, vol. 1. New Jersey: Ktav, 1999.

Rashkover, Randi. *Revelation and Theopolitics: Barth, Rosenzweig, and the Politics of Praise*. New York: T&T Clark, 2005.

Richardson, William J. "Heidegger and God – and Professor Jonas," *Thought: Fordham University Quarterly* 40(1) (1965): 13–40.

Through Phenomenology to Thought. Martinus Nijhoff: The Hague, 1964.

Richter, Cornelia. "Symbol, Mythos, Religion. Zum Status der Religion in der Philosophie Ernst Cassirers," *Die Prägnanz der Religion in der Kultur, Ernest Cassirer und die Theologie*, edited by Dietrich Korsch and Enno Rudolph. Tübingen: Mohr Siebek, 2000, 7–17.

Robinson, James M. and Cobb Jr., John B. *The Later Heidegger and Theology*. New York, NY: Harper & Row, 1963.

Rody, Tzvi. "Nazi Metaphysics (Or: Thoughts on Existentialism)," *Al Hamishmar* (August 9, 1946), 4.

Rojcewicz, Richard. *The Gods and Technology: A Reading of Heidegger*. Albany, NY: State University of New York Press, 2006.

Rolland, Jacques. "Getting Out of Being By a New Path," *On Escape*, translated by Bettina Bergo. Stanford, CA: Stanford University Press, 2003, 29–32.

Rome, Sydney and Rome, Beatrice, eds. "Martin Buber," *Philosophical Interrogations*, New York: Harper Torchbooks, 1970, 13–117.

Rosenstock, Eugen. "Rückblick auf Die Kreature," *Das Geheimnis der Universität*. Stuttgart: Kohlhammer, 1958, 209.

Rosenzweig, Franz. "Atheistische Theologie," *Zweistromland: Kleiner Schriften zu Glauben und Denken: Franz Rosenzweig: Der Mensch und sein Werk*, edited by Reinhold Mayer and Annemarie Mayer. Dordrecht: Martinus Nijhoff, 1984, 687–697.

Briefe und Tagebücher II, *Franz Rosenzweig: Der Mensch und sein Werk*, edited by Rachel Rosenzweig and Edith Rosenzweig-Scheinmann, in collaboration with Bernhard Casper. Den Haag: Martinus Nijhoff, 1979.

"Einleitung in die Akademieauasgabe der jüdischen Schriften Hermann Cohens," *Kleinere Schriften*. Berlin: Schocken Verlag, 1937, 299–350.

"Jehuda Halevi: Fünfundneunzig Hymnen und Gedichte Deutsch und Hebräisch," *Sprachdenken im Übersetzen, Franz Rosenzweig: Der Mensch und sein Werk*, edited by Rachel Bat-Adam. Dordrecht: Martinus Nijhoff, 1984.

Philosophical and Theological Writings, translated and edited by Paul Franks and Michael L. Morgan. Indianapolis, IN: Hackett Publishing, 2000.

The Star of Redemption, translated by William W. Hallo. Boston: Beacon Press, 1972.

"Transposed Fronts," *Philosophical and Theological Writings*, translated and edited by Paul Franks and Michael L. Morgan. Indianapolis, IN: Hackett Publishing, 2000.

"Vertauschte Fronten," *Der Morgen* 1(April 1930): 85–87.

Rotenstreich, Nathan. *Jewish Thought in the Modern Era*, vol. II. Tel Aviv: Am Oved, 1949 [Hebrew].

"The Right and the Limitations of Buber's Dialogical Thought," *The Philosophy of Martin Buber*, edited by Paul Arthur Schilpp and Maurice Friedmann. Chicago, IL: Open Court, 1967.

Roubach, Michael. "Die Rezeption Heideggers in Israel." *Heidegger-Jahrbuch* 9 (2009): 419–432.

Safranski, Rüdiger. *Martin Heidegger: Between Good and Evil*, translated by Ewald Osers. Cambridge, MA: Harvard University Press, 1999.

Šajda, Peter. "Martin Buber: 'No-One Can Refute Kierkegaard as Kierkegaard Himself.'" *Kierkegaard and Existentialism*, edited by Jon Stewart. Farnham: Ashgate, 2011, 33–61.

Schaeffler, Richard. *Frömmigkeit des Denkens*. Darmstadt: Wissenschaftliche Buchgesellschaft, 1978.

"Rezension zu M. Heideggers Vortrag über: 'Die Frage nach der Technik,' im Rahmen der Vortragsreihe: 'Die Künste im technischen Zeitalter, veranstaltet von der bayerischen Akademie der schönen Künste,'" *Zeitschrift fuer Philosophische Forschung*, 9(1) (1955): 116–127.

Schalow, Frank. "Thinking at Cross Purpose with Kant: Reason, Finitude, and Truth in the Cassirer-Heidegger Debate," *Kant-Studien* 87 (1996): 198–217.

Scheler, Max. "Reality and Resistance: On *Being and Time*, Section 43," *Heidegger, The Man and the Thinker*, edited and translated by Thomas Sheehan. Chicago, IL: Precedent, 1981.

Schine, Robert S. *Jewish Thought Adrift: Max Wiener (1882–1950)*. Atlanta, GA: Scholars Press, 1992.

Schmidt, Christoph. "Die theopolitische Stunde. Martin Bubers Begriff der Theopolitik, seine prophetischen Ursprünge, seine Aktualität und Bedeutung für die Definition Zionistischer Politik," *Die theopolitische Stunde: Zwölf Perspektiven auf das eschatologische Problem der Moderne*. Munich: Wilhelm Fink Verlag, 2009, 205–225.

"Monotheism as a Metapolitical Problem: Heidegger's War Against Jewish Christian Monotheism," *Heidegger's Black Notebooks and the Future of Theology*, edited by Marten Björk and Jane Svenungsson. New York: Palgrave, 2017, 131–157.

Schoeps, Hans Joachim. *Ja-Nein-und Trotzdem: Erinnerungen, Begegnungen, Erfahrungen*. Mainz: von. Hase & Koehler, 1974.

Jüdischer Glaube in dieser Zeit. Prolegomena zur Grundlegung einer systematischen Theologie des Judentums. Berlin: Philo, 1932.

"Secessio Judaica-Israel in Ewigkeit," *Bereit für Deutschland. Der Patriotismus deutscher Juden und der Nationalsozialismus*. Berlin: Haude & Spencersche, 1970 [1934].

"Tragische Existenz: Bemerkungen zu einem Buch über die Philosophie Martin Heideggers," *Philosophia* 1(2) (1937): 142–145.

"Zur jüdisch-religiösen Gegenwartssituation," *Der Morgen: Monatsschrift der Juden in Deutschland* 3(June 1937), 98–104.

Schonfeld, Eli. "Jewish Philosophy as Existential Hermeneutics: A Revisiting of the Relation between Philosophy and Judaism in Emanuel Levinas," *Jerusalem Studies in Jewish Thought* 24 (2015): 373–398. [Hebrew].

Schopenhauer, Arthur. *Parerga and Paralipomena: Short Philosophical Essays*, vol. 1, translated by E. F. J. Payne. Oxford: Clarendon Press, 1974.

Schrag, Calvin O. "Heidegger and Cassirer on Kant," *Kant-Studien* 58 (1–4) (1967): 87–100.

Schulz, Heiko. "A Modest Head Start: The German Reception of Kierkegaard." *Kierkegaard's International Reception*, edited by Jon Stewart. Farnham: Ashgate, 2009, 307–419.

Schwarzschild, Steven S. "Franz Rosenzweig and Martin Heidegger: The German and the Jewish Turn to Ethnicism," *Der Philosoph franz Rosenzweig (1886–1929): Internationaler Kongreß-Kassel 1986*, 2 vols, edited by Wolfdietrich Schmied-Kowarzik. Freiburg: Verlag Karl Alber, 1988.

"Judaism in the Life and World of Ernst Cassirer," *Il cannocchiale: Rivista di studi filosofici* 1(1–2) (1991): 327–344.

"The Theological-Political Basis of Liberal Christian-Jewish Relations in Modernity," *Das deutsche Judentum und der Liberalismus – German Jewry and Liberalism*. London and St. Augustin: Comdok, 1986, 70–95.

Schweid, Eliezer. "Religion and Philosophy: The Scholarly-Theological Debate between Julius Guttmann and Leo Strauss," *Maimonidean Studies*, edited by Arthur Hyman, vol. 1. New York, NY: Yeshiva University Press, 1990, 162–195.

Scott, Charles E. "Heidegger Reconsidered: A Response to Professor Jonas," *Harvard Theological Review* 59(2) (April 1966): 175–185.

Scult, Allen. *Being Jewish/Reading Heidegger: An Ontological Encounter.* New York: Fordham University Press, 2004.

Martin Heidegger and the Hermeneutics of Torah: A Strange Affinity. New York: Hunter College of the University of New York, 2007.

Seligmann, Raphael. "The Antinomies of Being." *Masot Philosophiot.* Tel Aviv: Devir, 1955, 232–235 [Hebrew].

"Heidegger," *Masot Philosophiot:* Tel Aviv: Devir, 1955, 135–142.

"Sein oder Nichtsein: Zu Heideggers Existenzphilosophie," *Socialistischen Monatsheften* 38 (1932): 432–441.

Shaw, Joshua. "Is Levinas's Philosophy a Response to the Holocaust?" *Journal for Jewish Thought and Philosophy* 18(2) (2010): 121–146.

Sheehan, Thomas. "Emmanuel Faye: The Introduction of Fraud into Philosophy?" *Philosophy Today* 59(3) (2015): 367–400.

Making Sense of Heidegger: A Paradigm Shift. London: Rowman and Littlefield, 2014.

Shell, Susan Meld, *The Strauss–Krüger Correspondence: Returning to Plato through Kant.* New York: Palgrave Macmillan, 2018.

Sheppard, Eugene. *Leo Strauss and the Politics of Exile: The Making of a Political Philosopher.* Waltham, MA: Brandeis University Press, 2007.

Shonkoff, Sam. "Sacramental Existence and Embodied Theology in Buber's Representation of Hasidism," *Journal of Jewish Thought and Philosophy* 25(1) (2017): 131–161.

Sieg, Ulrich. "Deutsche Kulturgeschichte und Jüdischer Geist: Ernst Cassirer's Auseinandersetzung mit der Völkischer Philosophie Bruno Bauchs. Ein Unbekanntes Manuskript," *Bulletin des Leo Baeck's Instituts* 88 (1991): 59–71.

"Die Verjudung des deutschen Geistes," *Die Zeit*, December 22, 1989.

Siegfried, Meike. *Abkehr vom Subjekt: Zum Sprachdenken bei Heidegger und Buber.* Freiburg: Karl Alber, 2010.

Sikka, Sonia. "Questioning the Sacred: Heidegger and Levinas on the Locus of Divinity," *Modern Theology* 14(3) (1998): 299–323.

Simon, Ernst. *Chajjim Nachman Bialik: Eine Einführung in sein Leben und sein Werk.* Berlin: Schocken Verlag, 1935.

"Hadat Shel Ha'Ratzionalismus," *Moznaim* 3 (1–6) (1934/1935): 110–113.

"Zwiesprache mit Martin Buber," *Der Morgen* 6 (September 1934): 314.

Skidelsky, Edward. *Ernst Cassirer: The Last Culture Philosopher.* Princeton, NJ: Princeton University Press, 2008.

Sluga, Hans. *Heidegger's Crisis: Philosophy and Politics in Nazi Germany.* Cambridge, MA: Harvard University Press, 1993.

Soloveitchik, Joseph B. *Halakhic Man*, translated by Lawrence Kaplan. Philadelphia, PA: The Jewish Publication Society, 1983.

The Halakhic Mind. New York: Seth Press, 1986.

"The Lonely Man of Faith," *Tradition: A Journal of Orthodox Jewish Thought* 7(2) (1965): 5–67.

"The Synagogue as an Institution and as an Idea," *Rabbi Joseph H. Lookstein Memorial Volume*, edited by L. Landman. New Jersey: Ktav, 1980.

Smith, Steven B. "'Destruktion' or Recovery? Leo Strauss's Critique of Heidegger," *Review of Metaphysics* 51(2) (1997): 345–377.

Spinoza, Baruch. *Theologico-Political Treatise*, translated by Samuel Shirley. Leiden: Brill, 1991.

Stern (Anders), Günther. "On the Pseudo-Concreteness of Heidegger's Philosophy," *Philosophy and Phenomenological Research* 8(3) (1948): 337–371.

Stern, Harold. "A. J. Heschel, Irenic Polemicist," *Proceedings of the Rabbinical Assembly* XLV (1983): 169–177.

Strauß, Eduard. "Eine jüdische Theologie?" *Der Morgen* 4(October 1932): 312–314.

Strauss, Leo. *Die Religionskritik Spinozas als Grundlage Seiner Bibelwissenschaft: Untersuchungen zu Spinozas Theologisch-Politischem Traktat*. Berlin: Akademie-Verlag, 1930.

"Existentialism," *Interpretation* 22(3) (Spring 1995): 319–338.

Gesammelte Schriften, edited by Heinrich Meier, vol. I. Stuttgart: J. B. Metzler, 1997.

Gesammelte Schriften, edited by Heinrich Meier, vol. II. Stuttgart: J. B. Metzler, 2001.

Gesammelte Schriften, edited by Heinrich Meier, vol. III. Stuttgart: J. B. Metzler, 2004.

"A Giving of Accounts," *Jewish Philosophy and the Crisis of Modernity: Essays and Lectures in Modern Jewish Thought*, edited by Kenneth Hart Green. Albany, NY: State University of New York Press, 1997.

"An Introduction to Heideggerian Existentialism," *The Rebirth of Classical Political Rationalism: Essays and Lectures by Leo Strauss*, edited by Thomas L. Pangle. Chicago, IL: University of Chicago Press, 1989.

"Kurt Riezler (1882–1955)," *What Is Political Philosophy? and Other Studies*. Chicago, IL: Chicago University Press, 1988, 246–250.

Leo Strauss: The Early Writings (1921–1932), translated and edited by Michael Zank. New York, NY: State University of New York, 2002.

"Letter to the Editor," *National Review* (January 5, 1956): 23.

"The Living Issues of German Post-War Philosophy," Heinrich Meier, *Leo Strauss and the Theologico-Political Problem*, translated by Marcus Brainard. New York: Cambridge University Press, 2006.

Natural Right and History. Chicago, IL and London: University of Chicago Press, 1953.

"Natural Right and the Historical Approach," *An Introduction to Political Philosophy: Ten Essays by Leo Strauss*, edited by Hilail Gildin. Detroit, MI: Wayne State University Press, 1989, 99–124.

"On the Interpretation of Genesis," *Jewish Philosophy and the Crisis of Modernity: Essays and Lectures in Modern Jewish Thought*, edited by Kenneth Hart Green. Albany, NY: State University of New York Press, 1997, 359–376.

On Tyranny, edited by Victor Gourevitch and S. Michael Roth. Chicago, IL: University of Chicago Press, 2000.

Persecution and the Art of Writing. Chicago, IL and London: University of Chicago, 1988.

"Philosophy as Rigorous Science and Political Philosophy," *Studies in Platonic Political Philosophy*. Chicago, IL and London: Chicago University Press, 1983, 29–37.

Philosophie und Gesetz: Beiträge zum Verständnis Maimunis und seiner Vorläufer, Gesammelte Schriften 2, 1995, 1–123.

Philosophy and Law: Contributions to the Understanding of Maimonides and His Predecessors, translated by Eve Adler. New York: State University of New York Press, 1995.

"Preface to the English Translation," *Spinoza's Critique of Religion*. New York: Schocken Books, 1965.

"Preface to Isaac Husik, Philosophical Essays," *Jewish Philosophy and the Crisis of Modernity: Essays and Lectures in Modern Jewish Thought*, edited by Kenneth Hart Green. Albany, NY: State University of New York Press, 1997, 235–266.

"The Problem of Socrates," *Interpretation* 22(3) (1995): 319–338.

"Progress or Return," *Jewish Philosophy and the Crisis of Modernity: Essays and Lectures in Modern Jewish Thought*, edited by Kenneth Hart Green. Albany, NY: State University of New York Press, 1997, 87–136.

"Reason and Revelation," in Heinrich Meier, *Leo Strauss and the Theologico-Political Problem*, translated by Marcus Brainard. New York: Cambridge University Press, 2006.

"The Religious Situation of the Present," translated by Anna Schmidt and Martin D. Yaffe, *Reorientation: Leo Strauss in the 1930s*, edited by Martin D. Yaffe and Richard S. Ruderman. New York: Palgrave Macmillan, 2014, 225–235.

"The Three Waves of Modernity," *An Introduction to Political Philosophy: Ten Essays by Leo Strauss*, edited by Hilail Gildin. Detroit, MI: Wayne State University Press, 1989, 81–98.

"An Unspoken Prologue to a Public Lecture at St. John's College in Honor of Jacob Klein," *Jewish Philosophy and the Crisis of Modernity: Essays and Lectures in Modern Jewish Thought*, edited by Kenneth Hart Green. Albany, NY: State University of New York Press, 1997.

"What Is Political Philosophy?" *What Is Political Philosophy? and Other Studies*. Chicago, IL: Chicago University Press, 1988, 9–55.

"Why We Remain Jews: Can Jewish Faith and History Still Speak to Us?" *Jewish Philosophy and the Crisis of Modernity: Essays and Lectures in Modern Jewish Thought*, edited by Kenneth Hart Green. Albany, NY: State University of New York Press, 1997, 311–356.

Tal, Uriel. *Christians and Jews in Germany: Religion, Politics and Ideology in the Second Reich, 1870–1914*. Ithaca, NY: Cornell University Press, 1975.

Taminiaux, Jacques. "The Interpretation of Aristotle's Notion of Aretê in Heidegger's First Courses." *Heidegger and Practical Philosophy*, edited by Francois Raffoul and David Pettigrew. Albany, NY: SUNY Press, 2002, 13–28.

"The Presence of Being and Time in Totality and Infinity," *Levinas in Jerusalem: Phenomenology, Ethics, Politics, Aesthetics*, edited by Joëlle Hansel. Dordrecht: Springer, 2009, 3–22.

Tanguay, Daniel. *Leo Strauss: An Intellectual Biography*, translated by Christopher Nadon. New Haven, CT and London: Yale University Press, 2007.

Taubes, Jacob. *Abendländische Eschatologie*. Bern: A. Francke, 1947.
  "Buber and Philosophy of History," *The Philosophy of Martin Buber*, edited by Paul Arthur Schilpp and Maurice Friedman. Chicago, IL: Open Court, 1967, 451–468.
  "The Development of the Ontological Question in Recent German Philosophy," *Review of Metaphysics* 6 (January 1951): 651–664.
  The Political Theology of Paul, translated by Dana Hollander. Stanford, CA: Stanford University Press, 2004.
Taubes, Susan. *Die Korrespondenz mit Jacob Taubes 1950–1951*, edited by Christina Pareigis. Wilhelm Fink: Munich, 2014.
  Die Korrespondenz mit Jacob Taubes 1952, edited by Christina Pareigis. Wilhelm Fink: Munich, 2014.
  "The Gnostic Foundations of Heidegger," *The Journal of Religion* 34(3) (July 1954): 155–172.
Thiselton, Anthony. *The Two Horizons: New Testament Hermeneutics and Philosophical Description with Special Reference to Heidegger, Bultmann, Gadamer and Wittgenstein*. Exeter: Paternoster, 1980.
Tijmes, Pieter. "Home and Homelessness: Heidegger and Levinas on Dwelling," *Worldviews: Environment, Culture, Religion* 2 (1998): 201–213.
Theunissen, Michael. *Der Andere. Studien zur Sozialontologie der Gegenwart*. Berlin: de Gruyter, 1965.
Thomson, Iain. *Heidegger on Ontotheology: Technology and the Politics of Education*. Cambridge: Cambridge University Press, 2005.
  "Ontotheology? Understanding Heidegger's *Destruktion* of Metaphysics," *International Journal of Philosophical Studies* 8(3) (2000): 297–327.
Torres Gregory, Wanda. *Heidegger's Path to Language*. Lanham, MD: Rowman and Littlefield, 2016.
Traub, Friedrich. "Heidegger und die Theologie," *Zeitschrift für systematische Theologie*, 9 (January 1, 1932): 686–743.
Trawny, Peter. 2015. *Heidegger and the Myth of Jewish World Conspiracy*, translated by Andrew J. Mitchell. Chicago, IL: University of Chicago Press.
  "Heidegger, 'World Judaism,' and Modernity," *Gatherings: The Heidegger Circle Annual* 5 (2015): 1–20
Trigano, Shmuel. "Levinas and the Project of Jewish Philosophy," *Jewish Studies Quarterly* 8(3) (2001): 279–308.
Troeltsch, Ernst. "Glaube und Ethos der hebräischen Propheten" (1916), *Aufsätze zur Geistesgeschichte und Religionssoziologie, Gesammelte Schriften*, vol. 4, edited by Hans Baron. Tübingen: J. C. B. Mohr, 1925.
Udoff, Alan. "On Leo Strauss: An Introductory Account," *Leo Strauss's Thought: Towards a Critical Engagement*. Boulder, CO: L. Riener Publishers, 1991.
Urban, Martina. "Persecution and the Art of Representation: Schocken's Maimonides Anthologies of the 1930s," *Maimonides and His Heritage*, edited by Idit Dobbs-Weinstein, Lenn E. Goodman, and James Allen Grady. New York: State University of New York Press, 2009, 153–179.
Van Buren, John. "Heidegger's Early Freiburg Courses, 1915–1923," *Research in Phenomenology* 23 (1993): 132–152.

"Martin Heidegger, Martin Luther," *Reading Heidegger from the Start: Essays in His Earliest Thought*, edited by Theodore J. Kisiel and John Van Buren. Albany, NY: State University of New York Press, 1994, 159–174.

The Young Heidegger: Rumour of the Hidden King. Bloomington, IN: Indiana University Press, 1994.

Vedder, Ben. *Heidegger's Philosophy of Religion: From God to Gods*. Pittsburgh, PA: Duquesne University Press, 2007.

Vega, Facundo. "'God Is Death': The Oblivion of Esotericism and Stimmungen in Leo Strauss's Heidegger," *Philosophy Today* 62(3) (2018): 823–845.

Velkley, Richard. *Heidegger, Strauss and the Premises of Philosophy: On Original Forgetting*. Chicago, IL: University of Chicago, 2011.

Verne, Donald Phillip. "Kant, Hegel, and Cassirer: The Origins of the Philosophy of Symbolic Forms," *Journal of the History of Ideas* 30(1) (1969): 33–46.

Voegelin, Eric. "On Debate and Existence," Eric Voegelin, *Collected Works*, vol. 12. Columbia, MO: University of Missouri Press, 1990.

Vogel, Lawrence. "Overcoming Heidegger's Nihilism: Leo Strauss versus Hans Jonas," *Heidegger's Jewish Followers: Essays on Hannah Arendt, Leo Strauss, Hans Jonas and Emmanuel Levinas*, edited by Samuel Fleischacker. Pittsburgh, PA: Duquesne University Press, 2008, 131–150.

Volpi, Francisco, "Being and Time: A 'Translation' of the Nicomachean Ethics?" *Reading Heidegger from the Start: Essays in His Earliest Thought*, edited by Theodore J. Kisiel and John Van Buren. Albany, NY: State University of New York Press, 1994, 195–212.

Wahl, Jean. "Martin Buber and the Philosophies of Existence," *The Philosophy of Martin Buber*, edited by Paul Arthur Schilpp and Maurice Friedman. Chicago, IL: Open Court, 1967.

Waldstein, Michael. "Hans Jonas' Construct of 'Gnosticism': Analysis and Critique," *Journal of Early Christian Studies* 8(3) (Fall 2000): 341–372.

Ward, Graham. *Barth, Derrida and the Language of Theology*. Cambridge: Cambridge University Press,1995.

Ward, James F. "Political Philosophy and History: The Links between Strauss and Heidegger," *Polity* 20(1) (Winter 1987): 273–295.

Wasserstorm, Steven M. "Hans Jonas in Marburg, 1928," *The Legacy of Hans Jonas: Judaism and the Phenomenon of Life*, edited by Hava Tirosh-Samuelson and Christian Wiese. Leiden: Brill, 2010, 39–72.

Webb, Stephen H. "The Rhetoric of Ethics as Excess: A Christian Theological Response to Emmanuel Levinas," *Modern Theology* 15(1) (1999): 1–16.

Weber, Elisabeth. "The Notion of Persecution in Levinas's Otherwise than Being or Beyond Essence," *Ethics as First Philosophy: The Significance of Emmanuel Levinas for Philosophy, Literature and Religion*, edited by Adriaan T. Peperzak. New York: Routledge, 1995, 69–76.

Weiss, Daniel H. *Paradox and the Prophets: Hermann Cohen and the Indirect Communication of Religion*. Oxford: Oxford University Press, 2012.

Weiss, Yfaat. *Lea Goldberg: Lehrjahre in Deutschland 1930–1933*. Göttingen: Vandenhoeck & Ruprecht, 2010.

Welte, Bernhard. "God in Heidegger's Thought," *Philosophy Today* 26(1) (1982): 85–100.

White, Carol, J. "Heidegger and the Greeks," *Blackwell Companion to Heidegger*, edited by Hubert Dreyfus and Mark Wrathall. Oxford: Blackwell, 2005, 121–140.

Wiener, Max. *Jüdische Religion im Zeitalter der Emanzipation*. Berlin: Philo Verlag, 1933.

Wiese, Christian. *The Life and Thought of Hans Jonas: Jewish Dimensions*. Waltham, MA: Brandeis University Press, 2007.

 "'Revolt Against Escapism': Hans Jonas's Response to Martin Heidegger," *Heidegger's Jewish Followers: Essays on Hannah Arendt, Leo Strauss, Hans Jonas and Emmanuel Levinas*, edited by Samuel Fleischacker. Pittsburgh, PA: Duquesne University Press, 2008, 151–177.

Williams, John R. *Martin Heidegger's Philosophy of Religion*. Waterloo, Ontario: Wilfrid Laurier University Press, 1977.

Williams, Michael A. *Rethinking "Gnosticism": An Argument for Dismantling a Dubious Category*. Princeton, NJ: Princeton University Press, 1996.

Withy, Katherine. *Heidegger on Being Uncanny*. Cambridge, MA: Harvard University Press, 2015.

Woessner, Martin. *Heidegger in America*. New York: Cambridge University Press, 2011.

Wolfe, Judith. *Heidegger and Theology*. London: Bloomsbury, 2014.

 Heidegger's Eschatology: Theological Horizons in Martin Heidegger's Early Work. Oxford: Oxford University Press, 2013.

Wolfson, Elliot R. *Alef, Mem, Tau: Kabbalistic Musing on Time, Truth, and Death*. Berkeley, CA: University of California Press, 2006.

 The Duplicity of Philosophy's Shadow: Heidegger, Nazism, and the Jewish Other. New York: Columbia University Press, 2018.

 Giving Beyond the Gift: Apophasis and Overcoming Theomania. New York: Fordham University Press, 2014.

 "Gottwesen and the De-Divinization of the Last God: Heidegger's Meditation on the Strange and Incalculable," *Heidegger's Black Notebooks and the Future of Theology*, edited by Marten Björk and Jane Svenungsson. New York: Palgrave, 2017, 211–255.

 Heidegger and Kabbalah: Hidden Gnosis and the Path of Posēis. Bloomington, IN: Indiana University Press, 2019.

 Language, Eros, Being: Kabbalistic Hermeneutics and Poetic Imagination. New York: Fordham University Press, 2005.

 "Not Yet Now: Speaking of the End and the End of Speaking," *Elliot R. Wolfson: Poetic Thinking*, edited by Hava Tirosh-Samuelson and Aaron W. Hughes. Leiden: Brill, 2015, 127–193.

Wolin, Richard. *Heidegger's Children: Hannah Arendt, Karl Löwith, Hans Jonas and Herbert Marcuse*. New Jersey, NJ: Princeton University Press, 2001.

 "Introduction: What Is Heideggerian Marxism?" In *Herbert Marcuse, Heideggerian Marxism*, edited by Richard Wolin and John Abromeit. Lincoln and London: University of Nebraska Press, 2005, xi–xxx.

Wolin, Richard, ed. *The Heidegger Controversy: A Critical Reader*. MIT Press: Boston, 1993.

Wolosky, Shira. "Two Types of Negative Theology; Or, What Does Negative Theology Negate," *Negative Theology as Jewish Modernity*, edited by Michael Fagenblat. Bloomington, IN: Indiana University Press, 2017, 161–179.

Wood, Robert. *Martin Buber's Ontology: An Analysis of "I and Thou."* Evanston, IL: Northwestern University Press, 1969.

Wrathall, Mark. *Heidegger and Unconcealment: Truth, Language, and History.* Cambridge: Cambridge University Press, 2011.

Wrathall, Mark and Lambeth, Morganna. "Heidegger's Last God," *Inquiry* 54(2) (2011): 160–182.

Wright, Tamara. *The Twilight of Jewish Philosophy: Emmanuel Levinas's Ethical Hermeneutics.* Amsterdam: Harwood, 1999.

Wurgaft, Benjamin Aldes. "Culture and Law in Weimar Jewish Medievalism: Leo Strauss's Critique of Julius Guttmann," *Modern Intellectual History* 11(1) (2014): 119–146.

"How to Read Maimonides after Heidegger: The Case of Strauss and Levinas," *The Cultures of Maimonideanism: New Approaches to the History of Jewish Thought*, edited by James T. Robinson. Brill: Leiden, 2009, 353–383.

Thinking in Public: Strauss, Levinas, Arendt. Philadelphia, PA: University of Pennsylvania Press, 2016.

Wyschogrod, Michael. *The Body of Faith: God in the People Israel.* New Jersey: Jason Aronson, 1996.

"Heidegger: The Limits of Philosophy," *Sh'ma* 12(231) (1982): 83.

"Heidegger's Tragedy," *First Things* (online journal) (April 2010). www .firstthings.com/article/2010/04/heideggers-tragedy

Yaffe, Martin D. and Ruderman, Richard S., eds. *Reorientation: Leo Strauss in the 1930s.* New York: Palgrave Macmillan, 2014.

Zaborowski, Holger. "Die Heidegger-Rezeption in Deutschland zwischen 1933 und 1945: Heidegger in der Kritik," *Heidegger-Jahrbuch* 5 (2009): 316–346.

Zahavi, Dan. "Phenomenology," *The Cambridge History of Modern European Thought.* Cambridge: Cambridge University Press, 2019, 102–127.

Zank, Michael. 2004. "Arousing Suspicion Against a Prejudice: Leo Strauss and the Study of Maimonides' Guide of the Perplexed," *Moses Maimonides (1138–1204) – His Religious, Scientific, and Philosophical Wirkungsgeschichte in Different Cultural Contexts*, ed. by Görge K. Hasselhoff and Otfried Fraisse. Würzburg: Ergon Verlag.

Zarader, Marlène. *The Unthought Debt: Heidegger and the Hebraic Heritage*, translated by Bettina Bergo. Stanford, CA: Stanford University Press, 2006.

Zemach, Shlomo. "Nazism, Sin'at Hayehudim, ve'Schopenhauer," *Moznaim* 10 (1–5) (1940): 232–247.

Ziarek, Krzysztof. "Giving Its Word: Event (as) Language," *Heidegger and Language*, edited by Jeffrey Powell. Bloomington, IN: Indiana University Press, 2013, 102–118.

Zimmerman, Nigel. *Levinas and Theology.* London: Bloomsbury, 2013.

Zuckert, Catherine. "Leo Strauss: Jewish, Yes, but Heideggerian?" *Heidegger's Jewish Followers: Essays on Hannah Arendt, Leo Strauss, Hans Jonas and Emmanuel Levinas*, edited by Samuel Fleischacker. Pittsburgh, PA: Duquesne University Press, 2008, 83–105.

Zuckert, Catherine H. and Zuckert, Michael P. *Strauss and the Problem of Political Philosophy*. Chicago, IL: Chicago University Press, 2014.

Index